BATTLE FOR JUSTICE

BATTLE FOR JUSTICE

How the Bork Nomination

Shook America

ETHAN BRONNER

See, N.Y.T 1/8/93
David Margolick
to "Bork"

ANCHOR BOOKS
DOUBLEDAY
NEW YORK   LONDON   TORONTO   SYDNEY   AUCKLAND

AN ANCHOR BOOK
PUBLISHED BY DOUBLEDAY
a division of Bantam Doubleday Dell Publishing Group, Inc.
666 Fifth Avenue, New York, New York 10103

ANCHOR BOOKS, DOUBLEDAY, and the portrayal of an anchor
are trademarks of Doubleday, a division of Bantam Doubleday
Dell Publishing Group, Inc.

Battle for Justice was originally published in hardcover by
W. W. Norton & Company in 1989. The Anchor Books edition is
published by arrangement with W. W. Norton & Company.

Library of Congress Cataloging-in-Publication Data
Bronner, Ethan.
    Battle for justice : how the Bork nomination shook
America / Ethan Bronner. — 1st Anchor Books ed.
        p.   cm.
    Includes bibliographical references.
    1. Bork, Robert H.   1. United States. Supreme Court—
Officials and employees—Selection and appointment.
3. Judges—United States—Selection and appointment.
4. Political questions and judicial power—
United States.   I. Title.
KF8742.B74   1990   90-35664   CIP
347.73'2634—dc20
[347.3073534]
ISBN 0-385-41549-4

For my parents,
Leah and Felix Bronner

Contents

Acknowledgments

Scores of people on both sides of the Bork divide helped me with this book. Many did not know me; they trusted me to use what they said thoughtfully and honestly. I have tried.

Among members of the Reagan administration, I thank Edwin Meese, William Bradford Reynolds, Terry Eastland, Howard Baker, Kenneth Duberstein, A. B. Culvahouse, and Thomas Griscom for their time, a precious commodity in government. I am especially indebted to John Bolton and Michael Carvin, who sat through many hours each of recollection and theoretical discussion. Thomas Korologos, a private citizen who worked for the administration on the Bork nomination, also was generous with his time.

Within the Senate, I thank the members of the Judiciary Committee as well as their aides who gave me substantive interviews. I would like to mention especially Senators Orrin Hatch, Arlen Specter, Joseph Biden, and Edward Kennedy and aides Randall Rader, Sam Gerdano, Ed Baxter, Jeff Robinson, and Mark Gitenstein. Jeffrey Blattner was exceptionally helpful, consistently intelligent. Jane Berman, committee spokeswoman, went well beyond the call of duty to provide me with documents and aid of all kinds. Special thanks to her.

A number of senators not on the Judiciary Committee also kindly agreed to reflect on the Bork battle with me; they included Alan Cranston, Warren Rudman, Richard Shelby, Wyche Fowler, and Dale Bumpers. I am grateful for their help.

On the Supreme Court, Justice Antonin Scalia did me the honor of sharing with me in a background interview his views on a number of topics related to the book. Justice Lewis Powell sat with me for more than two hours and followed up our interview by sending me several of his speeches. I thank him warmly and respectfully. Court spokeswoman Toni House was also most helpful.

Leaders of the anti-Bork campaign were forthcoming and generous. I especially thank Ricki Seidman, Melanne Verveer, Ralph Neas, Bill Taylor, Eric Schnapper, Kate Michelman, Althea Simmons, Anthony Podesta, Jackie Blumenthal, and Mimi Mager, who gave me dozens of hours of interviews and much needed help. Michael Pertschuk and Wendy Schaetzel of the Advocacy Institute talked over anti-Bork strategy with me and shared interviews they had conducted on the Bork controversy. Many thanks to them.

At Harvard University, I am grateful to a number of professors, but I especially thank Laurence Tribe and Michael Sandel for long, stimulating, and reflective conversations. Professor Tribe's secretary, Leslie Sterling, kindly provided masses of material. At the University of Chicago, I am indebted to Gerhard Casper, Judge Richard Posner, Carl Weintraub, and Ralph Lerner. At Yale, Paul Gewirtz, Harry Wellington, Bruce Ackerman, and Burke Marshall shared their thoughts. Burt Neuborne of New York University provided me with many insights, as he has for several years. Aviam Soifer of Boston University Law School helped me greatly both in discussions and in his astute reading and editing of several chapters.

Judge Bork, his wife, Mary Ellen Bork, and his son Charles shared some impressions and verified facts for me. I thank them. Bob Bork, Jr., sat with me for hours in formal interviews, chewed over issues and personalities for more hours, offered me material I might have missed, and helped me in many, many ways. I am deeply grateful to him.

A number of Judge Bork's friends and colleagues also put up with hours of interviews. I thank especially Leonard Garment, Raymond Randolph, Judge Ralph Winter, Howard Krane, Bruce Fein, and Judge Abner Mikva. I am most appreciative of the time and help offered by Patrick McGuigan.

There are many throughout the book who asked to speak on condition of anonymity; I am no less grateful to them.

My employer, the *Boston Globe,* is filled with more good people than any one institution deserves. Editor Jack Driscoll and Executive Editor Ben Taylor generously granted me a leave of absence from the paper, extended it, and then even took me back to work afterward; Alexander Hawes, Charles Liftman, and Diletta LaCortiglia set me up with desk, phone, and computer terminal inside the *Globe* building and watched out for my welfare with dedication and friendship; Washington Bureau Chief Stephen Kurkjian gave me a home away from home for several months; and Washington Office Manager Cynthia Taylor made me welcome. *Globe* telephone operators were terrific about taking my messages; the *Globe* library staff, led by Shirley Jobe, helped me through.

My colleagues Jonathan Kaufman and Charles Stein read the entire manuscript and offered many thoughtful points as well as support. *Globe* Deputy Managing Editor Kirk Scharfenberg first planted the idea for this book in my head, discussed it with me over the year and a half that followed, and read the book chapter by chapter as I wrote it. He provided intelligent, cogent suggestions. He has been a wonderful friend and editor; this book owes much to him.

I am very grateful to Morton Horwitz of Harvard Law School and Pnina Lahav of Boston University Law School, who discussed the book, in both substance and style, with me many times. They read several chapters and offered ways to improve them. They are dear friends and teachers.

I consider myself wonderfully fortunate to have Mildred Marmur as an agent. She is an author's dream, always providing superb advice and terrific support. Edwin Barber, my editor at W. W. Norton, did a splendid job, painstakingly going over every line with experienced hand and eye. Donald Lamm, president of Norton, did me the honor of reading an early draft and providing me with criticism and advice that were most welcome. Leslie Allen-Yeats provided first-class research assistance.

To those who offered me shelter and comfort when I could not afford hotels, I am indebted. In Washington, Richard Morin and Roxanne Rice and their sons, David, Joshua, and Drew, put me up and put up with me for several weeks, well beyond the call of duty, serving as a surrogate family; Matt Ridley gave me the run of his apartment, as did Alan and Michelle Wheatley. In New York, I stayed with my dear buddy Joe Davis. In Chicago, Wayne and Phyllis Booth were warmly hospitable.

My family was supportive throughout. My sister, Deborah Bronner, read the manuscript and made astute suggestions. My father, Felix Bronner, worked on every page, offering numerous and excellent changes. I thank him and my mother, Leah H. Bronner, for having taught me the value of ideas and the beauty of language. I dedicate this book to them.

At home in Boston, it was always an unmitigated pleasure to talk over the Bork controversy and everything else with Paul Stern and Beth Zeeman, lifelong friends. To my wife, Naomi Kehati, and our son, Eli, born just before work on the book began, I offer humblest thanks. They kept me balanced, happy, and in love.

BATTLE FOR JUSTICE

CHAPTER

1

The Most Powerful Man in America

"Toni, this is Lewis Powell," the associate justice said into the telephone at nine-thirty on Friday morning, June 26. "Do you think you would have time to stop by my chambers before we go on the bench?"

Not every justice dialed his own telephone calls. But then not every justice asked if you would "have time" to stop by his chambers. Powell was so polite and endearingly modest as to be of another era. Even his tidewater Virginia accent with the bizarre diphthongs seemed obsolete. Nobody talked that way anymore.

Thinking back over the past few weeks, Toni House, spokeswoman for the U.S. Supreme Court, realized that there had been something unusual about Powell's behavior. He had been requesting photographs, like that wonderful one taken by a *Washington Post* photographer of all nine berobed justices caught laughing as they prepared for their portrait, and that other one of the chief justice outside in the snow watching a clerk measure the accumulation with a ruler. For the first time Powell had developed an interest in mementos. He would call or send a note and ask her for copies of them. Odd, she remembered thinking. But she had made nothing of it.

Suddenly it made sense. Fifteen years as a reporter and editor for the now-defunct *Washington Star* had given House a keen sense for news. A slim blond woman who dressed in the silky professional chic of the capital, she was tough and controlled and proud of it. She was forever posting stern memos in the press room to warn reporters about being tidier or more responsible with Court materials. But even she was unable to contain herself this time and was nearly running down the stately hall of the Court building in her high heels, thinking of all the details that would have to be arranged in the coming hours. Of course, there would be a press conference, if he agreed, and endless phone calls and interview requests and pushy cameramen making their way into the normally hushed marble temple.

As she ran, she passed the office of the Associated Press, where Richard Carelli worked. Carelli, who had covered the Court for eleven years, glanced up and immediately suspected something. Over the next half hour he noticed an unexpected tension inside the Public Information Office of the Court, what he later referred to as some "rather fervent whispering.

"It was odd because it was the last day of the term," he recalled. "We knew what opinions were due, and there was nothing that big. It was supposed to be an anticlimactic conclusion."

Carelli saw Stephen Wermiel, who had covered the Court for the *Wall Street Journal* for the previous decade and said to him that something strange was going on. Maybe one of the justices was going to announce his retirement.

Carelli thought his job resembled covering the Vatican, but it was actually more akin to the old days of reporting on China from Hong Kong. At the Vatican there are men of high rank whose job it is to talk to reporters and analysts. There is no equivalent at the Court. Like reporters, House and her staff read the Court's pronouncements, but they never have access to the people making the decisions. They can't ask them what went into the decision, what negotiations there were, what compromises. Reporters can't ask the justices' clerks either since the clerks are sworn to secrecy and have more to lose than to gain by talking to reporters. Reporters never know when important decisions will be handed down; even by studying previous cases, they cannot confidently predict how justices will vote in the future. Thus journalists assigned to the Court must do more analysis than strict reporting, and they begin to acquire many of the qualities of the institution itself, becoming cerebral, reflective, and cautious.

As this was the last day of the term, the reporters would normally have set about their year-end analyses, seeking patterns, discussing subtle shifts in direction, pointing to the contributions of the new conservative justice, Antonin Scalia, and the new chief justice, William Rehnquist. But the focus today would shift to the retirement of the seventy-nine-year-old Powell.

The retirement of any Supreme Court justice, appointed for life, is an event. President Ronald Reagan had already named two justices—Sandra Day O'Connor in 1981 and Antonin Scalia in 1986—but Jimmy Carter had gone through four years as president without a chance to choose a single new justice. Since the nine members of the Court are often divided on sensitive social issues, any new appointment affords the president a chance to affect the nation long after he has left office.

But the retirement of Lewis Powell, House knew, was more significant still. A flexible conservative, Powell was the swing vote on a polarized bench. He provided the decisive fifth vote for the liberal wing on such issues as abortion, separation of church and state, and affirmative action. He was with the conservatives on the death penalty, protecting business interests, and aiding the prosecution in criminal cases. House was aware of what many Court watchers had been saying for a while: that the previous decade and a half had been as much the Powell Court as Court of Chief Justice Warren Burger.

A couple of years before, with Powell out ill for a month and a half, a number of 4–4 stalemates had occurred. In one end-of-term wrap-up that year Powell was called the most powerful man in America. House sent Powell a note at the time saying it was a pleasure and an honor to work for the most powerful man in the country. He sent back a characteristic reply: that he was most powerful only in his own home and only when his wife, Josephine, had gone shopping.

But Powell *had* made an enormous difference. With his retirement, especially in view of President Reagan's oft-repeated desire to impose his mark on the high court, the entire thrust of the institution was likely to change. Indeed, the Court had been undergoing a steady rightward movement since the early 1970s. Now, in 1987, rulings held dear by liberals were hanging on by a 5–4 thread. Gone were Earl Warren and William O. Douglas, the two progressive stalwarts. Liberals could count on only three very old men: Thurgood Marshall, seventy-nine; William J. Brennan, eighty-one; and Harry A. Blackmun, seventy-nine. A fourth justice, John Paul Stevens, sixty-seven, often voted with them. On the conservative side there were also four, three of them much younger: Chief Justice Rehnquist, sixty-two; Scalia, fifty-one; O'Connor, fifty-seven; and Byron R. White, seventy. In the middle was Powell.

Marshall was overweight and suffered from blood clots; Brennan had prostate and throat problems; Blackmun, too, had prostate ailments.

Powell had said in 1971, upon ascension to the Court, that he would stay only ten years. It had now been more than fifteen. Liberals prayed for his health and his will since he was with them on abortion and affirmative action, the most endangered issues if the Court's majority turned conservative. But Powell, fiercely independent and disdainful of partisan politics, was feeling the strain of the Court's labors. He had begun to think about his soon-to-be-born grandchild in Richmond, his Virginia home, and his fragile health.

House arrived at Powell's chambers. The gaunt, bespectacled justice, whose age really was beginning to show, rose in his gracious manner. Gesturing to the large couch, he asked her to sit down.

"Justice Powell, you're not going to do what I think you're going to do, are you?" she asked him before she had even settled down.

"Yes, Toni. I only decided definitely yesterday. Only the chief knows, and he's going to announce it from the bench at ten. I will tell my colleagues when we go in to robe."

Would he be willing to face the press? House asked. Powell said yes, he would be happy to talk to the regulars who covered the Court. Powell had grown rather fond of the Supreme Court reporters, thinking of them as responsible and thoughtful. House said fine, knowing full well there would be more than the regulars at the press conference.

When Powell said that only Rehnquist knew of his decision, he meant apart from his family. But for the past twenty-four hours, others had an idea of his plans. Senior White House aides, led by Chief of Staff Howard H. Baker, Jr., a former Senate majority leader, had gotten a tipoff. Soon after Powell informed Rehnquist of his decision, the chief justice had his secretary call Baker's secretary to set up a telephone appointment for the following morning at nine-thirty. Once word of Rehnquist's request became known in the White House, there was keen speculation as to the likelihood of a Powell retirement.

Twenty-four hours were scant notice. The previous year Chief Justice Warren Burger had paid the White House a visit long before his announced retirement. Administration officials were able to choose Rehnquist as his replacement and Scalia as the newest justice after careful scrutiny of their records and the political climate.

But Powell didn't do things that way. He believed that the Supreme Court, the government's third branch, should stay cordoned off from the executive branch. He had never felt any connection to the White House, either Reagan's or the one run by Richard Nixon, who had nominated him. Therefore, he saw no reason to give the president any warning. "I did not want it to have any implication that I was thinking of retiring because of who was president of the United States," he said later. "You know, I didn't go to the White House when Nixon announced my nomination. I stayed in Richmond, Virginia. I didn't feel any tie whatever to the White House. I barely knew the man. I'm sure he wouldn't have recognized me if he'd seen me.

"When I was nominated for the Court, the Justice Department offered to help me prepare for the confirmation hearings. I said thank you, no, thanks."

When Toni House returned to her office, she had an assistant make a photocopy of Powell's statement at a machine well away from the press room. When she handed out the day's opinions just after ten, she told the reporters in almost a casual way—House believed it her duty to preserve the Court's quiet dignity—that Powell was announcing his retirement. The room was thunderstruck. The day's rulings were quickly cast aside, and Carelli and the other wire service reporters ran to their computer terminals to spread the word.

For Washington's liberals, it would have been hard to invent less welcome news. As news agency teleprinters rang with bells to signal recipients of an urgent breaking story, and radio stations announced it, and Cable News Network broadcast it, the capital's telephones began buzzing. The lobbyists remembered precisely where they were when they got the news. They recalled it the way they recalled where they had been a quarter century earlier, when they heard that President John F. Kennedy had been assassinated.

Ralph G. Neas, executive director of the Leadership Conference on Civil Rights, a grouping of 180 organizations, was in his 1984 Renault just north of Georgetown, fighting muggy weather and traffic. While the news shocked him, it did not surprise him. Only a month earlier, at the annual meeting of his group, he was going over legislative priorities for the coming year. He said then that if Lewis Powell or anyone else retired from the Supreme Court, the Supreme Court nomination would become the top priority. He had no idea how prescient his words were. Neas, who was to head the unprecedented lobbying campaign against a Supreme Court nomination, stepped on the gas and planned the next half dozen telephone calls. As he put it later, "Everyone realized immediately what was going to be at stake, and our lives would be consumed, obsessed by the fight over the Powell seat."

Kate Michelman, installed not long before as director of the National Abortion Rights Action League, was giving a speech to a group of women's rights attorneys on Maryland Avenue in Washington, assessing progress and concerns of the previous year. She opened a note passed to her on the dais, looked up, and announced without a trace of irony: "Our worst fears have just been realized."

Paul Gewirtz, a liberal constitutional scholar at Yale Law School, was at a conference of judges in Virginia. The panel included Walter Dellinger of Duke University, Gerald Gunther of Stanford, and Paul Bator of the University of Chicago. Gewirtz, Dellinger, and Gunther were standing around chatting idly when they got the word.

"There was this explosion, this sinking feeling that after all this uncertainty, the moment of truth had come for the Court," Gewirtz remembered. "We knew the direction of the Court was at stake. For the next three days we talked about it endlessly. Endlessly."

Alexis de Tocqueville commented in his nineteenth-century exploration of this country, *Democracy in America*, that "the President may slip without the state suffering" and "Congress may slip without the Union perishing," because both can be replaced by the electorate. But, he said, "if ever the Supreme Court came to be composed of rash or corrupt men, the confederation would be threatened by anarchy or civil war." He was referring to the fact that justices are appointed for life.

The Court's role in the nation had grown immeasurably since de Tocqueville's day 150 years earlier. In the nineteenth century each state ran many of its own affairs; by the mid-twentieth century the Court had applied the federal Bill of Rights to the states so that national standards of free speech, freedom of religion, and free press were in force everywhere. State economic practices had been pushed into greater uniformity to keep up with the national economy.

During the Constitution's 150th anniversary in 1937, President Franklin Roosevelt likened the document to the Bible, saying it should be read over and over again. It was an apt simile. The Constitution had always served as the nation's scripture, but with the ongoing incorporation of the Bill of Rights in state laws, the national charter began to penetrate far more deeply into the lives of all citizens. As a result, debate over how to interpret the Constitution grew vastly and acrimoniously. In the postwar era judicial reasoning came to permeate political debate in the United States. The terms of constitutional discourse increasingly set the parameters for the nation's moral vision of itself. The notion that even local government ought to remove itself from regulating much personal behavior—a view arguably at odds with that of the framers—was a hallmark of Supreme Court decisions after the Second World War and especially in the 1960s and 1970s. Judicial definitions of liberty and privacy bloomed. They expanded to include the decision whether to terminate pregnancy and efforts to keep religious symbols and texture out of public life. To some, these expansions seemed part of the growth of an officially sanctioned liberalism. Individual rights were seen as "trumps" in both legal and political discourse. They were not dependent on the institutions of democracy but rather existed above and beyond them.

But with the ascendance to the Court of conservatives such as Rehnquist and Scalia, that public philosophy seemed threatened. The new members attacked the philosophical direction of the Court and society and sought to steer the ship on a more traditional course. Now Powell, who had steered his own centrist course, was gone. So, perhaps, was the Court. As Senator Edward Kennedy said of Powell's resignation on that day, "For the past fifteen years he has graced the Supreme Court as one of its most distinguished, respected and intelligent members, and all of us in Congress have especially admired him for his extraordinary integrity. Now the Senate will be watching carefully, as part of its advice and consent responsibility under the Constitution, to ensure that President Reagan does the right thing instead of the far right thing in filling the large vacancy that Justice Powell leaves."

In truth, no one—especially Lewis Powell—expected that one day he would be hailed by liberals as a hero. When nominated by Nixon in 1971 to fill the seat left by Hugo Black, Powell was not opposed by most liberal groups, but he was certainly not endorsed by them. He faced confirmation at the same time as William Rehnquist, who replaced John Marshall Harlan. The president of the National Organization for Women, Wilma Scott Heide, told the Senate Judiciary Committee then that it was clearly time for a woman justice. By the placement of two such conservative men on the high court, she said, "justice for women will be ignored or further delayed, which means justice denied."

Catherine Roraback, then president of the National Lawyers Guild, said of Powell and Rehnquist: "The views expressed by both men make it clear that they would be incapable of dealing fairly and impartially with issues arising out of the most pressing problems of our times: the struggle of blacks, other third-world people, women and other oppressed groups." Powell, she said, "does not bend or twist the Constitution; rather he totally ignores it."

While still a Virginia attorney, Powell had written an article for the *Richmond Times-Dispatch*—the editor was a longtime friend—in which he defended the right of the president to wiretap citizens without prior court approval if the administration thought there was intelligence to be gathered about threats to national security. The Vietnam War was raging, and protesters were being tapped at the behest of the White House.

"The outcry against wiretapping is a tempest in a teapot," wrote Powell, who had been president of the American Bar Association. "There are 210 million Americans. There are only a few hundred wiretaps annually and these are directed at those who seek to subvert our democratic form of government. Law-abiding citizens have nothing to fear. . . . The only abridgment of free speech is not by the government. Rather it comes from the radical left—and their bemused supporters—who do not tolerate in others the rights they insist upon for themselves." The article was carefully read and lovingly reprinted in the White House.

It was also true that Powell, as chairman of the Richmond school board, had bravely resisted segregationists and had overseen efforts to integrate the schools. Nonetheless, he ascended to the high court nominated by a president who said it was time to shift the Court's emphasis toward conservative interests.

But five months after joining the Court in 1971, Powell surprised his critics by denouncing his own position on wiretapping. He wrote an opinion striking down the administration's right to engage in the practice without judicial approval. Presidents had been ordering wiretapping without court approval for twenty-five years. Powell's opinion was especially strong because the case at hand involved real damage to American security interests. An office of the Central Intelligence Agency in Ann Arbor, Michigan, had been bombed. A man charged with the bombing found that federal agents had listened in on his conversations, and his lawyer called the surveillance unconstitutional. But Powell still found the wiretapping without judicial warrant a violation.

"History abundantly documents," he wrote for a unanimous Court, "the tendency of government—however benevolent and benign its motives—to view with suspicion those who most fervently dispute its policies. . . . Fourth Amendment protections [against unreasonable searches] become the more necessary when the targets of official surveillance may be those suspected of unorthodoxy in their political beliefs."

A year later Powell joined the historic 7–2 *Roe* v. *Wade* decision, which legalized abortion nationwide.

Powell, the essence of the southern establishment, brought up by strict, religious parents, was expanding his outlook and taking part in reshaping the nation's broad concerns. This at a stage in life when most people believe they have acquired their allotted wisdom. He remembered consciously trying to distance himself from his conservative instincts and background. He said, looking back on the wiretapping episode, that his article had been written with almost no research or thought, from the perspective of an advocate, which he had been all his life. "It is different when you are a justice. You wear a different hat, have a different responsibility."

Here was a powerful example of Lewis Powell's belief that one learns as one grows. Born and raised in Virginia, graduated from

Washington and Lee University and Harvard Law School, Powell was in manner and polish a product of the antebellum South. He had never been a restless intellectual, a rebel, or a questioner of values handed down to him. He recalled, for example, volunteering to fight Hitler at the age of thirty-three. He joined a bomber unit that had fifteen hundred troops—all male and all white.

"Coming from the South, I never gave it a thought," he said later. "It seemed perfectly natural. Looking back now, it is hard to imagine that was my view. But I grew up in that divided atmosphere."

The more involved he got in public life, the more he displayed signs of sensitivity to those less fortunate than he. Apart from his role in integrating the Richmond schools, he was also, as president of the American Bar Association in 1964–65, a vigorous lobbyist for an increased federal role in providing legal services to the poor.

Asked what decisions he took most pride in during his years on the bench, he cited two aimed at reducing racial discrimination. The first, the *Allan Bakke* case, struck down a racial quota for medical school admissions but laid down the constitutional basis for upholding voluntarily adopted affirmative actions. The Court was divided 4–4, and Powell's opinion defused the issue in Solomonic fashion. The second, the *Batson* case of 1986, overturned the right of prosecutors to disqualify potential jurors on the basis of race. "I was glad to have the opportunity to write that one," he said.

To the pragmatic Powell, his personal evolution argued cogently for the evolution of the Constitution in application to society's changes. He had little patience for the Reagan administration's advocacy of a return to the original intent of the Constitution's framers.

"I have seen so many changes just in my life," he reflected. "I remember in the late twenties hearing radio for the first time. My father had one of the first automobiles in Richmond. I have been alive eighty of the two hundred years of our Constitution. This country is very young. How can you say the Constitution should be frozen in time, that it is not a living document that must be interpreted?" He said the liberties Americans enjoy are guaranteed not by majority rule but by the Court's enforcement of the Bill of Rights.

Powell had never wanted to be a judge. A wealthy corporate lawyer, he relished the role of advocate and played it effectively in his soft-spoken way. "I enjoyed the law, the stimulation and combat of the courtroom. My technique in court was never flamboyant, and I am not eloquent, but I have persuaded a number of juries in my day," he remarked with a soft twinkle in the eye.

His name had been suggested for the high court in 1969, but Powell had written a letter to Attorney General John Mitchell saying that at age sixty-two he was too old. In 1971, with Nixon's choices running into serious opposition from the American Bar Association, Mitchell abruptly called Powell at the Waldorf-Astoria Hotel in New York where he was having breakfast with a client.

"I am authorized by the President to offer you an appointment to the Supreme Court," Mitchell said.

Powell declined again, reminding Mitchell of his letter two years earlier and adding that he hadn't got any younger. Mitchell said this time was different because Powell was no longer simply a possible nominee; he was the president's first choice. Mitchell asked him if he would be home that night. Powell said yes. He had barely walked into his house in Richmond when his wife answered the telephone. It was the White House. Nixon came on the line and spoke of Powell's duty to the South, to the law, to his country. Powell asked for twenty-four hours to consult his family but knew when he hung up he could not say no to the president.

"I've never been sorry I said yes," Powell reflected. "I was stupid to say no in the first place." The only regret Powell had in his decade and a half on the Court was the monasterylike isolation it imposed on his life. Because of his strong belief that the Court should have no partisan nature, he never voted during those years. He rarely socialized. He remembered coming to Washington to begin his tenure and wondering why none of his lawyer friends ever called to welcome him or invite him to lunch. After a couple of months he called one of his closer friends and asked if he had offended him in some way because the friend had never offered Powell a lunch invitation in his new city. The friend said his law firm had business with the high court every term. "I'm not going to take any justice to lunch and you're not going to come to lunch," Powell recalled him saying.

So Powell socialized with his brethren on the Court, worked six- and seven-day weeks, and spent what spare time he had with his family. Toward the end of the 1987 term he began his yearly ritual of thinking about retiring. But this time he felt the weight of the Court's work load more acutely than in the past. He was nearly eighty, had been on the Court fifteen years. Both seemed like nice round numbers. He talked to Josephine and his four children.

His son, Lewis III, who worked for Powell's old law firm in Richmond, came to lunch one Saturday in June. They talked about both their futures. Lewis was ambivalent about what his father should do. On the one hand, Lewis and his wife were expecting their first child, and he wished for his father the time and enjoyment of other grandparents. On the other, he believed that his father was a superb justice and that his country needed him.

But as Lewis talked about the service his father had given his country, he said something which his father later described as decisive: "Dad, it's a whole lot better to go out when some people may be sorry than it is to wait until when you decide to go out people say, "Thank God we got rid of that old gent.' "

Powell's departure meant one thing to most Court watchers: Robert H. Bork, federal appeals judge for the District of Columbia and favorite of the Reagan administration, would be nominated.

When Kate Michelman of the National Abortion Rights Action League returned to her office from giving a speech, she found two television network crews waiting. What would her organization do if Bork were chosen? It would mount an unprecedented campaign against his confirmation by the Senate, Michelman shot back. "We have researched his background, and we know what he stands for," she said.

When Althea Simmons, chief Washington lobbyist for the National Association for the Advancement of Colored People (NAACP), heard of the Powell departure, she was in Nassau, the Bahamas, about to address the annual convention of Delta Sigma Theta, the black women's sorority and service organization. News came via a call from her legislative aide in Washington, and her response was: "Oh, my God. That's Bork. We've got our work cut out for us. Pull our Bork files." When she went to the podium to deliver her talk, she told the audience: "Justice Powell has resigned, and Robert Bork is on his way to the Supreme Court. We've got to get to work."

But Bork himself was skeptical. When word of the Powell resignation reached the judge, Bork was in his chambers just down Capitol Hill from the Supreme Court working on an *en banc* opinion with fellow conservative judges Douglas Ginsburg, James Buckley, and Kenneth Starr.

En banc was a technique Bork had learned to use effectively. The nation's twelve federal circuit courts are forums of appeal whose decisions are handed down by three-judge panels. But the number of judges that sit in a given circuit can vary from half a dozen in New England to more than two dozen in the West, and any three-judge-panel decision can be challenged to the full bench of judges in a process known as *en banc.* Such a challenge can come from either party in the case or from another judge. Bork had developed a history of challenging opinions handed down by liberal panels in his circuit and of bringing along other conservatives, newly named by the Reagan administration.

In his first two years on the circuit, 1982–83, Bork had been a rather lonely voice since the court was still dominated by appointees of President Jimmy Carter. By 1987, after seven years of Reagan appointments, the majority was shifting to the conservatives, and Bork stood as their undisputed leader, benefiting as much from seniority as from intellectual force. He would use *en banc* with some frequency, incurring the anger of the court's liberals.

But even those battles were losing interest for Bork. He had not hired any clerks for the coming year and was thinking hard about resigning from the court. The D.C. Circuit deals with a lot of administrative and other passionless law, and Bork found such housekeeping tiresome. In a 1985 speech to the Thomas More Society, Bork said, "If Sir Thomas had had some of the regulatory cases that are our standard fare, he wouldn't have needed a hair shirt." A friend remembered Bork's complaint that what was wrong with his judgeship could be summed up by a recent case of monumental trivia. A man was required to travel by air for his company but vomited every time he flew. The plaintiff was suing to retain his job without having to fly. Bork averred that when all the arguing had ended, it was *he* who felt like vomiting. It just wasn't what a restless intellectual like Bork wanted to do with his time.

Moreover, Bork had been crushed in 1981, when Reagan named Sandra Day O'Connor to Potter Stewart's seat, and again in 1986, when he had expected a tap after Chief Justice Warren Burger had resigned. In fact, friends recalled his saying that he would not have moved to the D.C. Circuit at all had not the administration suggested to him that federal court service was a necessary interim post.

Then, in a terrible blow, his younger colleague on the same court, Antonin Scalia, was tapped for the seat of William Rehnquist, newly named chief justice to replace Burger.

On this particular Friday, June 26, Bork was working on an *en banc* opinion. Buckley mentioned the Powell resignation and said Bork looked like the nominee. Bork dismissed it. "The administration has a well-entrenched tradition of passing me over," he said.

Bork was not alone in his concern that the administration would pass him over one more time. His supporters worried, too. Patrick McGuigan, a young, fervent Oklahoman, was director of the Judicial Reform Project for the Free Congress Foundation, a grouping of conservative organizations. He was in his cramped office in a town house near the Capitol when his summer intern peeked in the door. Had McGuigan heard about Powell's resignation?

"I immediately called John Richardson, the attorney general's chief of staff," McGuigan recounted. "John, tell the attorney general and everyone else that if you guys don't do Bork this time, I'm going to slash my wrists.'"

McGuigan added that he would explain to his people that this one was worth fighting for. He then called Peter Keisler, a twenty-seven-year-old Yale Law School graduate and former Bork clerk who was working in the White House counsel's office. He repeated his desperate message. Next, McGuigan called Dan Casey, director of the American Conservative Union, and said they ought to inundate the White House and the Hill with pro-Bork telephone calls.

"That ought to be a pretty easy sell, don't you think?" asked Casey.

"I don't trust the jerks to do the right thing, do you?" countered McGuigan.

"Not really," agreed Casey.

Bork's admirers in the Justice Department had their own jitters. Their two bosses, Attorney General Edwin Meese and his top adviser, Assistant Attorney General William Bradford Reynolds, were in flight over the Atlantic. So Charles Cooper, head of the Office of Legal Counsel, called a meeting in his office with, among others, John Bolton, the department's liaison to Congress, and Terry Eastland, the department's spokesman. The aim was to plot a strategy to get Bork nominated as quickly as possible.

These were the self-described ideological foot soldiers of the Reagan Revolution. Tough, smart, and zealous in their devotion to right-wing principles, they saw Powell's resignation in epic terms. The moment of truth had arrived. Conservatives could finally regain control of the Supreme Court and the nation's moral and legal agenda. These young Reaganites had come to government service brimming with hope. For them, it *was* morning in America and they would return their nation to its roots and traditions. What they decried as a racial and gender spoils system—the efforts of previous administrations and courts to help blacks and women as groups, rather than to correct wrongs suffered only by individuals—would end. In their Justice Department, young white men would be no less deserving of government help than anyone else. Justice would be provided to *all* Americans rather than set one group against another. Americans were decent and God-fearing. No need existed to spy out racism and sexism in every corner of the land. The existing system, which occasionally offered jobs to blacks over better qualified whites, and developed elaborate schemes of equal pay for equal work to promote gender equality, and set aside percentages of government contracts for minority-controlled firms was unjust. It must go.

The work of conservative reform proved more difficult than imagined. Radical change comes hard and slowly in a stable country. Much of what the Reagan foot soldiers objected to had become institutionalized and widely accepted.

Now came the godsend. The Court, which had legitimized so much in existing liberal programs, could also put a stop to them if it had the right people up there. But the men at Justice were afraid that the newly pragmatic White House, now run by moderate Tennesseean Howard Baker, the chief of staff, would scuttle the nomination. It would push for a candidate easier to confirm in the defiant, newly Democratic-controlled Senate. Such a nomination would be a colossal waste of a unique opportunity.

Charles Cooper, a handsome Alabaman with ice blue eyes, who had clerked for Rehnquist, finally reached Reynolds on the airplane as he and Meese returned from Europe. They agreed that Bork was, without question, their choice. They would lobby for him. John Bolton got on the phone and went so far as to suggest that when Meese landed, he go by helicopter to the White House and that the selection of Bork be made that very night. This should be accompanied, he believed, by public pressure on Senator Joseph R. Biden, Jr., of Delaware, chairman of the Judiciary Committee, to hold early confirmation hearings.

Bolton and his colleagues wanted to mount a fierce pro-Bork offensive, one impossible for Baker or the Senate to counter. This time everything they cared about was on the line. As one of them said later, "If you can't get Bob Bork on the Court, you might as well shut the door and turn all the lights out."

CHAPTER

2

High Stakes

If right-wing activists and Justice Department officials were alarmed and wary, they were justified in being so. Within the new group running Reagan's White House, not Chief of Staff Howard Baker nor Counsel Arthur B. Culvahouse nor Communications Director Thomas Griscom was a Bork devotee. They each knew Bork was a federal judge in Washington, a smart, vociferous conservative to be found on all right-wing lists for nomination to the Supreme Court. But Baker and Culvahouse, soft-spoken southern gentlemen, were themselves closer in style and outlook to Lewis Powell than to Robert Bork. They were pragmatists, accommodators, concerned more with unity and accord than with rigid principle. They rarely used harsh words. They had come to the White House only months earlier to restore order and dignity to a presidency damaged by the Iran-contra scandal. The administration had secretly sold arms to Iran in hopes of freeing American hostages held in Lebanon. Profits from the sales were sent to right-wing Nicaraguan rebels, known as contras, despite a congressional ban on such aid. The plan failed, and both Congress and a special prosecutor were investigating. In addition, the Senate had been lost to the Democrats the previous November. The new men in the White House were not in search of a fight.

Indeed, had Powell given more notice, Culvahouse might have pressed for someone other than Bork to replace him. The previous year, when Chief Justice Burger retired, Scalia had been fully checked out before the nomination was made. Staff had prepared a book on him and had lined up the Italian-American community to campaign, if necessary, for the first of its number to be granted a lawyer's highest honor. Although deeply and somewhat idiosyncratically conservative, Scalia had little real controversy in his record. Nicknamed Nino, he was also an irrepressibly charming man with a hearty, warm laugh, a weakness for opera, and many friends in both the judiciary and the academy.

The choice of Scalia over Bork in 1986 was a complex political calculation. Rehnquist had often been a lone right-wing dissenter during his fifteen years on the Supreme Court. The administration knew his promotion to chief justice would draw intense liberal opposition. To send up Rehnquist with Bork would promote an explosive combination that might place both nominations in jeopardy, despite a Republican majority in the Senate. It would make more sense, the administration determined, to offer a less controversial nominee along with Rehnquist, thereby siphoning off liberal energy toward the future chief justice. The plan worked. After acrimonious hearings over Rehnquist, thirty-three senators voted against his promotion, the largest ever against a chief justice. But he was in. And with the opposition spent on Rehnquist, Scalia waltzed through.

Many conservatives had a unique sense of loyalty to Bork. In the late 1960s and early 1970s, when liberalism had so swept legal thinking in the academy, Bork had been bravely building the foundations for a conservative jurisprudence. It was not, they thought, a crude results-oriented approach but a high-minded system aimed at wresting control of the nation's legal culture from the liberals. His admirers had a simple conviction that one of the nine seats on the high court was his entitlement. As much as everyone liked Scalia, Bork had earned it more. As one senior Justice Department official put it, "There was a feeling that Bob had been in the trenches longer than Nino." But other factors entered into the equation. Scalia was a decade younger and so would serve longer. Unlike Bork, he didn't smoke and wasn't overweight. As another top Justice Department man said later, "Sometimes you have to put your sentiments aside and make some cold calculations."

The lukewarm attitude toward Bork within the new White House staff had little impact. The president told Baker from the beginning that he wanted Bork's name on the list. And while Meese did not do as his subordinates had hoped—he didn't helicopter to the White House that Friday night and insist Bork be named immediately—he made his views known.

Few administration officials were as close to Reagan as Ed Meese. The attorney general and the president shared a past, a purpose, and a style. To Meese's detractors of the center and left, it always came as an annoying surprise to learn that he was genuinely liked by those around him. He was, in fact, felt to be an unusually dear and gentle man. No snob, Meese had a common touch. He extended warm greetings to high and low and expressed thanks to secretaries, drivers, and FBI agents. He had a ruddy complexion, a near-cherubic smile, and unending optimism.

Yet Meese preached a harsh conservatism that came from the gut. His obsession with the tools and drama of law enforcement were legend. While working in the Alameda County district attorney's office in the mid-1960s, Meese personally directed the arrest of 761 Berkeley University protesters, joining the officers in their action and later telling Congress that the demonstrators were an "aid and comfort to the enemy."

Meese's work drew the attention of Reagan, who had campaigned for the California governorship in 1965 with a promise to "clean up the mess" at Berkeley. Once elected, Reagan plucked Meese from the district attorney's office to be his legal secretary. Meese took the unusual step of delivering to Reagan's office daily summaries of law enforcement reports from around the state. J. Anthony Kline, who succeeded Meese in the job in 1976, when Edmund ("Jerry") Brown, Jr., took over from Reagan as governor, said the reports were an odd assortment.

"They were anything from highway patrol reports to student disruptions," recalled Kline, who later became an appeals judge. "We thought this kind of daily report highly unusual in a governor's office of a state with twenty-three million people. There were weightier things to consider than a homicide in San Bernardino. So we put a stop to it."

Meese grew up in a devout German Lutheran family that nightly recited the Pledge of Allegiance and prayed. His aging mother, Leone Meese, in an interview with the *Los Angeles Times* in 1986, described a rigid, unpretentious family life with hamburgers on the boys' birthdays, spring lamb at Easter, and biblical literalism every Sunday. Meese had a paper route as a boy and cleared park trails as a teenager. His father, a clerk at police court and then a tax collector for Alameda County, regaled his four sons with stories of police derring-do.

Young Meese first traveled east to attend Yale, where he was active in the Lutheran student organization and on the track team. In 1958 Meese married his high school sweetheart, Ursula Herrick, whose family mirrored the Meeses in outlook and manner. Her father had been Oakland's postmaster.

Meese attended law school at Berkeley, worked briefly in army intelligence, and joined the district attorney's office in Alameda County. The Meeses had a reputation first in California and later in Washington as an unpretentious couple who preferred Sunday barbecues to cocktail parties.

In the eyes of many, Meese's unfailing loyalty to Reagan and others was a great strength. But it was also his weakness. As one former associate put it, "He tends to surround himself with people who are his friends and then never to see evil or wrong in those people. He doesn't see the bad side of anyone he considers a friend."

Personal loyalty in professional circumstances proved to be Meese's largest stumbling block as he moved from the White House, where he had served as counselor to the president, to the Justice Department after the first Reagan term. His confirmation to be attorney general was held up for thirteen months while an independent counsel investigated the circumstances under which Meese had given federal jobs to two friends who helped him when he fell behind in mortgage payments on his California house. No criminal wrongdoing was found, and he was confirmed. But other scandals continued to touch him, and there developed a widespread feeling that Meese had contempt for the spirit of the law where his friends were concerned. After he left office in late 1988, Meese was severely reprimanded by the Office of Government Ethics for what it said appeared to be repeated violations of federal conflict of interest regulations. A subsequent report by the Justice Department's Office of Professional Responsibility concluded that Meese engaged in "conduct which should not be tolerated of any government employee, especially not the attorney general." It said disciplinary action by the president would be warranted if Meese were still in office.

When the Powell retirement occurred, Meese was already under a cloud of ethical conflicts. His problems were compounded by the question of his role in the Iran-contra scandal. Had Meese given

Oliver North, the brazen lieutenant colonel on the National Security Council, the opportunity to shred key incriminating documents? If so, had it been out of sympathy or incompetence? Members of Congress's special Iran-contra committee wanted to know and were due to grill Meese on it in several weeks' time. The committee's Democratic majority would ultimately single out Meese for harsh criticism over the affair.

Meese had let slip some nasty and naive quotations over the years. He had said of criminal defendants, for example, "You don't have many suspects who are innocent of a crime. If a person is innocent of a crime, then he is not a suspect." One Christmas, while many in the nation were lamenting the growing plight of the homeless, Meese said that "people go to soup kitchens because the food is free and that's easier than paying for it." And he had called the American Civil Liberties Union a "criminals' lobby."

The attorney general was also an object of increasing controversy within the legal and academic communities. He had provoked an enormous dispute on constitutional philosophy by preaching a return to a jurisprudence of "original intention." He suggested that it had been a mistake to apply the Bill of Rights to the states—an audaciously atavistic criticism that challenged a basic notion of postwar judicial practice.

Finally, Meese had lost some of his following in the intellectual right, which was growing annoyed that his personal and ethical problems were blocking movement on its legal and social agenda. Even his own staff let drop the occasional comment about Meese's endless troubles. Ultimately Meese played a minor role in the Bork battle, so caught up was he in defending himself against charges of corruption and incompetence and doing what he could to run the rest of the department. As he said later, "I kept track of what was happening. I got daily reports. But I was not involved in tactical details." Others in the department agreed with that assessment.

Baker and Culvahouse realized that Bork was destined to be the nominee since Reagan wanted him. But they believed that the nomination would suffer if Bork was seen to be strongly associated with Meese and the Justice Department. They wanted the nomination to be perceived as purely a White House affair and Senate leaders to feel they had a role in the process. So a list of nominees was presented to Judiciary Committee Chairman Biden, Majority Leader Robert Byrd of Virginia, and, on the Republican side, Minority

Leader Bob Dole of Kansas and ranking committee member Strom Thurmond of South Carolina. The list included a number of conservative and moderate federal judges, headed by Bork, as well as the name of Alabama Senator Howell Heflin, a conservative Democrat on the Judiciary Committee who had been chief justice of his state's supreme court. But considering Reagan's and Meese's strong predilection for Bork, it was largely a public relations exercise. Only massive and persistent objections by the Senate leaders would scuttle the choice of Bork.

Aware of Baker's and Meese's difference, liberals hoped that a wedge could be driven between the White House and the Justice Department. Sufficient pressure up front might force the nomination of a more Powell-like figure whose impact on the Court and the nation would be less dramatic than Bork's was expected to be, in view of the balance on the bench.

So, over the weekend, liberals made several moves, not all in a coordinated fashion. Ralph Neas, executive director of the Leadership Conference on Civil Rights, called the White House. He failed to reach Culvahouse but got through to Griscom on Saturday to warn him that selecting Bork or someone equally polarizing would cause a fire storm. Neas, on paper an odd choice to lead the nation's civil rights lobbyists—he was white, male, Catholic, and Republican—had known Baker and his men from their time together on Capitol Hill. Neas had worked for a number of years for Senators Edward Brooke and David Durenberger. He had long believed that moderate Republicans and bipartisanism were the key to civil rights progress.

Neas told Griscom about the kind of opposition a Bork nomination would engender in the civil rights community. He said Bork had criticized many landmark Supreme Court decisions that had benefited blacks and that he had spoken at times of the need for the Court to overrule such decisions. That was threatening talk for the nation's blacks, already angered by what they perceived to be the administration's hostility to their interests. Why pick another big fight? Griscom fully understood and dutifully reported their conversation to Baker. Baker was unmoved. The president wanted Bork, and Baker had grown inured to Ralph Neas's nudging and warning him over the years. It wasn't the sort of thing he would change his mind over. When Reynolds and Meese heard about the Neas phone call, they dismissed it as evidence of how desperate the liberals were about the Supreme Court's slipping out of their hands. It also increased their resolve to name Bork. If they stepped back from the nomination now, Meese felt sure that Neas would crow to his constituents that he had stopped Bork without spending a penny.

The next day, on ABC's "This Week with David Brinkley," another key architect of the fight against Bork made his pitch. Laurence Tribe, a Harvard Law professor, was lecturing in West Germany and about to begin a month's vacation in the south of France with his family when the Powell resignation was announced. Tribe was the author of the leading scholarly treatise on American constitutional law as well as numerous articles and books on the subject. He had argued successfully and often in the high court. It seemed increasingly that no event of constitutional import had really occurred until he commented on it. As soon as Powell resigned, Tribe's office telephone rang with calls from reporters, editorial writers, Senate staffers, legal and academic colleagues. His secretaries located him in Munich.

Via satellite, Tribe made his case on ABC that Sunday morning. He said that Bork's nomination would endanger the right to abortion and even birth control in the United States. "It appears he would not allow the Constitution to be used to protect even the right to use birth control," Tribe said. "I think if the Court as a whole rolls back these fundamental rights, it transcends politics, it transcends conservatism versus liberalism, it transcends fitness of an individual. The question is whether any president should have a mandate to remake the Constitution as this president wants to do, using slogans like 'judicial restraint.' "

From the first, Tribe thought that the main issue of this nomination was the danger Bork posed to the evolving right of personal privacy—or, as Tribe liked to call it, autonomy—especially in family and reproductive issues. It was a concern that had an impact on class and race, since the rich had always had access to safe abortions, and that touched the sensitive American nerve of individual liberty.

Also over that weekend, Jeffrey Blattner, a recently hired Judiciary Committee staff aide to Senator Edward M. Kennedy of Massachusetts, was busily gathering material by and about Bork. He had already had his transatlantic conversation with Tribe—Blattner had been a student and researcher of Tribe's, and they had the added connection of both having clerked for Justice Potter Stewart—and also held numerous other consultations with liberal lobbyists and scholars in New York and Washington. He and other Kennedy aides were to draft an anti-Bork statement that was ready the day before the actual nomination. Kennedy considered using the statement as a means to block the nomination but chose ultimately to wait till after Bork was named to deliver it.

Tribe, Neas, Kennedy, and the rest of the nation's civil rights and liberal establishment could not have been readier for a fight with that president or that Justice Department over the Constitution and the direction of law and justice in America. From the day Reagan took office in 1981, he and those around him made clear that government policies of the past two decades toward race, sex, and religion—the wild cards of American politics—would change radically. Reagan and his aides interpreted their election as a mandate for a drastically different approach. Instead of offering special opportunities to groups like women, blacks, and other minorities that had suffered wrongs in the past, the administration wanted to restrict help only to those who had personally suffered from discrimination. Instead of pressing companies and local authorities to hire and promote more women and members of minority groups, this administration would argue that hiring should be based solely on merit. Instead of pressing for greater school integration, this administration would not "compel children who don't choose to have an integrated education to have one," as Assistant Attorney General Reynolds had put it less than a year after Reagan took over.

Ardent conservatives such as John Bolton and Terry Eastland were suddenly government insiders. Conversely, civil rights activists found themselves unwelcome. The civil rights community, accustomed to an honored place at the table of any American administration, now found itself unceremoniously without access to high places. Every administration since Kennedy's had at least claimed an interest in moving the civil rights agenda forward. All sought to break down patterns of discriminatory housing, segregated schools, unfair hiring and promotion practices. This administration, on the other hand, stated unambiguously that its view of justice diverged from that of the established civil rights community. The cutting edge of the Reagan Revolution was at Justice.

William Bradford Reynolds led the way. A wealthy corporate

lawyer and graduate of Phillips Academy, Yale, and Vanderbilt Law School, Reynolds was put in charge of civil rights at the Justice Department. A tall and stern-visaged man with thinning blond hair and large rimless glasses, Reynolds was seen by most as a bright and disciplined Republican, but certainly no ideologue. He was moderate to conservative in his politics. There was even talk four years earlier of his working in Griffin Bell's Justice Department under President Jimmy Carter.

But Reynolds took up the call of the Reagan era with singular vigor like a lawyer who uses everything in his power to promote the interests of his client. He quickly found himself the focus of unabated hatred by the civil rights community. He opposed busing as a means of school desegregation; he opposed affirmative action for blacks or women, saying it was using racism to fight racism and inexcusable; he abhorred the notion of homosexual rights. He believed the government had played much too great a role in trying to promote the needs of the oppressed. That was not civil rights, he said. That was placing the interests of one group over another, precisely the evil he had been hired to root out.

Reynolds spoke often and provocatively about his views. He said he and his colleagues were defending church, family, and community against an onslaught from the "liberal criminal lobby," promoters of child pornography, abortion, and homosexuality. On affirmative action, he said in a 1983 speech: "We are all, each of us, a minority of one. . . . In no instance should an individual's rights rise any higher or fall any lower than the rights of others because of race. Whatever group membership one inherits, it carries with it no entitlement to preferential treatment over those not similarly endowed with the same immutable characteristics."

Reynolds was unimpressed with Justice Harry Blackmun's words in the 1978 *Bakke* decision on affirmative action: "In order to get beyond racism we must first take account of race. There is no other way. And in order to treat some persons equally, we must treat them differently." It was a credo that had animated American policy since the major legal battles over civil rights had been fought and won. But to Reynolds, it was anathema to the American way of life.

According to several accounts, Reynolds placed pressure on Solicitor General Rex Lee, the government's lawyer in front of the Supreme Court. He pressed him to use high court briefs as a means of achieving the Reagan social agenda, urging the Court to overturn affirmative action and abortion. He so involved himself with the work of the solicitor general, a position that normally allows considerable independence, that some called him a "shadow solicitor." Reynolds said he was replacing social engineering with adherence to the law; his detractors said he was ignoring established law for political ends.

In addition, Reynolds and other key department officials paid special attention from the beginning to the selection of federal judges. This was an emphasis that received strong support from conservative groups. Right-wing activist Patrick McGuigan of the Free Congress Foundation remembered the day after Reagan's landslide victory in 1980, which also put the Senate in Republican control, a combination that had not existed since 1954. McGuigan was called into the office of his boss, Paul Weyrich. Also in the office was Randall Rader, who later served as Orrin Hatch's aide during the Bork hearings.

"Well," Weyrich told them, "we've just won the White House. And we've got control of the Senate. What's left?"

"The judiciary," McGuigan and Rader both answered.

"Right," said Weyrich. "Let's get to work."

The courts had played an unprecedented role in the changes in society over the preceding forty to fifty years. They had set the tone, indeed often led the way, on desegregation, personal liberty, and separation of church and state. With the legislature and executive silent on burning social questions, the Supreme Court stepped into the vacuum.

Meese and Reynolds wanted to undo some of the Court's work. They announced that they would screen judicial nominees for proof of conservative judicial philosophy. They asked potential candidates their views on a number of Supreme Court decisions and judicial trends, saying they were looking for judges who would exercise "judicial restraint" and who advocated strict adherence to the words of the Constitution and legislation. Otherwise, they said, judges were not interpreting the Constitution; they were remaking it, imposing their views of justice on the country.

These goals, so neutral and reasonable on their face, were, in fact, complex and politically loaded. Shortly after Meese moved from the White House to the Justice Department in 1985, he began a series of speeches advocating a return to a "jurisprudence of original intent."

That meant sticking as strictly as possible to the aims of the founders who wrote the Constitution. Especially galling to Meese was a recent Supreme Court decision that forbade a moment of silent prayer at the beginning of each school day. To Meese, "far too many of the Court's opinions were, on the whole, more policy choices than articulations of constitutional principle." The justices' "voting blocs, the arguments, all reveal a greater allegiance to what the Court thinks constitutes sound public policy than a deference to what the Constitution—its text and intention—may demand." Echoing Stephen Douglas's attack on Abraham Lincoln's notion of evolving liberty, the attorney general dismissed the idea that the Constitution is a living document as "chronological snobbery."

The issue was as old as the nation. When Douglas and Lincoln held their famous series of debates on whether slavery should be banned, each based his argument partly on what he claimed was the aim of the Constitution's framers. Douglas declared at one of the pair's 1858 exchanges:

> Washington, Jefferson, Franklin, Madison, Hamilton, Jay and the great men of that day made this government divided into free states and slave states and left each state perfectly free to do as it pleased on the subject of slavery. Why can it not exist on the same principles on which our fathers made it?
>
> This doctrine of Mr. Lincoln of uniformity among the institutions of the different states is a new doctrine, never dreamed of by Washington, Madison or the framers of this government. Mr. Lincoln and the Republican Party set themselves up as wiser than these men who made this government, which has flourished for seventy years under the principle of popular sovereignty, recognizing the right of each state to do as it pleased.

Lincoln responded in kind. He made much of the fact that the word *slavery* was left out of the Constitution. He said: "Now, I believe if we could arrest the spread, and place [slavery] where Washington and Jefferson and Madison placed it, it would be in the course of ultimate extinction. . . ." He mocked Douglas's insistence on "original principles," saying:

> I am fighting it upon these "original principles," fighting it in the Jeffersonian, Washingtonian, and Madisonian fashion. . . .
> Judge Douglas is going back to the era of our Revolution,

and, to the extent of his ability, muzzling the cannon which thunders its annual joyous return. When he invites any people willing to have slavery to establish it, he is blowing out the moral lights around us. When he says he "cares not whether slavery is voted down or voted up"—that it is a sacred right of self-government—he is, in my judgment, penetrating the human soul and eradicating the light of reason and the love of liberty in this American people.

The issues raised by Meese, as by Lincoln and Douglas, came down to these: How should the Constitution be read and used? Is the nation's charter analogous to a slab of Carrara marble and the nation like Michelangelo, searching for the splendid form hidden inside? Or is the document's meaning more fixed? When it says a president must be at least thirty-five years old, there is little discussion. But when its language is vague and broad, when it speaks of "liberty" and "due process," does the nation have license to reinterpret those terms in the light of its own changing standards? Is the Constitution grand and eternal because it is an anchor under the sea of shifting values propounded by each new generation? Or, on the contrary, is the Constitution's greatness derived from its very flexibility and ambiguity, its ability to "grow" and "progress" along with society's evolving sense of justice? How important is the will of the majority? Democracy means preventing tyranny of the minority, but it also means stopping tyranny of the majority. How broadly and under what circumstances?

Meese and other conservatives argued that the work of judges has no legitimacy unless it can be linked specifically to the intent of those who wrote the Constitution. Otherwise, "interpretation" is nothing but the exercise of judicial power.

Much of the development of individual and group rights had emerged from the work of judges extrapolating from the Constitution. Many such rights were the ones Meese sought to pare back. He said that judging based on changing mores made for unstable law and the kind of liberal pronouncements typical of the preceding generation of Court decisions.

Evident from the debate, however, is the difficulty in determining intent. There were many framers. Whose intent counts? Moreover, they left few records. Finally, their phrases often seem *deliberately* large, perhaps to achieve compromise among themselves, perhaps because they knew the charter would have to live long and serve in circumstances they could not foresee.

Of course, to argue that intent is vague and therefore indeterminate is, by itself, unsatisfying. Judges must not be released from making an honest effort to link their decisions to the words, structure, and intent of the framers' document. A remaining difficulty is what to do when intent simply cannot be discerned. Most judges and legal scholars argue that such a case demands a resort to previous judgments and what might be described as collective will or understanding. Meese rejected the latter, arguing that when intent is not clear, judges should defer to state legislatures. His opponents agreed that such a policy would be in the democratic tradition, but it would be wrongheaded because it would endanger political minorities. The progress of the postwar years was marked specifically by the increased protection the courts had offered minorities. To follow Meese's formulation would be to endanger those accomplishments.

Meese's campaign raised a storm in the nation's legal community. For the first time in fifty years—since the New Deal—sitting Supreme Court justices sparred with a senior member of the executive branch. William Brennan, the bench's most prominent liberal, denounced Meese's words, saying original intent "feigns self-effacing deference to the specific judgments of those who forged our original social compact. But in truth, it is little more than arrogance cloaked as humility. It is arrogant to pretend that from our vantage we can gauge accurately the intent of the framers on application of principle to specific, contemporary questions."

Justice John Paul Stevens, a centrist appointed by President Gerald Ford, also took issue with Meese. The attorney general had, in his view, failed to evaluate "subsequent developments in the law as well as the original intent of the Framers." Justice Byron White, a Kennedy appointee who voted consistently with the bench's conservatives, called Meese's ideas "simplistic."

The power of the American courts flows from their power of judicial review. Always controversial, judicial review is nowhere mentioned in the Constitution, which spends only four hundred words on the judiciary as compared with several thousand on the executive and legislative branches. Indeed, the judiciary was to be "the least dangerous" branch, in Alexander Hamilton's phrase, and was set up with few tasks and little identity. Originally, Supreme Court justices had no permanent home. They spent part of their time riding hundreds of miles on horseback to listen to appeals, prompting one early justice to liken his job to that of a traveling postboy. Not only was there the inconvenience of making one's way along muddied roads and sleeping at uncomfortable inns, but the job also held relatively little prestige. Three of the first seven appointees resigned after serving less than seven years. John Jay resigned the chief justiceship to serve as governor of New York. Robert H. Harrison, one of President Washington's early choices, resigned five days later to become chancellor of Maryland.

The work of the Court was also limited in the early years of the Republic. Only 2 acts of Congress were declared unconstitutional before the Civil War. More than 130 have suffered such a fate since then.

Especially in the past half century, the power of the Court has grown vastly. Its pronouncements are closely monitored because they affect the lives of millions. Supreme Court justices, shrouded in their black robes and housed in their marble temple behind the Capitol, are today among the nation's most prestigious and powerful individuals. The evolution of the Court's place in American life paralleled closely the growth of the federal government and the perceived need for greater uniformity among the various states.

Federal judges are not elected but rather appointed for life. Their power, therefore, seems to lack legitimacy in a society whose fundamental principle is democracy, rule by majority. By what right does a court strike down a law passed by a majority of the elected representatives? In most countries with a parliamentary system the elected body is the highest authority. Yet American democracy works precisely because there are limits on it. That is, the Court rests on a paradox: It is fundamentally undemocratic, yet its mandate to require the president to obey the same law as a homeless beggar makes it one of the most important guarantors of the democratic system. Moreover, those with unpopular opinions feel free to participate in the political process because they know they are protected by courts. If they were not protected, such dissidents would likely fall silent and deprive political discourse of unorthodox views. While the judiciary is then, in the language of legal theory, countermajoritarian, it is not necessarily antidemocratic. When functioning properly, the courts enhance democracy.

This was the view set forth by Hamilton in 1788. He pointed out that since the judiciary has control of neither purse nor sword, it must depend on the executive to carry out its orders. But, he said, "there is no liberty if the power of judging be not separated from the legislative and executive powers." And, he added, "The interpretation of the laws is the proper and peculiar province of the courts. A constitution is in fact, and must be, regarded by the judges as a fundamental law. It therefore belongs to them to ascertain its meaning as well as the meaning of any particular act proceeding from the legislative body."

Judicial review has been all but universally accepted as appropriate since 1803, when Chief Justice John Marshall stated in the landmark case of *Marbury* v. *Madison*: "It is emphatically the province and duty of the judicial department to say what the law is."

But the contours and limits of judging have been a historic battlefield within the legal community. During the 1930s "judicial restraint" became a progressive rallying cry because the Supreme Court kept striking down congressional acts of the New Deal. Progressives argued that if the country was democratic, "nine old men" ought not to be stopping the work of congressmen, duly elected representatives of the people.

In 1937 Franklin Roosevelt, stymied in his grand projects for the country's recovery from the Great Depression, went so far as to try his "court packing" plan. If a federal judge or justice did not retire within six months of his seventieth birthday, the president proposed adding a new judge to that bench. With six of the Supreme Court justices then over or near seventy, the plan would soon have afforded FDR a majority.

Many in the nation enthusiastically supported FDR and chafed at Court intransigence. Even so, the nation and Congress sensed that something sacred was being undermined and politicized. The plan, in fact, caused an uproar and ultimately failed in Congress. But it may have had its impact. New Deal legislation was from then on upheld by the Supreme Court as Justice Owen Roberts, the swing vote at the time, switched sides. By 1941 Roosevelt had, in any case, appointed seven justices owing to natural vacancies. He had his majority.

Beginning in the 1940s, partly because of Hitler's racial war and the rise of third world nationalism, the philosophical push for individual rights and racial equality gained strength. Defending and redefining individual and civil rights took up an increasing share of the high court's agenda. Essentially, rights had always meant the rights of those with property. Now they took on a new meaning as the Court started routinely to strike down state laws restricting an individual's freedom. In a typical early case the Court declared that a follower of Jehovah's Witnesses could not be obliged to salute the flag. The Court reasoned that compelling someone to express a view was as wrong as forbidding him from doing so. Slowly key aspects of the Bill of Rights, such as freedom of religion and speech and freedom from unreasonable searches, were applied to the states by "incorporating" rights in the Fourteenth Amendment (which says that states cannot pass laws which "abridge the privileges and immunities of citizens" or deprive anyone of "due process of law" or of "the equal protection of the laws"). Such decisions, while revolutionary, squared with society's sense that as technology changed the world, so, too, must law change and adapt. A sense of national identity came to mean countrywide standards of individual rights. Moreover, it seemed evident that racial inequalities would not be overcome without federal authority. Change had to penetrate all corners. The country was smitten with the idea of progress. The Court was right in step.

Chief Justice Earl Warren's fifteen-year reign, from 1953 to 1969, epitomized this new approach to the Constitution and society. Its watershed 1954 decision, *Brown* v. *Board of Education*, required the nation's schools to desegregate. The 1896 Court decision of *Plessy* v. *Ferguson*, legitimizing "separate but equal," was wrong. Subsequent decisions desegregated other institutions, provided the accused with a virtual bill of rights, and constructed a high wall between church and state. The Court based the church decisions on the First Amendment, which declares that "Congress shall make no law respecting an establishment of religion. . . ." Today Americans consider such separation fundamental to their society. Yet as late as 1931 the Supreme Court declared, "We are a Christian people." Not until 1947 did the Court issue its first church-state separation ruling. And in 1962 the nation's religious leaders were scandalized when the Court outlawed prayer in school.

But the Warren Court and the early Burger Court, like the eras they represented, suffered on occasion from zeal. Even liberal legal scholars expressed doubts about the rationales of a few key decisions. Yes, the judiciary had bravely filled a vacuum. But should that become a pattern? Some felt the courts were on the verge of over-stepping their authority. Some of the high court justices themselves felt this way and, in the following decade, began to rein themselves in, stepping back from the broad proclamations of the 1960s and early 1970s. At the same time, many of their early decisions, seen as scandalous at the time, became enmeshed in the popular conscience as natural and just. Yet the symbolism of unelected judges telling everyone what to do lived on in the heart of the right wing, and the judiciary became a whipping boy for conservatives.

The Reagan administration adopted the phrase *judicial restraint*, used by liberals fifty years earlier, but it now took on a new meaning. Instead of referring to the need to hand down narrow rulings based on existing law, judicial restraint was redefined to mean over-turning the wrong work of the previous decades. "Wholesale change" became the ironic rallying cry of conservatism, and the size of Reagan's electoral victory was declared the legitimator of the mission. The key, administration officials openly declared, was to place the right people on the federal bench and thereby return to a more legitimate jurisprudence.

During the first years of the administration judicial nominees were drawn from among the nation's most thoughtful and ardent conservative judicial theorists. Federal circuit courts, once liberal domains, began to edge rightward. Bork, in a 1987 speech, joked that Reagan had ruined American legal education by taking the best conservative scholars out of the law schools and placing them on the bench. When Reagan took office in 1981, federal judges were divided about three to two between Democrats and Republicans. On Reagan's departure from office eight years later, the ratio was reversed.

The nation's liberals—especially the civil rights community—had long thought of the courts as their special protectors. Stunned now by the electorate's apparent rejection of their programs, they began by offering only tepid opposition to a few of the judicial nominees. But when they organized themselves for battles they really cared about, they found to their surprise that they could win. Congress still listened to them. Over the objections of the administration, civil rights activists helped engineer an extension of the Voting Rights Act in 1982 and the declaration of a federal holiday in memory of Martin Luther King, Jr., in 1983.

In 1985 the administration settled in after a landslide presidential victory, and Meese took over as attorney general. Civil rights activists were of two minds. On the one hand, they stewed with anger and frustration. Their hard-won ground was slipping away. On the other, these activists knew they could get results. Suddenly they were presented with the potential for a major symbolic victory, one that would spur them to fight till the end of the administration.

Meese moved to promote William Bradford Reynolds to the rank of associate attorney general, the department's number three spot. The move would have little substantive impact. Meese could rely on Reynolds whatever Reynolds's title. This reality notwithstanding, here was a moment to rebound against the Reagan policies.

Reynolds's hearings, in June 1985, were a pivotal moment in the relations between civil rights activists and the Reagan administration. Witness after witness berated Reynolds and his policies, labeling them un-American, dangerous. Benjamin Hooks, executive director of the National Association for the Advancement of Colored People, spoke fervently to the Senate Judiciary Committee, which had to approve of the promotion. Hooks declared:

> Mr. Reynolds and the Department of Justice are waging an unprecedented, aggressive and unnerving campaign to reverse more than two decades of well-established principles for remedying the ravages of past discrimination and for ensuring that patterns and practices of discrimination should be eliminated.
>
> We talk about the Constitution being color-blind, sex-blind, or gender-neutral—and it is our hope that some day it will be. But if the past is any guide to the present and future, then color-conscious remedies will have to be used to alleviate color-caused individual problems.

Hooks noted that the Constitution initially took color fully into account, counting blacks as three-fifths of whites. Then he cited the post-Civil War amendments, which stated that the freeing of slaves, equal protection, and the right to vote were needed not by whites but by blacks.

Hooks echoed Lincoln, attacking Reynolds for his belief in sticking to neutral principles rather than dealing with the realities of discrimination: "Great moral problems deserve answers. . . . Neutrality is not the answer. . . . Can we as a nation be neutral on the question of slavery? Can we be neutral about lynchings, beatings, brutalities? . . . We cannot be neutral about that and we cannot be neutral about this situation. Members of the committee, the world is looking at you, and we ask that you do not confirm Mr. Bradford Reynolds because to do so would be to congratulate him and to vindicate the positions he has taken. . . ."

Hooks was joined by virtually every standard-bearer of civil rights in the country. Especially significant was the testimony of the Lawyers' Committee for Civil Rights Under Law, a bipartisan grouping of private attorneys first set up by President Kennedy in 1963. The organization had never before opposed a presidential nomination.

The lawyers' committee's point was forceful: Differences between it and Reynolds were not, as claimed, merely over the use of busing and quotas. It went to the very heart of the government's role in achieving justice for minorities. Reynolds's division had failed to apply the energy of its predecessors to areas of fair housing, discrimination against the handicapped, and voting rights. Through such a policy, the group said, the department had undercut those rights. For the first time the federal government was being seen as an opponent of civil rights.

Reynolds was also caught skewing history at a previous committee hearing. Senator Arlen Specter, Republican of Pennsylvania, pointed to Reynolds's earlier shading of the truth. The issue had to do with laws in Burke County, Georgia, struck down by the Supreme Court because of discrimination against blacks. Reynolds had told the committee in 1982 that although sympathetic to the suit against the county, he had lacked the resources to get the Justice Department involved. Departmental documents requested by the committee for the 1985 confirmation hearing clearly contradicted Reynolds. They showed Reynolds telling Solicitor General Rex Lee that any government intervention should be on the side of the white county government.

The nomination was mortally wounded. The Republican-controlled committee rejected Reynolds's promotion by a vote of 10–8. Specter and moderate Republican Charles Mathias of Maryland voted with the Democrats in opposition. That Reynolds had misled the committee was politically important; it helped the two Republicans and such conservative Democrats as Dennis DeConcini of Arizona to register negative votes. But the rejection was clearly something larger, hinging on more fundamental issues.

Reynolds was rejected on policy grounds. The policy was this claim: that the country now opposed special treatment to groups that had suffered unfairly in the past. The argument fell on barren soil. The committee members sensed that the time had not yet come when rigid legal notions of color blindness could be applied to social policy. Such ideas, when properly packaged, sounded fair, but in practice they prolonged injustice. America was a nation of pragmatists. Its elected representatives were saying color blindness was impractical and possibly something worse—an excuse for ignoring the legacy of slavery. The Reynolds defeat was not Reagan's last nomination to fall, at least in part, over such a difference in views.

For Ralph Neas, who fought Reynolds with extraordinary vigor, the defeat was a turning point. Neas had helped engineer the 1982 Voting Rights Act, successfully pressing for a twenty-five-year extension of a key section, more than three times longer than any previous extension.

In the beginning years of the administration Reagan's men had the upper hand in the rhetorical contest on race, capitalizing on white frustrations over affirmative action and busing. The officials spoke about quotas, and people listened. But the sense of threat that affirmative action had posed during the difficult 1970s began to subside somewhat in the 1980s. Ironically, the low unemployment and low inflation of the Reagan years hastened the change in attitude.

Furthermore, the officials themselves were helping people like Neas. Meese and Reynolds in particular had little credibility in Congress and the high court. Neas began to understand that as long as controversy continued to hover over them, as long as they were tarred by the brush of special prosecutors and Senate rejection, their plans would be further stymied.

"Because of their extremism, Meese and Reynolds actually contributed to a sense of reaffirmation on civil rights," Neas reflected toward the end of the administration. "Their department became increasingly viewed with disdain by both moderates and conservatives. There is just no doubt that they compiled the worst civil rights record in fifty years."

Neas, having had ample practice during the preceding seven years, played a key role in organizing the opposition to Bork. He had learned what symbols to promote, what language to use, how best to lobby the legislators and rouse the passions of ordinary citizens. In the beginning of the administration Neas and his colleagues were on the defensive, plaintive last paragraphs to news stories controlled by the administration. By the end of the Reagan era the roles had been reversed.

Neas had learned about television sound bites, about the value of choosing a few compelling phrases and simply repeating them again and again to every reporter who called. When Bork was nominated, Neas spoke of Bork's writings as a "thirty-year paper trail that cannot be shredded"; he insisted, further, that the nomination "is about what people have worked their whole lives for." His words were reprinted everywhere. Now a packager of the news, he easily took the offensive.

Neas worked out of a cramped basement office near Washington's Dupont Circle and spent much of his time trying to steer the coalition of diverse groups he headed called the Leadership Conference on Civil Rights. Founded in 1950 as an umbrella organization for thirty groups, the Leadership Conference's mission had always been keyed to the historic report of President Truman's Committee on Civil Rights entitled "To Secure These Rights." Its campaigns had aided passage of the Civil Rights Acts of 1957, 1960, and 1964, the Voting Rights Act of 1965, and the Fair Housing Act of 1968.

By the time of the Bork battle the Leadership Conference had grown to include 180 groups representing blacks, Hispanics, Asians, organized labor, the major religious groups, women, the handicapped, the aged, minority businesses and professions. In many ways these groups were strange bedfellows. Some, for instance, opposed affirmative action and abortion while for others such issues topped the agenda. On one thing they all agreed, however: They did not like the policies of Ronald Reagan.

Neas, forty-one, was the high-profile director and chief lobbyist of the Leadership Conference. Ruddy-faced and tousle-haired, Neas had been chief legislative aide for Senator Dave Durenberger, Republican of Minnesota, and a respected Capitol Hill insider when he took the job. He had worked for five years in the same position for Senator Edward Brooke, Republican of Massachusetts, the first black senator since Reconstruction. Partly because of Brooke's interests, Neas became deeply involved in civil rights issues, which remained for him an abiding passion.

Neas accepted the position of executive director of the Leadership Conference in 1981 at the dawn of the Reagan era. It was odd for a group with such a large black contingent to pick a white Republican male. Indeed, Neas, not the coalition's first pick, came aboard amid some ill feeling. He fitted no mold most members recognized. When some whites were fighting racism in the South, Neas was in a military academy in Illinois; he went on to Notre Dame and the University of Chicago Law School, not well-known bastions of civil rights activism.

It was also surprising that Neas accepted the position. Many of those closest to him had advised against it. The Reagan years were going to be a period of severe retrenchment in civil rights. To put it bluntly, this was a poor career move for a young man on the rise. So went the advice.

But Neas recognized it was the job for him. He believed deeply in its goals, and he knew that people admire those who fight the odds. Win or lose, you come out ahead. Controlled and meticulous, he held his cards close to the vest yet was an expansive, obsessive promoter and coalition builder. He was the sort of man who never tired of buttonholing legislators in the hallway, of writing memos and making phone calls, of seeing his name in the newspaper and his face on television. Neas was a champion smiler, a man who imparted a sense of intimacy while giving little away. Like many a Boston Irish politician—he was originally from Brookline, Massachusetts—Neas also had the slightly clerical air, common touch, and instinctive sense for power of those schooled in the Catholic Church. He was masterly at handling people, the kind of Washington professional who could beat you up and make it feel like a rubdown. As chief aide to liberal Republicans on the Hill he had often acted as broker between Democrats and the Republican leadership. Since the Leadership Conference on Civil Rights was run by consensus rather than majority, such skills were vital.

Neas also seemed to have a complex sense of debt to God, an unspoken vow to use his acumen for a higher cause. It was, in effect, a pact with Providence that partly absolved him from the sins of politics. He knew humility was a heavenly virtue, but it was, in honesty, a foreign trait. Acting in the cause of a more righteous society, Neas permitted himself the kind of gusto toward his own accomplishments of which he might otherwise be ashamed.

His debt was one cultivated partly through religious upbringing. He liked to cite the statement from the Second Vatican Council that all discrimination should be eradicated because it is contrary to

God's law; he also took note of the passages from St. Luke that command attention to the poor, the sick, and the needy. A 1968 Notre Dame graduate, Neas was a child of 1960s ideals and, like so many young Catholics, a fervent admirer of the Kennedys. He believed that he had a purpose on earth, that God had devised a life plan for Ralph Neas. Small signs of that plan abounded.

In 1979, shortly after he began his work for Durenberger, Neas had an encounter with destiny that vastly increased his sense of debt. He had gone with Durenberger to Minneapolis to meet state political leaders, joining his boss even though dragged out by a bad cold. As he headed for the baggage claim area, he felt numb and cold, his right leg grew weak, and he almost fell. He decided to get some rest.

Two days later, at a luncheon meeting which he addressed, Neas slurred his words and found himself virtually unable to eat. Alarmed, he called a doctor and was told to drink orange juice and get more sleep. The prescription was impossible to follow. Neas alternated between the bed, a chair, and the floor in an effort to fight the pain that was now creeping through his body. He called the hospital and arranged to be taken there, fearing the worst. He prayed and called his parents and his girl friend.

Preparing for the trip to the hospital, Neas pulled himself into the bathroom with the idea of shaving. Trying to keep his wits about him, he smiled into the mirror. The man in the mirror did not smile back. The right side of his face had fallen two inches. He couldn't move it. His body was slowly succumbing to paralysis.

Neas returned to his bed, recited an act of contrition, then made his way to St. Mary's Hospital in Minneapolis. The diagnosis was Guillain-Barre syndrome, a disease of unknown cause that progressively paralyzes the muscle-controlling nerves. For the next seventeen days Neas retained an ability to talk. During that period he found out things that nourished his religious sense of hope. One of the first people he met at the hospital was seventy-three-year-old Sister Margaret Francis Schilling, who was celebrating her fiftieth year as a nun. On her twenty-fifth anniversary she had contracted Guillain-Barre syndrome. Moreover, two of the doctors who were to treat Neas were also graduates of Notre Dame. Even under ordinary circumstances, Neas was one who searched for omens among the mundane details of his life. Here were accidents of fate that provided him succor. When offered the chance to go to the more sophisticated Mayo Clinic, he chose to stay where he was.

Slowly Neas became completely paralyzed, and for much of the following three months he lay in intensive care. He approached death on a number of occasions. Sister Margaret sat frequently at his bed, soothing his anxieties as best she could, reminding him of the virtues of patience. His body drooped grotesquely. Although unable to move, he felt intense pain. When touched, he wanted to scream, but his paralyzed vocal cords produced no sound. Liquid built up in his respiratory system. He could neither excrete nor breathe on his own. He lost fifty pounds. He feared he was going blind. He listened in agony one frightful night as a priest administered general absolution at his bedside.

At a Notre Dame dinner hundreds of miles away, five hundred people prayed for Neas's recovery. His friends and family prayed and wrote to him constantly.

Then, as mysteriously as it had come, the illness eased out of his body. Neas recovered his speech and his movements; he was able to breathe; he began to eat. For a year he walked with a cane.

After his recovery his mother tried to persuade Neas to settle down, marry, take a job in private practice. But the fight for his life had the opposite effect on him. It invigorated him, adding a cosmic dimension to his sense of destiny. It caused him to redouble his commitment to politics, which he saw as the priesthood of the real world. His struggle taught him vulnerability, and as he said later, it proved pivotal in his decision to take the Leadership Conference post. He also recognized a good story and told it often. Neas's brush with death was an opportunity that God had provided, both in substance and in public relations. So was the job offer from the civil rights community. He set to work with a sense of mission.

The inspiration may have been godly, but the work was distinctly earthbound. Neas's job was to cajole, to stroke, to glad-hand, and to produce memoranda that were specific without alienating coalition members. Over the Reagan years his legislative victories mounted in number. He fought for legislation benefiting the disabled and the elderly as well as for more traditional civil rights causes. In 1987 he began speaking about the danger to civil rights if Reagan had the opportunity to name another Supreme Court justice. Just six weeks before Powell's retirement Neas told the annual meeting of the Leadership Conference on Civil Rights what the group's agenda would be for the coming year. But, he warned, if Powell or any other of the nine justices should resign, "everyone agrees that we will put all other issues aside and the Supreme Court nomination will become the top legislative priority of the Leadership Conference."

This happened on June 26, and Neas instantly understood two things: that his life would be taken up completely by the Supreme Court nomination over the coming months and that he and his colleagues had to force the administration onto the defensive over the nomination. Unless Reagan sent up a moderate, someone in the Powell tradition, the country should understand that the Leadership Conference on Civil Rights would unleash all its energy and political might to wage the fiercest legislative fight of its history. This was a battle over the legitimacy of the past and so a struggle for the future.

CHAPTER

3

Levity and Ferocity

Robert Bork was a man of war. He struggled with everyone, especially himself. A restless, ambitious intellectual, he half-jokingly declared his motto to be "Wreak yourself upon the world!" A hulk of a fellow, he had a weakness for food, drink, smoke, and, especially, talk. Gruff yet self-deprecating, he relished contrariness; he was softhearted about hardheadedness, sentimental toward rigor and logic.

His political enemies were the liberal intellectuals who came of age in the late 1960s, yet he took to looking like one of them, cultivating a scraggly red beard and leaving untamed the frizz on his balding pate. Bork was a professor and judge, yet such professionals were the people he never ceased attacking. What Bork had written of antitrust law—that it was a paradox, a policy at war with itself— could have served as the title of his self-portrait. The legal system, with its rules and limits, provided for him a secure order, a kind of gyroscope. Law was the Ulyssean mast to which he strapped himself.

As a youth Bork was lanky, curly-headed, and pensive. He took up boxing and won his school championship. Next to his unsmiling photograph in the high school yearbook he placed an apt quote of pugilistic sophistication: "Do you want a contusious scab, maybe?"

"He was always competitive and aggressive," his elder son, Bob, said. "He likes boxing less because it is a sport than because he is a tough guy. It's reflective of his personality. He doesn't like baseball, for example. He watches football because it is a bone-crunching contact sport."

Bork began verbal jousting in his teens. In contrast with his appearance later in life—large, scruffy, with an ironic curl to his lips—he rarely cracked a smile as a kid. By his own recollection, he spent most of his time "reading books and arguing with people." He was a leading member of his school's debating team.

Bork's mother, Elizabeth, was an English teacher, something of an autodidact, aloof and occasionally ornery. She introduced reading to her strongheaded son through sleight of hand. "She tricked me," Bork recalled. "I didn't want to read as a kid. She read *Tom Sawyer* aloud to me and, at a crucial point, she refused to read any more. So I had to pick up the damn book and read the thing. And I got hooked and I've been reading furiously ever since."

From her husband and only child Elizabeth Bork demanded tidiness—something Bork was to spend his life refusing to deliver. She and her son used to argue long into the night. Bork's father, Harry, a purchasing agent with a steel company, was a simpler sort. He would call from upstairs that his house was not a debating society and that his wife and son ought to go to sleep. A hunter and gun collector, Harry Bork found pleasure in going down to the house's cool basement and practicing on a firing range he had built with spare steel parts.

They lived in Pittsburgh, where Bork was born in March 1927. The family moved from a more modest section of town to the white middle-class Republican suburb of Ben Avon when Bork was in the ninth grade. He spent his high school years in a trim stone house with a one-car garage on a leafy street. William Karn, two years older and living in the house next door, remembered young Bork's brief interest in snakes. He was encouraged by his mother, who bought him books on the subject and allowed him to have a couple as pets.

Taking a cue from his mother, Bork relished the exposure of cant. In his junior year he was news editor of the school paper, a fine forum for him. The war was raging in Europe. Although news reports showed that Hitler's armies were advancing on the Soviets, government propaganda always spoke of the retreating Nazi troops and advancing allies. Fed up with the hypocrisy, Bork wrote in the school paper: "The Russian army is still advancing backward and the German army is still retreating forward."

On another occasion some of the school seniors were shown in the local paper examining an army jeep; the photo's caption said the students were planning to contribute to the war drive by buying war bonds. Bork snorted in the following issue of the school paper that the seniors were barely able to buy war stamps, let alone war bonds. One of the seniors challenged Bork to a boxing match. Bork was pleased.

At fifteen Bork read *The Coming Struggle for Power*, a Marxist analysis of capitalism by John Strachey. "It hit me like a ton of bricks," he remembered. "It was very powerful stuff and I thought that was probably the truth."

Bork soon announced he was a socialist, shocking in his buttoned-up suburb. But here there was no conspiracy with his conservative mother. It was aimed as much at her as at others. Horrified, she visited his high school history teacher, Raymond Kuhl, to complain about her lad's dangerous leanings. Neighbor Karn and Bork once went, with devilish enthusiasm, to a Communist cell meeting in Ben Avon. Passions cooled a bit when they were treated to a Russian film about combines and reapers and annual grain harvests. When the meeting's leader suggested to Bork afterward that he drop by a bookstore—the party's local front—Bork declined. But Bork continued to admire Eugene V. Debs, the Socialist labor leader and presidential nominee.

Because many teachers in Ben Avon had been called up to military service, Bork's parents sent him east for his final year, to the Hotchkiss School, an exclusive preparatory academy in Lakeville, Connecticut. Upon graduation, Bork wanted to join the Marines, but his mother refused to sign the required parental permission forms. It was one of many confrontations between them, and Bork knew how to handle it. He told her that if he had to await his army draft, he would volunteer for the paratroopers and then she would be sorry she had withheld permission for the Marines. She relented, and he signed up and studied to be a translator for frontline troops interrogating Japanese prisoners. But before he had a chance to go to Japan, the war was over, and he ended up serving his time guarding supply lines for Chiang Kai-shek's army in China.

His favorite teacher from Ben Avon, Raymond Kuhl, advised Bork to go to the University of Chicago, a caldron of intellectual ferment under the direction of Chancellor Robert Maynard Hutchins. Bork entered the university in 1947 at the height of its fame and fell permanently under its influence.

Hutchins, a handsome visionary, had taken over the university in 1929 at the age of thirty. He had already served two years as dean of Yale Law School. At Chicago he abolished the powerful football team, got rid of fraternities, and reduced academic specialization. He believed that much of what was learned during the first two years of college largely repeated what had been studied in the last two years of high school. So he offered examinations as a means of skipping introductory classes and of halving the time required for a degree.

The idea was to develop a total commitment to the intellect. Hutchins abhorred pragmatism in education—he made a point of offering no music, engineering, or architectural courses—and defended nonconformity as vital to societal growth. He advocated a resurgence of traditional education and brought in Mortimer Adler as resident intellectual guide. Adler set up a program devoted to the classics of Western literature. Amid its neo-Gothic spires, in a middle-class enclave surrounded by inner-city slums, the University of Chicago flourished as an oasis of Aristotelian inquiry. Bork remembered that a simple jaunt across campus would bring him within earshot of half a dozen high-minded discussions on comparative literature and philosophy.

"Chicago was the kind of place which, by the education it offered and the extreme seriousness with which it was taken, had a way of arousing students to taking intellectual issues very seriously," said Karl Weintraub, former dean of the humanities and graduate of the same era. "There was a kind of fanaticism over how important it was to be serious about intellectual questions."

Wayne C. Booth, a distinguished literary critic and former college dean at Chicago, reflected: "It seems that there was a unique ability here at the time to excite young people about ideas, sometimes turning them into ideologues."

Chicago was a place of catholic taste and few sacred cows, but certain themes grew dominant. One was concern over the sorry decline of the intellectual tradition caused by liberalism. Chicagoans were taught to admire tradition and spurn contemporary fashion. A conservative English professor of the time named Richard M. Weaver in 1948 wrote an influential book called *Ideas Have Consequences,* a refrain found throughout Bork's later writing and speaking. Weaver admonished that the failure of intellectuals to take the force of ideas seriously was a symptom of the dissolution of the West. To him, modern liberal culture was corrosive. Also influential on the Chicago campus, although he didn't teach there, was Russell

Kirk. Kirk preached the inseparable link between property and freedom and the idea that social hierarchy is necessary and good. He was known for such sweeping statements as "[C]hange and reform are not identical and innovation is a devouring conflagration more often than it is a torch of progress."

Leo Strauss, a German refugee philosopher, ruled like an adored prince over the political science department and left his mark throughout the university.

"Strauss opened up an old vocabulary as though it had something to tell us," recalled Ralph Lerner, a professor at Chicago who studied with Strauss. "Things that contemporary scholars had written off turned out to be addressing questions which were important to us. They had to do with how we ought to live. What ought I to be striving for? He taught us that that was a meaningful question to which there was an answer. And the people who had most thoughtfully addressed that question were dead."

Lerner recalled that Strauss and others like him on campus had an entirely different approach from that typical of the day. Twentieth-century skepticism—the belief that great moral dilemmas had only personal answers but no absolute ones—was disdained at Chicago. Scholars elsewhere studied dead thinkers as flagstones on a trail of error. They were worthy of examination only to the extent that the study demonstrated the correctness of contemporary skepticism and values. But Strauss said precisely the opposite was true. Only through return to old principles would intellectual and moral inquiry become productive.

Part of that approach was belief in the old republican value of "virtue," of community service. Edmund Burke, the eighteenth-century British statesman who attacked the French Revolution as a denigration of traditional values, had become a major influence on much Chicago thinking. American philosophy and constitutional jurisprudence began to tilt toward liberalism; Bork and many of his fellow students meanwhile steeped themselves in the importance of republicanism, a return to traditional principles and hierarchical order.

A year ahead of Bork at the university in those days was Allan Bloom. Unknown to each other then, they became friends in middle age. Like Bork, Bloom was to gain fame in the late 1980s with a quintessential Chicago call for return to tradition. His field was higher education, and his warning came in a best-selling book called

The Closing of the American Mind. Bork was to law what Bloom had become to education—a conservative Cassandra of doom. Reaction to both men among liberal intellectuals was equally fierce, approaching the hysterical. They were denounced as frauds, as lacking in theory and insight. Such condemnation served to dismiss them without having to take issue with them.

While a Chicago undergraduate, Bork still claimed allegiance to what he called a New Deal type of socialism. He worked as a poll watcher for a professor who ran for Congress on a Socialist ticket. Bork flourished at the university, making Phi Beta Kappa. He wrote well and wanted to apply to the Columbia University Graduate School of Journalism. But officials there declined to send him an application. They didn't take seriously his two-year degree from the trendy University of Chicago.

Bork once described his religious background as "generic Protestant," but when he married, it was to fellow undergraduate Claire Davidson, the daughter of working-class European Jews, who was also a New Deal enthusiast. Neither cared for organized religion, and they practiced none. Bork decided to go to law school at Chicago upon the recommendation of a teacher who told him with acute prescience that law would allow the young man to "take philosophy into the marketplace."

At the law school he was quickly enamored of a thoughtful and tough young professor named Edward Levi. Levi was to become president of the university and later became the U.S. attorney general when Bork was already solicitor general. Bork was especially attracted to Levi's insulting humor. Bork once recalled being tickled the first day of class when Levi announced, "I won't keep you long today. I won't keep you long because I don't have anything to say to you. I don't have anything to say to you because you are too ignorant to talk to."

Bork had signed up with the Marine reserves as a means of support. The Korean War broke out after his first year of law school, and he was called up. A lieutenant, he spent 1950 to 1952 in training camps in Virginia and North Carolina and then returned to finish law school. In 1952 the Borks handed out leaflets for Democratic liberal Adlai E. Stevenson, Jr., presidential candidate. That was the last election either of them voted for a Democrat.

That same year Bork encountered a rigorous market-oriented conservative professor named Aaron Director. The thrust of Director's theories was that society prospered most when market forces were allowed to flourish, when businesses and individuals were left unfettered by government intrusion. Efforts to regulate market forces stemmed from romantic political goals and served only to increase human suffering, not to decrease it.

Director used economics to punch holes in current theory. Minimum wage laws, he argued, often restricted the number of jobs available to low-skilled and unskilled workers; rent control laws often reduced the amount of housing for the poor. Director contended that antitrust law in particular was a dinosaur with origins in nineteenth-century politics and prevented a free flow of goods and services. A totally free market, he believed, would increase efficiency and thereby help all consumers.

Director, too, had begun life as a leftist, but, Bork said, "the logic of . . . theory drove him from that position as later, through him, it drove me from socialism." Under Director's influence, Bork experienced what he frequently referred to as a conversion of religious proportions away from socialism toward conservatism. "I learned some basic economics for the first time and it gave me a free-market orientation rather than a socialist one," Bork said.

This conversion may have been intellectual, but emotionally it was part of a continuum. Director offered an overarching system of thought, a means of categorizing human relations, such as Marx and the socialist theoreticians after Marx had. Both frameworks were materialist, viewing the world through the lens of economic interaction. Moreover, the change allowed Bork to continue challenging those around him, to play the role of iconoclast among his peers. He switched, in effect, from true believer to true believer, attacking the "soft" liberal center of American political theory, but from the opposite end of the spectrum. He became a market-oriented conservative and a philosophical libertarian, opposing government intervention and regulation not only of the economy but also of social intercourse. It was a position that occasionally and unintentionally lent legitimacy to segregationists fighting federally enforced racial integration.

Instead of the leftist pricking the comfortable notions of suburban conservatives, Bork became the rightist doing the same among liberal academics. The conversion came so naturally that Director, a

Polish-born economist, did not remember it at all. He remembered Bork as very bright and willing and thoughtful—but not as a new convert.

Bork's childhood friend Bill Karn, later a lawyer in Pittsburgh, said he thought that Bork was always fundamentally a conservative whose socialism was a form of hell raising, a toss of the gauntlet, not deeply serious.

A Bork law school classmate recalled that after they had graduated and entered private practice, he and his wife and the Borks would play bridge on Friday evenings. Bork would seek to provoke them by advocating the dismantling of federal regulatory agencies so as to organize society around the principles of the free market. They would argue back on occasion but dismissed his provocations as Bork's slightly perverted form of fun. As the years went by, Bork's statements became increasingly provocative. He began to argue that all human behavior could be understood through the workings of the marketplace. The friend, a liberal, never took Bork's views seriously until Bork became Nixon's solicitor general. "Then I realized he was serious about that stuff," the former classmate remarked with a touch of wonder.

One thing more than any other appealed to Bork about Director's work: its claim to relentless reason unaffected by political forethought. He later called Director "the most savagely honest intellectual I have ever known," the highest Bork compliment. As Bork stated in his search for neutral legal principles some years later, "Recognition of the need for principle is only the first step, but once that step is taken much more follows. Logic has a life of its own, and devotion to principle requires that we follow where logic leads."

Bork's major scholarly contribution, a 1978 book twelve years in the making called *The Antitrust Paradox*, built on Director's concepts. It profoundly influenced the Reagan Justice Department, which promoted deregulation and purposeful laxity in the enforcement of antitrust law and encouraged mergers for the sake of efficiency.

The fact that Director's research forced on Bork a reevaluation of his own political beliefs made it more appealing. Through most of his life Bork was attracted to individuals who claimed that intellectual inquiry had led them away from earlier political convictions. The truth felt more real when it was unwelcome.

Bork's admiration for Director was, in part, the attraction of op-

posites. Director never published his theories; he was asocial in character, exhibited no passion, and was uninterested in the ebb and flow
of national politics. He was slow and methodical as a researcher, did
not raise his voice, and had few pretensions to intellectual leadership. Bork, on the other hand, became an ardent and very public
crusader. He felt restricted when confined to purely academic pur-
suits.

Armed with Director's theories, Bork stayed at Chicago a year
beyond law school to work under his instructor's supervision. That
year gave rise to the first of Bork's papers that made an impact. The
paper argued that when firms bought up smaller companies down-
stream in the production process—a move known as vertical integration—they were not necessarily acting as monopolies but sometimes simply becoming more efficient. It was an argument against
existing antitrust law and for freer markets. Bork was only twenty-
seven at the time. He won wide praise for the paper, which bucked
prevailing wisdom. The experience with Director provided Bork
with what he once described as "a new way of looking at the world
and an enormously rigorous and logical way—a method that seemed
to promise further explanations of things if one pursued it."

He would ultimately pursue such rigor, but first Bork entered private law practice. In 1954, after a year with a New York law firm, he
returned to Chicago with the large, prestigious firm of Kirkland and
Ellis, where he worked as an antitrust specialist.

Bork rose rapidly in the firm. He was almost certainly on his way
to a partnership when another former student of Director's named
Howard Krane came for a job interview. Although Krane's credentials were most impressive, he was turned away. A young associate
heard a partner talking about Krane in the hallway and understood
him to say that he had been rejected because he was Jewish. The firm
at the time had a limit on the number of Jews hired. The associate,
Dallin Oaks, told Bork. Not only was Bork's wife, Claire, Jewish,
but so were many of the men who had most impressed him in law
school, including Director and Edward Levi. Later Alexander
Bickel, also a Jew, became Bork's closest friend and mentor in constitutional law. The refusal to hire Krane was the kind of mindless
prejudice that had no place in Bork's world view. He was deeply
disturbed.

Oaks, a Mormon, understood the consequences of religious big-otry. He told Bork he would support him if he raised the issue. The two went to see several senior partners, and according to Oaks, Bork said to them, "We have a larger stake in the future of this firm than you do. We want this man considered on his merits." The partners agreed to reconsider. The quota system was abolished, and Krane was hired. He eventually became the managing partner of Kirkland and Ellis.

Krane and Bork became fast friends, almost inseparable, working together on antitrust cases, lunching daily, occasionally staying up all night figuring out the details of their cases. Krane, still a bachelor, took dinner with the Borks four or five evenings a week.

Krane remembered the Bork of those days not as a man obsessed with politics and philosophy but as an irreverent and skilled mental jouster. Together they invented a university football team that made use of antitrust terminology with a halfback called Vince Ancillary and a linebacker named Dummy Per Se. Dummy was once caught molesting Miss Use down by the patent pool.

They also dreamed up plots for mystery murders with a character called Dirk Dork and began to develop a story involving a murder in a law firm. But the story never got written. Krane admired Bork and used to tell him even then that Bork one day should sit on the Supreme Court.

Bork's other close friend at the firm was Oaks, his partner in the Krane crusade. Another Chicago graduate, Oaks, too, had fierce intellectual and political ambition. He ultimately became president of Brigham Young University, justice on the Utah Supreme Court, and one of the Mormon Church's governing Council of Twelve, in line to head the religious group's sprawling empire.

Oaks and Bork used to talk about finding greater intellectual ful-fillment elsewhere. In 1961 Oaks did just that. He left Kirkland and Ellis to teach at the University of Chicago. He remembered that Bork was shaken by the move because Oaks had acted on what the two of them had often talked about.

Bork grew more restless. He liked law practice, but he could see that it would not offer him a chance to make a lasting mark in life. Antitrust lawyer John S. McGee, who had studied under Aaron Director with Bork, remembered Bork's talking about leaving the law firm. "He told me he didn't want to spend his life practicing law and cash in at the end, leaving nothing but a trail of depositions, briefs and money," McGee recalled. "He wanted to leave something enduring."

Ward Bowman, who had also worked with Bork under Director, was on the faculty of Yale Law School. In 1962 a job opened up to teach antitrust. He recommended Bork for the position, and ultimately the offer came. So, at the age of thirty-five, Bork resigned his twenty-six-thousand-dollar-a-year junior partnership. He and his wife left the comfortable northern suburbs of Chicago, packed their three young children—Bob, Jr., Charles, and Ellen—into their Chevrolet convertible, and drove to New Haven, where he took a position as assistant professor of law for less than fifteen thousand dollars. His chance to make a mark had arrived.

The family settled easily into New Haven. They bought a rambling house, Claire Bork and the children made friends among other faculty families, and Bork quickly established himself as a house conservative and gadfly at the law school. At Chicago Bork had been one conservative among many. At Yale he was a minuscule minority. Apart from him there were Bowman, who had helped get Bork hired, and Ralph Winter, who joined the faculty about the same time and was later appointed by Reagan to a federal judgeship. To many of his liberal colleagues Bork seemed a quirky piece of exotica. Yale had built a reputation as a center of left-wing legal scholarship over the preceding three decades—partly as an antidote to the dominance of Harvard—but it was also a climate in which intellectual idiosyncrasy and nonconformity of all kinds were welcome.

One could count on a rousing debate with Bob Bork. He was always bucking prevailing wisdom, and he so loved to talk. Harry Wellington, who was to become dean of the law school, remembered Bork's positioning himself in the faculty lounge, smoking countless cigarettes, drinking huge cups of coffee, and challenging all comers on any subject.

Bork supported the presidential candidacy of Republican Barry Goldwater in 1964, a lonely position at Yale. Indeed, he was one of two members of the university's entire faculty willing to admit he favored Goldwater. He joined a group called Scholars for Goldwater at the urging of Chicago economist Milton Friedman, Aaron Director's brother-in-law. The group liked Goldwater's opposition to government intervention, his stated goal of cutting the federal bureaucracy, and his advocacy of escalating the war in Vietnam. Wherever Bork went, his disbelieving colleagues would ask him how he could possibly support Barry Goldwater. Bork said once that between the time he walked out of his house and arrived at his law school office, he held fifteen impromptu debates and arrived at work in need of another shower. The man was in heaven.

Bork wrote an article for the Yale student newspaper in praise of Goldwater. On campus Goldwater was considered such a right-wing radical, so antithetical to the Yale outlook, that the student editors of the paper had terrible difficulty finding anyone to write a piece in support of the Republican candidate. Bork at first begged off, saying he was an untenured assistant professor, in no position to stick out his neck quite so far. But the editors could find no one else, and he relented.

The same year Bork wrote a fateful article for the *New Republic*. In it he condemned the public accommodations sections of the proposed 1964 Civil Rights Act aimed at integrating restaurants, hotels, and other businesses. Bork had no objection to racial integration. Quite the contrary. But he was filled with an unrelenting suspicion of government coercion. He felt that requiring white business owners to serve blacks against their wishes was like telling people whom to invite to a dinner party. Once the government got that involved in people's personal choices, where was the limit? Freedom, the nation's greatest virtue, was threatened.

As he explained it a quarter century later, "I agree that the attack on racism was correct. The question was whether government could say to people who had racial preferences, 'You must associate [with blacks],' and I was looking for a principle to justify that."

His August 1963 article stated:

The discussion we ought to hear is of the cost in freedom that must be paid for such legislation, the morality of enforcing morals through law, and the likely consequences for law enforcement of trying to do so. . . . In a society that purports to value freedom as an end in itself, the simple argument from morality to law can be a dangerous non sequitur. . . . Of the ugliness of racial discrimination there need be no argument. . . . But it is one thing when stubborn people express their racial antipathies in laws which prevent individuals, whether white or Negro, from dealing with those who are willing to deal with them, and quite another to tell them that even as individuals they may not act on their racial preferences in particular areas of life. The principle of such legislation is that if I find your behavior ugly by my standards, moral or aesthetic, and if you prove stubborn about adopting my view of the situation, I am justified in having the state coerce you into more righteous paths. That is itself a principle of unsurpassed ugliness.

Those last four words—"principle of unsurpassed ugliness" rang in Bork's ears during the battle over his Supreme Court confirmation. His references in the article to the rights of barbers and chiropodists ("If it is permissible to tell a barber . . . that he must deal with all who come to him . . . [S]aying that a chiropodist cannot refuse a Negro patient . . .") were especially ill chosen. Bork may not have known it, but those were codes at the time for the feelings of racists who did not want to have to touch blacks.

To many, Bork's was a fringe position based on dogged and unsubtle insistence on libertarian "principle." Outside of the South he was joined by only a handful in the academy and on the editorial pages. Indeed, Bork himself came to regret and eschew his position.

When Bork's article appeared in the *New Republic*—then a left-liberal publication—its editors took a rare step. They printed their own reply, saying they disagreed emphatically with him. They made the point that Bork's notion of the freedom of the individual was half baked; restaurant owners and innkeepers were not, in fact, free to deny service to whites who were well behaved. The aim of the Public Accommodations Act was simply to extend that rule to people of other races. They also attacked Bork on grounds to become familiar through the years: They quoted Oliver Wendell Holmes, who said law was more the result of experience than of logic. Bork, critics said, was following logic too far. "Government without principle ends in shipwreck; but government according to any single principle, to the exclusion of all other, ends in madness," the editors said.

That article played a great role in Bork's failure to attain the Supreme Court. Few of his writings would so incense black Americans or so succor those looking for evidence that he harbored racist sentiments—untrue though it was. Even his friends and supporters would look back on the piece embarrassed that Bork had taken such a theory-bound stand. They would mutter that they couldn't figure what Bork was thinking at a time when right-minded whites were struggling to help blacks achieve equality. At the least, Bork's piece seemed to suggest an insulation from reality. Bork was not alone in his views, but virtually everyone else on his side really *did* harbor racist views or answer to constituents who did.

A decade after the article appeared, during his confirmation hearings to be solicitor general, Bork said he had changed his mind about the public accommodations law because it had worked fine. From then on he explained the 1963 article as the experimental musings of an academic pushing his notion of freedom. He said his ideas were the result of discussions he had been having with Alexander Bickel, his Yale colleague; the article no more than one end of a kind of faculty lounge debate.

In 1964, however, Bork seemed to take the ideas more seriously than that. He provided Goldwater with a critique of the Public Accommodations Act on constitutional grounds for use in his campaign.

Over the next several years Bork refined his libertarian ideas about freedom and the dangers of government intervention. Along the way he gained notoriety as a key conservative in the Ivy League. (There were, after all, not many.) One colleague remembered that after Goldwater's defeat, Bork said that while his wish was a pipe dream, the man he really wanted as president was Ronald Reagan.

In 1968 the *New Republic* invited him to write again, this time in defense of the presidential candidacy of Republican Richard Nixon. In the piece, "Why I Am for Nixon," Bork argued that Nixon and liberals shared the same goals but that Nixon merely wished to gain those goals through conservative, and more effective, techniques. He said liberals were wrong to doubt Nixon's sincerity. In a thought that he later applied in discussing his own defeat, he said, "[A]s audiences lose confidence in their ability to judge the technical competence of public performers, they are likely to begin judging qualities such as sincerity which, often quite erroneously, they imagine themselves able to detect."

Illustrating his contention that liberal techniques—i.e., government intervention—betrayed their own goals, and remembering what he had been taught by Aaron Director, Bork cited the minimum wage as the cause of higher black unemployment. He wrote:

> Laws that raise the minimum price of labor mean that the first
> to be fired and the last to be hired are the less skilled. Given the
> present distribution of skills in the work force, hikes in the

federal minimum wage mean unemployment for Negroes and particularly for Negro teenagers trying to enter the labor market. The introduction of the $1 minimum wage in 1956 created the first striking disparity between white and nonwhite teenage unemployment rates. Each new increase has hit rural and urban Negroes harder than whites. The net effect of these laws is to deepen poverty and make welfare measures more expensive and less effective.

That same year, 1968, Bork was nearing the end of his book on antitrust law. He took a sabbatical leave in England to do so. In England, on a barge trip with his family, Bork had trouble shaving because the bathroom was so cramped. His children begged him to let his beard grow. He did and never shaved it off.

While in England, he wrote a long article for *Fortune* in which, one final time, he applied his early libertarian ideas of individual freedom to constitutional law. The article, entitled "The Supreme Court Needs a New Philosophy," was an incisive and cogent argument in favor of an activist reading of individual rights in the Constitution. It was his last public fling with individual freedom as the cornerstone to the Constitution; it summed up precisely and elegantly the liberal and libertarian views that he was to scorn so vituperatively only a few years later and for the rest of his career.

He wrote: "The text of the Constitution, as anyone experienced in words might expect, is least precise where it is most important. Like the Ten Commandments, the Constitution enshrines profound values, but necessarily omits the minor premises required to apply them. The First Amendment is a prime example. To apply the Amendment, a judge must bring to the text principles, judgments, and intuitions not to be found in bare words."

He sought ways for judges to expand on existing rights and to justify other rights not specifically mentioned in the Constitution, rights such as privacy. He said the Bill of Rights was an incomplete, open-ended document. The work of its completion fell to the Supreme Court. He tried to work out a general theory of the relation between majority and minority rights. He wrote that "my freedom to swing my fist ends where your nose begins. The problem is to define the jurisdiction of the majority's nose. If it is permitted to begin where the majority starts to feel pain, the principle might prevent minorities from so much as twitching a finger."

After returning from abroad, Bork began to abandon that line of inquiry. As angry students and liberal sympathizers picked up the banner of freedom and individual liberty, Bork dropped it. Liberty had been a conservative rallying cry aimed at preserving the rights of the propertied from the reach of the masses. But liberty was co-opted by the left, and Bork and others on the right began emphasizing central authority and law and order over personal freedom.

Bork attributed his shift to the influence of Bickel, with whom he had taught a constitutional law seminar at Yale. Their course, in which the two often shouted at each other for several hours, each exhibiting wilting wit, was one of the school's most popular during those years. Bork would advocate libertarian constitutional principles, and Bickel a more measured, traditional approach. Once, while trying to promote his notion of a hard, sharp doctrine to control judicial review, Bork got frustrated with Bickel's insistence that only tradition and wisdom would serve that function. "Mr. Bickel's legal philosophy is a cross between Edmund Burke and Fiddler on the Roof," Bork told the class. Bickel liked that phrase and repeated it often later.

But after Bork's return from England the seminar started to fall flat. When Bork asked Bickel what happened, Bickel, now his closest friend, said, "You're not saying those crazy things you used to say."

Bork had, in fact, abandoned his libertarian search for new freedoms. The majority's nose, he had decided, was untouchable. Whatever the Constitution said clearly and explicitly, fine. But beyond that the minority had no discernible rights.

Bork's second conversion—from libertarian to social conservative—like his first—from socialist to libertarian conservative—resulted from many things. Forces were at work on Bork—and on Bickel—forces that became a defining factor in the country: Students rebelled against the war in Vietnam and against prevailing middle-class values. Blacks and women demanded power. Institutions that Bork had come to hold dear, such as the university, were under threat.

A headline in the *New Haven Register* on April 27, 1970, reads: YALE LAW LIBRARY HIT BY SUSPICIOUS BLAZE. A photograph above it shows hundreds of charred lawbooks piled up on the sidewalk across from the neo-Gothic facade of the law library. Police barriers close off the street. A couple of people are examining the books. A short distance away from them, briefcase in one hand, whiskered face held by the other, is a lone and worried figure, Robert Bork. Although unidentified by the newspaper, it is unmistakably he. It is a telling tableau. What the newspaper termed a suspicious fire had damaged the library and the books, holy implements in the temple of learning.

Bork's last notions of expanding liberty were sapped by what he saw around him in the heyday of the student rebellion. Excessive freedom had produced barbarism. Standards—academic, personal, civil—were falling. Methodical analysis was being replaced by liberal orthodoxy. And most members of the academy were joining in, providing the theoretical underpinnings of this so-called revolt. Bork resisted fiercely. During one long student strike at Yale he was one of two professors who insisted on giving classes.

During the sixties the lines of cultural war were drawn in America. Liberals and conservatives changed sides on the question of liberty, which now referred increasingly to the rights of minorities and the dispossessed. Bork had now moved over to the conservative side. It was, in many ways, an easy switch because it involved a return to his early Chicago training. He lamented the decline of authority, the loss of interest in the ancients, the dangers of permissiveness. In language and temperament he became a part of the nascent neoconservative movement and began to write for the *National Review* and the *Wall Street Journal*.

Slowly, as he felt the societal order face threat of decline, Bork ceased to be an iconoclast. He maintained his wit, but he lost his patience for good-natured intellectual jousting and became at times a testy advocate.

In an article in 1975 about Bickel's last book, *The Morality of Consent,* Bork was writing also of himself:

One precipitating factor in Alex's turn to political philosophy was the university tumult of the 60s. That turmoil, accompanied by threats, violence, assaultive rhetoric, all in the name of angrily asserted transcendental ideals, was a miniature French Revolution, a "chaos of levity and ferocity," in Burke's phrase. Alex was astonished and outraged, not merely with students prepared, in a spasm of mindless self-righteousness, to destroy institutions it had taken generations or even centuries to build, but even more with those faculty members who, at the first obscenity or classroom disruption, instantly abandoned the ideal of rationality. The residue of that anti-intellectual, anti-institutional time is still with us, legitimated by our tolerance.

The last sentence made clear Bork's sense of the work still ahead. For Bork, solicitor general when he wrote those words, it was time to stop the liberals from their take-over of the universities and judiciary, where so much of the nation's cultural and political agenda was set. The sixties and their aftermath produced a clash of societal visions: Liberals argued that the nation could be made more equal; conservatives stressed human limits; a push toward equality, in the conservative view, was fruitless, dangerous, and verged on state tyranny.

Ever the happy warrior, Bork set about to slay the sacred cows of constitutional law with his usual gusto. In short, he urged a return to original principles. He saw parallels between antitrust and constitutional law. Like antitrust laws, contemporary constitutional theory was based, he believed, on suspect liberal political goals rather than on rigorous, fact-based theory. Like antitrust law, constitutional law lacked serious theoretical foundation and was defenseless in the face of growing political manipulation. A reexamination of constitutional origins would build a new and permanent foundation.

The theories on antitrust promulgated by Bork and other Chicago analysts in the 1960s and 1970s were at first rejected as idiosyncratic. However, they gained ground among lawyers and academics, and during the Reagan years they became official policy. The surprising rise of his views emboldened Bork to promote his constitutional theories with renewed energy. Just months before Bork was nominated to the Supreme Court, he told a Philadelphia audience that the change in antitrust policy had been something of an epiphany for him. He had thought such a shift impossible when he began writing about the issues. "That accounts for the tone of much of my early writing—sarcastic and confrontational," he said. "I thought if you couldn't win, at least you could cause pain on the way out."

Echoing Richard Weaver's 1948 book title, Bork told the audience that "ideas have consequences." He added that the chances of restoring legitimacy to constitutional theory were excellent because of what he called Bork's wave theory of law reform. According to Bork's concept, courts often make law before an adequate theory has been formulated. The first wave of theorists begins with those deformed notions and builds. As he put it, "A rich, erudite and mindless literature grows up." Eventually the law makes little sense to *real* thinkers—such as himself—and "the second-wave theorists return to first principles . . . and they begin to construct better theories of how courts should decide cases. Since the second-wave arguments are much better, they slowly come to dominate the intellectual world, the new ideas slowly percolate through to the courts, and the law is on the road to respectability." Just as he helped lead the second wave in antitrust, so he would do in constitutional law.

Bork was now middle-aged—he turned forty in 1967. Faced with student unrest and liberal stridency, he recast his constitutional philosophy. The libertarian was becoming a Burkean, warning of the usurpation of power by left-leaning academics. He became convinced that the source of America's problem was not uneducated legislators making bad laws but educated intellectuals forcing their views into the body of law. On one side of the cultural war were the liberal intellectuals. On the other were Bork and a handful of other academics, joined by the "silent majority."

Bork chose as his own President Nixon's slogan of "strict constructionism." It was a term invented to restrict interpretations of constitutional intent to what the text said and not to what it might mean in today's context. Bork argued that only those liberties made explicit by the Constitution could be legally defended.

This thinking Bork laid out in a series of lectures published in the *Indiana Law Journal* in 1971. One of the most intelligently provocative law journal articles of its time, it shocked many. It became Exhibit 2 in the burying of Robert Bork sixteen years later.

The article puts forth the principle that unless the Constitution specifically addresses a value, there is no way for a judge to choose it over any other. The judge must withdraw and leave the choice to the legislatures. Bork attacked the 1965 case of *Griswold* v. *Connecticut*, in which the Supreme Court said that Americans enjoy a right of privacy even though it is unstated in the Constitution and that this right covers such things as the use of contraceptives by married couples.

At the time it was against the law in Connecticut for a married couple to use contraceptives. Griswold, the executive director of the Planned Parenthood League of Connecticut, and its medical director, a licensed physician, were convicted under the law. Their offense—giving married persons information on contraception and prescribing a contraceptive for the wife's use. The Court held the statute unconstitutional.

The decision, written by Justice William O. Douglas, said several amendments created "zones of privacy." The right to privacy was found in "penumbras formed by emanations" of those amendments. While widely criticized as loose constitutional reasoning, the *Griswold* notion of privacy became a touchstone in contemporary jurisprudence.

Bork said the Douglas decision was specious and unprincipled in deriving a new constitutional right. He thought it nothing more than middle-class judges placing their own values into the Constitution. In doing so, they usurped the rights of legislatures to make those value choices. He said, "Every clash between a minority claiming freedom and a majority claiming power to regulate involves a choice between the gratifications of the two groups."

Bork then compared the desire of a couple to use contraceptives in a state that bans their use with the desire of a utility company to defy a smoke pollution ordinance. He said the two cases were identical from a judicial point of view because neither right was found in the Constitution. "There is no principled way to decide that one man's gratifications are more deserving of respect than another's or that one form of gratification is more worthy than another," he wrote, adding, "It follows, of course, that broad areas of constitutional law ought to be reformulated."

The word *gratification* greatly offended many of his colleagues, especially because Bork referred to the "Equal Gratification Clause" in mockery of the Equal Protection clause of the Fourteenth Amendment that had been used to expand liberties such as privacy.

Most distressing in Bork's philosophy, from a liberal point of view, was his insistence that if legislatures passed intrusive laws, the laws had to be upheld if the Constitution did not specifically prohibit them. One old acquaintance recalled a dinner table argument she had with Bork during those years. Bork was holding forth: Judges have to stay out of anything not explicitly laid out in the Constitution. What, she asked, if a state passed a law requiring all male citizens to wear beards? Should the courts uphold the law? Of course, Bork replied triumphantly. But states wouldn't pass such laws, he added. If you fear they would, you have no faith in democracy.

76]   BATTLE FOR JUSTICE

In the 1971 piece Bork went on to discuss his view of First Amendment protection of speech, the most explicit and controversial part of the article. Rights, such as free speech, he said, exist to perpetuate the process of self-government, not to escape or destroy it. Therefore, "The category of protected speech should consist of speech concerned with governmental behavior, policy or personnel. . . . Explicitly political speech is speech about how we are governed. . . . It does not cover scientific, educational, commercial or literary expressions as such." Bork also said that speech advocating the overthrow of the government or acts of illegality was not worthy of protection. He was thinking of the rebels of the era.

Such a notion—that only political speech advocating legal acts was worthy of judicial protection—was shockingly narrow. If adopted, it would undo Supreme Court decisions of the previous decades cherished by the vast majority of Americans. Bork knew that his opinions would upset people. But that was where his analysis took him and he happily followed.

C H A P T E R

4

Public Figure

Had it not been for his wife Claire, Bork might never have gone into constitutional law. He was casting about for a second field to teach, apart from antitrust, and she said to him, "What's the biggest field in the law, the most exciting intellectual field?"

He said, "Constitutional law."

She said, "Teach that."

A woman of humble origins, willowy, dark-haired Claire Bork was street-smart and ambitious for her husband. Former colleagues remember that when the notion of his becoming solicitor general was floated, she was enthusiastic. She spoke of the possibility of his being named later to the high court.

She was also, in the words of a friend, a tiger to her cubs, a shrewd manager of home and family. She had dropped out of the University of Chicago to marry Bork and help put him through law school. But she ultimately got a real estate license and was planning, before her illness made it impossible, to finish her degree and go to law school.

Despite her fierce protectiveness, Claire softened Bork. They had a strong partnership, sharing everything. They grew intellectually and politically in harmony with each other. One day Bork showed up to work with dark rings under his eyes. When a colleague asked what the matter was, Bork said he had spent the night arguing with his wife. "About what? Money?" asked the colleague. "No, vertical integration," replied Bork, referring to an aspect of antitrust law.

Claire was driving through New England in 1971, visiting summer camps for her second son, Charles, when she felt a numbness in her hands. She was soon after diagnosed with cancer and told she had only six months left. With chemotherapy and assiduous support from friends and family, she lived more than nine years, enough to see her children grown. She kept her illness a secret from the children for some five years. All they knew was that their mother needed rest, but they never made much of it. She belittled the seriousness of her condition to them until the very end.

Barbara Black, who later became dean of Columbia Law School, was Claire's closest friend in New Haven. Wife of the renowned liberal constitutional scholar Charles Black, Barbara Black was the first person Claire told when the cancer reached her lungs. In the eulogy Barbara Black delivered at Claire's funeral, she recounted how Claire was a woman who could do anything, managing the business of the house with the merest corner of her mind.

"But the thing that Claire was, in my experience, uniquely talented at was a perceptiveness about people, individually and in relationships, about their needs, motivations, feelings. She was a genius at understanding people," Black said.

Discussing Claire's devotion to her family, Black recalled how profoundly touched she was by something Bork had said to her one evening shortly before his wife's death. They were sitting in the living room, the kids whizzing in and out, banging doors, being noisy and cheerful, and Bork said, "Look what I've got; I never knew I'd have this, I never thought I would. She gave it to me."

Bork, an only child, had had a strained relationship with his parents. He had never known the kind of domestic happiness Claire had brought him. She, and everything she represented and built, had become the anchor in his life. Soon she would be gone. The imminence of her demise, the feeling that such moments, ephemeral though they be, must be held tightly and cherished elevated the ordinary.

During Claire's illness and after her death Barbara Black was like a mother to Ellen, Bork's only daughter and youngest child, who was nineteen when her mother died. Ellen had her mother's spunky intelligence and dark-haired beauty. But the relationship between Ellen and Black would break off in agonizing abruptness seven years later, when Black, a liberal and influential academic, stayed silent over Bork's nomination to the Supreme Court.

Black found herself at that period in an excruciating quandary and discussed it with Harry Wellington, former Yale dean and friend of Bork's who felt the same way. Black couldn't abide the idea of Bork's fierce conservatism on the high court; her friends and colleagues were pressuring her to come out against his confirmation. But there was Bork, for whom she had great affection, and young Ellen, and the overpowering memory of Claire. Black could not forsake them, yet neither could she bring herself to say positive things about Bork for fear it would help win him confirmation.

The battle over Bork raged. So huge and unwieldy had it become that Black felt it was impossible to say something small and personal and leave it at that. She turned down requests from reporters to talk about it and resisted the pressure of friends on both sides. Ellen Bork, then a spokeswoman for the State Department's Central America section, was fiercely loyal to her father. She loved him and agreed with his conservative politics. To her, Black's position was unthinkable. For Ellen, her refusal to help Bork was so traumatic that she refused to speak to Black for a year.

Wellington also stayed out in large measure, despite constant insistence from both sides that his testimony would be key. He begged forgiveness from Bork later in a note in which he said one's duty to country came above one's duty to a friend. He said he knew Bork would understand. It made Bork blind with fury, and he vowed never to see Wellington again. Bork almost forsook his tradition of going to the Harvard-Yale football game the following November for fear he would run into the former dean.

One close friend of Bork's said, "I just couldn't understand Wellington and Black. Maybe I'm old-fashioned, but I believe you stick up for your friends. If Bob decided he wanted to be a ballerina and the New York Ballet called me up, I'd at least say he had nice feet."

In 1972 Bork became more politically involved, advising Nixon on legislation to limit busing in school desegregation cases. He stood virtually alone in the law schools in support for the bill. He also joined a group called Academics for Nixon and signed a full-page advertisement in the *New York Times* in support of his candidacy for a second term. Toward the end of the year Nixon aides contacted him again, partly on the advice of Bickel, who was increasingly conservative but still a Democrat. Bickel told them that instead of consulting him on legal issues, they ought to involve a smart Republican, a man like Bob Bork, in their administration. The aides asked Bork if he would like to be solicitor general, the lawyer who represents the government in front of the Supreme Court.

Here was a wonderful opportunity for Bork to put into practice what he had been preaching for so long. He would at last address the Court he had spent so much time criticizing. And for the tiny clique of conservatives at the Yale Law School, it offered a moment of small celebration. One student, later an official in the Justice Department, remembered the day Bork was named. He and Ralph Winter, a professor who would go on to be a judge, were sitting in the cafeteria and joking that the student newspaper the next day ought to headline the story with NIXON APPOINTS ONE-FIFTH OF THE LAW SCHOOL CONSERVATIVES. That was counting Bork, Winter, Ward Bowman, and two students.

It was a heady move for Bork and one fraught with danger. The Watergate scandal was edging closer to the Oval Office every day; fourteen months later Nixon would be forced to resign in disgrace. In June 1972, just a year before Bork took up his job, a team of men paid by Nixon's campaign had broken into the Democratic National Committee headquarters in Washington's Watergate complex. After the burglary was discovered, the administration engaged in a massive effort to cover up its sponsorship of those apprehended. How involved was Nixon in the original plan? In the cover-up? The nation wanted to know. During the investigation of the events it was discovered that the president had tape-recorded every one of his conversations in the White House; investigators sought the tapes.

Only five weeks after joining the administration, Bork was summoned by White House Chief of Staff Alexander Haig, who asked him if he would resign and become Nixon's chief defense lawyer in the growing scandal. Bork recalled Haig's telling him: "Only you can save us; a collision course is upon us."

Bork told Haig he would first have to listen to the contested White House tape recordings. Since Nixon wouldn't let anyone, including his own lawyers, hear the tapes, Haig and Bork agreed he was the wrong man for the job.

The next month brought a delicate problem of indicting Vice President Spiro Agnew for income tax evasion stemming from a kickback scandal while he was governor of Maryland. Bork had to find a legal formula that would allow for Agnew's indictment without showing the way toward an indictment of Nixon. He did it, and Nixon accepted his brief. Agnew was forced out, replaced by Gerald Ford, who became president upon Nixon's own resignation.

Two months later Bork was enmeshed in the Saturday Night Massacre. It occurred on October 20, 1973. Allegations regarding the extent of wrongdoing in the Watergate affair were then so widespread that Nixon asked Harvard Law Professor Archibald Cox to act as special prosecutor to investigate the circumstances surrounding the Watergate affair. To assure Cox of a free hand—his condition for accepting the job—Nixon promised him absolute authority in the investigation.

As Cox looked into the situation, he asked the president to hand over the crucial White House tapes. Nixon resisted, offering an edited version of the tapes. Cox stood firm and said he might seek a contempt citation against the president.

Nixon ordered Attorney General Elliot Richardson to fire Cox. Richardson refused and quit. The President then turned to William Ruckelshaus, deputy attorney general, who also said no and quit.

Bork was next in line. He was known to have had doubts about the appointment of a special prosecutor to begin with. He also believed that under the Constitution it was clear that Nixon had the right to fire Cox and eventually would do so. Rather than quit, Bork agreed to become acting attorney general and gave Cox his notice.

During the 1982 hearings on his nomination to the federal judgeship, Bork defended his role in the affair. He said Nixon was going to have his way and Bork's own resignation would serve no purpose. Further, his leaving would have had terrible consequences for an already shell-shocked Justice Department.

"At that point, you would have had massive resignations from the top levels of the Department of Justice," he told the Senate Judiciary Committee, adding that the department would "have effectively been crippled." Both Richardson and Ruckelshaus said they had urged Bork to carry out the orders and praised his actions. They said they both had given commitments to Congress not to interfere with the work of the special prosecutor, but Bork had given no such commitment and was therefore free to act.

As for Cox's work, Bork said he was confident at the time it would continue under other auspices. He said he had retained Cox's staff and suggested that Leon Jaworski, a widely respected prosecutor, be named to replace Cox. When and even whether Bork pushed for the naming of another prosecutor would be a matter of dispute. Some of those serving him at the time supported his recollections, but others took issue with his version of events, saying it was a week and a half before, under pressure, Nixon agreed to name another special prosecutor. The Judiciary Committee accepted Bork's explanation in 1982.

Bork's three-and-a-half-year tenure as solicitor general, though distinguished, had its share of political complications. He advanced his conservative beliefs, as on the constitutionality of the death penalty, the illegality of busing, and the power of the president over Congress. Yet those who worked with him had universally high regard for him as a man and lawyer. When Bork did not agree with the government's stand on a particular issue, he would often back off, allowing others in his office to argue the case. And he acted in intellectually honest ways that sometimes angered Nixon's conservative supporters. Once he acknowledged a prosecutorial mistake that freed the producers of the film *Deep Throat* from an obscenity charge; another time he urged the high court to allow Congress the power to impose minimum wages on local governments. Supreme Court justices remembered him as a fine and capable advocate.

Jewel LaFontant, a rarity in Republican circles since she was a black woman, had been in the American delegation at the United Nations when President Nixon offered her a position in the solicitor general's office. She was placed in charge of the very large civil division. The other deputy solicitors general resented the political nature of her appointment. The tradition had always been that the solicitor general's office was staffed exclusively with the best constitutional lawyers the department could find. They felt that LaFontant, with all due respect, did not fit that category. So they isolated her. A secretary told LaFontant one day that the other deputies had meetings from which she was excluded. She asked how the secretary knew. She replied that she was told to call all the deputies and the names were read out. The secretary said, "And Mrs. LaFontant?" The response was, oh, no, just the men.

LaFontant went immediately to Bork. As she told the story:

He exhibited strongly his dismay and sputtered his unhappiness about this attempt to exclude me and to discriminate against me. The very next day was the beginning of my attending so many briefings—I was bombarded with meetings—that

I wondered to myself whether I had been wise in complaining in the first place.

But Judge Bork handled this in his usual low-key way, quiet but determined and fair manner—no confrontation, no embarrassing accusations—things just changed. He had seen to it that I was treated the same as the others.

LaFontant said Bork also encouraged her efforts to increase the number of women in the Justice Department.

He was remembered fondly by colleagues from those years for beginning his days sitting on a couch in his office, smoking, drinking coffee, and filling in a crossword puzzle while briefs and legal papers were piled up all around him. Such insouciance had its drawbacks. The *Los Angeles Times* reported that Chief Justice Warren Burger once complained to Bork about his frequent lateness in filing briefs.

It was widely known that Bork had ambitions for the Supreme Court. At Christmas 1974, Yale law students produced a skit roasting judicial conservatives. Bork's tennis playing was used as a vehicle to mock his ambition. The students sang that Bork so wanted to play tennis that he would run down his mother, trample little old ladies, get up at 5:00 A.M., all just to play tennis, because "Bob Bork would do anything to get on the Court."

When, in 1975, Justice William O. Douglas retired from the Court, it was thought that Bork might be chosen to fill the vacancy. But President Gerald Ford felt that the public still associated Bork's name with the Watergate scandal; he picked John Paul Stevens, a moderate from Illinois.

With the electoral victory of Jimmy Carter in 1976, Bork considered going into private practice in Washington, a city he had grown to adore. But Dean Wellington, still a good friend, pressed him to return to Yale, offered him a prestigious chair, and Bork agreed.

It turned out to be a difficult time. Bork was seen by many at the school as Nixon's henchman for having fired Special Prosecutor Cox during the Watergate episode. Moreover, Bork was less of a playful theorist at that stage. Older, savvier, and more politically connected, he had lost his taste for academia and had become impatient for change. As Wellington analyzed it, "I had worked hard to get him back. I remembered him as a wonderful, provocative teacher. But those years in Washington were ones that would transform anybody. They had made him impatient with teaching, out of swing. The lead time between what you say and what happens is, after all, a lot longer in academia than in government."

Not just Bork's professional life had undergone metamorphosis, moreover. His personal life was in upheaval.

His Yale colleague and best friend Alex Bickel, who had given Bork so much intellectually and emotionally, had died of cancer at the age of forty-nine in 1974. Bork eulogized Bickel at the heavily attended New Haven funeral. It was a deeply moving testimonial. Bork's mastery of language, his wit and his passion were all in evidence:

> Alex Bickel's gifts were so great and so many that we would have envied him if we had not loved him. For years we knew that he was an extraordinary man. But the warm haze of personal friendship and the diversions of colleagueship obscured at first what gradually became clear—that he can be called, without hesitation or embarrassment, a great man. . . .
>
> I almost hesitate to speak of Alex as a friend, for that was a relationship so precious that talking may put at risk the full richness of the memory. But I must, because one of the man's great talents was his gift for friendship, and others have had the experience with him that I had. It is rare to have a friend with whom one shares every level of experience, from drinking and joking, to intensely personal concerns, to discussions of law and legal theory, and speculations about the order of things. It is true that, as the activity ascended in the intellectual scale, my share tended to shrink, mostly because of Alex's talents but also, it must be stated candidly, because of his flow of words. I once told him that it was the dream of my life to appear against him in the Supreme Court because that was the only place where, by the law of the forum, I would get half of the time for talking. . . .
>
> At a time of my own personal tragedy I went to Alex and Joanne [Bickel's wife] and cried out my grief. Later, on a night of good fortune, I went to them and celebrated late. As I left, touched by Alex's unmixed joy for me, I said to him, "In good times and bad times, I come to you first." I had not realized until I said it that it was true. . . .
>
> I must speak of the manner of his dying. With many friends,

one prefers to remember them in full vigor and wipe from mind the memory of the end. Not so with Alex Bickel. The way in which he went to his death will always remain for me and for the others who witnessed it one of the most profoundly moving experiences of our lives. For eleven months he knew that death was the likely outcome; for several of those months he knew it was the inevitable outcome. As soon as he learned what his illness was, he made a conscious resolve to die well. . . . With increasing difficulty in moving, toward the end almost totally paralyzed and blind, he read while he could, listened to reading when he could not, talked of ideas, of people and, unbelievably, tried to comfort his friends. . . .

He retained to the last his enjoyment of sardonic wit. When the headaches were very bad and the drugs making him drowsy and thick-tongued, I would telephone and, before starting a subject, ask, "How is it today, Alex?" He would say, "Not so good. Not so good. But don't worry, I can still take care of you." And I was always relieved to find out, once again, that he could. . . .

Because his life had been happy, he said he did not mind death. He recalled that when Charles James Fox lay dying, he told his wife, "It don't signify. It don't signify." For the first and only time in my presence, and then only for a moment, tears ran down Alex's cheek. And for once Alex was wrong. It does signify, and it will signify—to scholarship, to the nation, and to all who knew him for as many years as are left to us.

Having buried Bickel, Bork returned to Yale in 1977 as the first Alexander M. Bickel Professor of Public Law, a chair created in his friend's memory. Bork came bearing the weight of his life's central tragedy: Claire's cancer was spreading. Within a couple of years her medical bills became astronomical, and Bork took on well-paying corporate clients who would come to New Haven and pay him two to three hundred dollars an hour. His classes were less interesting—even his famed antitrust class, known to the students as protrust, had lost its bite—and he hurried home after teaching to tend to his wife.

He did finish his book on antitrust, which had been put aside when he went to the Justice Department. He also kept up his profile in conservative circles by giving speeches. His words had a different quality to them now from a decade earlier. Increasingly he was preoccupied with public morality, the decline of authority, and the need to preserve institutions.

The major focus of his anger was egalitarianism and the efforts of liberal intellectuals to achieve it. He extrapolated from his study of antitrust to society at large, stating toward the end of his book: "There is no prospect either in antitrust or in the society generally that equality of condition will be achieved, but antitrust demonstrates some of the costs of moving toward it." He then listed the destruction of wealth through inefficiency, the accumulation of power in the government, and the replacement of free markets with government-regulated markets. Finally, he said, egalitarianism leads to the ultimate sin: a shift from laws made by elected representatives to laws decreed by courts and bureaucracies.

Bork dedicated his career to fighting those evils. He pointed to the enemy—academics, journalists, lawyers, government officials— saying such people had an interest in moving law in the direction of their tastes and needs. That is why, he argued, free speech had become such an important part of the law. It was in the interest of the intellectual class to insist upon it.

And that is why such people favored egalitarianism. It placed a greater burden on the federal bureaucracy, which they populated. But, he warned in speech after speech, such people are making America feel guilty about itself, crippling its sense of confidence, its ability to punish criminals, to choose a moral direction. For Bork, egalitarianism went hand in hand with permissiveness.

In a speech at Carleton College in Minnesota during the 1977–78 academic year, Bork laid out his case, one he repeated over and over:

The trend now is running heavily against institutions and their authority, and that is worrisome. It is now apparent that for the past twenty years the health of our institutions has been in decline. . . . What is new, arising within the last decade or two, is a strong shift toward the assumption that the only truly moral society would be one in which outcomes were completely equal. . . . It is clear that a society whose morality is egalitarian but whose structure is necessarily filled with inequalities is very likely to be a society that is uneasy about itself, a society that feels guilty. We do. . . . An egalitarian dislikes hierarchies, which imply superiority. . . . He is therefore inclined to moral relativism about personal behavior. . . .

This leads to a denial of the right of the society to impose moral standards.

From a concern over moral relativism Bork went back to his long-standing worry: the desire of liberals to regulate businesses, producing heavy, intrusive, and dangerous regulation. Such a desire to redistribute goods goes against what Bork called the "natural tyranny of the bell-shaped curve" in the distribution of the good things of the world. In other words, inequality is the world's natural condition, and those who seek to change it through government action will bring state tyranny. A return to first principles, to the aims and beliefs of those who founded the country, would free the country from this absurd and alien ideology that sought to equalize rich and poor. That same ideology also sought to equalize sexual tendencies. It had to be fought.

And fight it he did. He publicly opposed government-imposed affirmative action for blacks and women, and in 1978 he fought at Yale an effort to ban law firm recruiters who discriminated against homosexuals. He had not been active in campus politics, but that issue exercised him. In a memo to the faculty, Bork wrote: "Contrary to the assertions made, homosexuality is obviously not an unchangeable condition like race or gender. Individual choice plays a role in homosexuality; it does not in race or gender; and societies can have very small or very great amounts of homosexual behavior, depending upon the degrees of moral disapproval or tolerance shown." He added that homosexuality was criminal in many states.

Despite his opposition, the proposal succeeded.

In December 1980 Claire Bork lost her fight for life. Bork found himself more alone than ever in New Haven with both Bickel and Claire gone. His children were grown; the large house was empty. As he told an old friend, "It's tough enough living in New Haven. Imagine doing it as a widower."

He spoke to Howard Krane, now managing partner of his old Chicago firm, Kirkland and Ellis, and agreed to return to the firm in its Washington office as a senior partner. Salary: four hundred thousand dollars a year. Financially comfortable for the first time, Bork did something he had never done: He indulged himself materially. He bought a half-million-dollar house next door to one owned by

Vice President George Bush and down the street from Supreme Court Justice Potter Stewart. And he bought a new BMW 528. He threw spaghetti parties, inviting friends like Stewart and William Safire, the conservative columnist of the *New York Times*.

Such stability, however, was not to be Bork's lot. No sooner had he begun the payments on his house and car than recently installed President Reagan announced Bork as his choice to fill a vacancy on the District of Columbia Court of Appeals, often called the second most important court in the nation.

Bork was not eager to take the job. He could scarcely afford the cut in salary. Further, the heavy load in administrative law at the D.C. Circuit didn't much appeal to him. As he said two years into the judgeship to reporters, "You remember those last lines in 'The Heart of Darkness,' 'The horror, the horror'? I kid friends that my last words will be 'The trivia, the trivia.'"

But if there was the stick, there was also the carrot. Bork was sent a clear signal: If he wanted to join the Supreme Court, he would have to go on the appeals court first. He took the job and went into debt.

Unmarried, with grown children, Bork now found himself pushed further toward a monastic existence through the solitary nature of a judgeship. "It was a real shock when I first took this job," he recalled afterward. "The phone rings and you think it's for you, but it's for your clerk or your secretary—because they lead normal lives. I wasn't married then. I'd sit here all day long and go home and talk to the dog."

Most of Bork's cases on the appeals court had little political content. He wrote more than a hundred opinions and voted in several hundred others. His opinions were of high intellectual and legal quality and always splendidly written. His five years on the bench also showed his strong-minded conservatism. He tended to deny plaintiffs the right to go to court unless the law explicitly granted them that right. He showed strong deference to the executive branch over Congress. And manifesting his belief that government was too involved in the affairs of businesses, he rarely pushed government agencies to perform when others accused them of failure to do so.

Bork was a powerful voice for conservatism, and his liberal colleagues on the bench accused him of activism on a few key issues. By and large, they acknowledged, he was a responsible and thoughtful judge, but he picked his battles; on those he worked hard for what they thought of as his agenda. As one colleague put it, "He really cared about his ideological positions. On those he was a risk taker. On certain cases he felt compelled to write. It was almost as though he had to control the situation."

The most striking example was a 1984 case called *Dronenburg* v. *Zech,* regarding the Navy's right to fire a nine-year veteran for consensual homosexual activity. The right of the military to regulate wide areas of behavior had long been upheld. Yet Bork took the *Dronenburg* case as an opportunity to attack the doctrine of privacy developed by the Supreme Court.

"We would find it impossible to conclude that a right to homosexual conduct is 'fundamental' or implicit in the concept of ordered liberty unless any and all private sexual behavior falls within those categories, a conclusion we are unwilling to draw," he wrote for the majority. He added, in order to make clear that such activity was not the realm of the judiciary: "If the revolution in sexual mores that appellant proclaims is in fact ever to arrive, we think it must arrive through the moral choices of the people and their elected representatives, not through the ukase of this court."

Bork then took a swing at the Supreme Court for having "created" new rights of privacy. He said that since those rights lacked an "explanatory principle," lower court judges could not determine how to apply them and were not bound by them.

Summing up his belief that the Constitution contained no unenumerated rights, he said, "When the Constitution does not speak to the contrary, the choices of those put in authority by the electoral process, or those who are accountable to such persons, come before us not as suspect because majoritarian but as conclusively valid for that very reason."

An effort by the liberal judges on the court for an *en banc* rehearing in the case failed. They were outnumbered by the growing corps of Reagan appointees. Abner Mikva, a Carter appointee who led the four judges in dissent, had tried originally to negotiate with Bork, whom he had known since their days in law school and with whom he remained friendly despite political differences. He went to Bork's chambers and said, "Look, Bob, the opinion is clearly correct. Most of us agree the military has special powers. But I don't understand using this as an opportunity to trash the Supreme Court when it has nothing to do with this case. Why do it?"

Bork was firm in his response. He would not change a comma.

In the dissent Mikva attacked Bork head-on. He said that Bork's "extravagant exegesis on the constitutional right of privacy was wholly unnecessary to decide the case before the court. . . . We find particularly inappropriate the panel's attempt to wipe away selected Supreme Court decisions in the name of judicial restraint. Regardless whether it is the proper role of lower courts to 'create new constitutional rights,' surely it is not their function to conduct a general spring cleaning of constitutional law. Judicial restraint begins at home."

What Mikva misunderstood—purposefully in this case—was that judicial restraint had been redefined in the Reagan era by Bork and others. It now meant not a slow, measured jurisprudence but a vigorous return to original principles.

In a 1987 case one of the D.C. Circuit's other leading liberals, Harry Edwards, attacked Bork and the conservatives he led on the bench by saying that their efforts to have so many cases reheard *en banc* was based on "self-serving and result-oriented criteria." Edwards accused Bork and the others of politicking and of ruining collegiality on the bench by seeking *en banc* rehearings in order to vindicate their positions.

Such talk was, of course, empty to Bork. He saw his job as returning the law to where it belonged, not watching it spread in the wrong direction. He denied any political motive, only jurisprudential principle. And the fact that his liberal colleagues were, to his mind, stuck in their politicized view of the judiciary made them resent his work. There was nothing to be done about it.

While on the bench, Bork continued to speak around the country, mostly to right-wing groups. In fact, he sometimes gave so many speeches that he neglected his work on the court. He would simply tell the chief judge that this was his "speech month." Little was to be gotten out of him that month. Some interpreted the speeches as an effort to curry favor with the Reagan administration. Bork railed against liberal control in the academy and on the bench and the need for wholesale change. Some of his friends thought the speeches unwise and unseemly. Most judges refrain from intense public exposure. One old friend, a fellow conservative, said ruefully, "Nobody knows exactly what effect Claire's death had on him. But I believe he would never have made those speeches if she had been alive. She would have put a stop to it. She was sensible politically and had a much broader view than he did of how others see things."

Ironically, at one such speech in the summer of 1982 Bork met Mary Ellen Pohl, a former nun with fervently conservative views, especially on the importance of supporting the contras in Nicaragua. Bork had refused to go out with any woman in the year and a half since Claire's death.

Yet he fell quickly for Mary Ellen, fine-boned, graceful, supportive, and deeply religious. He was fifty-five; she, forty. As a young woman in 1966 Pohl had entered the Society of the Sacred Heart, an elite cloistered order of nuns which represented the best of the "old" Catholicism. Just as Bork had been horrified by the developments of the 1960s within his temple—the university—so was Pohl shaken by the radical changes in her order over the following decade. A year after she entered the society—home to Kennedy, Ford, and Buckley women—the nuns tossed aside many of their most revered traditions. They emerged from the cloister and spurned the holy sister's habit in favor of pins or crosses worn on civilian clothes. Mass was made "relevant" to contemporary sensibilities. Pohl fought the changes at provincial councils to which she was elected. But she was unsuccessful.

As Mary Ellen mourned a loss of religious tradition, so Bork mourned for the course of law. Both abhorred a sudden, mindless rejection of the old in favor of egalitarian and utopian impulses, a rejection that brought far more harm than good. Pohl said of those years in the society:

> It came as a great shock to me because I had entered this order with a great tradition and I liked it the way it was. . . . [T]he new attitude seemed to be, "Let's get rid of all that and then reread the foundress's works and restructure our lives accordingly," but it didn't result in any new traditions coming about, and the changes just continued. . . . When the doors are suddenly opened, there is this great temptation to do and not to think. In many cases they were trying to create a social miracle, like bringing black children from a totally different environment to Noroton [the order's school in Connecticut]. It didn't have a prayer of working. . . .

In 1981 Mary Ellen Pohl grew irreconcilably disillusioned with the changes in the Society of the Sacred Heart. She left with hopes to marry and work for conservative political and social causes. When she first heard Bork speak, she was enamored of his wit and eloquence and conservatism. The experience was, in the words of a friend, "love at first listen."

After five months of dating in 1982, she and Bork were married in a large wedding at Washington's St. Matthew's Cathedral. Howard Krane was the best man. Ushers included Mikva, Scalia, conservative columnist George Will, and Raymond Randolph, with whom Bork had worked as solicitor general and who was to play a vital role during the Supreme Court confirmation battle.

The marriage was a little difficult for Bork's children. Of course, they tried to be pleased for their father, but it was hard to accept Mary Ellen at first. She was so different from their beloved mother. Even so, on the day of the wedding, Bob, Jr., went to his father and told him what had never been said: that the kids were happy for him.

For a few of Bork's New Haven friends, who had known him best as a family man, his new wife seemed a bit off-putting. She was so coiffed, so well turned out, so comfortably upper-crust in manner. It was not Mary Ellen's penchant to invite people around to the house, throw her legs up on a table, and gossip, as Claire had done. Mary Ellen's idea of a good time was an elegant restaurant and restrained talk regarding the issues of the day. Of course, Bork himself was somewhat stiff, arriving at New Haven Sunday barbecues in jacket and tie while almost everyone else was in shorts. But Claire had kept him down to earth. Mary Ellen encouraged his more formal and political side. Together there was something very Washingtonian about them.

Marriage to Mary Ellen also brought Bork closer to an important aspect of the New Right agenda about which previously he had had little to say: the need to lower the high wall constructed by the Supreme Court between church and state. Bork had long opposed the 1973 Supreme Court decision of *Roe* v. *Wade*, which legalized abortion. He had come to that opposition on purely constitutional grounds, however: He objected to the way the Court had expanded the 1965 privacy decision to include abortion. In 1981 he stated his disapproval of the decision, telling Congress, "I am convinced, as I think most legal scholars are, that Roe v. Wade is itself, an unconstitutional decision, a serious and wholly unjustifiable judicial usurpation of state legislative authority."

His constitutional views of *Roe* aside, friends from the mid-1970s remembered he had no personal objection to abortion. That changed during the 1980s. Senator Bob Packwood, Republican of Oregon, a strong backer of abortion rights, asked Bork in a private meeting during the confirmation battle for his views of abortion. Bork responded by referring to recent articles he had read about fetal pain and euthanasia.

Bork also gave at least two speeches on the need to reintroduce religion and religious symbolism into public life, saying that most Americans linked religion and morality. If we wanted one, we needed the other. That such religion would be solely Christian seemed to bother him little.

At the Brookings Institution in 1985 Bork said: "A relaxation of current rigidly secularist doctrine would in the first place permit some sensible things to be done. . . . I suspect that the greatest perceived change would be in the reintroduction of some religion into public schools and some greater religious symbolism in our public life. . . . The deliberate and thorough-going exclusion of religion is seen as an affront and has become the cause of great divisiveness."

Bork had never had religious training. Nor had he shown much interest in it before. Now his change of heart emerged: "There may be in man an ineradicable longing for the transcendent. If religion is officially removed from public celebration, other transcendent principles, some of them very ugly indeed, may replace them."

During the years leading to his nomination, Bork also developed a strong interest in federalism—the need to return to the states much of the power that had been taken from them. He delivered several speeches on the issue, stating that liberal intellectuals had been in the forefront of nationalizing morality through the judiciary. As he said in 1982, "[M]atters such as abortion, public school discipline, drinking ages, acceptable sexual behavior and the like have always been considered, throughout our history, as matters for local police power reserved to the states. It is conventional and correct to question the legitimacy of judicial incursions into these fields because they were previously thought committed to democratic choices."

Bork continually objected to the privatization of morality, calling it both unconstitutional and immoral. "When the Constitution, honestly interpreted, does not speak to the contrary, communities should be allowed to have a public morality," he said in 1986.

Bork had found historical and constitutional backing for his belief that the nation must again fashion ways to allow communities to forge moral character through law. That minorities and those holding unpopular views might be trodden upon seemed not to worry Bork in any substantial way.

Like Ronald Reagan, Bork believed that the emphasis on individual rights and equality had gone too far. It had produced relativism and permissiveness, increased crime and alienation on the parts of ordinary folks. The nation had lost its moral compass. The intellectuals who ran the courts and universities were at fault. Bork favored a muscular conservatism; he tended to see the world as a battleground between good and evil. Asked to name the book that had greatest impact on him, he pointed to Whittaker Chambers's *Witness.* It was an impassioned autobiography and apologia by a former Communist who sought to challenge the West to build a movement more powerful than communism.

With such notions, Bork's development of a New Right legal agenda was complete. No longer a rebel, Bork was the strong, lawyerly voice for the Reagan social program. Reagan himself implied it when he nominated Bork to the high court.

Bork wanted to fight the expansion of individual and minority rights because it was illegitimate; he opposed busing and affirmative action because they were intrusive regulation; he opposed homosexual rights and abortion because they were not in the Constitution and, as he stated in 1984, opposed by the majority of Americans; he favored the death penalty and greater firmness in dealing with criminal suspects; he supported increasing religion in public life because religion was the touchstone of morality; he advocated a return to more states' rights, with little regard for what majorities might do to those who did not fit in; he believed in a strong executive and condemned the intrusiveness of the Democratic Congress.

He backed up these views by advocating a narrow view of constitutional interpretation, a return to "original principles." Intellectually and emotionally such a position allowed him the kind of clean, systematic approach with which he had always been most comfortable. Like Marxism, like Director's market conservatism, originalism had strict, self-encased rules. There was little, if any, room for judges to give meaning to the charter's broad phrases. Through such judicial work, of course, political and social minorities had been granted a measure of equality in American society. By assailing the legitimacy of such decisions, Bork was ineluctably attacking the progress those groups had achieved.

Bork argued steadily that the coincidence of his judicial views with the Reagan political agenda was just that, a coincidence. He was nobody's tool and always open to argument. He never seemed to entertain the notion that like the liberals he so disdained, he and his conservative colleagues also moved often from the gut to the head, and not vice versa.

Others of his stripe saw it differently. Richard Posner, a prominent conservative federal judge in Chicago, put it this way in 1988: "It is questionable whether there has been anyone in the history of law who could really divorce his jurisprudential views from his personal and political ones. I think to be convinced of the importance of judicial conservatism, you have to dislike the policies of the courts. It's hard to get excited, without being remarkably detached, about judicial conduct that violates principles unless it is bringing about results you don't like."

At 6:30 A.M. on Wednesday, July 1, 1987, Robert Bork left his red-brick three-story house in the Potomac Palisades section of Washington and drove to 716 Jackson Place NW, a minute's walk from the White House. The nineteenth-century town house was used to lodge former presidents when they came to town. None was in residence that day. It was this house, with its pre-Victorian furnishings, that White House Counsel Arthur B. Culvahouse had chosen as a place to discuss with Bork his nomination to the Supreme Court.

It was 7:00 A.M., and Culvahouse, tall, blond, and open-faced, was waiting. As the confirmation process got under way and his exposure to Bork increased, he was to become a fan. At the moment he was not. He knew only that trouble lay ahead.

Bork and Culvahouse climbed to the third-floor dining room, where they sat facing each other. Culvahouse pulled out of his briefcase a handwritten list of some twenty questions, referring to it as his "skeleton" questionnaire.

The counsel had nicknames for a couple of them, such as the Gary Hart question, named for the former Colorado senator who had withdrawn from the 1988 race for the Democratic presidential nomination because of his sexual indiscretion: Had Bork ever had any extramarital affairs?

"No," Bork replied.

Now, Culvahouse said, the John Fedders question, after the former head of the investigative branch of the Securities and Exchange Commission whose wife had sued him for divorce: Did Bork beat his wife or children?

"No, but don't ask them," Bork offered, trying to inject humor. Culvahouse was stone-faced.

"Look, I've led a pretty dull life," Bork added in another attempt to loosen things up.

"That's good," Culvahouse responded coolly.

Bork did his best to answer the other questions simply.

The questioning over, Culvahouse told Bork that he could expect a call from Chief of Staff Howard Baker in the next few hours. Brimming with expectation, Bork went to his chambers at the federal courthouse. Just after noon Baker called and told Bork he should meet Baker's executive assistant, John Tuck, at Third and D streets, a discreet street corner, so as to avoid the eyes of the media. While prominently mentioned as the leading choice for the nomination, Bork was still under wraps. The White House wanted to keep him that way until the press conference.

Bork went with his secretary to the appointed spot. Dressed in a blue blazer and gray flannel slacks, he was perspiring heavily in the midday heat. He got into Tuck's station wagon. There was no air conditioning. Tuck took a circuitous route, driving down Independence Avenue, past the Jefferson Memorial, to enter the White House. But his car and passenger were seen by a reporter for Cable News Network, who immediately went on the air to report that Bork was the nominee.

Tuck took Bork to Baker's handsome and airy office in the White House's West Wing. There he met Baker; Culvahouse; Kenneth Duberstein, the deputy chief of staff; Thomas Griscom, director of communications; and William Ball, White House liaison to Congress. All congratulated him. They accompanied him up to the Oval Office.

Although they were soldiers in arms in the conservative movement, Bork had never known Reagan well. He had not worked for Reagan in 1980 as he had for Richard Nixon and Barry Goldwater in 1968 and 1964. Reagan, of course, had named Bork to the D.C. Circuit in 1982, but they had had minimal contact before that.

"I'd like to offer you the nomination to the Supreme Court. Will you accept it?" the president said solemnly to the judge.

"I've been thinking about it for ten to twelve minutes, and I think

I like the idea," Bork responded with a satisfied twinkle. He had trouble adjusting to the self-seriousness of the White House.

The president didn't get it. "Does that mean yes?"

Incredulous, Bork stiffened and gravely responded, "Yes, sir. I'd be honored, Mr. President."

From there, the two moved to the Queen Anne chairs in front of the fireplace and the White House photographers were asked in. With staff members on the couches, Bork and Reagan smiled at each other in awkward silence. In a rarity, Bork couldn't think of anything to say.

Baker explained to Bork that the president would announce his nomination to a press conference a few minutes later; Bork was to take no questions and make no remarks. It seemed strange to the nominee that he would not be allowed at least to express his gratitude publicly to the president and say how much he looked forward to the confirmation process. But as far as he could tell, the White House men were on top of the situation, and he figured they, not he, were the political professionals.

As the group entered the press conference, Sam Donaldson, the White House correspondent of ABC News, and Bill Plante, of CBS, were sitting in the front row and feigned shock at the sight of Bork. "Surprise, surprise, surprise," they offered aloud.

With Bork at his side, President Reagan announced the nomination and said of his choice: "Judge Bork, widely regarded as the most prominent and intellectually powerful advocate of judicial restraint, shares my view that judges' personal preferences and values should not be part of their constitutional interpretations."

The battle was joined.

CHAPTER

5

Advice and Dissent

After the announcement Bork accompanied William L. Ball III, an affable southerner with a honey-coated accent, to his West Wing office. As Bork settled into an armchair, Ball flicked on the television to the C-SPAN network, which broadcasts live the proceedings of the Senate. He wanted to see if there was any reaction yet to the nomination made less than an hour before.

There was.

Even before the picture blinked on, Ball and Bork could detect the inimitable Brahmin accent of the senior senator from Massachusetts, Edward M. Kennedy. He declared:

Robert Bork's America is a land in which women would be forced into back alley abortions, blacks would sit at segregated lunch counters, rogue police could break down citizens' doors in midnight raids, school children could not be taught about evolution, writers and artists could be censored at the whim of government, and the doors of the federal courts would be shut on the fingers of millions of citizens for whom the judiciary is—and is often the only—protector of the individual rights that are the heart of our democracy.

America is a better and freer nation than Robert Bork thinks. Yet in the current delicate balance of the Supreme Court, his rigid ideology will tip the scales of justice against the kind of country America is and ought to be.

The damage that President Reagan will do through this nomination if it is not rejected by the Senate could live on far beyond the end of his presidential term. President Reagan is still our president. But he should not be able to reach out from the muck of Irangate, reach into the muck of Watergate, and impose his reactionary vision of the Constitution on the Supreme Court and on the next generation of Americans. No justice would be better than this injustice.

Watching the proceedings on a television was Kennedy aide Jeffrey Blattner. He admired the way the senator unwound, delivering the statement with style and force. But he realized it was a risky speech. When it was over, he said to himself, "Now we better win."

Kennedy's was an altogether startling statement. He had shamelessly twisted Bork's world view—"rogue police could break down citizens' doors in midnight raids" was an Orwellian reference to Bork's criticism of the exclusionary rule, through which judges exclude illegally obtained evidence, and Bork had never suggested he opposed the teaching of evolution—but equally startling was that Kennedy discussed Bork's world view at all. The speech was a landmark for judicial nominations. Kennedy was saying that no longer should the Senate content itself with examining a nominee's personal integrity and legal qualifications, as had been the custom—at least publicly—for half a century. From now on the Senate and the nation should examine a nominee's vision for society. In fulfilling its constitutional duty of "advice and consent" on judicial appointments, the upper house should take politics and ideology fully into account. This was part of a growing assertion of power by the Congress and an unambiguous acknowledgment of the political nature of the Supreme Court, popularly portrayed as above politics.

To Bork and Ball, Kennedy's words seemed such a departure from tradition and such a distortion of the nominee's record as to be of no consequence. They shrugged off the speech as the ravings of a desperate politician. Kennedy, they thought, had blown it.

They were dangerously wrong in their assessment. Kennedy did distort Bork's record, but his statement was not the act of a desperate man. This was a confident and seasoned politician, one who knew how to combine passion and pragmatism in the Senate. Unlike the vast majority of those who were to oppose Bork, Kennedy believed from the beginning that the nomination would be defeated and that the loss would prove decisive in judicial politics.

He never apologized for the statement. It had a function. "I wanted to make clear what was at stake in this nomination," he said afterward. "The statement had to be stark and direct so as to sound the alarm and hold people in their places until we could get material together. I was confident we could win this one."

So Kennedy led the charge against Bork. He began by calling out the standing army of liberal family loyalists.

Something undeniably special came with a Kennedy phone call. For many of those reached, including small-town mayors and leaders of mid-size unions, a talk with Kennedy was a major event. Through Kennedy you touched history; you were linked to the vigor and idealism and romance of the American century. And many still wondered if Kennedy would one day be president. As the *New York Times* put it on his twenty-fifth anniversary in the Senate in November, 1987, "Four presidential elections hence, in the year 2000, Edward Kennedy will be a year younger than Ronald Reagan was in 1980."

The recipients of Kennedy's calls would be able to call in their staffs or phone their friends and begin the conversation with "Ted Kennedy just called and . . ." It still worked magic.

This, despite all the stories over the years of Kennedy and women, Kennedy and drink, Kennedy and cheating in college, Kennedy and Chappaquiddick. For conservatives, his moralizing about duty to one's fellowman, about equal justice under law stuck in the throat. The wild boy with the four-hundred-million-dollar trust fund and the blondes on his yacht and gin on his brain could go preach somewhere else, thank you very much. He was the liberal conservatives loved to hate.

The first part of the Reagan era had been a low point for Kennedy. Long a symbol of big government liberalism, he had lost his bid for the Democratic nomination to Jimmy Carter in 1980, when he seemed unable to explain why he wanted to be president. As the winds of conservatism blew through Washington after Carter's defeat to Reagan, Kennedy sank in visibility and relevance. His cause had lost its gloss, and he had lost his charm. Defeated, divorced, the nation's remnant of the Camelot years was written off by some as an inarticulate woman chaser, the embodiment of the directionless Democrats.

But the Reagan years proved to be a time of seasoning for Kennedy. He learned how to operate in the minority, how to forge alliances with right-wing legislators, how to work for health care, immigration reform, civil rights. He led the fight for AIDS research, for day care, for education, for advance notice of plant closings, for a higher minimum wage. He became, without question, one of the nation's great liberal lawmakers, earning a place in history apart from his family heritage. In 1987 alone, he moved more than twenty major pieces of his own legislation through the Senate, including one billion dollars for AIDS education and treatment, a civil rights bill that became law over President Reagan's veto, and a prohibition on employers' routine use of lie detectors on workers. The Reagan years also brought him to the decision that he would not run for president. The announcement, despite continued low-level specula-tion, was liberating for him. Before that decision, made in 1985, a Kennedy had been at or near the center of Democratic presidential politics for twenty-five years.

Suddenly, bold Kennedy legislative proposals were no longer dis-missed as posturing for the White House. "Running for president greatly increases your visibility but raises the question of your credi-bility," he said later.

And a quarter century in the Senate meant he knew the institu-tion and its rules better than most. Kennedy was fast becoming a king of the Hill.

By the time of the Bork nomination the glow of Reaganism was dimming. The nation was gaining perspective on the churning 1960s, and it had begun to yearn for some goals of social equality without the emotional baggage of the era. A toughened, pragmatic liberalism emerged, allowing politicians of all stripes to discuss fed-eral aid for child care and some forms of health insurance. Those had been Kennedy issues for a generation. He was ready to keep fighting for them, to shepherd them into law.

He was, at fifty-five, in the early autumn of his years. His back, badly broken twenty years earlier, pained him; he rarely complained aloud, but standing was often a chore. When he sat, he sprawled, searching for a position to relieve the pressure. His face was flushed; his teeth were yellowed; his hands sometimes suffered a slight tremor. Although he worked hard to control his weight, he seemed on occasion nearly to burst out of his expensive double-breasted suits and smooth Italian shoes. He smoked high-priced cigars.

His brothers and mentors—Joe, Jack, Bobby—were all gone, fro-zen in memory as bold, handsome, and young. They stood for promise, more attractive than reality. Their photographs were all over his office; they looked casual and happy, grinning in the light of a national dawn. He had been the baby brother, the one who had got his first Senate seat as a kind of birthright. But it was he who remained, the only one allowed a chance to turn gray. It was hard to accept, harder for him than for anyone. But when called upon to memorialize his brothers, he was often at a loss. "They were both my best friends and my political models," he said, his voice lowered, his hands fidgeting. "The last thing they would have wanted would be to be glorified or perceived as something they weren't. I don't really dwell on them. It's too much. It's not my disposition to look back. There is a whole new generation, a new set of issues. It's easier to look forward."

He was unable to write at any length about them without feeling empty inside. Even when he spoke about them, he would sometimes break down.

In the very early years, when his brothers were running the country, Edward Kennedy lived in their shadow. He chose to master the arcane ways of the Senate, to make his mark within that house rather than compete with them on the national stage. He worked hard, using his warm, easygoing nature. Despite resentment over his privilege—one wit proposed the creation of the Edward M. Kennedy Foundation to benefit wealthy and undeserving young men who wanted to start right at the top—Teddy earned the respect and friendship of his colleagues. He also brought home the goods for his state, pushing legislation favorable to Massachusetts fisheries and airlines. He knew the workings of the legislature better than Bobby. But after Jack was killed, Teddy often deferred publicly to his older brother out of loyalty and family discipline. They stuck together, as Kennedys did, gaining strength from their unity. They would walk huddled across the grounds of the Capitol, the younger one still taking insight and inspiration.

On that grim California day in June 1968, when Ted was riding in the elevator on the way to the autopsy room with Bobby's corpse, liberal activist Allard Lowenstein got in and exclaimed, "Now that Bobby's gone, you're all we've got. You've got to take the leadership."

Kennedy assured Lowenstein he would carry on. It was a wrenching transition, filled with drink and anger and fear, but he made it. Now, twenty years later, he was the one giving the cues, the

veteran pol, president of the clan. In place of youthful idealism he
offered boardroom savvy.

Kennedy threw himself into issues, as if only they could exorcise
his demons. He pressed his agenda with incomparable dedication.
Those who felt their interests threatened by the Reagan programs
turned to Kennedy. Eight months after the Bork defeat, the black
readers of *Ebony* magazine voted him the white man they most
trusted. The Leadership Conference on Civil Rights honored him
with its Hubert Humphrey Award. For the nation's poor, for its
minorities, Kennedy was the guardian in Washington.

But for Bork and his family, Kennedy's attacks on Bork were hard
to understand except as *ad hominem* assaults. Once, toward the end
of a long day of the Bork hearings at which Kennedy had repeatedly
assailed the nominee, the senator was walking alone out of his office.
Coming in the other direction was Mary Ellen Bork, accompanied
by Nancy Kennedy, a White House aide. Mrs. Bork had slept
poorly the previous night and was washed out from hours of sitting
in the glare of television lights. She had no desire to run into Senator
Kennedy. She was afraid she would burst into tears. But the senator
sought her out.

"Mrs. Bork, you must be so tired. It's a very difficult time, I know.
I hope you understand that it is nothing personal," Kennedy told
her, shaking her hand.

Then, before she had a chance to say much of anything, the senator turned on his heels and took his leave.

She couldn't believe he had dared speak to her at all. So surprised
and fatigued was she that she had no time for a response. It was a
moment she played back often in her mind, relishing some choice
words she wished she had addressed to the Massachusetts lawmaker.

Kennedy was unaware of how offended Mrs. Bork was by his
comment. He had said something similar to Bork himself at the
judge's courtesy call in early July. "Nothing personal, you understand." Bork did not understand.

To Kennedy, it really was *not* personal. Little in politics was. He
had led his entire life in the public eye; his life was fodder for the
supermarket tabloids. He could not be within camera distance of an
attractive woman without ending up on the cover of a gossip magazine. If he took everything said about him personally, he would
never survive. He had always been a symbol and had learned to
operate within the politics of symbolism. Heated rhetoric was part

of the game of government. When the day was over, win or lose, everyone could have a drink together. He had been trained to disjoin his inner feelings from the domain of public affairs. You could sense it when you were with him. His eyes revealed nothing. The man had venetian blinds on his soul.

When the Bork nomination was on its knees, and Bork decided to fight on anyway and take it to the full Senate, one of his supporters, Senator Phil Gramm, Republican of Texas, cheered him on. He said to reporters, referring to Kennedy's famed cheating episode on a college examination and reports that Joe Biden had once plagiarized in law school: "We know what the cheaters think about this. Let's see what the A students think."

When Biden saw Gramm, he was offended. He said, "That was a terrible thing to say. I'm no cheater."

When Kennedy saw Gramm, he said, "That was a low blow, Phil. But nice shot."

It was one of the things Kennedy admired about Reagan: He knew how to manipulate symbols for his causes yet could sup with his enemies. He said of Reagan once:

> He's absolutely professional. When the sun goes down, the battles of the day are really gone. He gave the Robert Kennedy Medal, which President Carter refused to do. He received my mother. . . . He's very sure of himself, and I think people sense that he's comfortable with himself, so why shouldn't I be comfortable with him? My family always had a healthy respect for him. . . . He had a philosophy and he's fought for it. There's a consistency and continuity at a time when many others are flopping back and forth. And that's an important and instructive lesson for politicians, that people admire that.

In his fight against Bork, as in all his battles, Kennedy did not handle the issues gently. He clawed them. Uninterested in the historical and theoretical bases of Bork's views, Kennedy shredded the legal niceties, searching for the larger societal meaning of what was at stake. When law professors briefed him on Bork's theories, he would seek ways to bring the issue down to a level everyone would understand. One scholar remembered him saying, "Look, the masses are not going to rise up over the issue of congressional standing. But they will over freedom in the bedroom."

He was dogged in his dedication. In August, September, and October 1987 he held meetings with liberal lobby groups; demanded endless hours of work from his huge, dedicated staff; sent a letter to every one of the sixty-two hundred black elected officials in the country asking for their help; stroked and poked his Senate colleagues in the cloakroom, on the floor, in the dining room; gathered key witnesses for the hearings; and exploited the inchoate sense around the country that when a Kennedy commits himself this fiercely to something, it is rarely in vain. He called on hundreds of his and his brothers' former aides, the people who made up the extended Kennedy political family, and asked them for legal and political analyses, speeches, newspaper opinion pieces, and contacts.

Anthony Podesta, a talented liberal lobbyist hired by Kennedy for the Bork fight, remembered going up to the Kennedy summer compound in Hyannis Port to help the senator make phone calls. He said that he went to Cape Cod dubious about how much work Kennedy really would do, given that he only had a few weeks off from the Senate. But Kennedy kept calling and Podesta kept phoning back to Kennedy's Capitol Hill office for more phone numbers to pass on to the senator.

Kennedy called Ernest Morial, former New Orleans mayor, and Sidney Barthelemy, the current mayor. In Alabama, he spoke with Mayor Richard Arrington of Birmingham, Mayor Johnny Ford of Tuskegee, and Joseph Reed, the Alabama Democratic Conference chief. In Atlanta he spoke at length with Mayor Andrew Young, a longtime family friend. All were black southern leaders.

At one point Kennedy woke up the Reverend Joseph Lowery at the Hyatt Hotel in New Orleans before the Southern Christian Leadership Conference's annual convention. Lowery, head of the SCLC, had planned to discuss Bork at the meeting. But after hearing from Kennedy, he turned the entire day into an anti-Bork strategy session. He told the convention about Kennedy's call, and one participant remembered how it fired up the crowd. From there the issue penetrated black churches across America. Preachers would hand out pen and paper and take ten minutes from the service for anti-Bork letter writing.

From the Cape, Kennedy called every one of the thirty executive members of the AFL-CIO. When he took his yacht out for a sail, Bork was still on his mind. He sailed up to the Maine coast, where he dropped in on Burke Marshall, Yale law professor and assistant attorney general for civil rights under President Kennedy. Stopping in at Marshall's island retreat on North Haven, Kennedy asked him if he would testify against the judge. Marshall agreed. Later in September Kennedy held a conference call with forty state labor leaders around the country.

Bork's defeat was ever present on Kennedy's mind that summer. A few weeks after the nomination the car taking Kennedy to his home in McLean, Virginia, was struck by a falling tree. The senator flew forward and hit the windshield. "I thought for a moment that there would be one vote less against Bork" was his immediate comment when he realized he was unhurt.

"The question was how to convince people that this should be a priority item, not just another cause to sign your organization's name to," reflected Podesta. "Ted would get on the phone and say, 'This is the most important fight we've had in the Senate in years. We need you to mobilize, to activate your people, to make this a top priority issue.' "

The letter Kennedy sent to the thousands of black officials included people at all levels—federal, state, city council, board of education. Written mostly by Michael Frazier, the Kennedy aide whose sole responsibility was liaison to the black community, the letter said: "The most important vote this year in the United States Senate will take place on the question of President Reagan's nomination of Robert Bork to the Supreme Court. Bork has been a lifelong opponent of civil rights, and he does not deserve a lifetime seat on the Supreme Court—and so I urge you to join me in actively opposing the nomination."

The letter, dated August 12, 1987, went on to say that in his twenty-five years of public life, Bork had "worked tirelessly against justice and progress." It said: "The Bork appointment could profoundly diminish the promise of our nation for the next decade and beyond. Everything we have worked for together in the past quarter century may be jeopardized if Bork is confirmed, and if the narrowly divided Supreme Court of today shifts in the direction of Bork's extremist ideology."

Frazier said that the idea for the letter was his and that he was the keeper of the list in the office. "The Senate was going into recess, and we had to have some way to keep this thing going, not to let it die." he said. "We were determined to show that Kennedy would go to the mat on this one."

There were two advantages to fighting this kind of nomination, as opposed to working for a piece of legislation. First, it allowed groups to focus on an individual. That had drawbacks for the senators, who had to look the man in the eye and meet his family. But for members of lobbying groups around the country it allowed vague feelings and fears to be crystallized in one person who would be seen only from afar. He could be demonized, caricatured, and made to embody all they hated. Secondly, the fight was limited in time. Three months, that was the commitment, whereas legislative fights could carry on for years. Moreover, this would be win or lose. No compromises were possible; no watered-down version could emerge. The stakes were high.

Kennedy, chairman of the Senate Labor Committee and longtime friend of organized labor, was especially effective with union leaders. Worried about Alan Dixon, Democratic senator of Illinois, who seemed inclined in Bork's favor, Kennedy called up Edward Hanley, head of the hotel and restaurant workers' union. The union was based in Chicago; Hanley and Dixon were close. Many of Hanley's members were close in temperament and attitude to teamsters. With Hanley, Kennedy didn't talk about women and minorities. He didn't discuss legal briefs. He made a few comments about Bork's attitude toward business and labor. But he said essentially: Ed, we don't call often. This one matters to us. Dixon's shaky. Give him a call.

So Dixon, a senator for whom such things made a huge difference—his nickname, Al the Pal, flowed from his unparalleled ability to cut deals and keep constituents happy with him—would get a call from Hanley. And after prompting from Kennedy, Dixon would also hear from Chicago Mayor Harold Washington and Representative Gus Savage, among many others. Dixon voted against Bork.

Podesta, who had once been counsel to the machinists' union, analyzed Kennedy's calls this way: "Our opponents complained a lot about the money spent in this campaign. But given a choice between ten thousand dollars and two phone calls from Ed Hanley, I'd much rather have the phone calls."

Kennedy called key financiers for other senators, including those of several southern Democrats. In one case, the man reached was due to hold a fund raiser for Senator Lawton Chiles, Democrat of Florida, the next evening. Chiles, who was to face what he described as ugly and unmatched pressure on this vote, came out against Bork.

Later, for unrelated reasons, he decided not to run again for the Senate.

The message communicated by Kennedy's calls was that this fight could be won. People knew that Ted Kennedy was no Don Quixote. If he invested his summer in this campaign, it could probably be done.

Kennedy's speech about "Bork's America" had been written the day before the nomination, and Kennedy considered delivering it that same day in an effort to block Bork's name. But he decided it wouldn't work.

The day of the nomination Kennedy was presiding over a subcommittee meeting on fair housing at which Assistant Attorney General Brad Reynolds was giving testimony. Meese called Kennedy at the meeting as a courtesy to tell him the nominee would be Bork. Kennedy told the attorney general he would oppose the nomination. Meese was unfazed. Kennedy then called two pillars of Harvard Law School, Archibald Cox and Paul Freund. He wanted to know if Cox planned to play a role in this nomination fight since he had been the victim of Bork's firing during the Watergate episode. Cox, ever the upstanding gentleman, told Kennedy he planned to stay out of the whole thing because it would be hard for him to be perceived as fair, but he also made it clear that he would not react publicly to Kennedy's attacks on Bork on Watergate.

Kennedy wanted to check in with Freund, a liberal with ties to the Kennedy family. Though retired, Freund was still considered one of the nation's most distinguished constitutional scholars. A man who had frequently been passed over as a Supreme Court nominee, Freund said he was disturbed by what he knew of Bork but would wait to take a position. Kennedy said that he preferred not to wait, that he was going to make a statement that day. Did Freund see anything wrong with that? Freund hadn't talked with Kennedy in a couple of years and was so surprised by the call that he found himself at a loss for words. He said simply that he was sure that whatever Kennedy chose to say would be fine.

Later in the day, when Freund heard what Kennedy had said, he was disturbed by its overwrought tone.

The materials for the Kennedy speech were gathered by Jeffrey Blattner, Kennedy's aide on the Judiciary Committee, a native of Pittsburgh, graduate of Harvard Law School, and former Supreme

Court clerk. Blattner was hardworking, energetic, quick-witted, and fascinated by hardball politics. He offered the building blocks of the speech, but it was written by Carey Parker, Kennedy's longtime chief legislative assistant. Blattner coordinated the substantive side of the battle in the Kennedy office, working under quiet, cautious Carolyn Osolinik, Kennedy's chief aide on judiciary matters whose political strategies were held in high esteem throughout the liberal community.

The moment Powell resigned, Blattner and Osolinik began gathering material on Bork as well as on a few other likely candidates. They plotted strategy and were in constant touch with Ralph Neas and other members of the civil rights and liberal community.

For the Kennedy office, veterans of several Reagan judicial nomination fights in the preceding few years, there was really no question that a confrontation was afoot. "The fact that this was a swing seat meant that unless Reagan threw in the towel and nominated a real moderate, there was going to be a fight," Blattner said later.

The idea of such a fight in the Senate was a new one. In the preceding half century a tradition had built up that the president had the power to nominate judges and the Senate's job was to confirm them unless there were signs of gross incompetence or corruption.

It was believed that a nominee's politics or ideology were off limits for two reasons. First, Americans were encouraged to think of judging as above politics, as an integral, self-enclosed system that required only intelligence, training, and integrity to perform well. Secondly a president's election was seen as a mandate not only to appoint the members of the executive branch but also to build the judiciary. Sheldon Goldman, a political scientist at the University of Massachusetts and one of the nation's closest monitors of federal judicial appointments, put it this way: "When the people elect a president, they also in a sense elect a judiciary."

Both concepts were under attack as the Reagan administration moved into the end of its second term. The first idea—that judging was more of a technical skill than an art—had been an issue of intense debate in legal academic circles for some years. When, in 1985 and 1986, Attorney General Meese pronounced the need to return to a jurisprudence of original intent, the debate broke into the open and became part of the nation's political dialogue.

The traditional concept of judging posits that the able practitioner applies the facts of a case to existing rules and comes up with a logically inevitable conclusion. The judge is a highly skilled mechanic. Under this model, a judge plays out a hand dealt by the outside world. He or she would be nearly as free of blame or congratulation for the result as would be a computer that had solved a complex problem. The judge is like Newton discovering gravity. Any judicial mistakes would be purely technical ones, questions of competence, not ideology.

Meese and his allies contended that by seeking out what the drafters of laws intended and by sticking to the wording of statutes and constitutional articles, the judge would come up with an inevitable conclusion, or nearly so. To them, this model was largely attainable. Where the Constitution or law was silent, the judge must suppress a desire to fill in the holes. He must return the question to legislatures, where the will of the people could be expressed.

In the decades leading up to the Bork nomination, another school of thought, a kind of polar opposite, gained limited currency. In that view, judging was like a sausage factory: It doesn't much matter what goes into the process as long as the final product tastes good. This school saw a judge not as a skilled mechanic but as a short-order cook. His work was evaluated not by his care for the machine but by the taste of his product.

As the debate intensified, it became apparent that neither position was entirely acceptable; some middle ground had to be staked out. Clearly a judge should stick to applying the major and minor premises—existing law and the facts of the case at hand—in as restricted a manner as possible. But the choices open to a judge were vast. For example, the existing law to be applied was not always self-evident. Which precedent should a judge choose? Several may conflict. And there was always the problem of applying the vague language of the law or a previous decision to the current case. No two cases were identical. Choice was involved, often between two societal values, such as the privacy of an individual accused of a crime and the public's right to be informed, or between order and liberty. Such a choice might be based partly on matters outside the case itself, such as a judge's own sense of what is just. As Senator Paul Simon said in March 1986, judges "must fill in gaps in the law and must resolve ambiguities about what the law is, and in doing so a judge inevitably draws upon his or her starting point views and outlook."

Chief Justice William Rehnquist, a conservative, said something similar in 1988: "Each of us [judges] comes aboard in the beginning of the process with certain philosophical baggage that may make us more or less sympathetic to particular legal arguments made in the case."

But just as clearly, a system of judging that depended entirely on what the judge had eaten for breakfast that morning—hence the term *burnt toast jurisprudence*—or what his aims for society were was unacceptable. Just because choice was involved didn't mean that every judge was really a short-order cook hiding behind a menu of rules. Most people accepted the notion that a judge was capable, at least sometimes, of applying complex rules which led to a result he did not like.

So a consensus developed that courts did have some creative role. The trouble was: How creative? The judges who sit on the federal bench are the people who determine what Senator Simon called "the real-world meaning of our Constitution and federal law," but there was acute disagreement over what that meaning was or should be. Nonetheless, it was publicly and widely agreed that judges' political outlooks had meaning in understanding their approach to the law. For that reason, a notion that such views were worthy of at least some consideration began to gain currency.

The challenge to the second assumption—that the president had the right to pick his judges with little Senate interference—flowed from the challenge to the first. Scholars, especially liberals, saw political motives to Reagan's professed interest in returning law to a more traditional bent. They were worried about Reagan's insistence on a specific agenda for the law—since it contrasted with their own—and began to urge senators to exert their role of advice and consent more vigorously. A glance at history and at the writings of the founders made it clear that the Senate had a legitimate role to play in acting as censor to nominees it considered inappropriate. Battered by the Bork and Meese claim that they had abandoned the framers in their modern reading of the Constitution, liberals saw an opening to promote their own cause through an invocation of the founders. Original intent, they seemed to be saying, was a double-edged sword.

Records of the Constitutional Convention of 1787 showed the delegates divided on who should appoint judges in the first place. Originally it was agreed that the power would rest entirely with the Senate, and only in a last-minute compromise was the president included. James Wilson of Pennsylvania expressed a typical reservation to the original plan when he said that granting the appointment power to such a large body as the Senate would result in "intrigue, partiality and concealment." John Rutledge and Alexander Hamilton worried about a president whose power looked monarchical. They said the chief executive would pick his candidates with greater care if he knew they would be scrutinized by the Senate. Gouverneur Morris summed up the final consensus, saying, "As the President was to nominate, there would be responsibility, and as the Senate was to concur there would be security."

The compromise led to Article II, Section 2 of the Constitution, which reads, in part: "The President . . . shall nominate, and by and with the Advice and Consent of the Senate, shall appoint . . . Judges of the Supreme Court and all other Officers of the United States, whose Appointments are not herein provided for, and which shall be established by Law. . . ."

Judges were to serve for life to guard them from the vagaries of the political system. So their appointments were different from those serving in the president's cabinet during his tenure; the judicial nominees would be examined more carefully. And the Senate was chosen as the check on the system for two reasons. The six-year term rather than two for representatives gave them greater insularity from day-to-day political pressures. Moreover, senators were elected not by popular vote but by the state legislatures (until the Constitution was amended in 1913).

From the beginning the Senate wielded its power of advice and consent. In 1795 President Washington nominated John Rutledge, who had already served as an associate justice, to be chief justice. At that time loyalty for the Federalist cause was manifested through support for the treaty with England negotiated by John Jay when he had been chief justice. Rutledge made a speech attacking the treaty, outraging many. His opponents went so far as to call into question his mental stability. He was said to be deranged and to have attempted suicide at one stage. A debate raged in the country, press, and Senate for five months. Notwithstanding Washington's popularity and his party's control of the Senate, Rutledge was denied confirmation by a vote of 14–10. Of the fourteen who turned him down, three had been framers of the Constitution.

Throughout the nineteenth century about one in four Supreme Court nominees was rejected by the Senate. Andrew Jackson's first nomination of Roger Taney was turned down because Taney had followed Jackson's orders to withdraw all government deposits from the National Bank. Ulysses S. Grant failed in three of seven nominations, even though the Senate was dominated by Grant's own party during his entire presidency.

In the twentieth century there were far fewer rejections with less overt attention to ideology. There were political battles over Court nominations—in the sense of partisan power struggles between Senate and president—but only a few that centered on a nominee's vision for the nation. The continuing move away from such concerns in the confirmation process was rudely altered by the Bork battle.

The most acrimonious fight in the history of the Court—until Bork's—was over Louis D. Brandeis. A Boston attorney and Harvard Law School graduate, Brandeis ultimately won confirmation and earned acclaim as one of the nation's great justices. Brandeis, known as the People's Lawyer for his social activism, was nominated by President Wilson on January 28, 1916. A political storm quickly ensued with six former presidents of the American Bar Association accusing him of being radical, antiestablishment, and anti-big business. Their letter to the Judiciary Committee called Brandeis "not a fit person to be a member of the Supreme Court of the United States."

Their objections were to Brandeis's penchant for crusading, his devotion to increasing equality and improving the lot of the poor and dispossessed. He had no interest in being a member of the club. There is little doubt that anti-Semitism also played a role. The opponents couched their motives in objections about his character and temperament, even his professional ethics. Despite their efforts, Brandeis was confirmed four months later by a vote of 47–22.

Fourteen years later the Senate turned down a nominee on ideological grounds, the only truly political rejection of this century until Bork's. On May 7, 1930, with the galleries filled to capacity and hundreds turned away, the Senate voted, 41–39, to reject Appeals Judge John J. Parker of North Carolina. He was the first nominee since 1894 to fail.

When nominated by President Herbert Hoover two months earlier, Parker had seemed a natural choice. A southern Republican with first-class credentials, he was backed by members of the bar and the Democratic senators from his state. But a week later the American Federation of Labor announced its opposition. It objected to a ruling of Parker's in a case that upheld a lower court's injunction against the United Mine Workers' right to organize nonunion members. The members had signed "yellow dog" contracts with their employers, forbidding them to participate in unions.

In theory, Parker was only respecting precedent, as would any lower-court judge. But to the AFL, Parker was upholding the order of a bygone era and showing antiunion bias. As the president of the federation said, "The significance is not that Judge Parker followed the precedent . . . but that his opinion reflects a judicial attitude entirely in sympathy and accord with the legal and economic policy embodied in the injunction. Confirmation will mean another 'injunction' judge will be a member of the Supreme Court."

Just as the labor issue emerged, another—that of race—joined it. The acting president of the NAACP announced that his organization would oppose Parker not for any decision he had handed down but for a racial slur he had made a decade earlier in a heated gubernatorial campaign speech. Parker had said that the "participation of the Negro in politics is a source of evil and danger to both races and is not desired by the wise men in either race or by the Republican Party of North Carolina." Parker had made the statement in response to repeated charges by his Democratic opponents that he intended to enfranchise blacks and to change the North Carolina Constitution to accommodate them.

Partisan politics also played a role in Parker's rejection. Progressive Republicans saw his nomination as a further opportunity to weaken Hoover, already battered by the stock market crash of the previous year and the perception of his chronic inability to handle the crises of his day. Other lawmakers had no desire to be seen by the organized black or labor communities as inimical to their interests. The NAACP had sent out telegrams to every one of its branches, especially in the North, where black voting was a growing political factor. It urged telegraphic protests to senators by every church, labor, civic, and fraternal group.

In a comment that would apply half a century later to the Bork controversy, the *New York Times* said: "In Judge Parker's case, the opposition to his confirmation touches in a definite, concrete way the fears of many Senators for their own personal fortunes. . . . Important organized minorities of considerable political power are antagonizing his appointment in a way to bring realization to certain Senators that they may feel the effect of organized resentment if they vote to confirm his nomination."

When Parker was defeated, the *Christian Science Monitor* labeled it "the first national demonstration of the Negro's power since Reconstruction days." The vacancy was then filled by Owen Roberts, who was unanimously confirmed. Ironically, Parker went on to a distinguished career as a judge more supportive of New Deal and antisegregation measures than Roberts. Justice Hugo Black once commented, "John Parker was a better judge after the hearing than before it."

The "Negro's power," as the *Monitor* had phrased it, grew with the civil rights movement. It was further manifested by the appointment of Thurgood Marshall, a black lawyer and solicitor general, to the Supreme Court by Lyndon Johnson in 1967. At the time southern Democrats accused Marshall of being too liberal and judicially activist. Senator Strom Thurmond of South Carolina said the Court did not need another liberal. He set about quizzing Marshall on the most obscure and arcane details of constitutional history, including the names of the framers of the Thirteenth and Fourteenth Amendments. Senator Sam Ervin of North Carolina said he opposed Marshall because he would add the crucial fifth vote to the four liberals on the Court, Chief Justice Earl Warren and Associate Justices William Brennan, William O. Douglas, and Abe Fortas.

Senator Edward Kennedy chided his colleagues for taking politics into account, saying the nominee's "background, experience, qualifications, temperament and integrity" should be all they ought to consider. Despite the bluster, Marshall easily won the expected confirmation by a vote of 69–11.

But the next year Johnson had less luck. Fabled liberal activist Chief Justice Earl Warren had announced his intention to retire. Eager to reward his longtime friend and adviser Abe Fortas, whom he had appointed to the Supreme Court three years earlier, Johnson nominated Fortas to be chief justice. The nomination died in the Senate, plagued by partisan politics, ideology, and concerns over Fortas's character and closeness to Johnson.

Johnson's power was ebbing. He was only months away from the end of his term, and he had announced he would not run again. Nineteen Republican senators said they thought the office of chief justice should be filled not by Johnson but by the winner of the upcoming election, who, they hoped, would be a Republican.

Fortas, a liberal on social issues, had other problems. His nomination served as a lightning rod for anger toward the Warren Court, especially in the areas of protection for criminal defendants and obscene speech. Conservative senators harangued Fortas about cases decided long before he had ascended to the bench. In one famous incident Thurmond shouted at Fortas, "Mallory! Mallory! I want that name to ring in your ears!" It was a reference to a 1957 case, eight years before Fortas joined the bench, in which a nineteen-year-old rapist was freed by the Supreme Court because his confession had been coerced. Once free, he robbed and raped again.

Fortas's close relationship with Johnson also made many resentful. He continued to act as an adviser to the president on an almost daily basis even when on the Court and on issues that might one day end up before him as a justice. While the full details of that relationship did not come out until afterward, it acted as a subtext throughout. What finally did Fortas in was the revelation that he had accepted fifteen thousand dollars for lectures at American University from funds provided by former clients. He withdrew his name and was forced from the bench entirely the following year over his acceptance of other money from a financier under indictment.

The Fortas fight, political in an essential way but centering publicly on questions of ethics, set the stage for the last two Supreme Court confirmation battles of the century before the Reagan era. Senate Democrats were seething over what happened to Fortas. When newly elected President Richard Nixon nominated Clement F. Haynsworth, Jr., in 1969, they attacked him over a conflict of interest. Haynsworth owned stock in companies affected by some of his rulings.

Senator Birch Bayh, Democrat of Indiana, said at the time that because this was the first time the Senate was asked to fill a Court vacancy caused by a retirement over ethical conduct, it was "only normal" that this committee would be particularly concerned about ethical conduct.

Haynsworth's nomination failed over the ethical issue, but he was also perceived to be unfavorable to unions and blacks, adding to liberal opposition to him. Many scholars thought later that Haynsworth was treated unfairly, that the opposition was spurred by anger over Fortas and aimed at Nixon. Haynsworth went on to a distinguished career as a federal judge.

It was widely assumed that whoever Nixon put up next would be confirmed because the Senate couldn't face another bruising battle. But Nixon, in an act of spite, chose G. Harrold Carswell, a mediocre Florida appeals judge with a segregationist background. As a young aspiring politician in Georgia he had declared: "I yield to no man as a fellow candidate or as a fellow citizen in the firm, vigorous belief in the principles of White Supremacy, and I shall always be so governed." During his confirmation battle he apologized and recanted, but an examination of his past showed other involvement with racism.

Carswell was also an easy target because of his poor record. Conservative South Carolina Senator Ernest Hollings said Carswell "was not qualified to carry Judge Haynsworth's law books." The dean of Yale Law School, Louis H. Pollak, said Carswell had "the most slender credentials of any Supreme Court nominee in this century."

Senator Roman Hruska of Nebraska, a loyal Nixon follower, was angered by the attacks on Carswell's poor record and made one of the most awkward and infamous statements in the history of Court nominations. "Even if he is mediocre, there are a lot of mediocre judges and people and lawyers," Hruska sputtered. "They are entitled to a little representation, aren't they, and a little chance? We can't have all Brandeises, Cardozos and Frankfurters and stuff like that there."

The Senate, following a concerted effort by Ted Kennedy, Birch Bayh, the civil rights community, and leaders of the law schools, rejected Carswell. It appears, in retrospect, an uncomplicated rejection. Carswell, after all, was an easy target. But in fact, the Nixon administration waged a mighty struggle to convince senators that they should not turn down yet another Court nominee. Only Carswell's lack of ability did the trick. Senators felt more comfortable hanging their rejection on competence than on Carswell's racist past.

Nixon accused the Senate of using competence and racism as pretexts for stopping judicial conservatives from getting on the bench: "When all the hypocrisy is stripped away, the real issue was their philosophy of strict construction of the Constitution—a philosophy that I share."

In a publicized letter to Ohio Senator William B. Saxbe, later attorney general, Nixon accused the Senate of denying him a historic right to see his choices appointed. That right, he said, had been granted to all previous presidents, and the advice and consent function of the Senate was clearly meant to be no more than *pro forma*. History shows Nixon to have been woefully wrong, but his statement reflected the prevailing wisdom then and since—until the Bork fight.

A measure of just how entrenched was the Nixonian notion—and of the impact of the Bork battle on dislodging it—can be seen in the thinking of Henry Paul Monaghan. As the Harlan Fiske Stone Professor of Constitutional Law at Columbia University, Monaghan held one of the nation's prestigious constitutional chairs. Monaghan, a conservative and strong advocate of original intent, testified for confirmation of Bork. He said that Bork's surpassing qualifications virtually obliged the Senate to confirm him. But seven months later, in an article in the *Harvard Law Review*, Monaghan recanted. He continued to call Bork a first-rate nominee and to lament his rejection. But after examination of the historical record he had decided that the Senate, after all, should feel no obligation to confirm Bork. As he put it in the article, "Rather (and to my surprise), all the relevant historical and textual sources support the Senate's power when and if it sees fit to assert its vision of the public good against that of the President."

Such surprise from a man who had spent decades studying constitutional law provided remarkable testimony to how the prevailing wisdom had shifted.

Eric Schnapper, a lawyer on the staff of the NAACP Legal Defense and Educational Fund, Inc., was a veteran of numerous judicial wars in the decade leading up to the Bork controversy. He said that after the draining battles over the failed Nixon appointees, it was difficult to rouse interest in opposing judicial nominees in the Senate. "Any inclination by anybody to fight judicial appointments died," he said. "Confirmation hearings became like Jewish weddings: Everyone stands up and gets introduced and it's a happy day in the life of the nominee."

After Carswell, the next controversial judicial appointment was Jimmy Carter's nomination of Cornelia Kennedy to the Sixth Circuit Court of Appeals in the Midwest. Schnapper said his studies showed Kennedy had ruled in favor of the defendant in every one of some one hundred civil rights cases. But senators and their staffs were ill equipped to evaluate her opinions and were reluctant to involve themselves in such a fight. "Nobody wants to do this kind of thing," Schnapper said. "When it's all over, you've ruined someone's career. It's not something a normal person enjoys." But the opposition to Kennedy was carried forward by Schnapper and his colleague Elaine Jones. Even so, Cornelia Kennedy was confirmed. The opposition did get five committee votes against and produced enough controversy around her to dampen her prospects of a rise to the Supreme Court.

Schnapper contrasted that lonely battle with a meeting a decade later of civil rights groups the day after President Reagan nominated Anthony Kennedy to occupy the seat Bork had failed to win. There were 250 people in the room, Schnapper recalled, and he didn't know 80 percent of them. "The mood had changed," he said. "There was an awareness of the importance of judicial nominations and of the possibility of stopping them. Suddenly there was a movement out there and people wanted to be part of it."

One of the biggest differences Schnapper noted between the Cornelia Kennedy effort and the fight against Bork was the readiness and awareness of Senate staffers. By the time of Bork a reasonably large investigative staff stood in place and had an enthusiasm for the work. In Schnapper's view, that began only in 1986.

In the early Reagan years deeply conservative legal scholars were placed on the federal bench with barely a murmur of opposition. In keeping with tradition, it was thought that since Reagan had been elected, he had a right to name his judges. They need only be competent and honest, and nearly all were. But as Reagan ran out of top flight academic conservatives, he began reaching into much younger and, occasionally, less qualified ranks. Liberals had been quietly wringing their hands. Now they began to protest. In addition, highly competent and intelligent Reagan nominees were being vetoed by the right wing for stands on abortion or gun control or for having at one time contributed to the American Civil Liberties Union. Such partisanship allowed Reagan opponents to say they entered the fray in *response* to a right-wing political agenda, not as part of their own.

In 1984 the liberals struck. Herman Schwartz, a left-leaning constitutional law professor at American University; William Taylor, a longtime civil rights lawyer who had worked for the government in the 1960s; and Nan Aron, founder and director of the Alliance for

Justice, a group of two dozen public interest legal groups, met to discuss ways to fight Reagan judicial appointments. They set up the Judicial Selection Project under the alliance and named Aron chairwoman. They put in place a mechanism for studying and lobbying against nominees considered unduly inimical to the interests of minorities, women, or civil liberties. The group was instrumental in blocking several lower-court appointments and later in the Bork fight.

Reagan supporters both in and outside the administration said often and loudly that their goal was to remake the federal judiciary, to undo the "activism" of the preceding quarter century. Some even expressed this aim in the clearest of political terms. Bruce Fein, who had been in the Justice Department working on judicial selection during the first term, told *Newsweek* in October 1985: "It became evident after the first term that there was no way to make legislative gains in many areas of social and civil rights. The President has to do it by changing the jurisprudence."

Administration officials would speak glowingly of their nominees' youth, saying they would be on the bench for a very long time. During Reagan's first term, 11.4 percent of all his appointees were under 40, a record for any recent president; the average age of his appeals court appointees during his first term was 51.5, the youngest average of the past five administrations.

He appointed Richard Posner, forty-two, and Frank Easterbrook, thirty-five, to the Seventh Circuit in Chicago. He appointed J. Harvie Wilkinson III, thirty-nine, to the Fourth Circuit; Kenneth Starr, thirty-six, to the District of Columbia, and Alex Kozinski, thirty-four, to the Ninth Circuit on the West Coast. All were highly intelligent and profoundly conservative. None had judicial experience to speak of, but all had expressed themselves fully in academic journals regarding their views on the direction of law. A nine-member President's Committee on Federal Judicial Selection sifted through the nominees' writings and speeches in search of genuine conservative ideology. Those present at interviews said potential nominees were asked about their views on abortion and on the rights of criminal defendants.

Some of these young nominees ran into trouble with their evaluations by the American Bar Association's Standing Committee on the Federal Judiciary. This committee gave candidates one of four ratings: exceptionally well qualified, well qualified, qualified, and not qualified. Over the years the ABA had come to exert considerable influence over the selection of judges. One of its criteria was experience in the law, and the younger nominees often received the low rating of "qualified." Frustrated liberals began to make much of the ratings, saying a new record for poor quality was being set for the sake of ideological purity. It was untrue. A comparison of the ratings of Reagan and Carter judicial nominees shows very little difference in quality. Carter, too, had had an agenda: to increase the number of women and members of minority groups on the federal bench. Ratings of some of these nominees were very low indeed and this despite ABA efforts to stretch criteria so as to make it easier for those benefiting from affirmative action.

As the number of Reagan appointments mounted, so did the issue of quality. A few of the candidates did have poor credentials. They provided a handle on the politically sensitive issue of heightened Senate scrutiny. Gradually, liberal groups and academics began to pressure the Senate to take its responsibility more seriously.

Common Cause, dedicated to good governmental process, issued a report in January 1986 entitled "Assembly Line Approval" which complained that the Senate Judiciary Committee was shirking its advice and consent duties: "[I]n recent years the Senate rarely has given serious scrutiny to judicial nominees. Some Republican Senators closely aligned with President Reagan have pushed to keep the confirmation process moving, as though that were the highest priority. Other Republicans and Democrats generally have gone along."

Strom Thurmond, the conservative South Carolina Republican who was Judiciary Committee chairman during the six years the Republicans controlled the Senate, was moving judges through faster than any chairman in twenty years, according to the Congressional Research Service. Nominees were being considered in group proceedings, as many as six or seven at a time. They faced virtually no investigation into their background and barely a few minutes of questioning.

Democratic Senators, alarmed at the prospect of scores of right-wingers taking over the federal benches, began making speeches on the floor echoing the concerns of Common Cause. Senator Alan Cranston of California delivered a long, historical argument for a more active Senate role. Paul Simon of Illinois, assigned the task by committee Democrats of examining judicial nominees, told the National Press Club in March 1986 that the Senate needed to increase its participation in the selection of judges. He said quality was the most obvious issue, but ideology also deserved attention. He thought senators ought to determine, within broad outlines, a nominee's views about the meaning of the Constitution and the role of federal courts. As Simon put it, "What are the nominee's views on key elements: majority and minority rights, presidential and congressional authority, federal power and state and local authority, and the meaning of the First Amendment?"

Simon confessed himself not fully comfortable with those yardsticks. He would feel more confident about applying them if a nominee's other qualifications were borderline or if the president seemed bent on packing the courts with too many judges of the same rigid ideology. He said also that a more active Senate role in the process should have a sobering effect on a president, preventing him from choosing overly and consistently ideological candidates.

Simon's unease over considering the ideology of a judicial nominee was commonplace in the Senate. It was also understandable. At the very core of the judiciary is the belief that judges are above the political fray, loyal to a system of rules known as legal reasoning. Though passions of the moment may wax and wane, the law will hold firm, providing the country with a solid foundation. The United States likes to think of itself as living by the rule of law, not men.

Even those most comfortable with examining the ideology of nominees would be unhappy if that were the *only* criterion. While the Court may reveal a political bias in interpreting the Constitution's broad phrases, its work is distinctly apolitical in other ways. As David Bryden, a professor of law at the University of Minnesota, has pointed out, justices' votes are not traded, party discipline is not imposed, and allegations that a justice has used his position on the Court to advance interests off the bench are rarely made and would be universally condemned as a scandal if found to be true.

Bryden added that if judicial merit were seen solely in political terms, there would be no need to select only lawyers as judges. Any profession would do. What could stop senators from insisting that nominees reveal in advance how they planned to vote on controversial issues? Why not amend the Constitution and abolish life tenure? Why would the Court continue to explain its rulings? Congress never does.

In other words, competence and intelligence had been and continued to be universally accepted as the main criteria in any confirmation process. Ideology was generally viewed, if at all, as a minor consideration. But for the Bork Supreme Court confirmation hearings, senators abandoned those long-held views, pushing ideology to a new prominence. That was a major shift in attitude.

After the Bork battle Senator Patrick Leahy of Vermont put it this way: "The Senate had not been paying enough attention in the past to the direction in constitutional law where those justices were taking us. There has been an evolution on our part with regard to philosophy. We see our responsibility more clearly."

The new Senate activism discomfited many. One sign of that was debasement of language used around the issue. Instead of saying that Bork went down for ideological reasons, most senators preferred to say Bork was defeated because he was "out of the mainstream." Laurence Tribe, the liberal Harvard professor, said Bork was out of the mainstream. Asked his view, Ed Meese responded that Tribe was out of the mainstream. Told of Meese's view, Ted Kennedy said Meese was out of the mainstream. And so it went. The debate over Bork was over ideology but cast in more comforting terms. The unspoken issue was the fight over defining the mainstream.

Simon's new activism stemmed partly from a young Yale law professor named Paul Gewirtz. Simon had been quoted in the press as downplaying political philosophy as a factor in the Senate's consideration of judicial nominees. Gewirtz had been informally debating with colleagues that very question; he believed that the opposite was true and that senators such as Simon should hear why. Put in touch with Simon, he laid out his ideas. To Gewirtz, it was a myth that what judges did was isolated from politics. He spurned the mechanical model, saying there was no such thing as a legal answer distinct from political philosophy. Simon was interested in Gewirtz's ideas and—rare for a man who writes most of his own material—asked him to work on his Press Club speech with him.

During the early and middle 1980s, when Gewirtz was debating the question of judicial philosophy, the test case he and his friends repeatedly cited was Robert Bork. He was the best example of Gewirtz's notion that credentials alone were not enough, since Bork's were so strong. In addition, Gewirtz knew Bork a bit from Yale and was fond of him in a distant sort of way. He thought, for example, that he would have no trouble voting for Bork for tenure at the law school. He thought of Bork as an appealing man and teacher. But familiar with Bork's judicial philosophy, he believed he could make a strong case for opposing Bork's confirmation to the Supreme Court. "The issue was one of having the power to decide what the Constitution means for the whole country, as opposed to provoking debate in academia," he said.

While Gewirtz was discussing the issue with his friends, another liberal law professor was developing a similar point of view. Laurence Tribe, the Ralph S. Tyler, Jr., Professor of Constitutional Law at Harvard University, was deeply worried about President Reagan's decisive 1984 electoral victory. Reagan would surely name scores more conservative federal judges and, more important, several Supreme Court justices. Most Americans seemed sadly oblivious of that presidential power, yet it would make a huge difference in their lives. Tribe wanted to convince a popular audience that a judge's personal philosophy would, without question, enter into judging and was therefore something the Senate and the nation should examine very carefully.

His book *God Save This Honorable Court* (1985) said in its preface: "People need to understand, it seemed to me, why those who interpret and enforce the Constitution simply cannot avoid choosing among competing social and political visions, and why it is that those choices will reflect *our* values—the diverse values of all those who might read this book—only if we peer closely enough, and probe deeply enough into the outlooks of those whom our Presidents name to sit on the Supreme Court."

Tribe presented a list of critical Supreme Court rulings on which he thought a careful probe of nominees should center. Two years later his book was to guide those shaping the argument against Bork's confirmation.

His first concern was the kind of personal liberty heretofore secured by decisions on individual and family privacy, decisions granting Americans the right to send their children to a school of choice, to live in whatever family makeup they chose, to use birth control, to seek abortion, and to keep government away from such things as sterilization of criminals. That was to remain Tribe's thrust from the beginning of the Bork fight.

His next concern was protection of minorities and women. In Tribe's view, while the legislatures had stridden forward in the area, the Supreme Court had often been alone guarding such rights.

Tribe then turned to decisions that improved the systemic nature of democracy, such as the cases from the mid-1960s that forced states to reapportion their legislative districts to one person, one vote and that struck down poll taxes. Neither decision stemmed directly from the Constitution's text, but Tribe, like the Court itself, believed they were implicit in the document's broad notions. They were precisely the kinds of decisions to which Bork and other proponents of original intent had objected.

Tribe also wrote about the balance of power between the executive and legislative branches. It was important, he averred, to maintain some power and identity for the individual states. But equally important was assurance that standards of individual liberty, especially the liberty to stand apart from the majority and to express oneself freely, be preserved.

God Save This Honorable Court put forth a notion of the Constitution as a living and "incomplete" document, dismissing strict construction as "appealing, and plainly wrong."

Tribe developed an argument for making the Court's balance a legitimate issue, one of the more delicate questions of the Bork fight. The context of a nomination should be considered along with the views of the nominee himself, he said. As he put it, "[I]f the appointment of a particular nominee would push the Court in a substantive direction that a Senator conscientiously deems undesirable because it would upset the Court's equilibrium or exacerbate what he views as an already excessive conservative *or* liberal bias, then that Senator can and should vote against confirmation. To vote otherwise would be to abdicate a solemn trust."

Tribe contended that such a consideration of balance could work not only against a nominee but in his or her favor. If, for example, the Court were seen to be moving strongly away from the nominee's views, it would strengthen the argument for confirmation.

This was a rather more complex view of the role of "advice and consent" than had existed previously in any formal way. Tribe was saying that a senator's job was not simply to rubber-stamp a president's choice or to satisfy himself that a judicial nominee's integrity, intelligence, and even philosophical leanings were to his liking. The legislator had to make a still broader evaluation of whether the nomination would be good for the Court and the country at that time. In Tribe's view, a nomination that would be appropriate in one year might be ill advised five years later because the Court could have changed.

Tribe's arguments were by no means accepted wholesale. But their echo resounded throughout the Bork battle and were referred to not only by those liberal lawyers and activists who largely agreed with the book's line of argument. One could see the book lending legitimacy to senators unwilling to judge Bork on his own merits but content to say that the nomination was "divisive" or wrong for the country at the time.

CHAPTER

6

Self-Made Men

Larry Tribe was to do more than provide ideas during the Bork fight. Although he entered the fray gingerly, he quickly became an intellectual architect of the opposition. During the hearings he was on the telephone daily with Hill staff, often by 7:00 A.M., providing counterarguments to ones made the previous day and suggesting lines of questioning. He was also the star anti-Bork witness, appearing alone for more than three hours. Before the hearings he held several meetings with Kennedy and Committee Chairman Biden and playacted the role of Bork for them. All present at the sessions agreed later that he outperformed the real Bork.

There was something aptly symmetrical about Tribe's playing Bork in those warm-up sessions. As the great battle developed, Tribe was increasingly depicted by his detractors as the Bork of the left, the one whose brilliance and integrity and legal credentials were beyond dispute but whose political and personal agendas were nakedly apparent. He was the sticky test case for those on the right who preached that ideology should not count in judicial confirmations. He was someone to be feared and, if possible, discredited. Just as some liberals dismissed the quality of Bork's mind—saying his judicial philosophy was a pitifully transparent justification for political goals—so those to the right of Tribe claimed his thinking was superficial and politically motivated.

Like Bork, Tribe was a standard-bearer for his side, among the most articulate and respected of liberal theoreticians. Both were self-made men, skilled wordsmiths obsessed with the power of ideas to move and shape public policy. They were sophisticated players on the public stage yet oddly naive about the long-term effects of such publicity. Taken by the pleasures of the spotlight, they hurt themselves politically. Each figured he was showing guts. But to their detractors they seemed to be campaigning in an unseemly manner for the Supreme Court. Like Bork, Tribe was mentioned constantly as a likely nominee to the high court.

But their similarities were less real than they appeared in the world of political symbols. For one thing, Bork claimed to seek neutrality. He spurned constitutional choices even as he made them. Tribe, on the other hand, asserted that one could not interpret the Constitution without taking a stand on complex and socially sensitive issues. He wasn't a nihilist; he didn't think the Constitution was an old bottle into which one cavalierly poured new wine. But he believed deeply in the need to *interpret* the charter's substance, to acknowledge one's prejudices without being blinded by them.

Tribe's prejudices were toward greater liberty and, especially, equality. He believed some parts of the Constitution provided the basis for welfare rights, although not for their judicial enforcement. He said that if he could have rewritten the Constitution, he would have specifically included provisions guaranteeing decent housing and employment for every person and, perhaps, a ceiling on inherited wealth. That didn't mean he found those provisions in the terms of the existing Constitution. He readily conceded that the sort of constitution he would want differed from the one he felt obliged to acknowledge the country had.

Nonetheless, Tribe thought there was play in the constitutional joints. What he most objected to in Bork's jurisprudence was the notion that only those rights specified in the Constitution are retained by the people. Tribe believed that the Constitution was written so that the principles of liberty and equal protection and opportunity could grow, at least in a limited fashion, with the nation. He was especially concerned about privacy as a constitutional concept. He wrote numerous articles seeking a way to justify a constitutional right to abortion, although he acknowledged that the 1973 *Roe* v. *Wade* decision was shaky constitutional law. And the Supreme Court case he lost that most upset him was the 5–4 decision against the rights of homosexuals to engage in private sexual conduct without fear of prosecution.

Quite apart from their philosophical differences, Tribe, at forty-six, was a more accomplished constitutional scholar than Bork and a more disciplined person. Bork had published occasional articles about the Constitution and one excellent book on antitrust, but Tribe had written one of the nation's most widely used treatises on constitutional law—a seventeen-hundred-page volume, updated and revised in 1987, a decade after it first appeared—and half a dozen other books on the subject. On related topics he had written another half dozen. While most of Bork's contributions were in the popular media or in the form of speeches, Tribe was a fountain of law journal scholarship.

Tribe was also an unusually successful litigator. He had won nine of twelve Supreme Court arguments in a variety of areas, from individual rights to corporate law, over an eight-year period. He successfully defended a Berkeley, California, rent control law and the right of news reporters and the public to attend criminal trials. He won a crucial Court victory for Pennzoil in its ten-billion-dollar battle with Texaco. And he had done well financially from his litigation.

Henry Paul Monaghan of Columbia, the ardent conservative and a harsh critic of Tribe's, called him "probably the most creative constitutional scholar around. He sees connections between A and B in a manner that is unparalleled. The problem is that I don't think such creativity is helpful in understanding the Constitution."

Tribe had a nimble mind. Attorneys who consulted with him gulped at his high fee but waxed poetic about his ability to grasp intricate legal arguments in minutes and to extend them to reaches they hadn't imagined. "He scales mountains," said one colleague.

Tribe's classes were oversubscribed; his telephones, always busy. He used precise and difficult language to form complex thoughts. He spoke in long, convoluted sentences, but what he said was provocative and often pithy or alliterative. When Reagan named Anthony Kennedy to the seat for which Bork had been defeated, Tribe was interviewed on all three television networks, telling ABC that Kennedy's decisions showed "more decency than dogmatism, more sensitivity than stridency."

His manner—tight, a touch humorless—and his ambition annoyed some people, especially the many who had reason to be jealous of him. It seemed that everywhere you looked—on television, in the newspapers—there was Tribe. There, staring you in the face yet again, was his kinky, piled-up hair and Cambridge crew-neck sweater and carefully selected adverbs. And you knew he kept every damn clipping and monitored his play. He had been known to complain to reporters when they hadn't published his words after an interview. His law school office and home study had full-wall mirrors.

A joke that made the rounds among Harvard law students was that Larry Tribe could never be president of the United States because this country had separation of church and state and Tribe thought he was God.

But many who knew him called him misunderstood. "Larry's a complicated person. Because of that consuming drive, a lot of people may get the impression that he is ruthless. But with his family and friends, including myself, he is a devoted father, husband and friend," said Albert Alschuler, a University of Chicago law professor, Tribe's Harvard roommate.

Tribe was also generous to liberal causes. He frequently helped fashion legal arguments for those defending abortion rights or affirmative action, sometimes volunteering to write long Supreme Court briefs. He never charged for his time on those occasions, and he contributed money to organizations that championed the rights of women and minorities.

When asked about himself, Tribe could be disarmingly honest one minute, calculating another. He had a boyish quality, using such expressions as *neat* and *blow my mind* when chatting informally. In summer he wore shorts and running shoes to his law school office and enjoyed walks—no-nonsense fast ones—along the Charles River. One afternoon a week he volunteered at the law school day-care center his wife, Carolyn, started, getting down on the floor with a bunch of four-year-olds. At home, in the elegant Victorian house near Harvard Square that Carolyn and he had fastidiously redecorated, he would happily sit in one of the family rooms and discourse about the law and the world. The Tribes held Democratic fund raisers at home and played host to book-signing parties by well-known liberals.

Tribe was something of a child prodigy. He was born in Shanghai in 1941 to Eastern European Jews, his first language was Russian, and he entertained a roomful of guests at his first birthday party by speaking it surprisingly well, his mother recalled. His father was interned by the Japanese, his younger brother was not yet born, and his early life was spent entirely among adults. At age four he taught himself to read.

After the war the family moved to San Francisco, where Tribe's father struggled as a car salesman. Tribe was a gifted artist and continually won art competitions. But he was pudgy, a foreigner, and socially inept. Childhood was not an easy time. He compensated by pushing himself, showing off to his parents, and lording his accomplishments over his younger brother.

"I was a really driven kid," he said one day. "I would wake up my parents at five in the morning with my latest painting, and they would ooh and ah. I liked that kind of stroking. I wonder why I was so driven."

He had liberal notions of progress and tolerance even as a young boy. In the seventh grade he painted for his junior high school a mural that depicted the road from the world of the caveman to the twentieth century. At the end of the mural stood the torch of knowledge and a collage of different religious symbols and people of various races in harmony. The mural still existed in the junior high school thirty years later. He continued to paint for a number of years, and his landscapes decorated his Cambridge home.

Tribe entered Harvard on a full scholarship at the age of sixteen and a half, determined to become a doctor. He had never heard of Harvard until a high school classmate with his own ambitions had mentioned it. Both boys were accepted, but only Tribe won the scholarship, and the classmate had to go elsewhere. Harvard became the defining institution of Tribe's life. When he first arrived, he was in shock. He had been the smartest boy in his class, but he discovered that so had most of his new classmates. "His first letter home was interesting," his mother said. "He said it was hard to walk around Harvard because every other boy was a Larry Tribe, too."

Actually it was worse than that. From a modest background, with parents who had not attended college, Tribe found himself surrounded by offspring of the eastern establishment, the sons of bankers and power brokers, graduates of Andover and Choate. They played unkind tricks on the naive young Californian. They would talk menacingly in German in the middle of the night, making him believe that Nazis were out to get him.

Tribe was afraid he wouldn't make it. But he joined the debate society, which served as a haven from abuse. More important, he finished freshman year second in a class of eleven hundred. He was beginning to get the message that not every Harvard student was a Larry Tribe. In his junior year his debate team won the national championships. Discovering along the way that he disliked laborato-

ries, he abandoned medicine for mathematics. Tribe became besot-
ted with the elegance of ideas. His love of math and science, which
continued throughout his life, had to do with a love for intricate
structural truth. As he said, " 'E to the i pi equals minus one' is one
of the most powerful proofs that God exists. It is one of the most
amazing facts in the world."

Awarded a National Science Foundation grant, Tribe entered the
Harvard graduate school in math. In his first semester he got all A's.
In his second semester he got all incompletes. It is not entirely clear
what happened. He said he was suddenly disaffected, overcome by
the abstract inhumanity of math. He was unable to talk to his new
wife, Carolyn, about it. Friends remember that Tribe recognized he
was not a mathematical genius, only very good, and that those few
who were geniuses would always outshine him. He decided to
switch fields. A bit late, he applied to the law school, was put on the
waiting list and then admitted.

One exigent teacher kept him off the law review his first year, but
he did better with each year and became an award-winning student.
He won a clerkship with a federal judge in California and from there
got another clerkship, with Potter Stewart on the Supreme Court.
He was offered teaching jobs at both Harvard and Yale and chose to
return to Cambridge. One of those who interviewed him at Yale was
Robert Bork.

Tribe started out teaching evidence and conflict of laws, feeling it
presumptuous to teach constitutional law, the domain of such giants
as Paul Freund and Archibald Cox. But he began writing in the
field, work which led to his 1978 treatise, and he quickly won emi-
nence as a constitutional scholar. Erwin Griswold, former dean of
Harvard Law School and former solicitor general, said of Tribe's
treatise: "It may well be that no book . . . has ever had a greater
influence on the development of American constitutional law."

Tribe's first argument before the Supreme Court was in 1980, ten
days after his father had died. He remembers being emotionally
numb, but he won the case, with Chief Justice Warren Burger quoting generously from Tribe's brief in the decision.

Some years earlier Tribe had come to know Sargent Shriver,
brother-in-law of Ted Kennedy, and had become issues director in
Shriver's short-lived 1976 presidential bid. Through Shriver, Tribe
got to know Kennedy and became a supporter and adviser.

Not long after Tribe's book on Supreme Court selection came out in 1985, he was asked to discuss his views with Democratic senators. He went to dinner with Kennedy, Biden, and Howard Metzenbaum of Ohio and laid out his case. A year later, after Chief Justice Warren Burger retired and Rehnquist was named to succeed him, Tribe wrote a letter to the committee along with Philip Kurland, a moderately conservative and highly respected constitutional scholar from the University of Chicago. They wrote that the Senate was obliged "to assure itself that a nominee's substantive views of law are within the broad bounds of acceptibility in American public life. . . . The Republic may demand—and its Senators ought therefore to ensure—that its life-tenured judiciary does not disdain the Bill of Rights or the Fourteenth Amendment's command for equal protection of the laws and due process."

Tribe did not wish to enter the Rehnquist battle. It was too risky for someone who argued frequently in front of the Court. But Kennedy used some of Tribe's arguments to marshal opposition to Rehnquist based on the justice's deeply conservative ideology. Rehnquist had often been a lone dissenter on high court rulings.

Kennedy's efforts were a beginning. The issue of ideology was discussed openly for the first time in a long while. But most senators were still shy about it, and since Rehnquist had already been on the Court for fifteen years, his elevation to chief was not something many were willing to bleed over.

Kennedy did manage to garner thirty-three votes against Rehnquist, the largest number of negative votes against a sitting justice in history. So the frustration he felt over the loss was accompanied by hope. When the Bork nomination was announced, the Senate was in Democratic hands after the elections the previous November. Beginning with the thirty-three against Rehnquist the year before, Kennedy figured that he should at least gain the forty-one votes needed for a filibuster.

Tribe at first also wanted to stay out of the Bork battle. He assumed, as did nearly everyone, that Bork would be confirmed, and he saw no reason to make an enemy out of a future justice. He also was short of time, trying to finish the second edition of his treatise. Finally, Tribe knew that taking a strong stand against Bork would add to the belief that he was a liberal henchman. He readily acknowledged he was generally liberal but felt he had been unfairly branded. He believed his constitutional views were more complex than a simple label would suggest.

But it proved impossible to stay out. Everyone kept calling him. He *had* written the book on the issue. Furthermore, Bork's views of the Constitution were, he felt, utterly wrong, even dangerous for the country. He knew Bork casually, from that Yale interview twenty years earlier and from a written exchange they had had on constitutional law. But nothing more. Ever so slowly Tribe was brought fully into the process, meeting Kennedy and Biden aides, talking by phone to Metzenbaum's staff. He pressed the issue of privacy and individual freedom over and over again, saying it was the area where Bork was most vulnerable, most out of step with the nation. He believed that Bork was conservative not only on privacy but also on speech, women, blacks, *everything* really worth fighting.

By the time of the Bork nomination liberals were girding for a fight over judicial appointments. They were feeling frustrated over Rehnquist, queasy about having given Scalia such an easy ride—he was confirmed unanimously—and angry about several other nominations they had fought unsuccessfully. One of them was Daniel Manion, an obscure forty-four-year-old Indiana lawyer, who won confirmation to the Seventh Circuit Court of Appeals in Chicago in 1986 despite a huge campaign against him. The extremely conservative Manion had been sympathetic to the John Birch Society and favored posting the Ten Commandments in classrooms. Moreover, he was woefully lacking in credentials. His legal briefs contained errors of grammar and syntax and seemed devoid of intellectual distinction. He had virtually no experience in dealing with federal or constitutional issues. Scores of law school deans and professors announced their opposition to him. But with the Republicans in charge of the Senate, he squeaked by on a 50–49 vote.

J. Danforth Quayle, Republican senator of Indiana and later vice president, was Manion's sponsor. He worked tirelessly to get the votes on the floor, using questionable tactics. He persuaded Nancy Kassebaum, Republican of Kansas, who had initially voted against confirmation, to withdraw her vote. He did so by encouraging her to join Arizona's Barry Goldwater in a courtesy arrangement known as pairing, which allows two senator on opposite sides of an issue to agree not to vote because one of the two cannot be present. Through pairing, their votes cancel each other out. Quayle told Kassebaum that Goldwater favored Manion's confirmation when he, in fact, had not yet made up his mind. Kassebaum's withdrawal created a tie, broken by the Senate president, then Vice President Bush.

The large mobilization against Manion by legal academics and by such liberal lobbying groups as People for the American Way failed but turned out to be helpful later in stopping Bork. Newspaper advertisements against Manion and the general sense of outrage in the academy raised the alarm. The tension passed through to the Rehnquist nomination.

Each battle had failed to rouse truly widespread opposition. Manion's was a nomination to a lower court, and Rehnquist was simply moving up from associate to chief justice, a matter more of symbolism than substance. The Bork stakes were higher on both counts. And liberal attempts to block both Manion and Rehnquist were important dress rehearsals, both organizationally and emotionally.

Ted Kennedy would have played a key role in a Bork fight under any circumstances. His decision to do so was strengthened because the chairman of the Judiciary Committee was Joseph R. Biden, Jr., Democrat of Delaware. Kennedy could have taken over Judiciary again when the Democrats won back the Senate in 1986. He had been Judiciary chairman during the Carter years. But Kennedy chose instead to head Labor and Human Resources in order to concentrate on issues of health care and wages. He would keep an eye on the workings of Judiciary without actually having to chair the committee.

It was not that Kennedy didn't like Biden. He did. Everyone liked Joe Biden. He was tall and handsome; he had an ear-to-ear grin and a boyish passion and keen political sensibility. He had a fine sense of humor, and he was a shrewd, hardworking, and collegial legislator. Biden was also a first-rate speaker both of prepared texts and off the cuff. One congressional staffer thought Biden had the highest ratio of eloquence to intelligence he had ever seen; Kennedy had one of the lowest. Kennedy was bright, but often he couldn't get the words out. Biden always sounded terrific. He and Kennedy, both Irish Catholics who had overcome wrenching personal tragedy, had known each other for a long time and had much in common. But theirs was a complex and wary relationship.

From the beginning of his political career, Biden was compared with the Kennedys. He understood the political value of the comparison, but he also resented it. Sitting in his handsome near-baronial house in Wilmington one day, he said he had always been dogged by portrayals of him as a young Ted Kennedy. Then, pointing to the things in front of him, he said: "We're as different as this table and that fireplace." He acknowledged that he had striven to highlight their difference but that Kennedy had seemed indifferent to the problem.

Only forty-four at the time of the Bork hearings, Biden had already been in the Senate for fifteen years. He was elected two weeks shy of the constitutionally mandated thirtieth birthday. He was a young man with the world in his palm. Six weeks later his wife, Neilia, and their three children, en route home with a Christmas tree, were hit by a truck. Neilia and Biden's infant daughter were killed. His two sons survived.

After taking office, Biden refused to move to Washington and commuted daily two hours from Wilmington, Delaware, to help bring up his sons, Joseph III and Robert. In 1977 he married Jill Tracy Jacobs, a teacher of emotionally disturbed teenagers, and they had a daughter, Ashley.

Biden was touching and noble in ways, with his rousing oratorical skill and optimism and the ability to rise above personal tragedy. He was tough, too, with a mix of self-confidence and brooding wariness that often comes from deep-seated insecurity. He was born in Wilmington, a town filled with wealthy people named du Pont. It was a place that could compete for highest number of Rolls-Royces per capita. Biden was of modest stock. He grew up on the other side of town, the son of a car dealer who wanted his boy to be a professional because professionals get respect. No one in his family had ever gone to college.

As a youth Biden stuttered slightly. He thought briefly about the priesthood, then law. Not an intellectual, he did well for himself, going to the University of Delaware and to Syracuse University Law School on a full scholarship. Those around him knew he would succeed. Yet his lack of distinguished credentials, either familial or educational, needled him in small ways. He was driven to show others his worth. At the same time, his background provided him with a shrewd and highly effective common-man style. His questions and debating technique said: "I'm nothing special, just a regular guy. But I can see what you're doing, and we regular folks don't have to take that crap."

To the surprise of many, Biden was to perform brilliantly against Bork in the hearings, smiling his regular-guy smile all along, acting embarrassed about challenging such a distinguished scholar, but gaining the rhetorical upper hand. For that, liberals would be eternally grateful to him and far more indulgent than they had ever been before.

But there was something about Biden's ambition, about the fastidious way he allowed himself to be packaged that made some liberals nervous. Biden had bought into the marketing notion of generational politics. He tried to sell his youth, combining high-pitched idealistic rhetoric with middlebrow pragmatism. Most Senate résumés were lists of positions and accomplishments. Biden's was a piece of advertising copy, beginning with the sentence "Joseph R. Biden, Jr., of Delaware, is one of the new generation of leaders in the U.S. Senate."

Biden had been slow to join the fight against Reagan's judicial nominees. Opposing presidential appointees on ideology had made him nervous. "What's going to happen with ideology when *I'm* president?" he would ask his staff. He was slow on Manion and hesitant on Rehnquist. In an earlier fight that mattered to liberals, against a young conservative named Alex Kozinski who was nominated to the Ninth Circuit in California, Biden did little.

He sought a middle position on abortion—calling it a personal choice but opposing federal funds for it—and introduced antibusing legislation, while calling himself a champion of civil rights.

In an effort to shed the baggage of traditional Democratic liberalism, Biden used Kennedy as an example of what he was not. Kennedy didn't take it personally, but it was revealing of Biden's balancing act.

While distancing himself from Ted Kennedy, Biden tried—as many Democratic politicians did—to co-opt the legacies of John and Robert. He would portray himself as their contemporary equivalents. This was due partly to Biden's longtime aide, Mark Gitenstein, chief counsel to the Judiciary Committee and Biden speech writer. Gitenstein, a soft-spoken southerner who felt that Biden was a new Robert Kennedy, laced Biden's speeches with Kennedy lines. This was also the tendency of Patrick Caddell, the insightful and difficult Democratic pollster and adviser who had helped Biden win his first Senate election in 1972 and was a key Biden aide in the presidential race. Robert Kennedy was Caddell's greatest hero.

Biden had declared for the Democratic presidential nomination only three weeks before the Bork announcement. His campaign was just getting going, and he had made the point frequently that he would not be subservient to the so-called special interest groups—that is, labor, civil rights, and women's groups. Walter Mondale's allegiance to those groups in 1984 was widely perceived to be the reason for his rout at the hands of Reagan. Biden felt strongly that he had to distance himself from liberal groups.

Kennedy believed that without the lobbying groups, Bork could not be beaten. The groups would get the grass roots activated, put pressure on senators, build an atmosphere of momentum and strength beyond Washington.

Finally, there was a most unfortunate statement by Biden only a year earlier, the kind of shoot-from-the-hip comment he seemed unable to avoid, the kind that ultimately ruined his presidential campaign. Biden loved to talk. Sometimes he did so without thought or information. He occasionally exaggerated or shaded the truth in small ways; he would, for example, tell Delaware constituents that he had introduced a bill when in fact, he had been one of many cosponsors who signed on afterward. Aides gently warned him of the dangers of such statements, but he brushed them off.

Biden's campaign faltered smack in the middle of the Bork hearings because of allegations that he had appropriated, word for word, a speech by British Labour party leader Neil Kinnock contrasting his accomplishments with those of his working-class ancestors. Biden had credited the speech to Kinnock on other occasions and had even publicly admired Kinnock's speech. But that day in late August he neglected to mention the speech's source, and it did enormous damage. Unlike his town meetings in Delaware, the national stage resulted in his every word being scrutinized. The candidacy died when someone located a videotape of Biden scolding a man in New Hampshire who questioned his academic credentials. His Achilles' heel jabbed, Biden spouted off inventive details about his stellar accomplishments in college and law school. His records at both had been modest. To many of those who knew him, the outburst was not an isolated event. Biden was clever. He had a good feel for language, and he cared deeply about his country. But his yearning for recognition led to gaffes.

Such an occasion occurred the previous November. In a long interview with the *Philadelphia Inquirer* over his planned presidential bid, Biden explained that his upcoming chairmanship of Judiciary was a mixed blessing. The sheer volume of work would force him to spend more time in Washington and less on the campaign trail. The article discussed the issue of Supreme Court nominees, calling it politically delicate for Biden.

"[T]he new Justice might tip the balance on such emotional issues as abortion. And yet recent custom would call for confirming the nominee, assuming no taint of scandal," the article said.

"Biden would be caught in the middle, faced with incurring either the wrath of the interest groups or the anger of a popular president. His inclination, he said, would be to vote for a distinguished conservative; Kennedy's bent, he said, might be to vote against such a nominee.

" 'Say the administration sends up [former Solicitor General Robert H.] Bork and, after our investigation, he looks a lot like another [Associate Justice Antonin] Scalia,' Biden said, referring to the conservative jurist whom the Senate confirmed unanimously earlier this year. 'I'd have to vote for him, and if the groups tear me apart, that's the medicine I'll have to take. I'm not Ted Kennedy.' "

Biden, who announced his opposition to Bork a week after the nomination, spent enormous amounts of energy and time trying to explain away that comment. He was largely unsuccessful and suffered editorial lampooning and the accusation that he was doing no more than toadying to liberal interest groups. Eventually the issue faded, but Kennedy and his staff thought at the beginning that they had to pressure Biden, who still sensed the need to distance himself publicly from Kennedy and old-style liberalism. He would insult Kennedy, but it was partly because he needed him and wished for his approval. Once Biden spoke movingly on television of his dead wife, and Kennedy sent him an admiring note. Biden was so touched and pleased that he spoke highly of Kennedy for weeks.

Kennedy would prod Biden. Some who knew them both believed Kennedy's Senate floor speech was aimed partly at making it impossible for Biden not to oppose Bork. The Democratic standard-bearer couldn't feel that strongly about something and have a Democratic nominee demur. Biden acknowledged that one of the reasons he announced his opposition earlier than he might have wanted was to prevent Kennedy from running the show.

In a confidential memorandum dated July 6, Diana Huffman, Biden's staff director on the Judiciary Committee, reminded Biden of a discussion they had had the day after Bork's nomination was announced and Kennedy had made his speech: "As we discussed on Thursday, it is important for you to take control immediately of the

Committee's handling of the Bork nomination. That includes setting the tone and theme of the debate, as well as controlling the timing of the hearings. . . . Other Democrats, let alone the Republicans, are already trying to frame the debate. It is important that you begin to shape it immediately."

In another memo, dated July 7, Huffman made the point more specifically: "You agreed with Leahy and Kennedy that the Committee should conduct a general oversight hearing on the Administration's judicial selection process. . . . Originally the idea was that Leahy or Kennedy would chair, but that could allow them to set the tone of the debate for Bork. RECOMMENDATION—CANCEL THIS HEARING."

Biden took the advice, as well as other advice Huffman offered regarding two hearings on other judicial appointments scheduled for late July. One, in particular, Bernard Siegan of California, was considered even more judicially conservative than Bork. To Huffman, that meant danger for two reasons: "If we conduct his hearing before we consider Bork, Bork, will by comparison, look very reasonable. It would also put untenable demands on the groups to oppose both at the same time. RECOMMENDATION—CANCEL BOTH HEARINGS. YOU WILL TAKE HEAT FROM THE REPUBLICANS, BUT CAN EXPLAIN THAT YOU ARE CLEARING THE DECKS TO CONSIDER THE SUPREME COURT NOMINEE. YOU SHOULD URGE LEAHY TO HOLD ONE OR TWO HEARINGS ON NON-CONTROVERSIAL NOMINEES TO FULFILL YOUR PLEDGE TO CONTINUE TO MOVE ON NOMINEES."

Undeterred, Kennedy sent Biden confidential memos on the hearings, offering advice. An August 4 Kennedy memo reminded Biden that Bork's testimony would fall precisely on the day of the Constitution's bicentennial and that they should exploit to the fullest that coincidence.

"In light of this auspicious occasion, it may be a good idea to follow Bork with distinguished scholars who can testify about how Bork's whole approach to interpreting the Constitution is inconsistent with the Farmers' commitment to individual liberty," Kennedy wrote. He expected at that point that the American Bar Association would give Bork a rating of "well qualified," adding that Bork opponents had to be prepared for support for Bork in the bar. He wrote: "While there may be pressure to schedule the bar leaders right after Bork, you may want to schedule this panel late in the hearings, late on some afternoon." Kennedy also warned against giving the lobbying groups too high a profile at the hearings, advising that they be allowed to testify only toward the end.

When Biden had spoken to the *Philadelphia Inquirer,* he knew almost nothing of Bork except that he had an impressive résumé and was frequently mentioned as a nominee. Once Powell had resigned, Biden's staff began combing Bork's record and getting calls from the interest groups saying just how seriously they would take a Bork candidacy. The same day John Bolton of the Justice Department called Biden aide Gitenstein to tell him to expect a Bork nomination. Gitenstein, aware of the *Inquirer* gaffe, said not to misinterpret anything Biden had said on Bork so far. And Biden told White House Chief of Staff Howard Baker the day after the Powell resignation that the administration ought to present a list of potential nominees to avoid an unnecessary fight.

There was disagreement on Biden's staff about how opposition to the nomination would play in the presidential political arena. Biden himself saw a Bork nomination as just about the worst thing that could happen to his campaign. He and his campaign staff knew such a nomination would deprive him of campaign time and enmesh him in a political jungle. As Stuart E. Eizenstat, a Democratic strategist, said a few days later, a fight over Bork would bring to the forefront "social issues we Democrats would prefer to see kept in the background."

Two days before the nomination White House Chief Baker and Attorney General Meese did as Biden suggested and held two meetings on Capitol Hill, one with Republican leaders—Minority Leader Robert Dole and ranking Judiciary Committee member Strom Thurmond—and one with Majority Leader Robert Byrd and Biden.

Biden sought to prevent a Bork nomination without saying so explicitly.

When he emerged from his meeting with Meese and Baker, he told reporters that there were some "very good people on the list" of twelve possible nominees and others who were "viewed as having hard edges. If one of them is chosen, it will be a very hot summer and a very hot fall." But he declined to tell the reporters whether Bork was one of those.

Biden pointed to the meeting afterward, saying that he had made his opposition to Bork plain. But that was not how Meese and Baker remembered it. Biden did not say, in their version, that he himself personally opposed Bork, only that the judge was one of several candidates sure to face a hard time. Meese and Baker already knew that, but they had also calculated Biden's need to separate himself from the interest groups. In sum, they walked away from the meeting figuring they could handle the heat a Bork nomination would generate.

One large factor eluded them: The anti-Bork effort would be carried forward *outside* the Senate. It would not be limited to the hearing room. Further, the themes of the Biden presidential campaign and the anti-Bork campaign would neatly dovetail over the coming weeks. Biden's campaign staff would come to see the Bork nomination as an unparalleled opportunity for their candidate.

It was pollster and adviser Caddell who understood the connection immediately. Caddell believed that Bork precisely represented what was wrong and unattractive in the Reagan world view. He could be beaten.

As Caddell saw it, the Reagan White House had always been out of step with the country on social issues, principally those connected with sex and religion. It was on such issues that a young, dynamic candidate could return the executive branch to Democratic hands. For him the Bork nomination was manna from heaven since it allowed his candidate, Biden, to pound those issues for free on national television, propelling himself right to the presidency.

As Tom Donilon, another top aide to Biden's presidential campaign, put it, "It was no accident that the Biden and Bork strategies were similar."

But Biden needed to get out from the pressure of the lobbying groups. It was uncomfortable, and when he did announce his opposition, he did not want it to be seen as a response to their demands.

So a week after the Bork nomination, on July 8, as the nation was gripped by the Iran-contra scandal and the charms of a brash right-wing lieutenant colonel named Oliver North, Biden called a meeting. Present were representatives of six groups—the Leadership Conference on Civil Rights, the NAACP Legal Defense and Educational Fund, Alliance for Justice, the Women's Legal Defense Fund, the Mexican-American Legal Defense and Educational Fund, and People for the American Way. Biden wanted to tell them to back off. They could count on him but please give him time. The liberal groups had been hinting darkly that they didn't know what to do about Biden. One prominent lobbyist had even suggested that if candidate Biden couldn't commit himself to the Bork hearings full time, he should resign his chairmanship.

The representatives figured all they could get from Biden would be a delay in the hearings until after the August recess, thereby giving them time to organize. When he spoke, they were astonished at how clearly and strongly he stated his views. They hadn't even dared solicit a promise that he oppose Bork. He announced it unprompted. But he asked that his plans be kept confidential until he made them public. All agreed.

Biden was taking command, eclipsing Kennedy, reassuring the groups, laying the groundwork for his leadership. But disaster hit, as he should have predicted. Word of his assurances to the groups leaked out within hours and appeared on the front pages of the *New York Times* and the *Washington Post* the next day. Biden now suffered the worst of both worlds. The stories gave the impression that Biden had agreed to lead the fight against Bork because of pressure from the groups.

"I learned a lot about dealing with the press from that period," Gitenstein remarked. "We tried constantly to correct the misimpression. But it was hopeless. Nobody believed us."

Biden made up for it, though. As the summer progressed, he immersed himself in the substance of the Bork battle, taking briefings from scholars both on advice and consent and on Bork's judicial philosophy. He delivered a key speech on the Senate floor in late July explaining why the Senate had a historic role to scrutinize nominees' philosophies, especially if they were nominated for them. And his behavior as chairman and questioning during the hearings won him wide praise.

For the lobbying groups, the Biden commitment was further evidence of the extraordinary momentum they had generated only a week into the process. The day after the nomination a meeting was called at the Leadership Conference, and the response was overwhelming. Representatives of eighty groups came, and the meeting room was packed beyond capacity. Ralph Nader, the consumer advocacy titan, couldn't get in. He was stuck in the hallway.

The coalition agreed to avoid single-issue advocacy, specifically controversial issues such as abortion and affirmative action. This nomination must be fought on a variety of points. They quickly agreed to set up four task forces: legal research, Senate lobbying, grass-roots organization, and public relations.

In the days leading up to the Biden meeting, nearly every day saw another dramatic anti-Bork announcement. The National Federation of Business and Professional Women's Clubs, a staid organization of 125,000, 40 percent Republicans, said it would be happy to dedicate a third of its public policy budget of $250,000 to stopping Bork. The National Education Association voted at its annual convention to oppose Bork, and the National Association for the Advancement of Colored People unanimously passed an anti-Bork resolution. Benjamin Hooks, NAACP executive director, thundered: "We will fight it all the way until Hell freezes over and then we'll skate across the ice."

CHAPTER

7

Raw Meat

Toward the end of the week of September 14, 1987, listeners to small radio stations in Alabama heard the following news item from a man named Henry Griggs in Washington:

[Voice of Griggs] "As Senate hearings on the nomination of Robert Bork to the Supreme Court continue, a number of civil rights leaders raised opposition to Bork, saying his stands on constitutional rights of minorities are critical. The Reverend Jesse Jackson had these comments: [Voice of Jackson] 'Judge Bork is a threat to the future of civil rights, workers' rights and women's rights. The achievements of the last 30 years are threatened by Judge Bork not only because he disagreed with those decisions and the Civil Rights Act of '64 or the Voting Rights Act, but he also would have the power on the Supreme Court to overrule or undercut those decisions. He is not just conservative; he is backwards. He is activist in his intent to undercut progress.' " (End report.)

Henry Griggs was not a news reporter. He was a public relations man for the American Federation of State, County and Municipal Employees, a huge trade union active in liberal causes. For August and September 1987, AFSCME lent Griggs to the anti-Bork effort full time. An important part of his job was to make radio spots that sounded like news and to call hundreds of radio stations around the country, offering the spots without charge. The aim was to get the reports included in the regular news broadcasts.

The term for such spots is *actualities*. Usually no more than snatches of speeches, they are used by many political campaigns. But in the Bork campaign they were more than that. They were meticulously produced and aggressively promoted with a wide variety of spokesmen and differing themes.

"Actualities are free, low tech, and highly effective," Griggs commented. "The idea is to get them as close to a radio report as we can get. For a lot of small radio stations around the country, it's great. They have budget cuts and often only have one or two reporters. They don't have that much stuff, but they have lots of time to fill. The trick is not to give them anything that is half-and-half. It's got to be a full-court press for your side. It's a kind of invisible publicity. People don't realize when they hear it that the station didn't send out a reporter and that we're the ones providing it."

Aided by comprehensive guides to radio stations around the country, Griggs sorted out formats and audiences countrywide. He targeted black stations with Jesse Jackson and NAACP Executive Director Benjamin Hooks. In the Southwest he offered interviews with Antonia Hernandez of the Mexican-American Legal Defense and Educational Fund. On the West Coast he provided officials of the Sierra Club warning that Bork would be bad for environmental protection.

One Griggs job was to keep a stable of interview subjects available for stations with last-minute needs. For example, he stayed in touch with a big Pittsburgh station that carried the Pirates' baseball games. When a rainout occurred, the station had three hours to fill. Griggs, with an eye on weather reports, would quickly offer a Bork-related interview. The Griggs campaign was quite successful. Morning and evening news broadcasts on small stations accepted some three-quarters of his offerings. He made two to three per day during the hearings.

"Often the station would take only the sound bite of the interview and take my intro off, but sometimes they would play the whole package I sent them," Griggs said.

The White House had a toll-free actualities number that played snatches of President Reagan's speeches supporting Bork's confirmation and other administration goals. But the two efforts were very different. The anti-Bork forces reached out to tiny stations in Tempe, Arizona, and St. Petersburg, Florida. Those stations rarely called the White House actualities line. And the anti-Bork spots came fully packaged and produced.

Griggs's radio work was complemented by that of a colleague, James ("Skip") Prior, in television. Prior was telecommunications coordinator at AFSCME, directing what the union dubbed the Labor News Network. Run out of the basement of AFSCME's massive Washington headquarters building, the network had a first-class studio that was put to frequent use during the Bork fight.

Prior's products were called not actualities but video news releases, or VNRs. They were occasionally fully packaged interviews but often simply the chance for television stations to interview Bork opponents without having to set up the interviews in advance. The anti-Bork campaign would gather effective spokesmen in the studio and call around to small stations in targeted states, offering free direct satellite hookups. Stations nearly always took them. The local anchor would then ask the guests why they so objected to Judge Bork's nomination. The speakers would oblige with long, well-rehearsed explanations.

Actualities and video news releases were but one aspect of the media campaign. The day after Reagan nominated Bork, People for the American Way, a high-profile, well-financed liberal lobbying group, sent out "editorial memos" to twelve hundred newspaper editorial boards and individual reporters, according to Melanne Verveer, the organization's vice-president. It continued to do so several times a week, expanding the list to seventeen hundred in the course of the campaign. The organization, by far the biggest spender in the anti-Bork camp, spent $1.4 million on its campaign, including $684,000 on advertising in newspapers, television, and radio. But the key to the anti-Bork strategy was not money. All the anti-Bork groups together did not spend more than a few million dollars. And the Justice Department and White House had more potential manpower and resources at their disposal than the opposition. The key to the battle lay elsewhere.

"The idea was to frame a strategic message," said Phil Sparks, Griggs's former boss at AFSCME and one of the liberal community's savviest public relations men. "We put out a three-page memo, listing the key themes and making sure that everyone in the coalition was singing from the same sheet. We also identified the two hundred most important reporters on this issue in Washington and constantly sent them huge amounts of stuff."

Much of the media strategy was framed by a liberal consulting firm known as the Communications Consortium, which advertised its list of nearly two thousand key media people, including such gatekeepers as assignment and news editors. Emily Tynes, who worked for the group, said her guiding notion was: If you could have a headline in the *New York Times*, what would you want it to say? She said the key to good media strategy was to give a sense of ownership on an issue, to set the terms of its debate.

Over the course of the summer the nation's high brow journals—nearly all of them more liberal than conservative—aided the anti-Bork forces. Anthony Lewis, the influential liberal columnist for the *New York Times*, devoted half a dozen columns to decrying Bork's narrow view of constitutional liberty. Magazines such as the *New Yorker*, the *New York Review of Books*, and the *New Republic* printed long, thoughtful, and angry pieces linking Bork to an unprincipled activism of the right and the Reagan social agenda and condemning him in the harshest of terms. Ronald Dworkin, a left-wing constitutional scholar at New York University, had long opposed Bork, both when they were colleagues at Yale, and later in print. He called Bork's positions "radical" and "antilegal." Renata Adler, a liberal Republican who had taken her law degree at Yale and wrote on legal issues in a highly intellectual fashion, labeled Bork's views on the Constitution "hard to read, cynical, poorly reasoned, and ideologically extreme to a degree that is unusual even on the outermost fringes of our public life." Philip Kurland, the conservative constitutional professor at the University of Chicago, attacked Bork in the *Chicago Tribune*. Kurland charged that Bork adjusted his views to political sentiment on the right at any given time to promote himself. The notable exception to this anti-Bork barrage was the *Wall Street Journal*, whose pro-Bork editorials matched in emotional timbre the most fervent anti-Bork material.

Bork's critics were steeped in the constitutional thinking of the past quarter century. To harness their rage made it much easier to label Bork as "outside the mainstream."

Apart from seeking to frame the debate, the Communications Consortium workers played the role of media monitor, seeking out trends and themes in Bork coverage during the hearings.

"Every morning someone would come in at six-thirty and do a summary of press coverage," Tynes said. "Then there would be a meeting to develop the message for that day. My job was damage control, to see how the message was playing in the targeted areas."

Tynes recalled an incident. A leader of the anti-Bork coalition had unforgivably told a reporter that support of Bork by attorney Lloyd Cutler—former counsel to President Jimmy Carter and an establishment Democrat—was a "setback." Such a remark was forbidden. Tynes had to spend a great deal of time getting everyone to tell reporters, as casually as possible, that this was not what was meant, that in fact, things couldn't be better.

Most agreed that the anti-Bork forces worked magic. When the battle was over, Bork and his advocates made much of the full-page newspaper, radio, and television advertisements. Their concerns were partly misdirected. Paid advertising around the country amounted to between one and two million dollars, not a magnificent figure in the circumstances. Of more importance was what public relations people called "free" or "earned" media—in other words, the news media.

"Never before had I felt so much like raw meat," commented Linda Greenhouse of the *New York Times*, speaking about liberal message framing. "Even while you knew it was happening, it seemed impossible to do anything about it. You couldn't avoid it. It was like Mount Rushmore in the middle of the flight path."

Groups like People for the American Way had learned to use paid advertisements to get free media. Indeed, that was one of its main goals. By producing a catchy commercial, the organization itself made news. That is, television news producers were attracted to the ads as phenomena in and of themselves. They would do a story on the ads, using them as proof of the commitment of the group and show the ads for free.

As David Kusnet, vice-president of People for the American Way, said of the use of an ad by news organizations: "It's different from all those generic authority figures in business suits talking into a camera. It's different from all those talking heads. We found with Bork . . . that if you have a media product, it gives you enormous advantage in getting free media."

He added that the very production of television or radio advertisements says to the world that the group is committed in its endeavor and that a serious fight is ahead. "You really don't exist in this country unless you're on TV," he added.

Media analysis is a tricky business. A large cottage industry aims to portray news reporting as unfair or biased. While the Bork battle revealed little evidence of such bias, it did bare the media's limits on two fronts: the reporting of complex issues and a tendency to play to national penchants for pragmatism and populism.

The media see it their job to render esoteric subjects accessible to the general public. By definition, the media are popular reducers. In legal questions, that means almost inevitably that the description focuses on the *impact* of a decision, rather than on how coherently the argument is structured. It is precisely to the latter that Bork claimed to address his writings. Like most of their readers and viewers, reporters tend to think of subtle legal and intellectual arguments as little more than artifices for an end product.

Reporters are attracted to tense and unusual issues. If established figures or organizations—say, Ted Kennedy or the American Civil Liberties Union—produce harshly critical assessments of a presidential nominee, that is news. What was said, the political context of the statement, the likely impact, and the response from the administration are the story. A detailed analysis of a statement's accuracy is of lower priority and often beyond a reporter's ability except in general terms. When Kennedy made his "Bork's America" speech on July 1, everybody reported it. The more sophisticated news organizations made clear that the speech was unusually sharp. They pointed to the partisan nature of the looming battle. But even columnists who later criticized the Kennedy attack as irresponsible did so only in sweeping terms. An explanation of the origins of the charges—each had a basis but sometimes little more—and the resulting distortion would be too painstaking for any media outlet. Hence the charges were fully aired, but not their rebuttal.

This was also true of a highly influential study by the Public Citizen Litigation Group, a Ralph Nader organization. Issued in early August, the Nader study was the first full-scale examination of Bork's judicial record. It claimed that one could predict a Bork judgment by simply examining the litigants. He was, it said, unwaveringly probusiness, progovernment, and anticonsumer. While the study had merit, it contained a few errors and a statistical bias: It used only fifty-six cases out of more than five hundred in which Bork had taken part. The Nader group chose these fifty-six because they were split cases—cases in which one or more judges dissented from the majority. The Nader group argued reasonably that such cases were noteworthy because disagreement implied controversy; these cases had a greater likelihood of reaching the Supreme Court.

But from this 10 percent of Bork's cases unfair general statements were constructed. Those conclusions were reported by news organizations and became a constant theme by anti-Bork forces throughout the campaign. Nothing would prove more helpful than to claim that Bork had biases against certain groups and had set himself to implement an antipopulist agenda for the court. To say that a Bork ruling could be accurately determined in advance suggested a lonely radical on the bench. In fact, Bork was part of a unanimous panel 90 percent of the time and in the majority 95 percent of the time. He ruled the same as the bench's most liberal judges about four times out of five.

The politically conservative Center for Media Studies in Washington examined television network and *Washington Post* coverage of the Bork nomination between July 1 and October 9, 1987. It found that "the topics covered most often reflected the major concerns of Bork's critics. Civil rights dominated with almost twice as much coverage as any other topic." It also found that "of 381 source judgments that clearly indicated praise or blame, 63 percent were negative and 37 percent were positive." Also, "sources discussing his ideology ran 4 to 1 negative at the *Post* and 6 to 1 negative at the networks. . . . Throughout the entire three months, only 16 sources defended Bork's ideology on TV news compared with 89 critical source statements."

The *story,* in other words, was in the criticism of Bork. Reporters reported the story with a nod toward fairness by having an opposing viewpoint at the end.

Another measure of success of the anti-Bork forces in controlling the terms of the struggle was found in the behavior of public opinion pollsters. A typical polling technique posits negative and positive statements about a candidate. On the basis of the statements, those polled are asked to approve or disapprove of the candidate. In the case of the Bork nomination the negative statements about Bork were far more compelling than the positive ones. There is no evidence that pollsters consciously loaded their questions. But the way the debate had been framed publicly led them to do so inadvertently.

Between September 18 and September 28, for example, the Roper

Organization polled twelve southern and border states for the *Atlanta Journal/Constitution*. The results were that 51 percent opposed Bork and 31 percent favored him. Those figures were enormously influential with southern senators.

Roper asked: "Supporters of Bork's nomination say he is an experienced and eminent jurist and would make strict interpretations of what the Constitution says and means. Critics of Judge Bork say he would turn back the clock, limit the rights of women and blacks, and make abortion illegal. Would you like to see the Senate approve Bork's appointment to the Supreme Court or turn down his nomination?"

The criticism of Bork was much more pointed and alarming than the praise was appealing. In fact, what was good about Bork seemed hard to grasp from that statement. Those unsure of how they felt about the nomination might well have responded to the graphic detail of the attack on him and remained unaffected by the support.

Louis Harris and Associates offered even more weighted questions in its survey the following week. Bork's positive qualities were presented first as "If President Reagan says that Judge Bork is totally qualified to be on the Supreme Court, then that's enough for me" and, secondly, "Judge Bork seems to be well informed about the law." The negatives it offered were: "Judge Bork seems to be too much of an extreme conservative, and, if confirmed, he would do the country harm by allowing the Supreme Court to turn back the clock on rights for minorities, women, abortion and other areas of equal justice for all people" and "Judge Bork has said, 'When a state passes a law prohibiting a married couple from using birth control devices in the privacy of their own home, there is nothing in the Constitution that says the Supreme Court should protect such married people's right to privacy.' That kind of statement worries me."

The Harris poll showed a heavy anti-Bork preference in the country, 59 to 27 percent.

In Harris's poll, the Bork quotation was an invention—although the sentiment *was* Bork's. Even so, one could imagine questions that might produce different results. If, in support of Bork, a pollster had said that the nominee wanted to wrest lawmaking from the hands of unelected and effete judges and return it to the chosen representatives of the people, more Bork support might have emerged.

Such evenhandedness was hard to attain in a popular context. Since the anti-Bork forces emphasized the *results* of his views, and pro-Bork forces only his ability to examine legal issues dispassionately, the argument was naturally more compelling on one side than the other.

This pattern was repeated and enhanced during the hearings as well. Democratic senators would lash out at Bork for favoring the wrong things for the country. Bork would reply with a painstaking legal explanation of why he criticized a certain decision. The accusation tended to make the evening news, and the explanation did not. The terms of the debate made it harder for any viewers unschooled in the law to side with Bork. He seemed to offer technical, esoteric explanations for real-world concerns. It made people suspicious.

Ironically, Sparks and Tynes, the anti-Bork media consultants, had learned their lessons from the right wing.

"In the past decade, the right learned how to get popular support for a notion and, through the use of polls and media, spread it," Sparks said. "For every dollar spent on creating an issue, they spent three on promoting it. They really had a better feel for the sense of the nation than we did."

Emily Tynes agreed. She noted that the antiabortion movement had learned from its 1960s opponents and had taken to using songs, rhetoric, and staged events to carry its cause to the people. The right also promoted issues through television and the co-opting of popular images, a standard Madison Avenue technique.

Liberals felt themselves unable to compete, and, Tynes said, the progressive movement was in a malaise during most of the Reagan era. Tynes, a black woman, had nearly given up on political activity. For her the Bork victory was "a shot in the arm, pure adrenaline. We spoke to how people were feeling."

Jackie Blumenthal helped write anti-Bork advertisements put out by People for the American Way. She felt the ads were less important as keys to stopping Bork than as a public announcement of a liberal counteroffensive.

"When Powell resigned, there was a simultaneous electric shock," she said. "We had been sitting on our hands for eight years waiting for the exact issue that would allow us to state what had been going wrong. For eight years the conservatives had been beating our brains out. Our ads broke the notion of our kowtowing to the new ethic in town. They were a sign that that period was over.

We felt it was time for us to say, 'You can't set the tone anymore.' "

These ads came under frequent attack as a distortion of the judicial selection process. But Jackie Blumenthal defended them, saying they were "kindling to make this a truly political, ideological battle, not partisan, but political."

People for the American Way had been started in 1981 by Hollywood producer Norman Lear, creator of "All in the Family" and other innovative television shows. Lear liked to say that his was probably the only organization in America that began as a TV spot. Lear's notion was that the group would enter the fray for control of the national agenda through the use of media and symbols. He understood that Americans like America, that they feel good about their country. This was something the right had understood; Lear wanted the left to realize it. That was one reason for the self-consciously—almost self-parodying—patriotic name for his organization. Lear wanted to counteract the hours of far right evangelical preaching on television and what he saw as the right's ability to control the national dialogue.

People for the American Way was particularly involved in battles over textbook banning and for freedom of information. It ran newspaper advertisements over judicial nominations, such as Daniel Manion's, and rapidly built up a budget of more than ten million dollars and a staff of about a hundred.

Focusing on the Bork nomination was a natural for the group. As Blumenthal put it, "Jerry Falwell needed an enemy to prosper. He and others used liberalism, the Trilateral Commission, communism. So we have done the same with figures like Bork. But the right didn't match us on this one. They showed an unbelievable failure of intelligence over Bork. They didn't know what this was about."

The advertisement that became a lightning rod for right-wing indignation was one Blumenthal helped put together for television, with Gregory Peck as narrator. It was Lear's idea to do a television commercial. Although he rarely got involved in the daily workings of People for the American Way, he had taken a special interest in the Bork nomination and contacted Peck, who had also become concerned over Bork. Jackie Blumenthal's two young sons and her deputy and the deputy's husband were the actors in the spot, put together in twenty-four hours because of Peck's schedule. The television family was shown on the steps of the Supreme Court looking up at its slogan, "Equal Justice Under Law." A gentle breeze ruffled their hair, as Peck introduced himself on the sound track and accused Bork of opposing civil rights, privacy, and much free speech protection.

"Robert Bork could have the last word on your rights as citizens, but the Senate has the last word on him," Peck said. "Please urge your senators to vote against the Bork nomination, because if Robert Bork wins a seat on the Supreme Court, it will be for life—his life and yours."

As David Kusnet, the organization's vice-president, explained it, the ad showed two positive symbols—the Court and the American family—interacting with each other. Juxtaposed on top of them was a looming Bork threatening the people and the institution. The ad won an award from *Millimeter* magazine, a trade journal for the film and broadcasting industry.

Perhaps the greatest irony of the Peck advertisement was that it was received with cynicism by the Washington press corps when People for the American Way presented it at a news conference. Few reporters wrote about it; few news programs aired it. The ad received little attention; it was aired only eighty-five times, tiny by advertising standards, and on mostly obscure stations for two weeks. Few Americans saw it, and few reacted. But on the last day of its airing White House spokesman Marlin Fitzwater attacked it, bringing it the attention it had never received. Once it was an object of controversy, it played for free over and over again on network news programs.

Most striking about the anti-Bork public relations campaign was its move away from classic left-wing tactics into a world dominated by the right—marketing. Demonstrations, while not entirely suppressed, were discouraged. Anti-Bork workers were instructed not to stage sit-ins at senators' offices or thrust banners in people's faces. Such techniques suggested advocacy at the political margin. The idea was to present the anti-Bork message as the very essence of traditional American values, as a front line against radicalism.

Arthur Kropp, president of People for the American Way, made such a point in a speech after Bork was defeated. Appropriately, Kropp's speech was to the Stanford Business School. Students of business would later devote master and doctoral projects to examining the anti-Bork campaign in detail as an example of first-class management. In his speech Kropp explained that demonstrations were often counterproductive. He said:

> What the camera always focuses on is the most outlandish person in the demonstration. It detracts from the issue.
>
> We did this without the traditional liberal saber rattling and protest marches because that was not the impression we wanted. It was an example of how the media and communication now play a dominant role. Once the progressives started using mass media and moving away from the old-fashioned politics of confrontation, the right wing began to lose its grip. What we did was to be innovative in the area of marketing. I believe we won because we had a good cause and because we presented it so that we didn't alienate but rather attracted people.

The marketing of Ronald Reagan offered a similar case study. One thing struck liberals, as they polled American attitudes: On an issue-by-issue basis, many people disagreed with large parts of the Reagan program. Yet those same people were attracted by the overall message that Reagan offered. No matter how badly things went in the Reagan administration, the president's popularity rarely fell below 50 percent.

That meant two things: first, that individual issues could be wrested away from their ideological base and, secondly, that the development of an overall message in any campaign was vital. People would go with you if they were attracted to the feel of your campaign, even if they disagreed with many aspects of it.

Two weeks after the Bork nomination was made, the Advocacy Institute, a liberal group dedicated to teaching the tools of public interest advocacy, published a paper called *The Bork Nomination: Seizing the Symbols of the Debate.*

The paper, written by institute directors Michael Pertschuk and David Cohen, expressed succinctly the media and marketing techniques employed by the liberals. It warned that the positive labels used by the White House for Bork—"brilliant, fair-minded, seasoned, genial"—"will be accepted uncritically by the media, and will thereby frame the issues and characterization of the nomination debate unless challenged consistently—and uniformly—by a plausible and compelling set of alternative labels and countersymbols."

The paper made the point, widely granted at that stage, that the fate of the nomination would be determined by those senators in the center of the political spectrum. Therefore, the winning symbols must be centrist.

"It would be helpful if journalists came to view Bork as a 'right wing loony,' but it is not likely," the paper said. "Like it or not, Bork falls (perhaps barely) at the borderline of respectability."

The paper went on: "Bork must come to be seen as an extreme ideological activist serving as Reagan and Meese's political agent, dispatched to achieve what they could not achieve in Congress, with the result of changing the Constitution, uprooting four decades of settled constitutional precedents."

It suggested labels for Bork, such as "judicial extremist," "judicial reactionary," "enemy of the Bill of Rights," "right-wing ideologue," adding, "[I]deologue is plainly a more negatively charged symbol than ideology because it incorporates fixedness, rigidity."

Finally, the paper turned to how Bork's opponents must cast themselves. "Opponents need to characterize themselves as true conservatives: preservers of the Burger/Nixon Court's legacy . . . and of the Court's delicate balance. The opponents of Bork are conservers of personal rights—the privacy of the bedroom, public health and safety, a fair and honest marketplace, preservers of the environment, restrainers of excessive government intrusion."

The goal was fifty-one senators. To get to those senators, the anti-Bork coalition had to go out to the people. If the campaign were left as an inside-Washington maneuver, Bork, himself an insider, would win.

Ricki Seidman, legal director of People for the American Way and an experienced political campaigner for liberal causes and candidates, said: "We could have all the substance in the world on our sides and go talk to senators. But to get their votes on this one, we needed to have their constituency against Bork. Rousing interest in legislation is hard enough. The Court is so removed. No one knows about it. We had to look for strategies that would serve as attention getters. People are not worried or knowledgeable about the Supreme Court but they are about the question of turning back the clock on civil rights and the Reagan agenda. We had to make clear that the Court and Bork are linked to those things."

Within a month of the nomination the public relations specialists in the coalition all agreed that polls would be central to a comprehensive, thoughtful campaign. The Boston firm of Marttila and Kiley, which had links to the Biden campaign and had done work in the past for AFSCME, was hired to carry out the poll. AFSCME offered forty thousand dollars to pay for it.

The poll, carried out in mid-August, was a watershed. It set out not only to test feelings about the nomination but also "to gauge the potential effect on voters' attitudes of many elements of Bork's record and background that have been subject to criticism in recent weeks." In other words, which issues could be best exploited? The poll reinforced the gut feelings of the anti-Bork leaders that the thrust of their message was appropriate. But it also offered important guidance on several overlooked points.

First of all, only about a third of Americans knew the Court had nine members; therefore, a campaign built on the concept of Court "balance" promised to have little impact. While balance continued as an underlying motivator and was frequently discussed with knowledgeable audiences, its prominence in coalition literature faded.

Secondly, the conservatives' belief that most Americans were unhappy with the Supreme Court, that they saw it as usurping the power of legislatures, was misguided. Only 27 percent thought that the Court was too conservative and 23 percent that it wielded too much influence on the country's affairs.

As Tom Kiley put it in his summation of the poll, "Supporters of Robert Bork, who is already positioned as a very conservative choice, cannot predicate their campaign on the existence of a public mandate for change on the Court. Quite the contrary; when it comes to the Supreme Court, most Americans are inclined to support the status quo."

Thirdly, the poll showed the American people to be more jaundiced about the judicial selection process than many inside Washington had believed. The vast majority of Americans—70 percent—believed that Reagan had chosen Bork for his political philosophy. Those polled seemed to scoff at the notion that Bork had been selected for his competence. The public saw the Court as an instrument of political power, not as the keeper of some abstract set of principles.

Fourthly, by a surprising five-to-one margin, Americans believed the Senate should carefully scrutinize a presidential nominee from all points of view, not merely his competence and personal integrity.

A fifth point noted in the coalition's analysis was that the nomination became increasingly unattractive the more Bork could be painted as someone with biases against groups or causes. It would not be enough to show that Bork was extremely conservative; he would have to harbor some kind of agenda.

In addition, there was populist resentment of officials and others, whether businessmen or academics, who sought to interfere with the freedom of individuals to conduct their lives as they wished. Bork's failure to support a constitutional guarantee of privacy—his opposition to the Supreme Court decision that struck down a law forbidding the use of contraceptives—could be deeply mined for that theme. The poll made clear that abortion should not be stressed in the headlines since it was a divisive issue. But the contraceptive case could be used as a kind of code.

Finally, Kiley warned the coalition against too much substance in its efforts to appeal to the nation: "To engage public opinion, Bork's opponents must keep their message clear, simple and direct. Again and again, we find that forays into constitutional law or judicial theory have the effect of impeding public understanding of the fundamental objections to Bork's nomination."

Nikki Heidepriem, a political message consultant hired by the anti-Bork forces, said that casting Bork as a right-wing ideologue seemed to her a bad idea because that put liberals in the bind of one day fighting off the notion that one of their nominees was a left-wing ideologue.

"Then we had the idea of simply labeling him a rigid ideologue, someone off the charts with a stifling interpretation of a living document," she said. "The key surrogate for that notion was privacy. That allowed some southern Democrats to talk about populism without our having to do it since it had bad connotations for blacks and ethnics. Privacy as an overarching concept gave us a chance to talk about control, as in choice, and integrity of the home as government becomes more intrusive. It was especially effective in the South."

And so, while fearing Bork would turn back the clock, the anti-Bork coalition actually *did* turn back the clock to beat him. It forced the debate into the domain of issues long settled, raising the specter of birth control police, poll taxes, and literacy tests.

Seidman of People for the American Way, put it this way: "From day one, we agreed to avoid the *A* words—abortion and affirmative action. At our first meeting, the day after the nomination, there was a keen sense of avoiding single issues. We decided we would concentrate on civil rights, not affirmative action, on birth control, not abortion." Seidman recalled being with Ralph Neas of the Leadership Conference and running into Louisiana Democrat Bennett Johnston in the Senate hall. Johnston, a conservative, was a leader among southern Democrats and a key vote. Neas told Johnston that the Bork battle would be broad-based, not a referendum on abortion and affirmative action. "I'm really glad to hear that, Ralph," was Johnston's encouraging reply.

For seven years liberals had been bemused and angered by Reagan's ability to set an agenda through mood and symbol. The 1984 Los Angeles Olympics, with their frenzied flag waving, were the classic example. The Soviet bloc had boycotted the games. Yet Americans chanted the slogan "We're number one." Through repetition and the meticulous staging of the Olympics, the nation seemed to believe that its victories in the games symbolized its place in the world. The chant wasn't a lie—the United States did well in the Olympics—but it was half true because there was little competition. Half-truths are the most effective tools of the advertiser.

It was partly through such advertising that liberal packagers constructed an image of Robert Bork. They had learned from their enemies. They took Bork's own words and decisions and pared away subtleties, complications, and shadings. What remained was neither lie nor truth. It was half-truth. Like the half-truths of the Reagan years, it played well.

One notorious half-truth stood out as effective. It involved a unanimous 1984 decision Bork had written on behalf of a three-judge panel relating to the sterilization of women workers at a chemical company known as American Cyanamid. The company had determined in 1978 that it could not reduce the amount of lead in the lead pigment department of a West Virginia plant to a level safe for fetuses. Since the Occupational Safety and Health Act (OSH Act) required employers to protect employees from harm to their fetuses, the company banned women of childbearing age from the department.

The company told women that if they wanted to undergo surgical sterilization, they could work there. Five women underwent sterilization to avoid losing their jobs.

The nine justices of the Supreme Court in November 1986 in a light moment as they prepare for their official portrait. Prior to retiring, Justice Lewis F. Powell, Jr., requested this photograph as a memento. Standing from left: Sandra Day O'Connor, Lewis Powell, John Paul Stevens, Antonin Scalia. Seated from left: Thurgood Marshall, William Brennan, Chief Justice William Rehnquist, Byron White, and Harry Blackmun. *(credit:* Lucien Perkins, *Washington Post)*

Associate Justice Lewis Powell announcing his retirement from the Supreme Court, June 26, 1987, a few months before his eightieth birthday. *(credit:* UPI/Bettmann Newsphotos)

Attorney General Edwin Meese.
(*credit:* UPI/Bettmann Newsphotos)

William Bradford Reynolds, assistant
attorney general for civil rights.
(UPI/Bettmann Newsphotos)

Ralph G. Neas, executive director of
the Leadership Conference on Civil
Rights. (Leadership Conference
photo)

Robert H. Bork, marine private first
class in 1945. (Family photo)

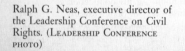

Solicitor General Robert Bork with his first wife, Claire, in 1974. Claire Bork died of cancer six years later. (FAMILY PHOTO)

Bork and his second wife, Mary Ellen, in 1987. (credit: UPI/BETTMANN NEWSPHOTOS)

President Reagan congratulating Bork just before announcing his nomination to the Supreme Court. Watching, from left, are White House Chief of Staff Howard Baker, White House Communications Chief Thomas Griscom, Attorney General Edwin Meese, and Deputy White House Chief of Staff Kenneth Duberstein. (credit: PETE SOUZA, WHITE HOUSE)

President Reagan announcing his nomination of Robert Bork to the Supreme Court on July 1, 1987. (Pete Souza, White House)

Senator Edward M. Kennedy (D-Mass.) questioning Bork at the judge's confirmation hearings. (U.S. Senate photo)

Senator Paul Simon (D-Ill.), member of the Judiciary Committee. (U.S. SENATE PHOTO)

Laurence H. Tribe, professor, Harvard Law School, a key Bork opponent. (HARVARD UNIVERSITY NEWS OFFICE)

Senator Joseph Biden (D-Del.), chairman of the Senate Judiciary Committee, questioning the nominee. (U.S. SENATE PHOTO)

John Bolton (center), Justice Department liaison to Congress, joins Judge Bork (left) for a chat with Senator Biden during a break in the hearings. (U.S. SENATE PHOTO)

The Bork confirmation hearings open in the Senate Caucus Room, September 15, 1987. (U.S. SENATE PHOTO)

Reporters listen on the first day of the Bork hearings. (U.S. SENATE PHOTO)

Judge Bork being presented to the Senate Judiciary Committee. At the witness table, from left: Representative Hamilton Fish (R-N.Y.), former President Gerald Ford, Judge Bork, Senate Minority Leader Robert Dole (R-Kan.), and Senator John Danforth (R-Mo.). Behind the witnesses is Bork's family. From right are the Bork children—Robert, Jr., Charles, and Ellen—followed by Mrs. Potter Stewart, widow of the justice and friend of the Bork family, and Mary Ellen Bork. (U.S. SENATE PHOTO)

Committee Democrats, from left, Howard Metzenbaum (Ohio) and Dennis DeConcini (Ariz.). (U.S. SENATE PHOTO)

From left, Senators Orrin Hatch (R-Utah) and Strom Thurmond (R-S.C.) listen to Judge Bork testify. (U.S. SENATE PHOTO)

Judge Bork making a point during his hearings. (UPI/BETTMANN NEWSPHOTO)

Judge Bork testifying. (U.S. SENATE PHOTO)

Senator Patrick Leahy (D-Vt.) listens
to testimony. (U.S. SENATE PHOTO)

Senator Gordon Humphrey (R-N.H.)
at the hearings. (U.S. SENATE PHOTO)

Senator Arlen Specter (R-Pa.) questions Judge Bork. (UPI/Bᴇᴛᴛᴍᴀɴɴ Nᴇᴡꜱᴘʜᴏᴛᴏꜱ)

From left, Republicans Charles Grassley (Iowa) and Alan Simpson (Wyo.) listen to Bork testify. (U.S. Sᴇɴᴀᴛᴇ ᴘʜᴏᴛᴏ)

Former Transportation Secretary William Coleman and former Representative Barbara Jordan (D-Texas) greet each other before testifying against Judge Bork's confirmation. (UPI/BETTMANN NEWSPHOTOS)

Atlanta Mayor Andrew Young testifying against Judge Bork. (UPI/BETT-MANN NEWSPHOTOS)

Senator Howell Heflin (D-Ala.), Judiciary Committee member, at the hearings. (UPI/ Bettmann Newsphotos)

Senators Joseph Biden and Edward Kennedy confer during the hearings. (U.S. Senate photo)

October 1, 1987, the day that a majority of senators announce their opposition to Bork, the nominee meets with President Reagan, Deputy Chief of Staff Kenneth Duberstein, Chief of Staff Howard Baker, and Attorney General Edwin Meese in the Oval Office. (PETE SOUZA, WHITE HOUSE)

The Senate Judiciary Committee votes 9–5 against confirming Judge Bork on October 6, 1987. From left: Gordon Humphrey (R-N.H.), Arlen Specter (R-Pa.), Charles Grassley (R-Iowa), Alan Simpson (R-Wyo.), Orrin Hatch (R-Utah), Strom Thurmond (R-S.C.), Joseph Biden (D-Del.), Edward Kennedy (D-Mass.), Robert Byrd (D-W. Va.), Howard Metzenbaum (D-Ohio), Dennis DeConcini (D-Ariz.), Patrick Leahy (D-Vt.), Howell Heflin (D-Ala.), and Paul Simon (D-Ill.). (UPI/BETTMANN NEWSPHOTOS)

The day after the committee vote, Mary Ellen Bork addresses Republican senators on what she felt was the mistreatment of her husband's nomination, as Judge Bork listens. Standing and sitting in background, from left: Minority Leader Robert Dole (Kan.), Judiciary Committee minority chief investigator Robert ("Duke") Short, White House liaison to Congress William L. Ball III, and lobbyist Thomas Korologos, who helped handle the nomination for the White House. Seated, clockwise from left: Senator Rudolph Boschwitz (Minn.), Senator William Armstrong (Colo.), Senator James McClure (Idaho), Senator Larry Pressler (S.D.), Senator Thad Cochran (Miss.), Senator Strom Thurmond (S.C.), Mrs. Bork, and Judge Bork. (U.S. SENATE PHOTO)

President Reagan and Judge Bork confer on October 9, 1987, as Bork prepares to announce he will not withdraw his name. (PETE SOUZA, WHITE HOUSE)

Just before Judge Bork announces his intention to stay in for a full Senate vote on his nomination, President Reagan looks at Bork's prepared statement. Listening to Bork from left: Chief of Staff Howard Baker, Vice President George Bush, President Reagan, Attorney General Edwin Meese, and Deputy Chief of Staff Kenneth Duberstein. (PETE SOUZA, WHITE HOUSE)

Judge Bork tells a White House press conference that he will not withdraw from nomination and that the full Senate should vote on his confirmation. (PETE SOUZA, WHITE HOUSE)

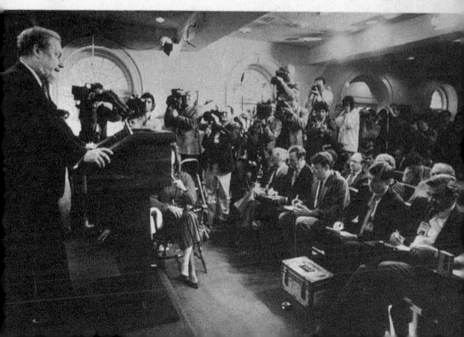

Judge Douglas Ginsburg telling a press conference on November 11, 1987, that he is asking President Reagan to withdraw his nomination to the Supreme Court. (UPI/Bettmann Newsphotos)

Justice Anthony Kennedy being sworn in at his confirmation hearing, December 14, 1987. (UPI/Bettmann Newsphotos)

When the federal agency charged with worker safety—the Occupational Safety and Health Administration, known as OSHA—inspected the plant, it fined American Cyanamid ten thousand dollars for the policy. It said that offering sterilization to its workers constituted a "recognized hazard" which was in violation of the OSH Act.

The body that reviews OSHA decisions disagreed. It ruled that the term *hazard* in the act was not meant by Congress to extend to an offer of sterilization. *Hazards* meant processes or materials that caused injury or disease to employees as they worked or engaged in work-related activities. Since the offer of sterilization—as heinous as it may be—did not fit into that category, the law was being inappropriately used; the fine need not be paid. OSHA did not appeal the decision.

But the women's union, Oil, Chemical and Atomic Workers, did appeal. In 1983, five years after the five women had been sterilized, the case came to the federal Court of Appeals for the District of Columbia. The union had sued the company under another law, arguing that requiring only women to be sterilized constituted sex discrimination under Title VII. There it was more successful. The company ultimately paid compensation to the women, settling the suit out of court.

When Bork and two fellow judges faced the case, their sole job was to decide if American Cyanamid should pay the ten-thousand-dollar OSHA fine. Had the policy of suggesting sterilization constituted a "hazard" under the OSH Act? It was not the panel's task to rule whether the policy broke any other federal or state law or was offensive to common decency.

An administrative law judge had already held that it was economically infeasible for the company to reduce the level of lead in that section. Bork's panel concluded that the industry could not be made safe for childbearing women, although that conclusion was contested by the union.

Bork's panel had before it the ruling of both the administrative law judge and the OSHA Review Commission saying that the option of sterilization was not a violation of the OSH Act. The administrative law judge had told OSHA that he thought it was fining the company under the wrong law. He said, "I have seen nothing in the law, in the legislative history or of any case decided under section 5A1, that could be convoluted to include sterilization under the situation that we face here as a recognized hazard. No way."

Bork's ruling spoke of the "distressing choice" facing the women and of the "moral issues of no small complexity." But, it said, the role of the court was simply to decide whether the term *hazard* in the OSH Act included pointing to an option to be sterilized. It concluded that the administrative law judge and OSHA Review Commission were correct, that the law could not be stretched to include that. The decision noted that the union might do better arguing that such a policy was an unfair labor practice under the National Labor Relations Act. The company did not have to pay the fine.

More liberal judges might have expressed greater indignation over the policy; a few would likely have ruled differently. Bork's acceptance that it was economically infeasible for the company to reduce lead levels revealed a penchant toward business not shared by every member of the judiciary. But the ruling was hardly extraordinary. Even Laurence Tribe, so firmly against Bork, was bothered by the attention given the *American Cyanamid* case.

"To treat the choice that was put to those women as a workplace hazard was stretching that law to purposes it was never meant to serve," he observed afterward. "I think Bork's decision in that case was defensible and attempts to use it to show him to be a prosterilization ogre were terrible. It was part of attempts to stir up fears about him as a person, which I tried not to do and regret that others did."

Of all the cases described to those queried in the Marttila and Kiley poll, *American Cyanamid* produced the most dramatic response. Seventy-seven percent of those polled said they were "much less inclined" to approve of Bork after hearing of that case.

Tom Kiley, in summarizing and analyzing the polling data, said the case was one that demonstrated the role of populism in the anti-Bork effort: "The excesses of big business, in particular, have served to shift the popular resentment toward government Reagan exploited in the early 80s and redirect it toward the wealthy and powerful interests that the President now symbolizes. *The campaign must focus on Bork's consistent record of support for the privileged and the powerful.*"

Kiley worried about using the *American Cyanamid* case for that purpose, however. He said it might not be a credible example because the decision was unanimous and "there may be some points of fact that would make it easily refutable." But Kiley did give a nod in the direction of public relations reality: "On the other hand, this particular case produced a more outraged response than any of the other 18 items we tested."

The anti-Bork message makers understood what they had to do. They went with outrage. In newspaper advertisements by People for the American Way, the National Abortion Rights Action League, and Planned Parenthood, the public was told that Bork upheld a company policy giving women workers a choice between sterilization and their jobs.

For millions of Americans, that decision symbolized what was wrong with Robert Bork. It stuck in their minds long after the Bork nomination had been defeated. It showed that Bork opposed women's rights, favored big business, and—get this!—approved of sterilization. It all came together in this one case. No matter if the case was misrepresented in the telling. One of the two other judges on the panel said later: "They made Bob look like some kind of Nazi scientist in that case. It was inexcusable."

The truth was flouted in many other instances as well. In an advertisement that ran in major newspapers just before the hearings, the National Abortion Rights Action League stated: "You wouldn't vote for a politician who threatened to wipe out every advance women have made in the 20th century. Yet your senators are poised to cast a vote that could do just that."

In its newspaper ad, Planned Parenthood trumpeted: "If your senators vote to confirm the administration's latest Supreme Court nominee, you'll need more than a prescription to get birth control. It might take a constitutional amendment." The ad also stated that Bork had "upheld a local zoning board's power to prevent a grand-mother from living with her grandchildren because she didn't be-long to the 'nuclear family.'" Bork had had nothing to do with that 1977 case, known as *Moore* v. *City of East Cleveland*, nor had he ever commented on it.

At the local levels already boiled-down position papers from the Washington anti-Bork coalition were further reduced, leading to absurdities. In West Virginia, for example, an ad hoc newspaper known as the *Bork Blocker* said in September: "Simply stated, Bork would return America to the 'separate but equal' era of the late 1800s." In fact, Bork had always defended the Supreme Court's 1954 school desegregation ruling, which reversed the separate but equal doctrine.

Another West Virginia leaflet said that among Bork's views was the belief that "Women could be subjected to sexual harassment on the job, and fired if they refused to submit to unwanted sexual advances by their supervisors." This referred to Bork's ruling that sexual harassment could not be made punishable under a sex discrimination law—a narrow view, to be sure, but a far cry from the way it was presented.

In Alabama anti-Bork activists exploited a line in a July story in *Time* which called Bork an agnostic. The label might have suited Bork at an earlier period in his life, but his religious beliefs were much less clear by the time of his nomination. In any case, religion should have had no relevance to his qualifications for the bench, especially in the liberal world view. That did not stop those who saw a good issue. Hank Sanders, a spokesman for the Alabama New South Coalition, said of Bork in newspaper interviews: "He began as a socialist . . . and now is on another extreme not even accepting God's existence." The coalition's board chairman, J. L. Chestnut, Jr., issued statements saying, "It is hardly conservative to reject the existence of God pending further proof from God that he exists. That is downright radical." And in a resolution sent to Senator Howell Heflin, the coalition declared: "That Blacks are to be counted three-fifths human and women have no constitutional standing are part of the legacy of 'original intent.'"

The coalition leaders in Washington tried to keep discussion on a higher level but often accepted bogus issues at the local level if they produced results. An internal coalition memorandum in mid-September reported without comment: "They [in Alabama] are taking the approach that Bork's agnosticism is a problem; they have mailed to a list of Baptist ministers and are recruiting their support primarily on the basis of Bork's agnosticism. . . ." A week later an internal report stated: "Debra Huntley of the Alabama Democratic Conference is concentrating on the agnosticism issue which seems to be getting big play there."

To make sure that senators understood the political importance of opposing Bork, the anti-Bork forces attacked on a wide variety of fronts. That involved a search of Federal Election Commission records to identify senators' major contributors; leaflets and small demonstrations; face-to-face meetings with lawmakers; letter writing and phone calls; and tracking the movements of the senators in their states so that an anti-Bork representative was present at all public meetings.

The Leadership Conference on Civil Rights, where the campaign was centered, hired a grass-roots coordinator named Mimi Mager. For a campaign that would normally take two to three months to organize, she had two to three weeks. She worked hard. Her section financially supported coalitions in forty-two states and provided organizers to twenty-five coalitions in seventeen states.

Mager set up a desk operation of six in Washington, most of them members or consultants to other coalition groups. Each stayed in touch with coordinators in the states.

The organizers persuaded numerous city councils, including those of Chicago, San Francisco, Jersey City, and Pittsburgh—Bork's hometown—to pass resolutions against the nomination. Groups also developed varying rallying cries, such as "We're one justice away from injustice" and "Robert Bork is a walking constitutional amendment."

Michael MacDougall, an independent organizer based in Austin, Texas, was hired by the coalition to coordinate efforts in Texas, Oklahoma, and Mississippi. He also helped in the state of Washington and in Arizona. A veteran of numerous liberal grass-roots organizing efforts, MacDougall was struck by the unprecedented enthusiasm and energy.

"People were lining up to volunteer," he said. "I had no idea how easy it would be. Bork pushed buttons on people I'd never seen before. The degree they were willing to work and cooperate was amazing. It was especially amazing how people put their egos aside in this battle. I always have to deal with egos but not in this one. At first I saw the task as monumental, but once I got going, it was easy. Bork really brought out the selflessness in people."

MacDougall guided the effort in his states, made sure the message was consistent, put together ways of contacting members of various organizations, nudged hard-liners away from confrontational tactics. In Texas, for instance, just before MacDougall had a chance to settle in, the Texas Abortion Rights Action League had picketed a meeting attended by Democratic Senator Lloyd Bentsen. Bentsen made clear to a newspaper reporter that he resented such tactics. MacDougall had a talk with the league members as well as with the president of their national organization, Kate Michelman in Washington. They were told to back off and did so with alacrity.

"What was surprising to me was that there was no resentment in my going over their heads to Washington," MacDougall recalled. "Normally people get pissed off. But with the Bork effort, it was like they were excited kids. It was real high profile, a cosmopolitan, sophisticated revenge on Reagan."

MacDougall and other grass-roots organizers made sure that letters kept reaching key senators. They insisted that the letters be written individually and, if possible, on personal stationery, even perfumed, so as to avoid the appearance of a mass organized mailing. Senators paid much less attention to what one strategist called Astroturf mail. An example of the latter was when the office of Senator Heflin, a key undecided committee member, began receiving a flood of letters urging him to "Vote for Bark."

From the beginning it was believed at the top that Bork was partly a pretext to get a liberal grass-roots operation together that could be used in future political battles. Bork seemed to embody so much of what liberals disliked in the Reagan agenda that he was an excellent target of their wrath and frustration. As one early memorandum of the grass-roots task force, dated July 13, stated, "We are in for the long haul! We must keep in mind that the struggle continues beyond defeating Bork."

In Louisiana, a politically complex state with a Catholic south and fundamentalist north, MacDougall chose Mark Morial, son of New Orleans's first black mayor, to head the anti-Bork coalition. Morial was a sharp, handsome, ambitious young man in his twenties. MacDougall persuaded Morial that heading the group would be good for his future.

The local affiliates of the Washington organization took ad hoc names such as Louisiana Committee for a Fair Judiciary or Minnesota Coalition of 139,000 to Oppose Bork or the Rhode Island Coalition for a Balanced Court. They sent reports to Washington every two weeks.

A typical report, from Pennsylvania in mid-August, reads in part:

Working coalitions have developed in Philadelphia, Pittsburgh, Harrisburg, Erie, State College, Bucks County, Allentown, Scranton, and others being formed in York, Lancaster, Reading and the Phila. suburbs of Chester, Montgomery and Delaware.

Each coalition meets regularly, organizations are contacting their members, doing major postcard and petition drives and phone banking. The Pittsburgh City Council passed a resolution and similar measures are being attempted around the state.

Funds are being raised for a radio blitz across the state.

The report also offered whatever intelligence the coalition had on the state's two senators, John Heinz and Arlen Specter, both Republicans. Specter was the only Judiciary Committee Republican who might be persuaded to vote against Bork. He was undecided, but he had gone against administration nominees before, including Brad Reynolds and Daniel Manion.

The mid-August update said that Heinz had been quite accessible and impressed when Bork was brought up by citizens in some of the state's smaller towns. Specter, however, was more complicated. He was on vacation and would not see anyone till he returned. The report then stated: "The key to Specter are attorneys, contributors and the Jewish community in Philadelphia. We have identified several dozen influential folks and are in the process of having them contacted. . . . Joan Specter has been contacted and will continue to be but those in the know indicate that she will probably not be influential with her husband on this one."

The effort to get to senators through their friends, family, associates, former law partners, major fund raisers, and vote gatherers was relentless and meticulous. Senators seen as electorally vulnerable were threatened. Those who had received major funding from labor or civil rights groups had their debts called in. Around the country the message went out: This one matters.

At the annual meeting of the National Association for the Advancement of Colored People, Coretta Scott King, widow of the Reverend Martin Luther King, Jr., said to loud applause: "We must let our senators know that a vote against Mr. Bork is a prerequisite for our vote in the next election."

Hazel Dukes, NAACP board member and New York Democratic committeewoman, introduced New York Democratic Senator Daniel Patrick Moynihan to the NAACP convention as a veteran supporter, saying he would almost certainly oppose Bork. When Moynihan, who was up for reelection the following year, declined to commit himself, Dukes told the *Washington Post:* "I have the votes in New York to defeat him. When I get with his staff in New York, I'll get what I want. It's strictly politics."

Something similar happened to Florida's Lawton Chiles. He held a meeting on Bork with representatives of the NAACP, the National Organization for Women, and the Women's Political Caucus in his Washington office about three weeks before the vote. A centrist, Chiles said that he was undecided and offered some arguments in Bork's favor. Chiles pointed out that over the previous two decades of public life his own record on race and gender issues had been impeccable.

But Carlton Moore, NAACP president in Fort Lauderdale and later a city commissioner, told Chiles that if he voted in favor of Bork, he would be throwing twenty years of an impeccable record down the drain as far as the NAACP was concerned. If he were to do that, it would likely support his opponent in a primary. Chiles became flustered and said he would not be treated that way. But he did vote against Bork. When he made his decision, the Florida anti-Bork coalition was the first to know.

"Perhaps I stated the case a bit strongly, and I can understand why the senator was upset, but I wanted to represent the true feelings of the community," Moore said later.

Frank Jackalone of the Florida Consumer Union was grass-roots chief for the state. He contacted Bill Gunter, state insurance commissioner and a key liberal Democrat, and asked for his help in persuading Florida's other moderate Democrat, Senator Bob Graham. Gunter agreed and made a point of sitting next to Graham at the big football game between Florida State and the University of Florida held in Tallahassee in early October. He casually bent Graham's ear on Bork. Graham proved very receptive, and Gunter reported back to the coalition on Graham's thinking. Graham voted against Bork.

In Pennsylvania Arlen Specter was approached at Jewish New Year services by fellow members of his congregation who had been asked to do so by the coalition in that state.

In Washington State Daniel Evans spent a vacation at the isolated mountain retreat of a friend who surreptitiously reported back by telephone to the anti-Bork organization on his state of mind. But not all efforts to get the Evans vote were so subtle. He faced great public pressure within the state of Washington. The work backfired. Angered at the degree of pressure exerted on him by the anti-Bork forces, he ended up voting for Bork.

In Arizona Dennis DeConcini, a Judiciary Committee member and a moderate Democrat who was undecided on Bork, was given hints that if he voted for Bork, the Hispanic wing of the Democratic party there would put up a candidate against him in the primary. DeConcini's brother and wife were also approached.

It is difficult to assess the effectiveness of such lobbying. DeConcini voted against Bork but, like nearly all of Bork's opponents, had a long list of substantive reasons. When asked if he was concerned that another candidate would run against him in a primary, DeConcini said, "It is always in the back of your mind." But he declared that the threat was not what made him decide. Pressure, he said, was heavy on both sides.

One aim of the anti-Bork coalition was to impart a sense of unstoppable momentum. The coalition made sure that reports critical of Bork were evenly spaced, coming out when little else was happening so as to create news events. Leaders also sought constantly to expand the coalition membership, adding groups every week. Ultimately some three hundred organizations joined the anti-Bork movement. They included such groups as the Association of Flight Attendants, B'nai B'rith Women, the Disability Rights Education and Defense Fund, the Jewish War Veterans of the USA, the Organization of Chinese Americans, the National Council of Senior Citizens, the Sierra Legal Defense and Education Fund, and the YWCA. Most had never considered taking a stand on a Supreme Court nomination before. But this one was cast in such dire terms, it so concentrated the struggle between those hoping to shape the country that it was nearly impossible to remain neutral on it. As columnist George Will derisively put it, "The ease with which such groups have been swept together for the first time in such a campaign reflects, in part, the common political culture of the people who run the headquarters of the compassion industry."

Opposition became especially noteworthy among women's groups. Bork had opposed the Equal Rights Amendment, the Court's 1973 abortion decision, and the application of the Fourteenth Amendment to women as a group. Hence even moderate women's organizations felt their fate and power on the line.

The National Federation of Business and Professional Women's Clubs, Inc., whose membership is nearly half Republican and active especially in the South and Midwest, made a huge commitment to the anti-Bork effort. Monica McFadden, the group's Washington lobbyist, said this was a first for the 125,000-member organization. The Bork nomination provided the group an opportunity it had sought for several years: a public policy issue that stirred the membership.

"Here were all the issues we cared about embodied in one fight," she said. "Senators know we're not nut cases. We're very moderate as a group. The average age of our members is late forties, early fifties." She added that what excited many of the members was the way the Bork battle attracted younger women to the organization, offering it a chance to reinvigorate its role and purpose in the country.

Patrick Caddell, the Democratic pollster and Biden adviser, remembered addressing a lunch of staff members of the Republican National Convention in early September. He had been asked to offer a Democrat's perspective to a discussion with Ed Rollins, former Reagan campaign chairman and political adviser. Caddell, who enjoyed nothing more than being provocative, started attacking the Bork nomination as poison for the Republicans. He said there was no better way to drive moderates and young women into the arms of the Democrats than to threaten them on issues such as privacy and equal protection for women.

"I thought I was throwing red meat at them, but the response was amazing," Caddell remembered. "Many women there agreed. One woman said to me that the nomination could be a Pandora's box for the party."

Two organizations hesitated for many weeks about whether to take a public stand on the nomination: the American Civil Liberties Union and Common Cause. Both, while liberal in orientation, prided themselves on being process- rather than result-oriented and on fighting issues in a principled, nonpartisan fashion. The fact that the Bork battle was seen as the domain of liberal Democrats made their decisions harder because it opened them to charges of politicization. That became a major issue a year later, when Republican presidential candidate George Bush used the ACLU membership of his opponent, Massachusetts Governor Michael Dukakis, as a blunt instrument with which to club him.

For the ACLU, Bork's consistent majoritarianism, his derision of the kinds of individual rights the organization championed made it almost impossible to stay out. The problem was a fifty-year-old rule forbidding the group from taking a stand on high court nominees. At an emergency meeting at the end of August the ACLU joined the opposition. It was not unexpected, but it was newsworthy and significant. Common Cause, which had made the same decision some weeks earlier, said that because Bork rejected the traditional role of the Supreme Court, that of defender of the rights of minorities, it had no choice but to oppose his confirmation.

The work against Bork went forward long before the hearings began and well away from the Senate chamber where he would officially be questioned. It took the White House by surprise. The administration expected a difficult confirmation battle. It thought, however, that the fight would occur *inside* the hearing room, as it had with Rehnquist. All the while, it was priming its candidate on his role in Watergate and on technical legal issues. The country beyond Washington was virtually ignored until too late. While liberals had discovered an issue to embody their anger and frustration of seven years and were mobilizing their troops, the administration was in a state of confusion.

CHAPTER

8

Let's Not Ballyhoo It

Two hours after President Reagan nominated Bork, John Bolton, assistant attorney general in charge of relations with Congress, ordered a department car and drove down Pennsylvania Avenue to see the judge in his chambers. He brought with him several of the many forms Bork would have to fill out over the coming weeks, including an FBI background check and a Senate questionnaire. He wanted to get the process moving to remove any excuse for delay on the part of the Judiciary Committee.

Bolton's visit was in most ways routine for such an official. But it was one of his many efforts to exert a guiding hand in a process that continually eluded his control. The White House, which planned and executed the confirmation process, held Bolton and other Justice Department officials at arm's length.

Bolton was thirty-eight years old, an intense man, with wire-rim glasses and a thick reddish mustache. He was also a former student of Bork's and a fierce admirer. It was Bolton who had advised Meese to nominate Bork the same evening that Powell resigned. Bolton fretted throughout that the administration was packaging Bork as a moderate and soft-pedaling social issues that should have been pounded.

Of all the jobs Bolton fully deserved in a Reagan administration, congressional liaison made the least sense. Bolton was not known for his diplomatic skills on the Hill. Liberal lobbyists would chortle that guys like him only made their work easier since he alienated rather than persuaded those lawmakers not clearly associated with the right.

But Bolton was highly intelligent. He was a Phi Beta Kappa and summa cum laude graduate of Yale University and editor of the *Yale Law Journal,* and his profile was what the Reagan Revolution was all about: a mix of urban ethnic heritage and right-wing ideology. The son of a Baltimore fire fighter, Bolton was the first in his family to go to college. Steeped in blue-collar culture and values, he was a tough libertarian conservative with a sharp mind and an even sharper tongue. Having practiced privately with the prestigious Washington firm of Covington and Burling, Bolton joined the administration in its first days, working in the White House and the Agency for International Development. After a couple of more years back in private practice, he joined the Justice Department under Meese in December 1985.

When Bolton arrived at Bork's chambers that July 1 afternoon, the judge was chatting with three judicial colleagues, Stephen Williams, Douglas Ginsburg, and James Buckley, all conservative Reagan appointees. The jurists were in shirt sleeves; a secretary had brought in champagne.

Bolton offered his greetings and congratulations and quickly got down to business.

"Look, Bob," he said, "the White House has made it clear this is to be a White House show. Frankly we don't care about that. But just promise me this: Whatever advice they give you, you'll then come listen to me because we at Justice have your best interests at heart. Justice has no interests other than yours."

Bolton explained that the White House had a full agenda apart from the Court and could easily screw up a complicated and ferocious confirmation fight. To Bolton, as to many at Justice, the new fellows at 1600 Pennsylvania Avenue did not understand the significance of capturing the third branch of government. They lacked the balls to bring hard issues to the American people. They sought compromise and deals, but they failed to understand that with judicial nominations there are no deals. Senators cannot trade a bridge for a confirmation vote. It's straight up or down, and this one would take real work. The White House people understood the challenge so poorly that they blithely referred to the confirmation battle as "final passage."

Judge Buckley had had a somewhat arduous confirmation battle himself. He agreed with Bolton. There might well come a time when the needs of the White House and the demands of the confirmation process would diverge. When that happens, he said, follow Justice. Douglas Ginsburg was listening, hardly dreaming of what lay in store for him. Ginsburg noted that Ted Kennedy was already on the attack. Bolton, he suggested, had a point.

Bork listened somberly. Resignation, rather than jubilation, had been his mood most of the day. For one thing, he detested paper work and Bolton had just brought him a truckload. For another, he was confused about whom to listen to. He felt pulled in various directions. It seemed to him that a highly professional lobbying machine was gearing up at the White House. He had been told that. Yet Bolton now warned him that the White House might screw it up.

But a deeper issue troubled him in the hours and days following his selection. As much as he loved his second wife, Mary Ellen, he was struck by how tragic it was that Claire was not alive to witness his nomination to the Supreme Court. Here was a moment to which she had aspired. They had talked about it. When Claire lived and fought her illness with such resolve, the nomination, like so much else, seemed achievable. Her influence and management had, in part, brought him to this moment.

Sitting there with his political and judicial allies, Bork tried to relax. But he couldn't. As the champagne was uncorked and the telephone rang for the tenth time in twenty minutes with congratulations from conservative politicians and colleagues, Bolton took his leave. As he was backing out of the office, Bork looked up at him. Without apparent irony, the nominee said: "If this is such a great day, why do I feel so depressed?"

Inside the White House, consensus had it that if Bolton and his ilk ran the campaign, it would be doomed. Baker and Culvahouse were already worried about proclamations such as the one by right-wing fund raiser Richard Viguerie on the day of the nomination: "Conservatives have waited for over 30 years for this day. This is the most exciting news for conservatives since President Reagan's reelection."

Some days later *Human Events*, a rightist weekly journal, hailed the nomination, saying that "the president could advance his entire social agenda—from tougher criminal penalties to curbing abortion-on-demand to sustaining religious values in the schools, etc.—far beyond his term." It was exactly the kind of emphasis on results that Bork's handlers hoped to avoid.

For the White House, the calculation was clear: The struggle was over conservative southern Democrats and moderate northern Republicans. These were not people interested in a battle over abortion, school prayer, and affirmative action. Moderate Republicans drew their strength from voters pleased with Reagan's fiscal policies but less enthusiastic about his social conservatism. Many were suburban professionals with a keen appreciation for individual liberties. Too much attention to abortion or prayer in the schools could endanger that support. And southern Democrats depended on a delicate coalition of blacks and moderate whites to win elections. They were safest avoiding the divisive issues of affirmative action and other race-related concerns.

Both groups of senators had to be told of Bork's credentials, of his deference toward legislators, of his mainstream and distinguished career as a federal judge, one never reversed by the Supreme Court. In other words, Bork's strong association with the right had to be played down and his stature within the legal profession played up. If fought over issues and results, the Bork battle would be a losing proposition.

As Will Ball put it most tellingly afterward, "The idea was to set forth Bork's record, not to engage in a political battle."

Another concern underlay leaving the nomination in Bolton's hands: The Justice Department had faced numerous problems with the Senate in recent years. Attorney General Meese had taken a year to get confirmed; Brad Reynolds had been turned down as associate attorney general; several judicial nominations championed by Justice had run into serious opposition. While nearly all got through, resentment was building. It would be impossible to keep this nomination entirely away from Justice. But the message had to go out that this was a White House operation and one based on the traditional criteria of fine credentials. Ideology was to be avoided.

On Saturday, July 4, 1987, President Reagan made his first pitch for Bork as a highly qualified moderate. In his weekly radio message he spoke not of the need to overturn *Roe* v. *Wade* or to be tougher with criminals or to allow a greater measure of religion in public life.

He said: "Judge Bork is recognized by his colleagues and peers as a brilliant legal scholar and a fair-minded jurist who believes his role is to interpret the law, not make it." The president urged senators to "keep politics out of the confirmation process."

"There was a determined effort to make Bork the president's nominee, not Ed Meese's or Brad Reynolds's," recalled presidential Counsel Culvahouse. "We tried to pick up votes where the votes were—in the middle."

Howard Baker made a similar point. "Our strategy was to manage the Bork campaign here out of the White House because we felt it would be freer of the trappings of conflict here than out of the Justice Department," he said. The former Senate majority leader added that the White House was also better equipped and staffed to manage a difficult legislative battle than the Justice Department.

Another advocate for keeping the Justice Department at a safe distance was Lloyd Cutler, a prominent Democratic lawyer, former counsel to President Jimmy Carter, and a friend of Bork's. Cutler was given great leeway in working on the Bork confirmation. It was felt he had important credibility with the political center. Apart from his association with establishment Democrats, Cutler was one of the founders of the Lawyers' Committee for Civil Rights Under Law, set up by President Kennedy. Since civil rights groups were opposing Bork, it was a most useful credential.

On July 16 Cutler wrote a long op-ed piece for the *New York Times* announcing his strong support for Bork. The piece described the nominee as a principled moderate in the tradition of Felix Frankfurter. It dismissed as nonsense the notion that Bork was an extremist or a man with an agenda. Well written and detailed, the op-ed piece fell like a bombshell.

One week after the nomination Howard Baker held a meeting in the office of Minority Leader Bob Dole. Present were the Senate Republican leadership, the Republican members of the Judiciary Committee, and staff from both the White House and the Justice Department. Baker gave a rousing talk about the importance of the nomination and made it clear that the operation would be run out of the White House. Pointing offhandedly to Bolton, he indicated that the men at Justice would, of course, be helping out.

But Baker had more to worry about than shepherding a Supreme Court nominee around. He was trying to restore order to the White House and move along the president's programs, stymied by congressional hearings on the Iran-contra scandal during those very same weeks. A groundbreaking arms treaty with the Soviets seemed likely by the end of the summer. American ships were guiding oil tankers through the Persian Gulf war zone.

So Baker called in Thomas Korologos, an affable private lobbyist who had been congressional liaison in the Nixon administration. Korologos had handled more executive nominations than anyone else in Washington, including those of Henry Kissinger and, more recently, William Rehnquist. Olive-skinned, a bit chunky, with handsome white hair and rimless glasses and the expensive suits and sports obsession of a Washington power broker, Korologos worked on such nominations for the Reagan administration free of charge. It kept his profile high and paid large dividends in his private lobbying efforts.

"It's basically a coaching operation," Korologos said. "You explain to the nominees what confirmations are all about, take them through courtesy calls with senators. It's an arcane art. For Bork, we sat there and did it mechanically. We weren't neophytes. I'd done hundreds of these." As Korologos acknowledged later, that very experience with traditional battles blinded him to the unique nature of this one.

Korologos said his job was to package Bork. That did not mean to fabricate things, but simply to emphasize the helpful and play down the harmful. He worried, as did Baker and Culvahouse, about the cheering from the right.

"You had these conservatives jumping up and down about turning back the clock on the Warren Court, and that worried us," he said. "I said, 'Jeez, fellas, he's one of yours, but let's not ballyhoo it. The moderates are the ones we have to convince. We're not running for sheriff here. We're after fifty-one senators' votes. You can do all your ballyhooing at the swearing-in ceremony.'"

George Will, conservative columnist and close friend of Bork's, made the same point in print. He quoted Groucho Marx in *Animal Crackers* saying to the musically minded Chico, "How much do you charge not to play?" and said, "That is the question Bork's wisest supporters should ask some of his other supporters."

The Saturday after the nomination, the day of Reagan's first radio pitch for the nomination, Korologos visited Bork at his home. Both men sat tieless on the living room couch. Emma, Bork's golden retriever-like mutt, nosed around Korologos. High on Korologos's list was a discussion of what he affectionately called murder boards, mock hearings at which he and others threw difficult and embarrassing questions at the nominee in preparation for the real thing.

Bork resisted. Rehnquist and Scalia had advised him against them. They had said the questions were too general and the sessions unproductive and a waste of time. Moreover, it was not the sort of activity Bork relished by nature. He was not much of a politician in the traditional sense. The man was no verbal glad-hander. He would rather sit around with other lawyers and discuss the points of law that would come up.

Korologos also thought Bork should avoid interviews with the press. Senators, he told the judge, did not like to hear from a nominee in the newspaper before they had a chance to question him. Bork disagreed on that point as well. He had already given a background interview to David Beckwith of *Time* and planned to do at least another with him. He had also agreed to an interview with the *New York Times.* He said he would stay off the television but saw no reason not to talk to the print reporters, as he had been doing for years.

Bork had a warm relationship with the Washington media. He was close to conservative columnists George Will and William Safire. He and his family had grown friendly with *Time*'s Beckwith, who had covered Bork since his days as solicitor general. Bork had occasionally had Linda Greenhouse of the *New York Times* over to the house. He knew Al Kamen of the *Washington Post,* having given him a series of interviews in 1984. Kamen and Fred Barbash of the *Post* had asked to tape interviews because Bork's name was so frequently mentioned as a high court nominee. They said they would not use them unless Bork was nominated.

Bork, who had considered becoming a journalist himself, liked many Washington journalists. As solicitor general he occasionally lunched with them. Bork loved to talk. Journalists loved to listen.

Korologos gave in. He scheduled only one murder board and agreed that perhaps press interviews were not such a terrible thing. Korologos relented partly because Bob Bork was a most persuasive and stubborn individual. Like many people, Korologos was somewhat intimidated by Bork.

"It was a mistake not to make him do more murder boards," Korologos said. "I should have rolled him on that. But he was a genius, the Einstein of the law. It's a little hard to bang your fist on the table and say, 'This is how it's going to be.' So we did a few unusual things."

On the interviews, Korologos figured that with all the nasty things being said about Bork's nomination, perhaps a little humanizing would be a good thing. Okay, he said to himself, let the guy talk about his favorite color and sports team, about his family, about why he has a beard. Might do some good.

The beard was an issue of some contention within the Bork camp. A number of senators and their staffs let the White House know they thought the whiskers should go before the confirmation hearings. Bork's record was unsettling enough. He needed all the help he could get in looking all-American. But Korologos ruled out that idea immediately, figuring that good packaging meant invisible packaging. Shaving off a twenty-year-old beard just before public hearings would draw more negative publicity than the beard itself.

The decision to keep the beard did not prevent Bork from resolving to try to drop about fifty pounds and get off cigarettes. But as the summer progressed, he was unsuccessful. He got caught up in the minutiae of winning confirmation, counting the senators on both sides.

An administration official who went calling on senators with Bork remembers a break between such visits in early September. He, the judge, and another official went to the public cafeteria in the basement of the Dirksen Senate Office Building for a cup of coffee and a cigarette. Bork started recounting a meeting with Howard Baker at the White House that morning in which the leanings of various senators were discussed. The official was horrified to learn that Bork was being included in such discussions. The other official said that Baker, facing criticism from the right over his handling of the nomination, was feeling under pressure. Cigarette in hand, Bork turned to the official and said: "He thinks *he's* under pressure?"

Ted Kennedy could not have predicted it, but it was partly his first statement that caused such confusion within the administration. Brad Reynolds believed the White House overreached in its efforts to portray Bork as a centrist because the accusations against him were so extreme.

"His centrism was woefully overstated," Reynolds lamented. "Kennedy's statement had set the tone for the opposition and had the effect of intimidating those on the administration's side. They sought to counter that by overstatement on their own side as to how wrong that was. It was a question of tone. The White House felt strongly that we ought to tone down Bob's views. People here [at Justice] felt the strength was to state it harshly and boldly the way he does."

The White House campaign made Bork out to be a natural judicial successor to Lewis Powell, a comparison of dubious accuracy. Bork spoke constantly of the need for an overarching theory for the Court; Powell rejected such a notion, saying he had always believed that law should develop case by case. But Powell had become the centrist model, and the administration was determined to make Bork fit. As the president said on July 29 to law enforcement officials during one of his few summer speeches on the Bork nomination, "It's hard for a fair-minded person to escape the conclusion that, if you want someone with Justice Powell's detachment and statesmanship, you can't do better than Judge Bork."

The White House strategy was reasonable in many ways. How else to win confirmation except by persuading moderates of both parties? It had, however, a serious flaw, one not well pondered in advance: It opened up the administration and Bork to a charge of deception. This was precisely the kind of accusation that would offer waffling senators a hook on which to hang their rejection. It would allow them to say that Bork's integrity and predictability concerned them more than his ideology. It also offered liberals an important tactical advantage. Their contention that Bork was "out of the mainstream" seemed buttressed by official efforts to push him to the center. If Bork needed to be repainted as a moderate, what did that say about the judge's real colors?

The differences in approach between Justice and the White House led to an endless series of turf battles and minor tussles: Who would accompany Bork to see which senators; who would handle which forms; who would go on television talk shows; who would brief witnesses for the hearings? Justice, whose main task was research, sent to the White House position papers, speeches, op-ed articles, all with the hope of having the president or Baker sign or deliver them. But the White House continually demanded modifications or simply ignored them.

Terry Eastland, the chief spokesman for the Justice Department, said he wrote at least three Bork speeches for Reagan that were never delivered. Michael Carvin, of the Office of Legal Counsel, wrote an op-ed piece for the president that got sent back continually for changes and ultimately was not distributed at all.

Just over thirty, a graduate of Tulane and George Washington University Law School, Carvin was one of the Justice Department's bright young stars. He was a Brad Reynolds protégé, having worked as Reynolds's assistant on civil rights for five years. Carvin was big and blond with a penchant for eating cartons of junk food at his desk as he worked late into the evening, his shirt untucked, tie knot yanked six inches below his neck. He had a mordant wit. A New Yorker, Carvin remembered passionate political discussions around his family's dinner table. He was as devoted to a right-wing judicial agenda as could be imagined and would get enraged over hypocrisy or cowardice.

Asked once about the Supreme Court's role in protecting groups such as blacks and Hispanics, seen as "discrete and insular minorities," in the phrase of a 1938 Court decision, Carvin shot back: "You want to talk about 'discrete and insular minorities'? You know which ones I would protect? First, fetuses. Second, nineteen-year-old Italian-Americans in New Jersey who can't get jobs on their own fire departments because of affirmative action. Third, assistant park commissioners being hounded out of office by powerful local newspapers. To me, those are discrete and insular minorities."

For Carvin, a mixture of hypocrisy and cowardice characterized fights over the administration briefing book on Bork.

The book, called the White House Report on Bork, was completed in early August. It was written at Justice largely by Carvin and Stephen Markman in the Office of Legal Policy. Carvin and Markman wanted to include a section in the book with quotations from Kennedy, Metzenbaum, and Biden saying ideology should not be a factor in judicial nominations. But the White House said no, it did not want to alienate those senators.

When one White House official said he saw no reason to throw down the gauntlet to Kennedy and Biden, Carvin responded, "If we're going to get through the next three months without offending Biden and Kennedy, we're not going to get very far."

Spokesman Eastland, a key advocate of the New Right, said later: "In my view, when Kennedy made his statement that first day,

Reagan should have gone to the press room of the White House and put Kennedy back in his cage by saying, 'Who is the swimmer from Chappaquiddick to be making such statements?' "

The White House also edited out sections on affirmative action and abortion. Carvin and Bolton and others began to refer to the book as the "Bork as a Liberal Book." At one point the White House decided to respond to the liberals' charge that Bork would tip the balance of the Court to the right. It wrote that Bork's circuit court opinions were thoroughly in the mainstream, adding, "Judge Bork's appointment would not change the balance of the Court."

Disgusted, Bolton threw up his hands and said, "If he wouldn't change the balance of the Court, why the hell are we nominating him?"

On one issue would the White House advertise Bork's toughness: crime. It sent to Justice articles with anecdotes about judges who were hampering police work through legal technicalities. But Bork had ruled in almost no criminal cases and had written next to nothing about criminal law. Moreover, many Democrats were also eager to portray themselves as tough on crime.

Asked for speeches and articles emphasizing crime, Justice selected one that the White House vetoed. Tom Griscom, the White House communications director, said the speech contained an anecdote about a dead baby in a garbage can as part of an illustration about legal problems in search and seizure.

"I nixed that," Griscom recalled. "I said this is gruesome, and I can't see the president of the United States saying it. Americans don't react well to shock. It makes their skin crawl, makes them want to go out and puke. I said we can tell the people what Bob Bork supports without blowing their heads off."

Other efforts were under way. Raymond Randolph, the Washington attorney who had worked with Bork in the solicitor general's office and had become a friend, acted as the nominee's counsel throughout the process. He and Lloyd Cutler organized private initiatives, lining up prominent members of the bar around the country who supported Bork. One lawyer who attended the meetings suggested a search of Federal Election Commission records to identify key financiers of certain senators. But most others present said that would be inappropriate for a judicial confirmation and decided against it. Of course, the opposition was busy mining that vein.

Randolph said that throughout July there was a sense of security and calm in the White House regarding the nomination. "The sky was clear and they couldn't hear the thunder," he said ruefully. In fairness, he observed, there was little obvious cause for concern. Editorials from around the country were generally favorable to Bork and critical of Biden's about-face and Kennedy's early and harsh opposition. The impression gained ground that it was the Democrats who were playing politics with the sanctity of the high court. It was the Democrats who were accused of playing a game dangerous to the Republic in anticipation of the following year's elections.

As Gary Jarmin, a political consultant to conservative Christian groups, told *Congressional Quarterly* in mid-July: "If the Democrats beat up on Bork and make him look like a pariah on school prayer, abortion, civil rights, feminism and . . . all the other weirdo causes they embrace, it will come home to roost for them in 1988." Even many Democrats believed he was right.

Moreover, support for Bork was coming from prestigious members of the bar. Justice John Paul Stevens, a centrist who voted often with the liberal wing of the bench, said of Bork in a speech to the Eighth Judicial Conference in Colorado in mid-July: "I personally regard him as a very well-qualified candidate and one who will be a very welcome addition to the Court. There are many, many reasons that lead me to that conclusion."

In early August former Chief Justice Warren Burger told the annual meeting of the American Bar Association in San Francisco: "I don't think in more than fifty years since I was in law school there has ever been a nomination of a man or woman any better qualified than Judge Bork."

And a poll commissioned by the *National Law Journal* showed that 50 percent of 348 state and 57 federal judges asked said they would vote to confirm Bork if given the chance. Only 24 percent said they would not, with the rest undecided.

In the view of right-wing activists, however, the White House erred terribly by banking on the views of judges to sway the country. Terry Eastland put it this way: "To me, Reagan was like a big landowner with lots of No Trespassing signs and the left was like a bunch of ragged teenagers who start going on the land. The landowner ignores them, so they start to pillage. Still nothing happens. Then they strip the garage, and the owner says, 'It's no big deal.'

Ultimately the trespassers take over; they grab the owner, bring him down to the basement, and chop off his head. It was the failure to act in the first instance that cost the Reagan administration the game."

White House officials protested after the confirmation had failed that they had been unfairly accused of not working hard enough. Shortly before the final Senate vote Tom Gibson, then director of public affairs at the White House, drew up an extensive listing of pro-Bork activities by various sections of the White House. It was meant to be proof that they had worked hard. And they had. But a glance at the list makes clear that the bulk of the work began in mid-September, around the time of the hearings themselves. By then the anti-Bork offensive was well on its way to victory.

For example, the first lobbying telephone call to a senator by President Reagan on the Bork nomination was listed on September 30, after most senators had made up their minds. He did not call most southern Democrats. His first meeting with Republican Senate leaders took place on the day the hearings began, September 15.

Howard Baker called all the southern Democrats on July 21 and 22 but did no more personal lobbying until mid-September. In August he did sit for eight interviews and make a dozen speeches on the subject, mostly to Republican groups. Beginning in mid-September, when he was under fire, Baker gave a lot of interviews and speeches. He also personally lobbied sixty senators in September and October.

Various lower echelons in the White House produced op-ed pieces, letters to the editors, drafts of speeches, and so on for different administration officials to sign. Again, most of that work was done in late September and October.

While the White House tried to keep conservative groups from getting too publicly involved during the summer, many were doing so on their own anyway and resented the admonition.

Patrick McGuigan of the Free Congress Foundation in Washington recalled that a White House staff member called him once and asked him to prevail upon Daniel Popeo, legal director of the Washington Legal Foundation, from speaking out for Bork's conservative views. Popeo had made a number of just the kinds of supportive comments about Bork that worried the White House, saying Bork would overturn half a century of bad law.

McGuigan said he replied: "No way. I'm not going to call a guy who's like a brother to me and say those things."

The staffer replied that the worst thing that could happen would be for conservatives to use the nomination to promote their agenda. McGuigan shot back that no, the worst thing that could happen would be to lose the Bork war.

McGuigan meant that. Animated by a combination of religious fervor—he was a devout Catholic—and conservative political goals, he toiled like a beast for Bork. For McGuigan, the contest over Bork was a personal struggle. When the battle was over, McGuigan wrote a book offering his views on what happened. In the preface he thanked his wife for her understanding, writing: "My wife Pamela has for these many years endured hours, days and weeks of separation to support my work but never so intense a time of tension and sadness in our life as the final weeks of Bork's struggle, when it gradually became clear to me he would not prevail."

Conservatives were especially effective at generating mail to senators and ultimately beat the anti-Bork forces in number of letters sent. Religious fundamentalists, hopeful that Bork would contribute to overturning the abortion decision, were the most active, although some such groups stayed away, concerned that Bork was areligious. The Public Affairs Committee of the Southern Baptist Convention urged that its 14.6 million members "prayerfully consider writing letters to their United States Senators to support the Bork nomination." The author of the resolution, Les Csorba of the First Baptist Church in Alexandria, Virginia, said: "Judge Bork's opinions that the Constitution does not protect pornography, that homosexual activity is not a constitutional right, that some public recognition of the role of religion in our history should appear in textbooks, and his respect for the Establishment Clause, are consistent with the sentiments of the Southern Baptist Convention."

Dr. Robert Grant, chairman of the Christian Voice, wrote to his followers: "Robert Bork does not support the idea of a constitutional right to engage in sodomy. He may help us stop the gay rights issue and thus help stem the spread of AIDS. Don't wait—act now! We must return the law of our land to godly foundations while we have a chance."

Concerned Women for America, which championed traditional family values, worked hard for Bork. The group launched a huge direct mail campaign and ran newspaper advertisements in Pennsylvania and Alabama, homes of Senators Arlen Specter and Howell Heflin, undecided members of the Judiciary Committee.

McGuigan's group also ran radio advertisements in Washington,

D.C., to counter a similar campaign by People for the American Way.

In Chicago a group called Free the Court! generated grass-roots activity for Bork. The name suggested the need to liberate the Court from "liberal special interests," according to Steven Baer, its director as well as director of the United Republican Fund of Illinois. The group had no contact with the White House other than an encouraging nod of approval from officials there when Baer called to announce its formation. He set up Senators Biden and Simon as targets since both were committee members running for president and were against Bork. Baer's group sent a couple of dozen demonstrators to many of their campaign appearances in Iowa and Illinois.

"We wanted to spook the southern senators with coverage of our anti-Biden work," Baer said later. "Our work was small-scale. We only spent twenty-five thousand dollars. But we did manage to have Biden met by pro-Bork crowds. He was visibly irritated."

Baer's group sent a plane with a banner over the Iowa State Fair during a debate, saying BIDEN AND SIMON, BORK BASHERS, LIBERAL LAPDOGS. At the Illinois fair it handed out large tickets to a Biden and Simon Puppet Show, "starring Joe 'Absolutely Open Mind' Biden and Paul '50 Ways to Leave Your Principles' Simon, produced by bootlicking, sycophantic political ambition, directed by the liberal special interests that control the Democratic presidential primary process and the activist agenda of the Supreme Court."

The work drew some local press coverage.

But more significant were the right's failings in grass-roots efforts. A sign of that failure was the poor organization of a group begun in Southern California by Bill Roberts, onetime campaign director for Reagan. Called We the People, the group vowed to raise two million dollars but never brought in more than two hundred thousand.

Just before the hearings began, McGuigan called one of his friends at the White House to complain that Korologos had disparaged outside groups for not doing enough to help the confirmation. McGuigan protested that he had been killing himself over this thing and that it was the White House that had done too little. The official said Korologos was complaining about the corporate establishment, which promised help and did not deliver.

McGuigan said it was most important for the White House to begin raising money for the pro-Bork campaign. "This nomination won't get by unless some bucks get plowed into television advertising pronto," he said. Then, referring to the anti-Bork ad recorded by Gregory Peck, McGuigan added, "For God's sake, the other side has Abe Lincoln in their TV spots. You need to get the president on the horn to some of his rich buddies, and the word needs to go out that this needs to happen."

"We can't do that," the official replied. "It's just not appropriate for the president to raise money for a lobbying operation." This was partly a reference to the Iran-contra scandal when money for the contras was raised privately by those connected to the administration.

"I don't care how you do it," McGuigan replied. "I don't care if it's done with winks and nudges." The official said he would see what he could do. Nothing materialized.

Another serious setback was the failure of pro-Bork forces to persuade the National Rifle Association to help them. Perhaps the most effective conservative lobby in Washington, and one of the wealthiest, the NRA stayed out of the Bork fight despite two decisions Bork had handed down as a judge in its favor. The main reason the group sat out the fight was its concern over what it saw as Bork's cramped view of the Fourth Amendment prohibition against search and seizure. NRA leaders feared Bork would seek to close loopholes in the law regarding state troopers who stop and search vehicles, confiscating unregistered firearms. Anything that might detract from the free possession of guns was perceived as a threat by the NRA. When one of the most powerful conservative groups in the country, one which had frequently poured its funds into fights over judicial nominations, felt threatened by Bork's strict interpretation of the Constitution, it was an omen.

In early August the White House held its only official murder board for Bork. Gathered on the fourth floor of the Old Executive Office Building were nearly two dozen officials from the White House and Justice and several attorneys from the private sector, including Cutler and Randolph.

Kennedy's July 1 statement hung over the proceedings. Will Ball asked Bork: "What is Bork's America *really* like?" Bork looked intensely uncomfortable but said: "Is this where I give my Fourth of July speech? Okay, fine. Next question."

Some asked him open-ended questions such as: "What is your

view of the religion clause in the First Amendment?" Others asked him about the Boston school busing case during his years as solicitor general. At that time—1974—Bork had considered entering the case on the side of the disgruntled white parents. Because he didn't want to encourage their violence and because Attorney General Edward Levi was opposed, he had dropped the idea. Thirteen years later the details were fuzzy; Bork he said he couldn't remember.

Only Carvin and Bolton tried to bait him on difficult issues such as privacy. But the setting was inappropriate. With all those people there, little progress was made. Bork and the men from Justice considered the three-hour session a waste of time. Not everyone did, however. At one point Howard Baker came in for a few minutes. After he left, he ran into a group of reporters and told them that the prep session was going on and that Bork was so brilliant that he was going to win the battle single-handedly. To gain confirmation, Baker said, the administration need look no further than its own nominee.

Baker, of course, was bluffing a bit. But he did believe Bork would be so good that it would be hard to stop him. He and others were still under the spell of another marine who had humiliated a Senate committee, Lieutenant Colonel Oliver North of the National Security Council. North, with his boyish good looks, cracking voice, and earnest eyebrows, had charmed much of the nation while under Senate interrogation for his role in the Iran-contra scandal. Baker had little doubt that Bork would be the Ollie North of the law.

As Dan Casey, head of the American Conservative Union, put it, thinking back to his early feelings, "It was inconceivable to us that he wouldn't be confirmed. We were euphoric and cocky. We had just seen what Ollie North had done, and we figured Bork is a lot smarter. He'll run circles around those guys."

He and Baker did not know how well that sentiment played into the hands of Bork's opponents. Their only real worry was Bork himself, so if they could publicly build up concern over his testimonial skills, anything short of a brilliant performance would help them.

North's fame was hurting the pro-Bork effort in other ways. Phyllis Schlafly, of the ultraconservative Eagle Forum, told a newspaper in late July that she did not feel the right needed a massive public outpouring in support of Bork, that it was the liberals' burden to mobilize the country against the nomination. "I really think that most Americans know it is self-evident that Bork will be the next

Supreme Court justice," she said. "I haven't done anything yet. I've been too busy watching Ollie North."

And liberals used the details of the North story, especially the fact that he shredded key documents prior to the investigation, to add resonance to their case. Ralph Neas of the Leadership Conference, for example, said Bork had a twenty-five-year paper trail that could not be shredded. The National Organization for Women distributed buttons at its annual convention reading "Shred Bork."

As August ended, and the nation returned to work, the administration's public confidence over Bork took on a hollow quality. The papers were filled with ominous details of anti-Bork petitions, speeches, and telegrams. Television talk shows displayed anti-Bork spokesmen with iron resolve and quiet confidence asserting that theirs was a just and winning cause. It was increasingly clear that the opposition had gained the upper hand over the summer. Just as the men at Justice were beginning to comprehend that turning the tide was a monumental task, their cause suffered an unexpected and terrible blow.

The week before the hearings began, the rating of the Select Committee on the Federal Judiciary of the American Bar Association, normally a secret until the testimony, was leaked to the media. The fifteen-member committee was split. While ten voted Bork "well qualified," the highest rating, four voted him "not qualified" and one "not opposed." It was the first time in sixteen years that the ABA committee had been split on a Supreme Court nominee and the first time in the thirty-five-year history of the ratings that the initial ABA rating of a nominee included a vote of "not qualified." This lack of unanimity cut to the heart of the administration's promotion of Bork: his qualifications.

The discrepancy between that vote and the unanimous vote of "well qualified" five years earlier, when Bork had been nominated for the circuit court, was explained as the difference between qualifications for a lower court and for the Supreme Court. Those who voted Bork not qualified said they were concerned about his "judicial temperament," which they defined as "his compassion, open mindedness, his sensitivity to the rights of women and minority persons or groups and comparatively extreme views respecting constitutional principles or their application, particularly within the ambit of the Fourteenth Amendment."

The committee spent more than two months interviewing four hundred people and reading all of Bork's opinions and writings. But to the administration and other Bork backers, the expansive definition of "judicial temperament" was, like "judicial philosophy," yet another mask for politics. The four were liberals opposed to Bork's views, it was argued.

In fact, the four *were* liberals who almost certainly did not like Bork's views. But they said politics had nothing to do with their votes. One of the four, Jerome Shestack of Philadelphia, aligned with a group of lawyers working for Biden's campaign, said: "Politics has never come up in any of the committee's considerations and political considerations do not play the slightest role in anyone's deliberations."

Shestack meant that the opposition was not partisan. It was manifestly political in that it sprang from a vision for the nation that was at odds with Bork's. The nominee's sponsors understood there was a clash of visions at stake. It was because of that clash that Bork had been nominated. But they clung to the hope that Bork would not be judged on that level.

The weekend before the ABA leak was Labor Day weekend. Bork and half a dozen White House and Justice Department staffers gathered at Bork's house for two days of rehearsals. The informal setting contrasted with the one previous murder board.

An entire day was spent on Watergate because that seemed the only issue of integrity on which a rejection could be hung. All felt satisfied that Watergate held no smoking gun. The next day around the Bork dining room table was spent on issues. Another meeting was called for the following Saturday, September 12, just three days before the hearings were to begin.

What participants remembered most from September 12 was a little speech by Lloyd Cutler, the Democratic lawyer who had been a strong Bork backer. The speech later became a kind of mantra for the young lawyers who had been there, and they would often imitate Cutler's sonorous, stentorian manner when they repeated it.

"Bob, you have managed to arouse the united opposition of all labor groups, all women's groups, and all civil rights groups," Cutler said. "It's an extraordinary historical alliance, and it is going to be very tough to win this. You must separate yourself from the Meese-Reynolds school of jurisprudence." Cutler urged Bork to say in the hearings that *some* antiabortion laws were probably unconstitutional and to express a moderate position on other issues. For Cutler, such talk was not disingenuous. He believed that Bork was different from

Reynolds and Meese, that he was a more moderate thinker.

The others at the Bork dining room table were flabbergasted. Brad Reynolds, a hero to many of them, was sitting right there. In addition, the hearings were days away, and Cutler was pronouncing in ominous tones about a historic alliance against the nominee. Finally, Bork's record was so clear that he could not possibly get away with the kind of change in position that Cutler was advocating.

A number of those present spoke up, seeking to blunt Cutler's effect. Carvin said Bork had written extensively on the abortion decision and on affirmative action and simply did not believe some of the things Cutler was urging on him. Ray Randolph interjected that Cutler was right about the historic alliance and that only one other person had been in such a fix—Ronald Reagan—and he had done very well, thank you. People laughed, and that provided a transition out. But Cutler's pessimism continued to hang over the proceedings.

The previous Tuesday there had been a senior staff meeting at the Justice Department with Meese and Reynolds. Terry Eastland, who was not attending the preparatory sessions at Bork's house but who was picking up distressing signals all over, said that the department ought to begin drawing up a list of new Supreme Court nominees. It was the first time that view had been expressed aloud at the department. The others looked at Eastland aghast, as if he had uttered an obscene sacrilege. Most said he was crazy. The hearings hadn't even started. But a few also began to fear that his advice was sound.

The day before the hearings, Monday, the Bork team gathered in Will Ball's West Wing office for a final discussion. To qualm nagging doubts, there was a great deal of bravado about how well the nominee would do. Everyone claimed to be pleased to have prestigious people like former President Gerald Ford and former Chief Justice Warren Burger signed up as witnesses. They would certainly show who was out of the mainstream, for God's sake.

After the meeting broke up, Ball, Culvahouse, and Bolton found themselves at one end of the room together out of earshot from the others. Culvahouse turned to Bolton and asked: "So, John, how are you feeling about the hearings?"

"Not good," Bolton averred.

"I don't either," said Ball.

"Me neither," said Culvahouse.

CHAPTER

9

The Main Event

Early on the morning of Tuesday, September 15, 1987, more than one hundred restless people waited to enter the Russell Senate Office Building. The hearings were scheduled to begin at ten.

Newspapers that day ran long Bork stories and numerous anti-Bork advertisements. The previous evening at the Bright Hope Baptist Church in Philadelphia, anti-Bork groups led by Representative William Grey held a "Funeral for Justice" with printed obituaries, pallbearers, and a choir.

Inside the Senate the eight Democratic and six Republican members of the Judiciary Committee seemed evenly divided on the nomination: five in favor, five against, and four undecided. A cadre of extra staff labored to haul and sort through dozens of sacks of daily mail and answer the telephones. Illinois Senator Paul Simon alone had received 120,000 pieces of mail on Bork by the end of the proceedings. The telephones of Senator Leahy, Democrat of Vermont, got so jammed that he brought his car telephone up from the Senate garage to free a line in the office.

The Senate's Republican leader, Bob Dole of Kansas, a Bork supporter, said of the hearing that day: "Wherever you go, and some of us go a lot of places, this is generally question number one or number two in any town meeting in America."

Senator Arlen Specter, Republican of Pennsylvania, anticipated the onslaught. He had seen a fistfight nearly break out over Bork at a town meeting in Norristown, Pennsylvania, earlier in the summer. The battle was especially brutal for Specter because he was the only committee Republican undecided on the nomination. The two extra telephone lines installed in Specter's Washington office were taking two thousand calls a day; another thousand a day flooded his Pennsylvania offices. His receptionists took to answering the phone: "Senator Arlen Specter's office. Are you calling about the Bork nomination? Are you for or against?" Callers were about evenly divided.

Senator Kennedy and his staff had been working on the hearings nonstop over the preceding few days. Aides Jeffrey Blattner and Carolyn Osolinik accompanied the senator wherever he went so they could go over the Bork material between his scheduled appointments. They met with him in New York, where Kennedy was dedicating an old-age home in the Bronx. They went with him back to his Cape Cod home and from there, the next day, to a shipyard in Quincy, Massachusetts. While the senator spoke in Quincy, Blattner and Osolinik took the subway to his Boston office, where they were met by staffers Carey Parker and Tony Podesta. Laurence Tribe and his wife came to the office, and when Kennedy arrived, Tribe went over a number of questions with him, suggesting Bork's likely responses. Blattner and Osolinik flew back to Washington and worked until just after 3:30 A.M. They were at the senator's McLean, Virginia, house at 8:00 the next morning. It was a work schedule they followed throughout the hearings. Blattner, living on Snickers bars and Cokes, gained twenty pounds.

On the third floor of Russell the great Senate Caucus Room was ready. The chamber was renowned. It had held the Watergate hearings fourteen years earlier and the Iran-contra hearings just two months before. It looked regal with its ornate neoclassical amphitheater, its black-veined marble floor, and its thirty-five-foot-high gilded ceiling. Rows of tables awaited 150 journalists, and behind them, seats for other observers ran from one set of Corinthian-columned walls to the other. Journalists reserved places in advance—organizations were limited to one reporter per seat—and arrived to find their affiliations marked on signs taped to their spots, just as they were at the Iran-contra hearings. During the first week, when Bork gave testimony for an unprecedented five days, no seat was empty until late in the day. Lobbyists, friends and relatives of senators, and a few dozen members of the general public took up the places behind. Airport metal detectors and a dozen police and security personnel guarded the hearing room doors, even though one could not enter the building without passing through an identical set of barriers.

Two main television cameras were set up, one in a corner of the front of the hall and one at the very back. Twenty-three spotlights were trained on the ample leather witness chair. The tables for the senators and witnesses were covered in billiard-green felt cloth. Behind the senators were mahogany benches for staff members, who were armed with documents and suggestions. For the length of a football field outside the room, thick television cables ran along the floor leading to video monitors. A score of technical personnel for the networks huddled around humming banks of equipment, speaking nervously into portable telephones or headsets.

The stage was set.

This was more than a metaphor. For Thomas Donilon, senior campaign adviser to Biden, the hearing room was a vast stage set from which his candidate would propel himself into the homes and hearts of millions of voters. Biden's presidential campaign had been forced to cut back on his promotional appearances because of the Bork nomination, so Biden had to use the hearings for their maximum potential. Biden had prepared for the Bork hearings as for few events in his life. The administration's refrain over the preceding weeks that the brilliant, scholarly nominee would wipe the floor with the dim-witted chairman was too much for Biden to bear. He would not let it happen. He had closeted himself with anti-Bork experts day after day, on antitrust, on privacy, and on the First Amendment. He and his campaign staff wanted to leave none of the staging to chance. When Larry Tribe playacted Bork at Biden's Wilmington home, campaign officials videotaped the senator in the exchanges. The tapes were played back and studied. Biden asked his family and Carolyn Tribe to watch the tapes. Was his message getting across to nonlawyers?

Only two months before, Oliver North had won an emotional and rhetorical battle against U.S. senators in this room. The somber gray-haired men in dark suits asked lawyerly questions about North's involvement in illegal international maneuverings, and the handsome uniformed marine launched into heartfelt speeches about

Communists and freedom. Many Americans—often contemptuous of authority and sympathetic to underdogs—were smitten by North. Senators learned their lessons. Over the week of Bork testimony they reversed roles with their new witness. Bork continually laid out dry legal arguments, and his liberal opponents waxed poetic about God-given rights and simple justice and the American heritage.

During Iran-contra, senators had looked down upon the witness from a raised platform. This typical arrangement had given the impression of harsh bureaucrats sitting in judgment on a young patriot. Donilon instructed that the platform be removed from the room and the senators placed on the same level as Bork. And he pushed the chairs and tables of the senators and witness as close to one another as possible—man to man.

He also thought back to all those flattering photographs of North taken from directly in front and below, his chest festooned with medals and ribbons attesting to his patriotic sacrifices. None of that, Donilon decided. No photographers in the central bay between Bork and the senators. He had masking tape placed along the floor and left strict instructions to keep the photographers on the sides, where they would not shoot from below and where their lenses would capture in full, unheroic dimensions the judge's bulging waistline.

Finally, Donilon decided, when Biden made his opening statement, his staff would not occupy the seats behind him. He would deliver his speech—part flag-waving rhetoric, part constitutional scholarship, part regular-guy straight talk—directly to the camera, his head framed by the tall mahogany bench behind. Biden would look presidential.

Biden himself understood the opportunity; it was one he did not easily embrace. He reflected later: "Calling it an opportunity is a little like saying: 'I've been dropped in the water that is shark-infested. But, you know, it's an opportunity. If I make it to shore, I will set a world's record. No one has ever done this before.' "

Biden initially took the job of Judiciary Committee chairman with great reluctance, knowing that a high court retirement could cause incalculable complications to his likely presidential bid. Soon after the Democrats took control of the Senate again in 1986, Ted Kennedy called Biden to offer him the chairmanship of Judiciary. Kennedy thought he was offering a fine prize to the ambitious young Delaware senator, and he sought something in return: Biden could have the Judiciary chairmanship if Biden would allow Kennedy to keep his large Judiciary staff. Kennedy was a loyal boss trying to protect his staff members. But Biden told Kennedy not to give up Judiciary. Kennedy didn't seem to understand. Biden made it clearer: He threatened that if Kennedy turned down the chairmanship, he would take all of Kennedy's staff away. Kennedy laughed and called a press conference an hour later to announce his decision to take over Labor.

Of course, Biden could have demurred on the Judiciary chairmanship, passing it to the next ranking Democrat so as to concentrate on presidential politics. But paradoxically, he felt running for president meant he could not be seen to pass up the job. "Had I not taken the chair, I am certain the argument would have been: Biden rejects responsibility. Is this guy a flash in the pan? Is he not ready to take on a tough job?"

In truth, Biden needed a boost. Just three days earlier the *New York Times* had run a front-page story reporting that the Delaware senator had used verbatim parts of a speech by British Labour party leader Neil Kinnock without giving credit.

It was a deeply moving speech. Kinnock, with his Welsh working-class lilt and oratorical gift, appeared in a British television commercial, asking: "Why am I the first Kinnock in a thousand generations to be able to get to university?" Pointing to his wife, Glenys, he continued: "Why is Glenys the first woman in her family in a thousand generations to be able to get to university? Was it because all our predecessors were thick?"

On August 23, at the Iowa State Fair, Biden closed his campaign speech, saying: "I was thinking as I was coming over here, why is it that Joe Biden is the first in his family ever to go to a university? Why is it that my wife who is sitting out there in the audience is the first in her family to ever go to college? Is it because our fathers and mothers were not bright?"

Kinnock ridiculed the notion that his coal-mining ancestors were any less gifted than he, saying of them: "Did they lack talent? Those people who could sing and play and recite and write poetry? Those people who could make wonderful beautiful things with their hands? Those people who could dream dreams, see visions? Why didn't they get it? Was it because they were weak? Those people who could work eight hours underground and then come up and play football? Weak?"

Biden mimicked Kinnock, moving the locale of his ancestors' travails to Pennsylvania and extending their workdays. "Those same people who read poetry and wrote poetry and taught me how to sing verse?" continued Biden, whose father was a Chevrolet dealer in Wilmington. "Is it because they didn't work hard? My ancestors, who worked in the coal mines of northeast Pennsylvania and would come up after twelve hours and play football for four hours?"

His fists clenched, Kinnock concluded: "Does anybody really think that they didn't get what we had because they didn't have the talent or the strength or the endurance or the commitment? Of course not. It was because there was no platform upon which they could stand."

Biden clenched only one fist during his conclusion: "No, it's not because they weren't as smart. It's not because they didn't work hard. It's because they didn't have a platform upon which to stand."

The plagiarism story had run in the *Des Moines Register* and that evening on NBC.

The speech was a Biden staple; he had credited Kinnock often, both before and after. When confronted, his campaign staff called it a meaningless slip. But Biden neglected to give credit again at a speech only forty-eight hours later. Because Biden promoted himself as a uniquely visionary orator, and because he had presented the lines as his spontaneous musings ("I was thinking as I was coming over here . . ."), the plagiarism accusation cut deeply. The Biden campaign was especially troubled because it was clearly the campaign of another Democratic hopeful that had prepared the videotape. It seemed to Biden and his people that of all times to strike him such a blow this was surely the most contemptible—just when he was set to lead the charge to stop Bork, a goal shared by nearly all Democrats. The tape had been distributed by Dukakis's campaign manager, John Sasso. But Biden may have been wrong to see a direct link to the Bork hearings. Sasso had first tried to hawk the story to reporters nearly two weeks before.

Biden had also been under fierce attack from the right early in the summer because of his announcement that the hearings would not take place until mid-September. Conservatives calculated that to be the longest delay in a quarter century between nomination and confirmation hearings. Biden countered, saying Bork's long record required careful study; no senator wanted to spend his August recess in the hearing room. There was truth to both assertions, but it was equally clear that liberal groups and senators needed time to build a case against the nominee and stir grass-roots opposition. Biden was aiding that effort. Further, conservatives were livid that Biden had announced his opposition to Bork early. They did not see how Biden could run for president and still claim to chair the hearings dispassionately. A number called for his resignation from the committee chairmanship.

Biden ignored these rumblings and went on to work hand in hand with the liberal groups that had declared war on Bork. Sub rosa, his staff met weekly with group representatives and stayed in constant telephone contact with them. After each of these meetings Judiciary Committee staff director Diana Huffman said to the representatives: "Remember, this was all off the record."

The actors took their places: the senators and their aides; the reporters; the nominee accompanied by family, Secret Service men, administration officials, and former President Ford—Bork's first advocate. The interplay of power among the nation's three branches of government—executive, legislative, and judicial—was about to appear in unusually compact form. That the hearings took place precisely two hundred years after the signing of the charter establishing that relationship seemed more than a coincidence. That Biden and Simon, and a key witness, Dole, hoped to gain their parties nomination for the presidency the following year only added to the feeling that here was a moment blending politics and national self-definition. It was the political process at its most elevated and significant—and at its rawest and most partisan.

The president had recently declared himself: The confirmation of Robert Bork would be the top domestic priority of his remaining sixteen months in office. Two years earlier he had campaigned in Senate races telling the nation that Republican control of the upper house was vital to assure confirmation of his judicial nominees. And

Dole had called the Bork fight "the main event" of the year's congressional session. Moreover, lobbying groups on left and right had been using the Bork nomination for extraordinarily successful fundraising and membership drives. The National Abortion Rights Action League was gaining a thousand new members each week.

With his wife and sister and parents in the hearing room—this was a major political debut for the senator—Biden opened the proceedings that morning with grace and humor. No one could accuse Biden of mistreating Bork at the hearings. His deference to the nominee, accompanied by his wide grin, bordered on the obsequious. "I guarantee you this little mallet is going to assure you every single right for you to make your views known, as long as it takes, on any grounds you wish to make them," Biden told Bork that first day. Later he said: "Clearly I do not want to get into a debate with a professor. . . ." The *Washington Post*'s television critic Tom Shales wrote: "Biden did everything but rush over to Bork's water glass with an ice-cold refill."

Biden's efforts to overcome the perception that he bore ill feeling toward Bork sometimes took on quirky dimensions. Three days into the hearings, as the attention to the plagiarism charge grew, Biden called a press conference to announce his intention to continue running for president. Afterward he was standing around the witness stand, talking to Bork, who said, "Well, if this doesn't work out, maybe I'll run for president." Biden looked him in the eye and said, "Don't do that. You're too damn good." No one within earshot understood what Biden thought he was doing.

Biden welcomed former President Ford, Bork's first introducer, saying: "We miss you here in Washington. Quite frankly, most of us envy you; not only that you have been president . . ." The room broke into appreciative laughter.

Solicitor General Bork had served under Ford for two years after Ford took over as president when Richard Nixon resigned in disgrace in 1974. His endorsement of Bork was *pro forma,* no more than a sanctimonious repetition of the judge's résumé. He offered no insight into—or even acknowledgment of—the intense controversy surrounding the process that day.

Ford's appearance would have been uneventful but for one surprise. After the former president finished, Biden sought to allow Ford to take his leave. All knew, Biden said, how busy Ford was. At that moment the bland, moderate Democrat from Arizona, Dennis DeConcini, neither aggressive nor a showman, and undecided on Bork, interrupted.

He begged the indulgence of the committee, claiming he had not realized he would have questions, but after "very carefully" reading the former president's statement, he wanted to know: Had Mr. Ford read any of Judge Bork's opinions on the circuit court?

Ford was flustered. Well, he had read some synopses, as well as reports on Bork, both favorable and critical.

DeConcini pressed. "Mr. President, have you had a chance to read any of his law review articles, in particular the *Indiana Law Review* article of 1971, or any of his law review articles that are of a controversial nature?"

Ford: "I have not read individual law review articles. I have read synopses of some of those articles, comments pro and con by individuals who were interested."

DeConcini: "Thank you, Mr. President."

The day had barely begun and a strategic blow was landed on a former president tapped to be Bork's most prestigious supporter. Ford hadn't the slightest idea about Bork's record. He was there as a showpiece, and Dennis DeConcini, of all people, pointed that out. This exchange presaged DeConcini's tough questioning of Bork and his ultimate opposition to the nomination.

The Justice Department men had feared precisely such an embarrassment. Hearing that DeConcini might ask Ford a question, they had urged committee Republicans to pressure the senator—at least tell him how impolite such a move would be. Just before the hearings they had waited with Ford in Vice President Bush's Senate office, Dirksen 201. In this three-office suite, photographs of Bush and his large, handsome family lined the walls; tables held model airplanes like the one Bush had flown in the Second World War. Others were covered with little bronze and wooden elephants, the Republican symbol. There, on the red Leatherette easy chairs, pro-Bork witnesses waited their turns throughout the hearings.

As the Justice men sat with Ford, they passed him some material on Bork to study. But the point was lost on the former president, who chattered on about skiing and golf as if the occasion for this great gathering were a celebrity tournament.

Even White House aides had questioned a need for Ford's presence at the hearings. It was Ford, after all, who had pardoned Nixon after the Watergate scandal; therein might lie ammunition for the opposition. So they gently told Ford that he was doubtless extremely busy. They would certainly understand if he couldn't come. Ford didn't get the hint. He insisted, saying, "When I make a commitment, I stick to it." No one dared say no after that.

They had been able to impress upon Biden that Ford "had a plane to catch." Would Biden be so kind as to excuse the former president immediately after his statement? Biden complied, but DeConcini would have none of it.

"Ford had requested to come and had insisted on being first," DeConcini said afterward. "When you're going to be a witness, it's not inappropriate to ask: 'Have you read the stuff?' "

Aware that the television networks had decided to forsake the largely ceremonial morning session, Biden saved his opening statement for the afternoon. With his aides the only staffers missing from the seats behind, Joe Biden proclaimed:

And so let us make no mistake about the unique importance of this nomination, at this particular moment in our history. . . . For I believe that a greater question transcends the issue of this nomination. Will we retreat from our tradition of progress, or will we go forward, ennobling human rights and human dignity, which is the legacy of our two-century journey as a people? . . .

My areas of concern touch the relationship of people of different races in our land . . . the basic right of privacy, privacy in our marriages, and in raising our children . . . the right of free expression, be it political—for example, whether Martin Luther King could have been prohibited from advocating violation of immoral segregation laws—or be it artistic. . . .

I believe all Americans are born with certain inalienable rights. As a child of God, I believe my rights are not derived from the Constitution. My rights are not derived from any government. My rights are not derived from any majority. My rights are because I exist. . . . They were given to me and each of my fellow citizens by our creator and they represent the essence of human dignity.

It was a telling rhetorical flourish, the linking of progress to rights and the recognition of overarching natural law. It was a testament to a predominant view of certain constitutional rights that had crystallized only within the past generation. The Constitution itself never mentions natural law. Abolitionists and other advocates of greater equality early in the country's history had invoked natural rights in support of their argument. Rarely had they succeeded with the argument in legal battle.

For the nation's first century and a half, in fact, property rights had held sway, often invoked to justify dominance of the powerful over the dispossessed and the weak. Before the Civil War, courts allowed slaveowners to defend their legal "right" to pursue their escaped "property." Until the New Deal corporations successfully defended their "natural right" to stymie economic reform. In the 1930s progressives were hostile to the idea of omnipresent rights because rights belonged to the rich and had come to mean trouble for the poor. In the landmark *Lochner* v. *New York* case of 1905, the Supreme Court struck down a New York State law limiting the hours that employers could require of bakers. The Court said both employers and employees had the "right" to liberty of contract, which was fundamental and natural to man. The state could not interfere much with such contractual and economic relations. Rights, as understood by the courts, were subject to definition by the men in power. The Court offered little comfort to those on the out.

Beginning in the late 1930s, "rights" gradually came, in Supreme Court parlance, to mean *human* rights—civil and personal—enjoyed by those not in power. Landmark cases over the next fifty years— upholding the right not to salute the flag, the right to express unpopular opinions, the right of poor criminal defendants to a lawyer—seeped into the culture; soon most Americans thought of such rights as "natural," beyond dispute, thoroughly a part of the nation's founding. Rights became legal trumps, the basis of an evolving unwritten constitution. Biden's speech played to the belief that the framers would approve, even if they had not said so explicitly. It was like Abraham Lincoln's argument that the framers disliked slavery and had planned for its extinction—possible but not provable; nonetheless, rhetorically powerful. Biden's was a common man's reproach to Bork's majoritarian view of the Constitution. The argument rang true to millions of Americans familiar with the sentence "I've got my rights."

The rights, however, were of recent vintage, at least in their application in all fifty states. As Justice William Brennan said:

As late as 1961, I could stand before a distinguished assemblage of the bar at New York University's James Madison Lecture and list the following as guarantees that had not been thought to be sufficiently fundamental to the protection of human dignity so as to be enforced against the states: the prohibition of cruel and unusual punishments, the right against self-incrimination, the right to assistance of counsel in a criminal trial, the right to confront witnesses, the right to compulsory process, the right not to be placed in jeopardy of life or limb more than once upon accusation of a crime, the right not to have illegally obtained evidence introduced at a criminal trial, and the right to a jury of one's peers.

In the quarter century following Brennan's lecture, each of those rights had been declared fundamental to individual liberty.

Biden's natural rights assertion mixed two traditional schools of thought, one that such rights were God-given and the other that they were inherent in human dignity. Apart from that, his was not a serious argument from a scholarly viewpoint. How can one overturn the will of the majority through an assertion about the essential nature of the universe? It defied systematic interpretation and invited rampant subjectivity.

But Biden's *was* a serious cultural argument; it represented an extraordinary change the nation had gone through in the preceding several decades. From a legal point of view, natural rights were, for the first time in American history, predominantly thought to be on the side of those who had nothing else.

With Biden's opening statement done, Bork's hour had arrived. He had been sworn in before Biden's statement. Biden had asked: "Judge, do you swear to give at this hearing in response to questions the truth, the whole truth and nothing but the truth, so help you God?" Bork, standing, his right hand raised, and with the incessant whir and click of automatic camera shutters serving as background noise, responded: "I do, Mr. Chairman."

After two and a half months of impassioned debate the country had its first chance to see and hear the man at the center of the storm. Polls taken by the major media showed the nation to be evenly divided on his nomination. Bork's performance over the following days would play a vital role in determining the tilt of public opinion.

Although Bork's testimony at the hearings seemed quite natural, the practice had shallow historic roots. The bitter confirmation struggles over Brandeis in 1916 and John Parker in 1930 occurred without the nominees' testimony. Not until 1925 did a Supreme Court nominee sit before the Senate Judiciary Committee, when Harlan F. Stone was asked to reply to questions after his appointment had run into political trouble on the Senate floor. By 1939, beginning with Felix Frankfurter, such an appearance had become routine. Even then, although Frankfurter successfully defended himself against scurrilous charges of being a Communist sympathizer, he had first tried to avoid testimony.

In his famous opening statement, Frankfurter said: "I should think it improper for a nominee no less than for a member of the Court to express his personal views on controversial political issues affecting the Court. My attitude and outlook on relevant matters have been fully expressed over a period of years and are easily accessible. I should think it not only bad taste but inconsistent with the duties of the office for which I have been nominated for me to attempt to supplement my past record by present declarations. That is all I have to say."

Closer questioning of judicial nominees began in the 1960s, but Bork was to set a record—five days.

Through the morning Bork had sat silently at the witness table with Ford and Bob Dole. Dole had also offered a brief statement of support. Now he was alone. He sat impassive and stiff in his dark suit. His unruly hair and scruffy beard had been trimmed. A heavy smoker, he touched not one cigarette inside the hearing room or within camera distance.

During the administration's preparations there had been some debate: Should Bork should make an opening statement at all? That question had been settled. He would. Then came wrangling over the kind of statement. His former clerk, Peter Keisler, now on the staff of the White House Counsel's Office, acted as Bork's aide-de-camp throughout the hearings. Keisler had offered a draft of an opening statement that sought, at one point, to make light of the welter of advice Bork had been given, including that he should shave off his beard. Keisler hoped to help Bork soften his image through a moment of self-deprecation. But Bork rejected that; the event was too grave. He wrote his own statement.

Bork began by introducing his family; his mother did not come; he was confident she was watching on television. Then he thanked his introducers, Ford, Dole, Senator John Danforth, and Representative Hamilton Fish, and went on to agree with Biden on one point: The hearings were to be largely a discussion of judicial philosophy. He clarified his differences with Biden, saying that when a judge reads "entirely new values into the Constitution, values that the framers and ratifiers did not put there, he deprives the people of their liberty. That liberty, which the Constitution clearly envisions, is the liberty of the people to set their own social agenda through the processes of democracy."

He added: "My philosophy of judging . . . is neither liberal nor conservative. It is simply a philosophy of judging which gives the Constitution a full and fair interpretation but, where the Constitution is silent, leaves the policy struggles to the states, and to the American people."

Little more than a question of emphasis, but a crucial one. Liberty for Bork, as for liberals, meant freedom for individuals from tyranny of the majority. But liberty for Bork also meant—and here was the difference—the right of the group to set society's course. A town or state could tell a person that if a law or an ordinance was offensive, say, a restriction on pornography or one on antidemocratic speech or on the availability of contraceptives, one was welcome to move elsewhere. A citizen has no constitutional "right" to insist on changes in majoritarian practices. Such a dissenter's freedom to insist would mean less freedom for the majority, which, Bork said, was not what democracy or the nation's charter mandated. The only merited individual protections against majority rule were those explicitly stated in the Constitution.

Indeed, Bork had spent a quarter century assailing liberal, rights-oriented constitutional decisions in the harshest possible terms. Now, however, he withdrew into a lawyerly, cautious shell on the stand. His statements were measured and often seemed inconsistent with what he had been saying for decades.

Biden knew Bork's record. He was eager to pin Bork down on the 1965 *Griswold* case, in which the Supreme Court struck down a Connecticut law forbidding use of contraceptives even by married couples. That decision enshrined the notion of a constitutional right to privacy, a notion Bork had attacked numerous times. In his 1971 *Indiana Law Journal* article, Bork said: "The truth is that the Court could not reach its result in *Griswold* through principle."

At the hearing Bork retreated. Yes, the Court might indeed be able to strike down such a law. The way the Court did it in 1965, however, was invalid; perhaps there was a more constitutional way to get there.

This sideways movement frustrated Biden. "You have been a professor now for years and years," he complained. "You are one of the most well-read and scholarly people to come before this committee.... [H]ave you come up with any other way to protect a married couple, under the Constitution, against an action by a government telling them what they can or cannot do about birth control in their bedroom?"

Bork responded: "I have never engaged in that exercise." Later, when Biden pushed him again, he said: "There may be other arguments and I do not want to pass upon that."

Here were weak-kneed statements from a man known for verbal muscle. The testimony grew even flimsier when he was faced with the bulldozer driven by Ted Kennedy.

Kennedy rarely asked a simple question. His questions were, in fact, packaged inside accusations and declarations. He began on Bork's view of *Griswold:* "Doesn't that lead you to the view that you would uphold a statute requiring, say, compulsory abortion, if a legislature enacted it by majority?" It was followed by five paragraphs before Bork had a chance to respond. Kennedy said that in Bork's world the individual had precious few rights.

When Bork finally spoke, he said: "I have the greatest respect for the Bill of Rights and I will enforce the Bill of Rights. I have enforced the Bill of Rights." He then repeated his complaint that the *Griswold* definition of privacy had no contours, that it was a free-floating right. He was able after another exchange to make the point more forcefully by adding: "Privacy to do what, Senator? You know, privacy to use cocaine in private? Privacy for businessmen to fix prices in a hotel room? We just do not know what it is."

But attempting to answer the compulsory abortion question—a trenchant criticism of his theory—Bork said something he would surely not accept from another: "I have never found it terribly useful, in testing constitutional theories, to use examples that we know the American people will never enact. The founders of this nation banked a good deal upon the good sense of the people, as upon the courts."

Hypotheticals are the stuff of constitutional theory. Supreme Court justices frequently pepper lawyers with hypotheticals during oral arguments. Indeed, Bork's own writings were full of this technique, known as the slippery slope argument. Who was to determine whether the American people would never enact the examples? Over the years different legislatures had passed a number of now-incredible laws—to ban the teaching of foreign languages, for instance, and all private education. Others had sought to sterilize certain types of criminals. Bork offered no constitutional means of overturning such laws, even those regulating bedroom habits. His only argument regarding compulsory abortion was that no state would pass such a law, and if it did, the state would not enforce it. To suggest otherwise, he said, was to exhibit little faith in the people.

Kennedy turned to his specialty, civil rights. He asked Bork for an explanation of his 1963 article in the *New Republic* in which Bork opposed a federal law requiring businesses to serve blacks. Bork had said that such government intrusion into the private affairs of its citizens was inexcusable, that it was an unacceptable breach of individual liberty, and had described the landmark Civil Rights Act as premised on "a principle of unsurpassed ugliness."

Kennedy's question was again buried in a speech about the importance of progress on racial equality. He interrupted Bork's efforts to answer. Kennedy told Bork that while it was good to see that the nominee had praised the 1954 school desegregation decision, "I am troubled because I believe that your clock on civil rights seems to have stopped in 1954."

Kennedy's aide, Jeffrey Blattner, sitting behind the senator, was at the edge of his seat. This was Bork's moment, Blattner thought. All he has to do is look straight at the camera and say, "Senator, that article was the biggest mistake of my life. I will go to my grave regretting it. I ask the nation's blacks to forgive me."

Bork did nothing of the kind. As soon as Bork spoke, Blattner relaxed. The judge said he had announced his abandonment of that 1963 position at his 1973 hearings to become solicitor general but, in fact, had changed his mind before that.

Bork picked up a little energy when Kennedy asked why he had not said so publicly before that. It was not his habit, Bork said, to "keep issuing looseleaf services about my latest state of mind."

The point seemed fair, a sound rhetorical blow, but Kennedy had expected it. Two days before, he had asked his staff to prepare for him a list of the civil rights landmarks achieved between the 1964 Civil Rights Act and Bork's 1973 recantation. He then responded:

> The point that I would make here, is that you felt it was sufficiently important to publish your views at a time when we were having a national debate in the early part of the 1960s on civil rights legislation. We were having a national debate in 1968 on the whole issue of fair housing. We were having a national debate in 1972 on the civil rights legislation and you did not feel, even though these were matters that were right before the American people and the Congress of the United States, sufficiently aroused in terms of your altered or changed views, that you were prepared to publish those matters. I would just say I wish you had been as quick to publicize your change of heart as you were to broadcast your opposition.

It was a strong accusation. It got stronger. When Bork defended his previous position on liberty, saying that he had been worried about government coercion of individuals, Kennedy asked: "Were you not worried about the coercion that was happening to blacks in this country because of lack of opportunity for equal employment?"

Bork said that he had always found segregation abhorrent. Nowhere in his writings could one find a mark of racial or ethnic hostility. This missed Kennedy's point. Kennedy was not accusing Bork of being a racist. He was accusing him of lining up on the wrong side of history, of declining to help solve the nation's great moral struggles. Kennedy went next to the issue of poll taxes.

In the 1966 case of *Harper* v. *Virginia Board of Elections*, the Supreme Court struck down a Virginia poll tax for state elections, saying it deprived poor citizens of the equal protection promised in the Fourteenth Amendment. Bork had attacked that decision, saying that the Fourteenth Amendment was aimed at racial, not economic, discrimination. The Court, by its own acknowledgment, had expanded the Fourteenth Amendment beyond its origins in *Harper*, saying: "We have never been confined to historic notions of equality. . . . Notions of what constitute equal treatment for purposes of the Equal Protection Clause *do* change." But, Bork objected, on what principle had the Constitution changed? Who told appointed judges they should adapt the national charter to *their* views? Virginians wanted a small poll tax. Shouldn't they be allowed to have it?

Faced with Kennedy's question, Bork explained his argument that the Virginia poll tax had not been racially discriminatory and was only $1.50. He named Supreme Court justices and legal scholars who agreed with him that the Court had wrongly struck the poll tax down.

But Kennedy knew where he was heading with this line of questioning. "You and I may not have to worry about where each dollar goes but there are a lot of Americans who do and to suggest that a poll tax, if it is small enough, does not deprive a poor person of a fundamental aspect of citizenship, well, that reminds me of Anatole France's famous remark that 'the law in its majestic equality forbids the rich as well as the poor to sleep under bridges and to beg in the streets and to steal bread.' " The previous day Kennedy had asked aide Blattner to find him that quote because he knew he could use it.

Kennedy added that judges were supposed to treat poor as well as rich fairly. "I just think we have to be sensitive to the realities, not just legal technicalities."

Before his thirty-minute questioning period ended, Kennedy took up Bork's opposition to Court decisions in the 1960s requiring state legislatures to reapportion their voting districts so that each person's vote counted equally, the so-called one man, one vote cases. Bork had objected to one man, one vote. It was entirely clear, he said, that the framers had never called for such a rigid formulation. His explanation, clear and legally sophisticated, left many listeners far behind: "Now it should be said that my position was the position that Justice Stewart took in Lucas against 44th General Assembly in dissent. There you had a reapportionment plan with a state senate based on counties, I believe, which had been adopted by a referendum with a majority vote in every county in the state. . . . There is nothing in our constitutional history that suggests one man, one vote is the only proper way of apportioning. . . . Indeed, the executive veto, the committee system, districting, all those things are really inconsistent with one man, one vote."

Kennedy now let loose. "I think the people of this country, Judge Bork, accept the fundamental principle of one man, one vote even though they are not burdened with a law school education. . . . I do not think you have to be a law professor to know a little about simple justice. . . . With all your ability, I just wish you had devoted even a little of your talent to advancing the equal rights rather than criticizing so many of the decisions protecting rights and liberties. Lawyers can always make technical points, but justice ought to be fair."

With network cameras focused on him, Kennedy was playing Oliver North. He was appealing to the strong pragmatic, populist sentiment in the country, the kind that distrusted lawyers who "make technical points" and proceed to take away people's rights. His manner offended many intellectuals of both left and right. But Kennedy was not after their approval. He was aiming at a wider audience.

Bork had not understood the nature of the proceeding. In fact, the nominee was getting it all wrong. He had prepared for a bench trial, but with the entire nation watching, this was a jury trial. Bork needed to step back from cases and talk about values and rights. As *Washington Post* television critic Tom Shales wrote, "He looked, and talked, like a man who would throw the book at you—maybe like a man who would throw the book at the whole country."

It took three days for Bork to answer Kennedy. On Friday afternoon Kennedy charged that Bork had "shown his bias against women and minorities and in favor of big business and presidential power."

The litany seemed endless. Bork belatedly shot back: "Senator, if those charges were not so serious, the discrepancy between the evidence and what you say would be highly amusing." He then proceeded to say that he was not guilty of the things of which he had been accused by Kennedy. But Bork never stood up for what he was.

Here was an odd phenomenon: This man of enormous passion, this ex-Marine who had never backed away from a fight, came across to the American people as bloodless.

CHAPTER

10

Missed Opportunities

The Bork handlers had a bad time of it from the beginning. John Bolton worried early. The first day of hearings was only half over and Senator Howell Heflin, Democrat of Alabama, was complaining. "He's good on substance but there's too much judge talk," Heflin advised Bolton during a break. "He's too professorial."

This from a man who had been chief justice of the Alabama Supreme Court and was officially undecided. A bad sign. It gave Bolton the feeling Heflin was searching for reasons to oppose. Bolton attributed the problem to stiffness on Bork's part. In Will Ball's White House office that evening—after each day of the hearings, the Bork camp gathered there—Bolton repeated the Heflin comment. Bork had left the meeting for home and didn't hear it. The others claimed to see no big problem. Bork would relax, and if supporters continued to feed the right questions to the senators, all would be fine. Few allowed themselves an honest evaluation publicly that evening. The handlers were telling reporters that their man was doing great—and they were trying to believe it.

On the first day they had hoped Bork would look good during questions by Senator Strom Thurmond, Republican of South Carolina.

Thurmond, the ranking minority member, had served as committee chairman for the six years the Republicans had held the Senate. He wanted to help Bork, but in truth he had not gone out of his way over the summer to do much for him. Deeply conservative and the most senior Republican, Thurmond was a natural to be the administration point man on the committee. But Thurmond was not enthusiastic about the judge. He had strongly favored the naming of a southerner to replace Powell. In particular, Thurmond favored his former aide, William Wilkins, Jr., for whom Thurmond had gotten a federal judgeship in South Carolina. Thurmond pushed Meese and Reagan hard on the idea, and they had placed Wilkins's name on the original list of Supreme Court nominees. When Bork, the northerner and Yale intellectual, was named, Thurmond was miffed.

Thurmond was a most extraordinary member of the United States Senate. Pushing eighty-five, with surreally tinted orange hair, he was a combination of old-world etiquette and hard-nosed politics. He had been named president pro tempore of the Senate. Although his hearing was fading, he was alert and assiduously hardworking.

In the old days Thurmond had been the scourge of civil rights legislation. In 1964, for example, he had actually wrestled Ralph Yarborough of Texas to the floor outside a committee room to prevent him from making a quorum to act on a piece of civil rights legislation. Thurmond won that one, pinning Yarborough until the Texas liberal was rescued by the committee chairman. In the same year Thurmond switched parties, declaring that the Democrats were "leading the evolution of our nation to a socialistic dictatorship." Seven years earlier he had held the floor against a civil rights bill for twenty-four hours and eighteen minutes.

Apart from his famous accent—in his mouth, the nominee's name was "Jedge Bawk"—Thurmond often seemed to bear little resemblance to his old self by the time of the Bork hearings. True, his comments occasionally jarred contemporary ears. During the testimony of Kathleen Sullivan of Harvard Law School, he said: "I might say, when I was in school, I did not have any pretty teachers like Miss Kathleen Sullivan." But he had also insisted not long before: "I'm not a racist, and I've done everything I could to help the people of both races throughout my lifetime." He had mellowed slightly as the country, and especially the South, had changed. With South Carolina's blacks growing in numbers and power, he chose not to block extensions of civil rights laws and even voted for the Martin Luther King federal holiday. In 1971 he became the first southern senator to hire a black professional staff member.

Thurmond's work for Bork was polite and correct but without

visceral commitment. When Biden decided in July to delay hearings until mid-September, he called Thurmond, who did not object. Only later, when other conservatives made much of the delay, did Thurmond claim he had never agreed to the wait, and he accused Biden of dissembling.

Thurmond dutifully went through the questions his staff prepared for him. He asked Bork to clear his name of accusations by another federal judge that Bork had deceived him; he asked Bork to show he was not an obstacle to women's progress. Bork responded carefully and clinically but with little sweep. Then Thurmond served up a question that offered Bork a genuine platform.

"It appears to me that much of the attack on you is based on selective citation and taking your statements out of context," he said. "Is there any particular area where this has occurred on which you would like to comment?"

Bork declined, saying he would discuss such cases as the hearings progressed. It was an astonishing reply for a man who later took to the lecture circuit to complain about distortion after distortion left unanswered.

There were other lost opportunities. The next attempts were made by Orrin Hatch, the Utah Republican.

Hatch himself had actually been the administration's second choice for the Powell seat. Hatch had done more for the administration on its conservative judicial agenda than anybody else in the Senate. He had, for instance, fought for constitutional amendments to overturn Supreme Court decisions upholding abortion and banning school prayer. He had pushed through legislation allowing interstate sales of rifles and handguns. And he had been Rehnquist's lead defender during a difficult confirmation fight.

In the days after Powell's retirement, liberal groups were in some ways more afraid of Hatch's nomination than of Bork's. They knew that senatorial courtesy would make it difficult for Hatch's colleagues to turn him down. And they viewed Hatch as among the crudest of right-wingers.

Bork got the nod over Hatch for several reasons. A major one was constitutional. The Senate had that year raised the salaries of Supreme Court justices to $110,000 and the Constitution forbids a senator from taking a job whose salary he votes to raise during his term. Further, an important reason to choose Hatch over Bork would be to ride in on senatorial courtesy. But the administration believed it could get Bork through. So why give up a vital Senate ally like Hatch? Finally, Hatch was inconsistent in his desire to join the Court. In the last several years, when his name was floated, he would occasionally approach Justice Department officials, grab them by the arms, and say, "You know how much water I've carried for you guys. I deserve that nomination." But at other times he seemed unsure he could face the monastic existence. As he said later, "I subscribe to what Howard Baker once said: Funeral homes are livelier than the Court. And I know some Democrats like Ted Kennedy would like to see me out of the Senate. I'd miss terribly the ability to speak out and stand up on important issues."

Tall, well-tailored, and handsome, Hatch at fifty-three, was a shrewd politician. He had been in the Senate only eleven years, but the walls of his outer office at the Capitol were incomparably crowded with photographs of him and the powerful as well as two-foot-by-three-foot portraits of his family and of Reagan. In addition, he had framed numerous handwritten notes from his six children. In a sense, these notes had a curious effect. Some of them contained highly personal messages, such as the one from a daughter about how much she appreciated the confidential chat they had had the previous evening, how much it meant to her to have a fine father to whom she could turn in moments of indecision. A staunch Mormon, Hatch worked hard to promote himself as a protector of family and religious values. One jarring note was his frequent easy use of four-letter words.

Hatch was, in fact, an intriguing combination of ideologue and pragmatist. His work in Judiciary was rigidly conservative, but he often cooperated with liberals on his other committee, Labor and Human Resources. He and Kennedy cosponsored legislation to ban the routine use of polygraph tests by employers as well as to commit the federal government to spend one billion dollars on AIDS research. He also championed restricted government aid to day care at a time when many senators to his left could barely work up enthusiasm over the issue.

Hatch worked genuinely hard for Bork. He believed in the judge and saw that he needed protection from the liberal vipers. So his first question was a jab at Kennedy (he later said that Kennedy had "lied and cheated to the American public" about Bork, placing "politics above principle"). He said to Bork: "I think what you have been able to show here today is that these major issues are not easily explained in thirty-second sound bites that we people in Congress are used to popping off about; is that correct?"

Instead of picking up the cue—Hatch was trying to remind Bork that perhaps he *ought* to come up with catchy thirty-second answers—Bork took slight offense. "Well, Senator," he said, "If you are suggesting that I have proved that I cannot explain them, I do not want to accept that."

Hatch tried again a minute later, asking Bork to define *judicial activism*.

Bork responded with a careful answer of more than 150 words that made reference to "academic legal debate" and "most of those writing in the law schools these days." Hatch—not to mention network executives who had canceled daytime soap operas to broadcast the hearings—was getting nervous.

Hatch leaped to the rescue, saying: "In other words, in simple terms, judicial activism is when judges make law rather than interpret the law?" Bork agreed that was a fine shorthand definition.

Seeking to lead Bork by the hand and failing miserably, Hatch turned to *Roe* v. *Wade*, the 1973 ruling forbidding states from banning abortion. He asked Bork to explain what was objectionable about the decision and got a fine technical answer. Then Hatch listed all the famous scholars, liberal as well as conservative, who had assailed the *Roe* decision. Hatch was building to a rhetorical climax and needed Bork to help. He wanted to dismiss *Roe* by showing it to be utterly discredited and asked: "In your lengthy constitutional studies, is there any Supreme Court decision that has stirred more controversy or criticism amongst scholars and citizens than that particular case?"

Bork: "I suppose the only candidate for that, Senator, would be Brown against Board of Education. It is possible, you know, for the Supreme Court to be—"

It was stunning. Bork chose the one sacred decision of twentieth-century jurisprudence, a legal anchor of contemporary society, praised by all as the wisest and most courageous of rulings, and compared it with *Roe*. Of course, Bork was right. *Brown had* been controversial. But it had attained the status of a holy object. Comparing *Roe* with *Brown* was asking for trouble, nearly a death wish.

Hatch interrupted, refusing to let him finish his sentence.

"Or possibly the Dred Scott case," Hatch pointedly interjected. He was referring to the 1856 decision, the most ignominious and universally condemned of all Supreme Court rulings, that said a black slave was property even when on free soil. Bork, recovering, agreed it was an apt comparison.

Hatch said later: "It was very frustrating when you serve up a question that he ought to hit a home run on and he wouldn't do it. I told him he should say to other senators, 'Sir, this is a lie.' He said, 'I don't think I can do that.' I said, 'The heck you can't.'"

Hatch finally got the picture: He would have both to ask the questions *and* to provide the answers from then on, and he did.

After the first day Bork got a little better. He was more relaxed and occasionally showed flashes of wit. But he continued to make mistakes.

On the second day Arlen Specter referred to a 1954 decision that desegregated the school system of Washington, D.C. Since the District was run by the federal government, it fell under different rules from the states, and a different constitutional rationale was used from that in *Brown* v. *Board of Education.*

The case, known as *Bolling* v. *Sharpe,* had used a method Bork condemned as unconstitutional. Specter wanted to know what it meant to Bork to accept a decision that went against his constitutional principles. Bork compared this with New Deal decisions centering on the Commerce Clause of the Constitution, the reasoning of which Bork had also condemned.

Specter: "You accept in Bolling v. Sharpe to strike down segregation in the District of Columbia, and you accept it in the Commerce Clause. What happens to your principles?"

Bork: "Senator, I did not accept it in Bolling v. Sharpe. And when I say I accepted it in the Commerce Clause, I accept it because what has happened is irreversible.... [W]e do not try to tear up the nation in a vain attempt to take the Commerce Clause back to where it was in 1790."

Specter: "Final question. Do you accept Bolling v. Sharpe or not?"

Bork: "I have not thought of a rationale for it because I think you are quite right, Senator."

Al Kamen, who was reporting on the hearings for the *Washington Post,* felt his heartbeat pick up. Bork was saying he could not justify the decision to desegregate the D.C. school system thirty-three years earlier. Here was a story.

Kamen was not the only one to realize what a bombshell had been dropped. At the five-minute break right after that exchange, Bork's advisers told him that he could, under no circumstances, leave the discussion where it had been. He must say—and loudly, for all to hear—that he would never touch that precedent. Bork immediately understood.

As soon as the room was called back to order, Bork said to Specter: "I want to make it clear, absolutely clear if I can, that my doubts about the substantive due process approach to *Bolling* . . . does not mean that I would ever dream of overruling *Bolling* v. *Sharpe* . . . And furthermore I should make it clear, as I have said repeatedly, segregation is not only unlawful but immoral. And I do not want my doubts about a constitutional mode of reasoning to be turned into anything other than that."

A disaster had been averted. But the liberal lobbyists were working the journalists hard outside the hearing room, putting their "spin" on the proceedings. Bolton and Korologos were, officially, not supposed to talk to the press, a major handicap at a moment such as the *Bolling* one. They could have made clear that Bork had no intention of overruling it.

The administration was getting killed at the spin battle. At the meeting that night in Ball's office there was sentiment to compete with Ralph Neas and Kate Michelman in getting to the media their version of what was happening. Leslye Arsht, who was handling Bork press for the White House, was against Bolton and Korologos's talking to reporters. That was not their job. But in a rare moment of agreement between them, Bolton and Korologos decided to ignore what they were told. Beginning the next day, they stalked the halls during breaks, offering reporters positive assessments.

Bork continued to provide little help. He remained poor at picking up cues offered by his allies on the panel and at defending his past actions.

On the third day of hearings Hatch raised the question of Bork's objection to the 1966 decision, *Katzenbach* v. *Morgan*, striking down literacy tests, the issue Kennedy had made so much of two days earlier.

Here Hatch offered Bork an opportunity for indignation. "Some commentators have suggested that your comments in opposition to *Katzenbach* were an effort to reinstate literacy tests for voters."

Bork: "Absolutely."

A puzzled Hatch tried it one more time. "Let me ask you directly, so nobody has any question about it. Was your criticism of the Katzenbach case based on approval of literacy tests, or disapproval?"

Bork: "Absolutely not, Senator. I have, in matter of fact, no view of literacy tests. I have not looked at how they operate. . . ."

Hatch was left stranded.

Still more extraordinary instances occurred on Friday, the fourth day of hearings.

Gordon Humphrey, Republican of New Hampshire, wanted to bring the hearings around to a subject dear to every conservative—crime. He told a story about an elderly neighbor of his in Washington who had been robbed three times. The woman had bars installed on her windows and had become, like other aging Americans living alone, a prisoner in her own home. With that backdrop, Humphrey posed his question: "What responsibility do judges have to protect society and individual citizens from criminals?"

This was Bork's opportunity to earn easy points. He need only wax indignant over a justice system that had become weighted toward the defendant, a system showing insufficient sympathy for the victim and the victim's family. Conservatives agreed on those points. Crime had become such an emotional political issue that few liberals wished to quarrel over it anymore. But Bork seemed to want to show independence, to prove that he was the kind of judge whose answers fit no predictable political program. He offered a general statement regarding a judge's responsibility to balance a fair trial for the accused with justice for the victim. Then he said: "I am not an expert on criminal law." Since the White House had sought to sell Bork as a law-and-order judge, this was a disconcerting reply.

Humphrey tried again. He told another story: An Iowa man had brutally murdered a ten-year-old girl on Christmas Eve. When the man was in custody, a policeman carried on about how difficult it would be to find the girl's body in the falling snow; the accused man led the authorities to her body. After the man was convicted, an appeals court reversed the judgment on the ground that the state had to prove that the officer had not acted in bad faith in appealing to the defendant's conscience. Indignant now, Humphrey asked: "How far should judges go in protecting criminals at the expense of society?"

But Bork refused to bite the bait; criminal law, he repeated, was not his area of expertise. Of course, no one was asking him how many books he had written about the criminal justice system. A simple statement would have done, words regarding the need to be tougher on criminals and more understanding toward victims. No such luck. Humphrey gave up. Afterward he expressed anger, saying he had asked the crime question because the Justice Department had requested him to do so. Yet Bork wouldn't play his part.

Later that morning Howard Metzenbaum, Democrat of Ohio, one of the Senate's most cantankerous members, raised the American Cyanamid case.

Metzenbaum had earlier attacked Bork over Watergate and his views on antitrust. Now he loosed a stream of indignation over the case which had already been fully exploited in the anti-Bork campaign the preceding two and a half months.

"Judge, I must tell you that it is such a shocking decision, and I cannot understand how you as a jurist could put women to the choice of work or be sterilized . . ." said Metzenbaum, ignoring the fact that Bork had done no such thing.

Seventy-year-old Metzenbaum, silver-haired, tall, and stooped, had gained a reputation in the Senate as an obstructionist. Since his election in 1976 he had established a power base by his ability to prevent things from getting done. A multimillionaire parking lot magnate, Metzenbaum was especially troubled by anything that smacked of favors to big business. The *Wall Street Journal* later said of Metzenbaum: "In the U.S. Senate, where cooperation and comity are the grease that makes the wheels turn, Howard Metzenbaum is a bucketful of sand."

Metzenbaum saw himself as a guardian against special interests and corruption. In 1984 he led the fight against the confirmation of Ed Meese to be attorney general. But his enemies in the Senate sat back and watched with relish when, during the same period, it was revealed that he had received a $250,000 "finder's fee" for his role in the sale of a Washington, D.C., hotel. He returned the money but denied any wrongdoing.

Metzenbaum was a formidable interrogator. Bork, on the other hand, did little to alter the impression that he had in fact written an opinion offering workingwomen a choice between being sacked and being sterilized. Such an accusation had run in anti-Bork literature. Clearly the judge should have been ready for it. He was not. He approached the question casually.

In his response he hesitated, saying: "I am just trying to recall the case." He began talking about the Occupational Safety and Health Administration and "ambient blood levels" instead of ambient lead levels. Then he made one of the most egregious errors of his testimony.

Barely acknowledging the moral horror of the policy—he spoke only of "a distressing choice"—Bork placed the policy in an oddly positive light. He said the company might simply have fired the women without offering them the "choice" of sterilization. "Some of them, I guess, did not want to have children. . . . I suppose the five women who chose to stay on that job with higher pay and chose sterilization—I suppose that they were glad to have the choice— they apparently were—that the company gave them," he said.

Metzenbaum sat, nearly vindicated because that *was* a shocking thing to say.

Bork's clumsiness assuaged the consciences of the anti-Bork activists who may have felt guilt about exploiting the case in the beginning. The answer smacked of the kind of insensitivity to women and workers of which he was continually accused.

Eric Schnapper and Elaine Jones of the NAACP Legal Defense Fund were in a taxi on the way to Capitol Hill when they heard Bork's response to Metzenbaum. Schnapper was shocked. Upon arrival at the Senate, he and Jones rushed to the liberal "war room," an empty Senate room where the anti-Bork forces had set up camp. Schnapper urged women's groups immediately to put out statements condemning Bork's answer, and they did. Then they got in touch with the lawyer for the sterilized women.

At the urging of her attorney, one of the five sterilized women fired off a telegram and then a handwritten letter to the committee. She took violent exception to the notion that she had "welcomed" the choice.

"I had surgery because I had to have the job and felt I had no choice," wrote the woman, Betty J. Riggs of Harrisville, West Virginia, in the letter. "If I lost my job I would have lost my home and I also needed it to help support my parents, my father is totally blind and my mother had emphysema. . . . During this time we were harassed, embarrassed and humiliated by some supervisors and some fellow workers. They referred to us like animals, such as dogs being spaded or neutered. They told us we were branded for life. . . ." She added that two years later the department was closed anyway and she was demoted and transferred to another department, precisely what she had hoped to avoid through her sterilization.

Riggs, helped by her attorney, then struck one of the most reso-
nant anti-Bork chords in her letter: "I feel Judge Bork done me an
injustice. . . . I don't see how any Judge could rule that way. I don't
think he realized we were human beings with feelings, and further
more I don't think he cared, no one should have that power to alter
or destroy reproductive organs of any human being. . . . This Country is known for freedom. I think we'd better back up and take a
good look at these issues. Do we want someone who can dismiss this
very important issue so easily to have this power? . . ."

Hatch, ever valiant in his efforts to save Bork, engaged him on the
issue slowly and carefully the following day. While Bork did a much
better job of it then, the damage was irreparable. The sense that
Bork was cavalier and insensitive was burnished into the minds of
many who had watched on Friday.

Toward the end of that day DeConcini and his wife were going
over a videotape of the day's proceedings. Mrs. DeConcini, strongly
against confirmation, had taken a keen interest in the Bork hearings.
She was at the hearing room every day. As the couple listened to the
tape in a back room, a committee aide happened by. Bork was talking about the *Cyanamid* case on the tape. The aide remembered the
DeConcinis were visibly indignant. "I can't believe he's saying those
things," the senator exclaimed to his wife. Mrs. DeConcini was in
vehement agreement.

Earlier in the hearings DeConcini had said to Bork: "You leave
this senator unsatisfied as to how we . . . can conclude that you're
going to protect the citizens of this country in interpreting the Constitution on the Court as it relates to sex."

As the hearings progressed, Bork admirers tried to be optimistic. He
was, they felt, giving the lie to the accusation that he was a bug-eyed
zealot. He displayed calm and patience. To those offended by Oliver
North's rhetorical flag-waving, Bork showed himself a world apart.
He gave the sense that his true dedication was to the law, not to a
political agenda. His answers exhibited erudition and learning on a
wide range of legal issues.

But many who followed the hearings understood instinctively
that erudition and learning were not enough. Bork was missing
golden opportunities. He was talking legalese. His nomination had
become the focus of a vast public dispute over the direction of the
nation. He was not getting his message across.

Will Ball of the White House staff told Bork that he needed to "score a few more points." At one point, he said, perhaps Bork could bring the discussion around to the right to bear arms, a popular issue in the heartland. Bork said he had never really thought about that right. "Judge, goddamn, surely you've thought about the Second Amendment," protested Ball in his down-home southern accent. "Not really," Bork said, and the issue died.

Randall Rader, committee aide to Hatch, remembered going up to Bork as he ate a sandwich in Bush's office during the lunch break on the second day and saying: "You're doing a wonderful job, but I really think you need to get a tear in your eye and wipe it away and say: 'I would dearly love to defend the constitutional rights of women and blacks.' Make a flowery speech. Cast your eye down with emotion. Leave the room ringing a bit."

Bork responded: "Randy, I'm a lawyer, not a politician."

But some judicial conservatives would complain that Bork was not showing lawyerly ability. A good lawyer tailors his argument to the forum in which he is arguing. Bork misunderstood his audience.

One of the first to recognize the problem was perhaps Bork's most fervent admirer—his eldest child, Robert, Jr. A thirty-two-year-old business reporter for *U.S. News & World Report,* Bob was in many ways a younger, less formed version of his father. He was more nervous, less sure of himself, but also very bright and a fine writer. While his looks were laced with the dark traits of his mother, he had many of his father's characteristics. He was also large, with a bulging waist and tight, curly hair. He had his father's baritone voice and wicked irony, which he applied both to others and himself. He once said that he recited a prayer before each date, which was how he knew God didn't exist.

Bob loved his father enormously. He carried within him Bork's gestures and habits. He chain-smoked Camel filters and was deeply taken by conservative, market-oriented theories. His politics were hard right. But personally he had a gentle, vulnerable quality. His mother's death from cancer often haunted him. He romanticized his parents' marriage and thought of it as an ideal partnership between a man and a woman. He had never gone through a period of rebellion against his parents, politically or philosophically. The time when he might have done so, when he was a teenager, was when his mother fell ill. The children found strength at the time in Bork's devoted care for Claire and in family unity.

Right after the nomination was announced, Bob had offered to help his father. He would take a leave of absence from his job and put himself in charge of the flow of paper and contact with various people. Bork said there was no need.

Speaking of it later, Bob said, "In the way that Nancy Reagan looks after her husband's affairs, someone should have been there for him. I should have insisted."

But once the hearings began, Bob did take a leave to be with his father and do what needed to be done. He hung around the pro-Bork war room, the Senate conference room where Justice Department lawyers wrote questions for Republican senators and monitored the hearings. At one point, frustrated by the opposition's control of the media, Bob said he would bring his personal computer in and put out press releases. But he was told not to. Just before the committee vote he wrote a column for the op-ed page of the *Washington Post*, complaining about the distortions Bork's opponents had spread. He went on "Good Morning America" and a CNN talk show. By then it was too late.

He had tried to influence his father at the start of the hearings. On the evening of the first day he and the rest of the family went back to Bork's house. Neighbors, especially Mrs. Potter Stewart, widow of the justice and a close family friend, brought over homemade food. Friends were constantly coming and going. Bork had gone briefly to the White House for the day-end meeting. He came back only to be pulled into telephone consultation with various officials.

Just before supper, martini in hand, Bork settled into his usual chair in the living room by the fireplace. He picked up a detective novel, one of his principal diversions in life. Bob looked in, went haltingly into the room, and stood behind the couch.

"I think you did really well," he began softly. "You were really very impressive. But I have to tell you that you seemed a bit nervous. I was thinking that you ought to remember Aristotle's First Enthymeme: Know your audience. You have to explain more. A lot of people won't know what you're talking about. You have to try to use more plain talk. When you say, 'In X case,' you're talking shorthand that only lawyers will understand. It sounds too technical."

Bork was taken aback. "So you don't think anyone understood anything I was saying?" he asked in frustration.

"No, a lot of people understood," Bob protested, not wishing further to upset his father. "But the people that you really want to convince out there are not just senators but the public at large. I also don't have the impression that a lot of senators know a lot about this stuff. Remember when you were a professor. It should almost be like a classroom. It'd be nice to get a blackboard."

The next evening Bob told his father he had done much better, and after that he stayed away from evaluative comments. Bork, a stubborn man under extraordinary pressure, could not listen to much advice so late in the game. It only rattled him.

CHAPTER

11

Confirmation Conversion

If Bork missed opportunities to persuade a frightened public to trust his judgment, his testimony was marked by a still more remarkable phenomenon: He modified views he had held strongly and repeated widely for two decades.

Bork had built a career upon assailing many modern Supreme Court decisions as unprincipled, unreachable, indefensible. He had laid out his objections in detail. Dozens of rulings, in his view, needed to be overturned because one illegitimate decision can spawn so many others. The Court needed to be steered along a course of original intent.

Faced with close questioning on these points, however, Bork told a different story. Suddenly, or so it seemed, some of those decisions had become acceptable or so much a part of the legal fabric that they could not be unraveled; other rulings suddenly represented more or less his own position; and still others, he now suggested, could be reached by a different constitutional path from that taken by the Court.

Like the White House, Bork seemed to understand that confirmation depended on a softening of his harsh commentary. At least, that was the skeptic's view. As the week of his testimony wore on, Bork stepped back from—and then occasionally returned to—restrictive and radical statements he had made on free speech, constitutional protection of women, and the need for the Supreme Court to overrule bad decisions.

Senator Patrick Leahy labeled the modifications a "confirmation conversion," and the phrase stuck. Bork angrily denied it. There was a big difference, he said, between the provocative theorizing of an academic and the responsibility of a judge. "In a classroom nobody gets hurt. In a courtroom, somebody always gets hurt, which calls for a great deal more caution and circumspection than you are required to show when you give a speech at Indiana or some other place." He also argued that he had matured and mellowed over the years.

The problem was the longevity of some of Bork's early provocative statements. Many had been repeated in more recent years while Bork sat as a federal judge. Bork also had told interviewers that the approach he had taken to a subject a decade or more earlier still represented his essential view of the subject. So the notion that his thinking had evolved dramatically or that once on the Supreme Court, he would take a more measured approach seemed contradictory and opportunistic. As Kate Michelman of the National Abortion Rights Action League put it, "he can't in forty-eight hours undo thirty years of legal reasoning. He is recasting his philosophy because he knows he has to win confirmation. It's simply not believable."

The most dramatic example was in the area of free speech. The Constitution's First Amendment says, in part, "Congress shall make no law . . . abridging the freedom of speech. . . ." A complex question regarding that freedom is whether speech should be seen exclusively as a means toward an end—such as informed self-government—or whether it can be considered an end in itself, a self-expression or self-realization that is integral to a free, creative society. Increasingly, especially since the 1960s, Americans have taken the latter view. Being free to express ourselves allows us to grow not only as participants in democracy but as individuals. Moreover, protecting unpopular speech is a relatively low-cost method of promoting tolerance, a key virtue in a diverse society.

Bork rejected that view. He argued that free speech was an integral part of the democratic process and should be protected only to the extent that it promotes that process. This was a major pillar of Bork's majoritarian edifice: Liberties that enhance rule by majority merit protection, but liberties that threaten it need not.

In his 1971 *Indiana Law Journal* article, Bork stated: "Constitutional protection should be accorded only to speech that is explicitly political. There is no basis for judicial intervention to protect any other form of expression, be it scientific, literary or that variety of expression we call obscene or pornographic. Moreover, within that category of speech we ordinarily call political, there should be no constitutional obstruction to laws making criminal any speech that advocates forcible overthrow of the government or the violation of any law."

Bork reasoned that since the Constitution guarantees a republican form of government, citizens must be free to discuss and to write about political figures and issues. In other words, free speech concerning political matters flowed directly from the structure and functions of the government the framers created.

But there it ended. To throw constitutional protection around forms of expression that did not directly feed the democratic process had no rationale. Art and literature may have an effect upon the political process, he figured, but no more so than other human activities such as sports or business. No one would argue that sports and business were covered by the First Amendment. Why should poetry be?

As he said in the 1971 article, "The notion that all valuable types of speech must be protected by the first amendment confuses the constitutionality of laws with their wisdom. Freedom of non-political speech rests, as does freedom for other valuable forms of behavior, upon the enlightenment of society and its elected representatives. That is hardly a terrible fate."

Since only discourse that added to the democratic process deserved protection, calls for illegal action—especially for the overthrow of the government—would not enjoy constitutional protection.

Bork's early theories on speech were intriguing. But in the American legal tradition they were radical and reactionary. They took speech protection back to a previous generation, when people were locked up for advocating antigovernment positions. Most Americans of the 1980s took for granted that government could not interfere with most speech that attacks government policy. Yet it was a right of relatively recent vintage. Throughout the nineteenth and early twentieth centuries, the Supreme Court often declined to protect controversial speech. In 1911, for example, the Court upheld a libel conviction against a newspaper for statements critical of the president and secretary of war, and it affirmed a court order enjoining a union from stating that a company was on its "We don't patronize" list.

In the infamous *Abrams* case of 1919, five Russian Jewish immigrants were jailed for up to twenty years for their opposition to American intervention in the Russian Revolution. They had dropped from a building onto New York's Lower East Side leaflets denouncing the American role. The leaflets exhorted workers to "Wake Up!" and to "spit in the face of the lying, hypocritical, military propaganda." They referred to President Wilson as "his Majesty" and called for a general strike to prevent ordnance shipments to anti-Soviet forces. The high court upheld their convictions. One of the five died in prison, possibly during interrogation.

In 1925 the Supreme Court allowed the conviction of Benjamin Gitlow for publishing a virulent left-wing paper; in 1927 the Court agreed with the jailing of Anna Whitney for her participation in a meeting of the Communist Labor Party Convention. The meeting had adopted a platform urging revolutionary unionism over Whitney's objections.

In the 1940s and early 1950s, faced with anti-Communist legislation severely curtailing free expression, the high court did little. Only under pressure from the civil rights movement did the Court uphold citizens' First Amendment rights to picket and hold sit-ins.

Thus Bork's theories seemed all the more threatening; not long before, his view had been ascendant. Bork knew he was preaching sacrilege; indeed, he readily acknowledged it. But he said that was where "neutral principles" led him. It was that combination of boldness and inexorable logic which made Bork an exhilarating scholar to some and a political danger to others.

Seven years after the *Indiana Law Journal* article, Bork repeated his views on free speech protection in a talk at the University of Michigan. In that speech, as in the Indiana article, Bork attacked a 1969 Supreme Court decision which summed up current legal doctrine on speech protection. That decision, *Brandenburg* v. *Ohio*, stated that "the constitutional guarantees of free speech and free press do not permit a State to forbid or proscribe advocacy of the use of force or of law violation except where such advocacy is directed to inciting or producing imminent lawless action and is likely to incite or produce such action."

The defendant in the case was the leader of twelve hooded Ku Klux Klan members who gathered with firearms to burn a cross and condemn "niggers" and Jews. The Klan leader said: "If our president, our congress, our Supreme Court, continues to suppress the white, Caucasian race, it's possible that there might have to be some revengeance [*sic*] taken." That leader had been arrested under an Ohio law that had been used for generations against syndicalists. The Supreme Court overturned his conviction and the law.

The key to the decision was the notion of imminence, a recasting of the famous "clear and present danger" test used by Justice Oliver Wendell Holmes, Jr., in his dissent to the 1919 *Abrams* case. People could advocate hate and violence, the Court said, as long as their speech was unlikely to lead to imminent action.

Bork said in 1978 that the decision was fundamentally flawed because it protected speech advocating the destruction of democratic government. He said such speech was typically used to recruit people for terrorist or underground activity, and there was no reason it should be protected.

In 1984 Bork did retract, sort of, the most controversial aspect of his earlier theory of speech. Responding to an article that referred to his 1971 views, he said he had abandoned the idea that only explicitly political speech was protected by the First Amendment. He wrote that he had "long since concluded that many other forums of discourse, such as moral and scientific debate, are central to a democratic government and deserve protection. I have repeatedly stated this position in my classes."

This retraction, if succinct, seemed incomplete and altogether curious. It made no reference to art or literature and again linked the protection of the freedom of speech to its contribution to democratic government. Bork did not mention the protection of the advocacy of illegal acts. Moreover, two years before, at his confirmation hearings to become a federal judge, he repeated that his 1971 article was correct. He allowed, nonetheless, that he would follow Supreme Court precedent rather than his own theory on the bench.

Bork's restricted view of First Amendment protection was a spur to his opposition. Groups such as the American Civil Liberties Union and Public Citizen made much of that concern.

Senator Leahy, a liberal Democrat, took a special interest in the First Amendment question; he pursued it closely on the second day of hearings. It seemed clear to him that Bork had moved in his views on the subject. Where did Bork stand now?

"I have expanded to where I am about where the current Supreme Court is," Bork replied, causing a quiet stir in the room. A minute later what he said was still more surprising: "The Supreme Court has come to the Brandenburg position—which is okay; it is a good position. . . ."

Leahy, taken aback, asked if Bork really accepted the *Brandenburg* ruling. Bork said he did. Leahy asked him if he had ever before stated publicly that acceptance. Bork said he had not. By way of explanation, Bork then quoted Benjamin Franklin on the constitutional convention two hundred years earlier: "[H]aving lived long, I have experienced many instances of being obliged by better information or fuller consideration to change opinions, even on important subjects which I once thought right, but found to be otherwise. It is therefore that the older I grow, the more apt I am to doubt my own judgment and to pay more respect to the judgment of others."

It was a touching and apt quote but unconvincing to many who watched.

Senator Arlen Specter of Pennsylvania was the next questioner. He said he was so surprised by Bork's answers to Leahy he wanted to pursue the issue despite plans to discuss other topics. As he put it, if Bork had really moved to the current Supreme Court view on free speech, "I think these confirmation hearings may be very brief indeed."

Bork said he had indeed done so.

In the anti-Bork war room, where the proceedings were monitored by television, there was agitation. Bill Taylor and Eric Schnapper, both lawyers with long experience at such hearings, understood that something crucial was occurring. Actually they had expected Bork's shift, thinking it unlikely that the nominee would hold fast to all his controversial positions. But they disagreed over what to make of the move on *Brandenburg* and on subsequent questions. Schnapper felt the change should be emphasized because senators showed least patience with inconsistency and any appearance of dissembling. Taylor felt it was important to show that on the fundamental issues Bork had not really changed, that he was as vehemently conservative as his writings made him appear. In the end there was room for both arguments, and both were made.

Schnapper put together a sheet contrasting Bork's previous statements on *Brandenburg* with what he said that day at the hearings. His comparison was brandished during the subsequent break by liberal lobbyists, who held impromptu press conferences expressing outrage over the apparent shift. Senators Leahy and Metzenbaum said that along with Bork's extreme conservatism, a new problem was arising: credibility. The next night Schnapper stayed up till 5:00 A.M. drafting a booklet comparing a number of Bork's positions before and during the hearings. He called it "Bork vs. Bork." The press ate it up.

When the session resumed, Senator Heflin said it seemed that Bork shifted his position only when a carrot was held in front of him. Bork and his supporters bristled at the suggestion. He explained his intellectual development and demonstrated that he had undergone numerous shifts when there was nothing to be gained. He complained that he was first under attack for being rigid and now for being flexible. No matter what he said, it seemed, he would be assailed.

But there *was* a legitimate question here. Days earlier the Justice Department had issued a book titled *A Response to the Critics of Judge Robert H. Bork.* In it Bork was described as rejecting a major part of the *Brandenburg* ruling. "Judge Bork," it said, "does not believe that the first amendment protects those groups—the Ku Klux Klan, Nazis or Weathermen—who would supplant our constitutional democracy with a pernicious form of totalitarian rule that forsakes the rights and freedoms of all citizens." Perhaps Judge Bork did not believe that. But the Supreme Court did. And if Bork did believe it, why had both so many promoters and detractors got it wrong? The answer: Bork had not changed his mind at all. Upon further questioning, Bork's modification was itself remodified.

Asked by Thurmond the next day to discuss *Brandenburg* again, Bork said: "I have not changed my mind about what I said upon this subject. I could have accepted a First Amendment law that developed the way I thought in 1971 it ought to have from the beginning. . . . The law did not develop that way. It developed to require a closer nexus between the advocacy and the violent action. . . . That is a change in the thing, but it does not involve me changing my mind at all. . . . As an academic, I thought that was not theoretically justified. As a judge, I accept it, and that is all there is to that."

Other questions nailed it down. Liberals had complained that under Bork's theory, Martin Luther King, Jr., would have been subject to arrest for advocating civil disobedience. Leahy asked Bork about that. Bork replied that King was advocating the disobedience so as to test the constitutionality of a law. Bork reasoned that if the

law proved to be unconstitutional, then King's speech was protected.

But, Leahy protested, what if the law proved to be fine? Would
King still be protected for advocating disobedience to it? Bork said
he did not know. The point was that for Bork, you could advocate
an illegal act if the law you wanted to break turned out to be unconstitutional. But who could know in advance? What kind of protection was that? The whole idea of protecting speech was to protect
unpopular ideas.

Bork still thought speech should be protected only if it fed the
democratic process and still thought *Brandenburg* was wrong. But as
a high court nominee and judge he now said he would accept the
ruling as law. His years of advocacy for a distinctly different approach to the First Amendment were dismissed as insignificant.

Bork's contradictory testimony on free speech also represented
another lost opportunity. He failed to spell out what was objectionable to those on the right—and some on the left—about current
Supreme Court doctrine regarding protected speech. Ray Randolph, Bork's friend who was acting as his counsel through the
process, said afterward that Bork should have looked Specter in the
eye and said to the Jewish legislator: "Senator, we are talking about
men with guns and knives under their gowns calling for the exter-
mination of Jews and blacks. Is that really the kind of speech we
want to protect in our society? Do you honestly believe that if a
community forbids such speech, the First Amendment has been
violated?"

The Court had not always insisted that hate advocacy was protected under the First Amendment. Throughout the 1940s and 1950s
the Court distinguished between speech that was protected and
speech that was not. Its clearest expression of that was in a 1942 case,
in which a unanimous Court ruled that certain classes of speech
were not protected. The Court upheld a conviction of a Jehovah's
Witness for calling a city marshal a "damned fascist" and "God
damned racketeer." It discussed unprotected speech, saying: "These
include the lewd and obscene, the profane, the libelous, and the
insulting or 'fighting' words—those which by their very utterance
inflict injury or tend to incite an immediate breach of the peace."
The Court said such utterances "are no essential part of any exposi-
tion of ideas, and are of such slight social value" as to be outweighed
by "the social interest in order and morality."

In the 1960s much changed as the Court moved away from such a two-tiered system and insisted that it had no role in protecting certain values over others. In 1969 it protected the private possession of obscene materials, saying that the "right to receive information and ideas, regardless of their social worth, is fundamental to our free society." In cases of the early 1970s the Court essentially got rid of exemptions such as the one under which the Jehovah's Witness had been convicted.

Such decisions were a vital part of the changing American society in the late 1960s. They gave protesters against the Vietnam War and advocates of alternative life-styles the right to express themselves more freely. In a 1973 Indiana case the Court overturned the conviction of an antiwar protester who shouted, "We'll take the fucking street later." In a 1971 free speech case a protester in California was arrested for wearing a jacket in a court hallway bearing the phrase "Fuck the draft." The Supreme Court overturned his conviction. In an opinion that superbly reflected the era, conservative Justice John Marshall Harlan declared: "One man's vulgarity is another man's lyric." Harlan also stated the liberal credo of speech in that opinion. He said free expression meant "putting the decision as to what views shall be voiced largely into the hands of each of us, in the hope that use of such freedom will ultimately produce a more capable citizenry and more perfect polity and in the belief that no other approach would comport with the premise of individual dignity and choice upon which our political system rests."

To those who came of age intellectually and politically in the sixties, such growth in free speech doctrine was crucial. To protect only the speech favored by the government—even local government—was dangerous. Unorthodox viewpoints would get lost. If that meant allowing a few crazed Nazi and KKK members their rights to preach hatred, it was a risk worth taking. Faith in the people meant faith that the vast majority would reject such rubbish. And inherent in our system was the notion of maximum self-expression.

Bork and other conservatives strongly objected. To them the sixties were where America went wrong. They said values of democracy and community needed to be officially promoted by the government and the courts. If the people are free, they should have the freedom to decide as a group to ban speech they consider dangerous or obscene. Must expressions of racism be protected in order for all speech to be protected? Bork did not think so. The "slippery slope" that worried liberals left him unconcerned.

A famous example of this issue was the 1978 march on Skokie, Illinois, by a group of Nazis. Skokie's large percentage of Jewish Holocaust survivors persuaded the town to pass a law banning demonstrations by hate groups. The American Civil Liberties Union came to the aid of the Nazis with an ACLU official proclaiming the liberal credo "Free speech exists in the most extreme cases or it doesn't exist at all."

The federal appellate court in Chicago rejected the Skokie law and allowed the march. The court said that the government must treat all speech with neutrality and that the state can no more restrict a Nazi rally in Skokie than it can stop a civil rights march in Birmingham.

Bork himself addressed the Skokie case in his 1978 Michigan speech: "The fundamental issue raised by Skokie is not the affront to the Jewish citizens there, though that is serious enough; it is whether a creed of that sort ought to be allowed to find voice anywhere in America."

Here was a trenchant critique of modern liberalism: If government recoils from making value choices, then erosion will destroy the societal cohesion produced by shared beliefs. This was a concern on the right but also of some political and legal theorists to the left of liberalism. So-called communitarians on the left were eager to reinstate the possibility of communal unity through shared values. They believed that liberalism had failed. For courts to tell a community that it has no right to ban racist demonstrations only adds to a feeling of powerlessness and alienation of many Americans. Citizens' efforts to take control of their lives and environments were further undercut by the growing power of courts and bureaucracies. No wonder so many Americans dropped out of the political process, they said. No wonder fewer Americans voted than in any other industrialized country.

Bork might have made those points at the hearings.

But he did not. He said only that he had previously been worried that if such speech were allowed, it could actually prevail, a far less potent point that trivializes the issue. He said that to Leahy when he was explaining why he had opposed *Brandenburg* but had subsequently come to accept it. In criticizing the decision, he was thinking of pre-Nazi Germany, where wild men stood on street corners advocating the overthrow of the government and no one took them seriously.

As part of his backtracking, he then added: "I now think that this society is not susceptible to that, even in its worst days, and I also think that the First Amendment says we will take that chance."

The last statement was at best disingenuous. As Bork stated the next day, he had not changed his theory on protecting antidemocratic speech. He did not believe the First Amendment said anything of the kind.

This sort of waffling earned Bork the contempt of some fervent admirers. After three and a half days of Bork's testimony, Bruce Fein, former Justice Department official and Heritage Foundation scholar, said the nominee's performance had been "a magnificent triumph for the liberals. The basic message sent by the hearings so far is that the courts are about where they should be, that no great changes are needed. Bork is bending his views to improve his confirmation chances and it's a shame." Fein said one of the important aims of the hearings and of getting Bork on the Court was to send a message to lower courts regarding the need to pull back from the "activist" work of the Supreme Court of recent years. "But now you are not going to have any kind of dramatic pronounced impact even if Bork is confirmed because the impression he is giving is that things are all right in the judiciary. It dramatically diminishes the effect of confirming him."

Richard Viguerie, the direct-mail entrepreneur and conservative fund raiser, lamented that Bork and the administration were "missing a big opportunity to get a message across. Since when do conservatives want to fight and bleed and die to get moderates on the Supreme Court? Who cares about moderates? . . . He is running from the issues."

And Pat Robertson, the television evangelist running for the Republican presidential nomination, said that Bork had "gone before the television cameras and said he is in the mainstream and wouldn't do anything different from anybody else. . . . Some people are wondering why they should go to the mat for him."

Another key question—and another area of Bork modification—was the constitutional protection of women. Here again, the Court's decisions since about 1970 reflected fundamental changes in society.

And here again, Bork had bitterly attacked those decisions.

For nearly two centuries the Supreme Court had routinely upheld state or federal laws that discriminated against women. Nothing so jars modern ears as to read those decisions. Nothing so illustrates how Supreme Court rulings routinely mirror their era.

In 1873 the Court upheld an Illinois law forbidding women to practice law. A woman who was a leading legal editor had sought that right and was turned down. A concurring opinion by Justice Joseph P. Bradley read, in part: "The natural and proper timidity and delicacy which belongs [sic] to the female sex evidently unfits [sic] it for many of the occupations of civil life. . . . [The] paramount destiny and mission of woman are to fulfill the noble and benign offices of wife and mother. This is the law of the Creator." In 1908 the Court upheld an Oregon statute limiting the hours women were permitted to work, saying: "That woman's physical structure and the performance of maternal functions place her at a disadvantage in the struggle for subsistence is obvious. . . ."

In 1948, while claiming to recognize the "vast changes in the social and legal position of women," the Court nonetheless upheld a state statute prohibiting the licensing of women as bartenders, excepting wives or daughters of the male owners of the bars in which they would work. And as late as 1961 the Court unanimously upheld a Florida statute which included men on the jury list unless they requested an exemption, but exempted women unless they volunteered. The Court said that the "enlightened emancipation of women" notwithstanding, the state's classification was reasonable since "woman is still regarded as the center of home and family life."

In 1971 women's liberation was stirring. The Court began to offer women protection from discriminatory attitudes expressed in various laws. It unanimously invalidated an Idaho statute favoring men over women to administer estates of those who had died. In that case the Court alluded briefly to the Equal Protection Clause of the Fourteenth Amendment, one of the anchors of postwar jurisprudence. The relevant portion of the amendment says that no state shall "deprive any person of life, liberty, or property, without due process of law; nor deny to any person within its jurisdiction the equal protection of the laws."

The amendment, ratified in 1868 in the wake of the Civil War, was aimed primarily at protecting freed slaves. But in this century the Court used it to protect corporations, poor voters, aliens, and children born out of wedlock before applying it to women as a group.

Those decisions manifested a view of the Court's role rejected by Bork and the right: The less political power a group has, the more it needs special judicial protection. It was a cardinal principle of liberal legal thinking. To Bork, that took away the majority's right to run its own affairs. To many others, it protected minorities from the tyranny of the majority.

Throughout the 1970s the Court widened equal protection for women. It struck down federal statutes that presumptively provided benefits to military wives but not to military husbands; it invalidated a provision of the Social Security Act awarding survivors' benefits to widows, but not to widowers, responsible for dependent children; and it struck down a Utah law providing for parental support obligations for sons until age twenty-one but for daughters only until age eighteen. In the last case, the Court stated that "a child, male or female, is still a child. No longer is the female destined solely for the home and the rearing of the family, and only the male for the marketplace and the world of ideas."

In 1976 the Court made more explicit how it would apply the Equal Protection Clause to gender discrimination. The clause now was to require three different levels of legal scrutiny: strict scrutiny, intermediate scrutiny, and rationality. These were classifications the Court offered lower courts in deciding whether a state law could pass constitutional muster.

Under only the most compelling circumstances could a law discriminate on the basis of race or national origin. Any law that did so would face "strict scrutiny" to determine its constitutionality. Laws regarding economic discrimination had been and would continue to be examined only to see if they rested on some "rational" basis. That is, did the government or state legislature have any reason for its economic line drawing, as in favoring one business but not another?

Discrimination based on gender was nearly as hard to defend as that based on race, the Court said. Indeed several justices sought to apply a strict scrutiny test to gender discrimination. But they fell one vote short, and a compromise was reached in 1976. The Court acknowledged that there are cases in which gender discrimination may be accepted, such as in filling combat units or in hiring guards for imprisoned male sex offenders. It made clear that it would apply to gender discrimination laws a level of scrutiny "intermediate" between the strict and rational tests. Some referred to this intermediate level as heightened scrutiny.

To Bork, the very use of the Equal Protection Clause for anything other than race contradicted the aims of the framers of the amendment. In his 1971 *Indiana Law Journal* piece he ridiculed the expansion of the amendment to cover a wide variety of nonracial discrimination.

The only thing that could be said with certitude about the Equal Protection Clause, Bork averred, was that "it does require that government not discriminate along racial lines. But much more than that cannot properly be read into the clause." He added that "cases of race discrimination aside, it is always a mistake for the Court to try to construct substantive individual rights under the due process or the Equal Protection Clause." Bork had never publicly varied from that line of thinking. Civil libertarians and liberal women's groups saw this as reason enough to fight him so vigorously. Only weeks before his nomination to the high court, Bork said in an interview broadcast overseas as part of the Constitution's bicentennial: "I think the Equal Protection Clause probably should have been kept to things like race and ethnicity."

At the hearings Bork was asked his view of applying the Equal Protection Clause to women. He said that he was bothered by the groupings and classifications engaged in by the Court—strict scrutiny for one group, intermediate for another—and favored one test to be applied uniformly, a "reasonable basis" test. He argued that use of a reasonable basis would yield about the same results as the method used by the Court.

Bork was saying that the Equal Protection Clause *did* apply to women—a new position—but in a way different from the Court's way. He said that if the Court applied a reasonableness test, nearly all discrimination against women would be seen to be unreasonable and so unenforceable.

No one was sure what to make of this new position. On the one hand, Bork said: "It is much better to proceed under the reasonableness test. . . . Any person is covered. That means everybody is covered, men, women, everybody."

On the other hand, he wanted to use it under a scrutiny the equivalent to the lowest rung on the current ladder—the rational basis. What kind of protection was that? In 1961 the Court had stated, after all, that women were still regarded as the center of home and family life, so a Florida law had been "reasonable." It was not an approach that inspired confidence.

Bork said he called it a "reasonable" as opposed to a "rational" basis to make clear that the test was not the same as the existing third category. He also pointed out that the reasonable test was not his idea but that of Justice John Paul Stevens, who had also expressed discomfort with the current doctrine.

But the distinction between "reasonable" and "rational" was something of an artifice. Bork's new position on equal protection of women was largely cobbled together for him at the Justice Department by Carvin, Reynolds, and Markman. While Bork had long attacked the Court's classifications, he had never worked out an alternative. Faced with the angry accusations of women's and civil liberties groups, he and the legal conservatives at Justice came up with the new position.

It was first presented in Bork's name in the Justice Department book *A Response to the Critics of Judge Robert H. Bork.* The presentation conspicuously lacked quotations from Bork. The reason was simple: There were no quotations; Bork had never before taken that position.

The book stated that, apart from racial discrimination, "[i]n Judge Bork's view, all other classifications should be upheld so long as they are rationally related to a legitimate state interest." Thus it was clear that there was no distinction between the rational and reasonable tests. In Bork's newly articulated view, then, women were indeed covered by the Fourteenth Amendment. But state legislatures would receive greater deference in gender discrimination laws than under current Supreme Court doctrine. He argued that because society had changed so fundamentally in its attitude toward women, legislatures were unlikely to pass discriminatory laws against women. And if they did, the Court would examine whether the law was "reasonable" from the state's point of view. Modern society, he claimed, would view very little in that regard as reasonable.

In answer to Howell Heflin during the second day, Bork pushed a bit unnecessarily in an effort to show flexibility. He suggested that the Equal Protection Clause might be used to uphold abortion, an idea he would have ridiculed mercilessly in other circumstances. He was not overly encouraging of the approach to Heflin, but he said people were working on it, and perhaps they would succeed.

Heflin asked Bork if that approach did not contradict the judge's basic understanding of the Fourteenth Amendment.

"I do not think it is entirely contrary to my constitutional philosophy because I have been saying this morning that the Equal Protection Clause applies to women as well as to men—obviously because it would be ridiculous to say it applies only to men. . . . I would suppose that is where the argument [for abortion] would be built. . . . But I can go no further than that. . . ."

During hearings on a human life bill in 1981, Bork had sung a different song. He said: "Roe vs. Wade is, itself, an unconstitutional decision, a serious and wholly unjustifiable judicial usurpation of state legislative authority." This suggested that under no circumstances did the Court have the power to decide the abortion question.

Bork claimed that reasonableness and intermediate scrutiny would end up with the same results. He said that by contemporary lights, nearly all discrimination against women was unreasonable and would therefore be banned by the Court.

But his critics said the way the Court had used the rational basis test for the past century was not very encouraging. As Laurence Tribe of Harvard said later, the rational test almost never was used to strike down state laws. The state always gave a reason for the discrimination. The point of the rational basis test was to grant deference to the reasoning of the state legislatures, not the opposite.

Of course, Bork's entire philosophy rested on deference to the legislature, which was the point of the rational basis test. He was saying that while he had no objection to reversing gender discrimination, it should come from the legislative, not the judicial, process. That was how democracy worked. As he asked rhetorically in a Catholic University speech in 1982, why should courts be "entitled to tell the legislature their moral judgments are really prejudices and that their perceptions of social reality are skewed?"

That was why he had opposed the Equal Rights Amendment, a failed 1970s effort to enshrine equality for women explicitly in the Constitution. In a speech at the time Bork said: "The desire for judicial government is dramatically illustrated by the proposed Equal Rights Amendment. It would confirm the courts in their worst tendencies by handing them, without legislative guidance of any sort, the task of making the infinite number of political decisions required in deciding when men and women must be treated alike, when they need not be, and, perhaps, when they may not be. The fact that the courts have already started down that path on their own is no reason to legitimize it."

For liberals, gender discrimination, like racial discrimination, would not be overcome without the active involvement of the courts. The Constitution promised equal protection. The courts had a right and a duty to ensure it throughout the country. Relying on those in power to share that power voluntarily was unrealistic and unnecessary. The judiciary existed precisely to make sure the broad principles of the Constitution were not trampled upon by the political process.

As Patrick Leahy said on the fourth day of hearings:

> You know, democracy is a terrible system of government except it is the best we have. . . . Take the average person. They see a legislature that may go off and do quirky things for whatever political reasons, whether it is the national legislature or a state legislature. And they see an executive perhaps indifferent to their wishes as they see them, and so they always look to that one body, the Court, that seems more independent than the other two put together, less swayed by the passions of politics or the passions of the moment, and they go to them.

Some of the people Leahy referred to were watching these proceedings with interest. In offices and homes around the country, television sets and radios were tuned to the Bork hearings; from Dallas to Seattle to Pittsburgh, groups gathered to send letters and jam Capitol telephone lines. At noontime, lawyers in Providence, Rhode Island, set up tables to gather signatures of those opposed to Bork. In Montgomery, Alabama, representatives of seventeen groups for blacks, women, and labor unions gathered hands at a press conference on the third day of the hearings to urge the Senate to reject Bork. Every day of Bork's testimony the Alabama New South Coalition ran advertisements around the state saying, in part: "The Reagan administration has fired a parting shot of contempt for the rights of minorities and women in the nomination of Robert H. Bork. . . ." The ads included the phone numbers and addresses of Alabama's two senators, Howell Heflin of the Judiciary Committee and Richard Shelby. Readers were urged to contact the legislators. Many did so. In Philadelphia, on the second day of Bork's testimony, a rally for a workers' bill of rights turned into an anti-Bork demonstration.

Those feeling precisely the opposite were also watching and participating. The Judiciary Committee was flooded with telegrams and letters in support of Bork's confirmation. "Regret Senator Kennedy's demagogery. There is much support for you in Massachusetts and deep personal respect," said a telegram from Needham, Massachusetts. "You are a giant surrounded by pigmies. Stand firm," said another from Kilgore, Texas, and addressed simply: "Judge Robert Bork, Washington, D.C. "Take courage that you enjoy far more support than news media admit. . . . Pay no heed to the humiliation to which you will be subjected nor to the manifold gratuitous insults that will be offered," said another from Miami, Florida. And from Greenville, South Carolina: "The 'splitting of split hairs' appears to be a technique of your adversaries."

Where Bork really stood on free speech and the constitutional protection of women became most significant when examined in light of a third question: the overturning of previous high court decisions. Bork may not have liked the evolution of the free speech doctrine, but did he hope to change it? Bork may have been uncomfortable with intermediate scrutiny, but was he set on revising it?

Reversal was an especially complicated issue because Bork was an advocate of judicial restraint, a theory that traditionally meant courts ought not to move boldly, leaving that to the democratic process. But Bork also championed originalism—that is, the intent of the framers of the Constitution ought to guide the law. More than once Bork averred that a wrong decision needed to be overturned so as not to continue to breed other bad decisions. So while he favored incremental change by the Court, he also seemed to advocate monumental shifts.

Only three months before his nomination Bork spoke to the Philadelphia Society of a new wave of originalist judges and scholars who would rid the nation of the bad, nonoriginalist law that had been put into place.

"It may take ten years, it may take twenty years, for the second wave to crest, but crest it will and it will sweep the elegant, erudite, pretentious, and toxic detritus of non-originalism out to sea," he said with characteristic vigor that evening.

A few months before that, at a meeting of conservative law professors and students in a group known as the Federalist Society, Bork had said: "An originalist judge would have no problem whatever in overruling a non-originalist precedent because that precedent, by the very basis of his judicial philosophy, has no legitimacy."

And in 1985 in an interview with the *District Lawyer,* Bork was asked if he could identify cases that should be reconsidered. He said, "Yes I can, but I won't."

Yet one theme ran through all of Bork's remarks at the hearings: Overturning precedent must not be done lightly. He had often said that nothing but adherence to the framers mattered. In his opening statement he said something very different: "The past, however, includes not only the intentions of those who first made the law, it also includes those past judges who interpreted and applied it in prior cases. That is why a judge must give great respect to precedent. It is one thing as a legal theorist to criticize the reasoning of a prior decision, even to criticize it severely, as I have done. It is another and more serious thing altogether for a judge to ignore or overturn a prior decision. That requires much careful thought."

The very first question asked of Bork at the hearings had concerned the role of precedent, known in law as *stare decisis* (let the decision stand). Biden asked the judge which cases he thought should be reconsidered. Bork said he could not name them without going back to casebooks but added that two examples of the kinds of decisions that could not be undone were those relating to the Commerce Clause and legal tender.

The first category, the Commerce Clause decisions, referred to the New Deal Court's having vastly expanded the power of Congress after 1937 to regulate interstate activities. The expansion was based on the phrase in the Constitution's first article granting Congress the authority to "regulate Commerce . . . among the several States." The second reference, to legal tender, had to do with the fact that the framers apparently intended to prohibit paper money.

Both examples were trivial. Virtually no judge or serious scholar in the country would have advocated overturning either one. They served Bork as uncontroversial examples of law that was nonoriginalist but too established to overturn. Yet they provided little comfort to liberals who feared Bork would seek to overturn numerous civil rights and privacy decisions.

When asked by Thurmond what his criteria would be for overturning a decision, Bork said he would examine whether institutions and expectations had grown up around the decision because "there is a need for stability and continuity in the law. There is a need for predictability in legal doctrine."

The daring iconoclast who had heralded sweeping the "toxic detritus of non-originalism out to sea" suddenly sounded like a cautious clerk.

On the afternoon of the fourth day Kennedy asked Bork about his attitude toward precedent. He had a tape recording of a speech Bork had made at a college in 1985 at which the judge had dismissed the importance of the Court's respecting precedent. The tape had been sent to Kennedy by a member of a gay group. There was disagreement among the Democrats: Should it be played? One Kennedy aide feared it would look like a cheap trick, as if Bork were being sandbagged. Biden expressed the same concern. Nothing was more important to him than to appear to be treating Bork fairly. All agreed that Bork should have a transcript of the recording in advance. No one could accuse the Democrats of playing unfairly.

When Kennedy brought up the tape, Biden immediately intervened and asked Bork whether he had seen a transcript of the recording. Bork said yes.

But that did nothing to reduce the drama of hearing the man's deep baritone ring through the Caucus Room as he and the committee sat and listened: "I don't think that in the field of constitutional law precedent is all that important. . . . If you become convinced that a prior court has misread the Constitution, I think it's your duty to go back and correct it. . . . I don't think precedent is all that important. I think the importance is what the framers were driving at, and to go back to that."

Bork did little to explain the statement except to protest that it was an off-the-cuff reply after a dinner speech. In all prepared remarks in his life, he said, he included the idea that some law was too entrenched to uproot even if it was wrong in origin.

When asked if the privacy cases—those beginning with the 1965 *Griswold* decision on contraceptives and including the abortion ruling—were too entrenched to be overturned, Bork demurred. He said it would be inappropriate to comment.

Once again, Bork was modifying a previous stand. And yet just how?

CHAPTER

12

Intellectual Feast

On occasion, during the Bork hearings, constitutional debate was superseded by efforts to impugn Bork's decency. On the third day Vermont's Patrick Leahy asked Bork why he had never performed any free legal service for the needy, what lawyers call *pro bono* work. Bork replied that when he was in private practice in the late 1950s, his firm did not do much of it and his specialty, antitrust, would have been of little use. Leahy challenged him, saying that a man of Bork's talent could have done much to help those in need of legal aid.

Leahy was here engaged in a high-wire act. Since his unexpected Senate victory in 1974 he had been precariously balanced as a liberal in a largely conservative state. While Vermont was beginning to lean farther left, Leahy felt he needed cover for a negative vote on Bork. Never comfortable with a confirmation vote based on ideology, Leahy sought to challenge the nominee's commitment to equal justice.

Patrick Leahy was a tall, bespectacled, and balding man of kindly manner. He looked older than his forty-seven years, and he took comfort in returning frequently to his Middlesex farm and invoking to great rhetorical effect his simple Vermont roots. His Senate office was one of the most understated on Capitol Hill. While other lawmakers packed their walls with gawdy trinkets from their states and innumerable photographs of themselves with world leaders, Leahy's was the essence of New England diffidence. He had but one small family portrait on a table. A discreet étagère with antique crockery stood demurely in an office corner. A guileless print of a cat and dog hung on one wall; a small wooden sled, on another. The decoration reflected the man—charming and unpretentious.

But that afternoon Leahy shed his affable manner and badgered Bork, falling into a style of questioning he had perfected as a county prosecutor. His interrogation was so aggressively repetitive that Biden interrupted at one point, saying, "Senator, I think he's answered that question."

Leahy said he pursued that line of questioning because he feared Bork was out of touch with ordinary people, that he lacked compassion. An absence of *pro bono* work was evidence of that.

When Leahy finished, an angered Gordon Humphrey, Republican of New Hampshire, asked Biden to grant him two minutes. A former commercial pilot, Humphrey was on the Senate's right-wing flank, an unyielding antiabortion advocate and promoter of the anti-Soviet Afghan rebels. A man who never shied from using colorful language, Humphrey was a kind of polar opposite to Leahy, emblematic of rugged, rough-and-tumble New Hampshire as Leahy was of serene Vermont.

Humphrey resented the way the White House had chosen to portray Bork as a moderate, saying afterward: "I think we ought to frankly acknowledge that the philosophy of judges enters unavoidably into their decisions."

A forty-six-year-old loner in the Senate, Humphrey was known even to sympathetic Justice Department officials as a loose cannon. In late 1988 Humphrey had to apologize to a Republican congressional candidate in his state for saying she had no business running for public office because she had two young daughters and ought to stay home and care for them.

He was also notorious for spending his days in a small, windowless office deep inside the Capitol building staring at a bank of computer terminals—like an airplane console—listening to tapes of classical music, communicating with his staff through computer messages.

He constantly accused Bork's opponents of shameful tactics; the Leahy line of questioning was, for him, a perfect example. Granted the two minutes, Humphrey went through Bork's nearly four years in the Marines, his twenty-four years of teaching and public service, all at modest pay, and asked how anyone could possibly fault Bork for not performing *pro bono* work. He had an excellent point.

Leahy had to defend himself. Glancing down Bork's history of earnings, he interjected that he noticed something about Bork's income that perhaps the senator from New Hampshire had overlooked. He said that in 1979 Bork had made nearly $200,000 in consulting fees, in 1980 nearly $300,000, and in 1981 around $150,000. Perhaps the nominee was not so selfless after all.

Bork's face went red. He looked down and then said those were the only years he had done consulting work. "And there was a reason why I did it and I do not want to go into it here."

Suddenly Leahy understood that he had committed an unspeakably cruel gaffe. Those were the years Claire Bork had been struggling valiantly with cancer; Bork had been forced to earn money to pay her medical bills. Leahy tried to recover, saying that he fully understood and that no one doubted the legitimacy of the fees.

But Humphrey, never a man of subtlety, wanted the point made explicitly and asked: "Were those years, in which you were engaged in outside employment, years which coincided with heavy medical bills in your family?"

Bork, nearly inaudible, said: "Yes." He placed his flushed face in his hands and rubbed his eyes. Thomas Korologos, the White House lobbyist, sitting behind Bork, twisted his wrists. That was the signal he and Biden had agreed upon to request a break. The chairman complied. Bork and his family went out to a balcony overlooking the street. The judge drew slowly on a cigarette. Nobody spoke.

It was already late in the afternoon at that stage, and the Bork team members thought that, under the circumstances, perhaps they could call it a day. Bork seemed so rattled by the reminder of Claire Bork that it seemed better to stop. In addition, the next questioner was Arlen Specter, Republican of Pennsylvania, who seemed to enjoy nitpicking at constitutional arguments. Specter was asked if he would be willing to wait until the next day. He refused. He said he was sorry Bork had been asked an unpleasant question, but he was prepared to go and wanted to do so. Biden gave his go-ahead.

Specter had missed most of that day's session because he had flown with Reagan to Philadelphia for the official celebration of the Constitution's bicentennial in the city where the charter had been drafted.

The administration was worried about Specter. He was uncommitted on Bork and had a history of independence and liberalism that made his vote far from certain. He had voted for Rehnquist, but he had opposed Manion and several others. When the opportunity arose for him and Reagan to go to Philadelphia together, the men at Justice realized it would be a fine opportunity for the president to engage in a little pro-Bork lobbying. In fact, while Bork and his family stood on the balcony that afternoon, John Bolton took a call from Brad Reynolds at the department, who told him that Reagan had lobbied Specter hard on the trip and came back with encouraging results.

Nothing could have been farther from the truth.

During the Philadelphia celebrations Specter was seated next to Reagan. Specter's senior colleague from Pennsylvania, Senator John Heinz, brought to the podium a beautiful young black girl, who was about nine years old. She asked Reagan about Bork, saying she was concerned that the judge would not protect her civil rights. The surprised president leaned down and with a smile, put his hand on the girl's shoulders, and replied: "I'm sure Judge Bork will protect the rights of blacks, and the rights of everyone, and I wouldn't have nominated him if I didn't think so." Then Reagan turned to Specter and said: "Did you hear that, Arlen?"

"Yes, Mr. President."

That was it. Reagan never mentioned Bork to Specter before or after. When Bolton went up to Specter and confidently asked about his trip with Reagan, the senator said, "You know, it was very surprising. I would have thought he would talk about the nomination, but he hardly mentioned it."

That evening, as the Bork team gathered in Will Ball's White House office for its nightly assessment of the hearings, Reynolds told everyone that the president had lobbied Specter and Heinz and that reports were that it had gone very well. Bolton, caught again between a ballooning sense of doom and the need to show deference to his superiors, said he had heard a somewhat different story.

Whatever lobbying Reagan might have done would probably have been useless. Specter, whose large nose and ample jowls gave him a passing resemblance to Richard Nixon, was a profoundly stubborn man. Born to immigrant Jews in Kansas, a graduate of the University of Pennsylvania and Yale Law School, Specter took great pride in his intellectual and political independence. It was his opposition, for example, that made the difference in stopping the confirmation of Brad Reynolds to the post of associate attorney general. He had also opposed the MX missile in 1985, dismissing White House threats to cut off fund-raising help for his 1986 reelection campaign. Ultimately he voted for the MX but then announced he would not have Reagan help him raise campaign funds.

Specter, fifty-seven, was one of the most dogged men in the Senate. He had lost several races in Pennsylvania for mayor, governor, and senator before winning the Senate seat he so coveted in 1980. His victory was won through sheer unrelenting effort. As one reporter recalled, Specter knew he would beat Democrat Pete Flaherty that year. It was a simple question of toil. The reporter paraphrased Specter's analysis as follows: "He was going to win it, and he knew he was going to win it, and the reason he was going to win it was because Flaherty didn't want it enough. He wasn't willing to take that extra flight to Altoona, to shave a second time each day."

Specter had built his reputation as a tough public prosecutor in Philadelphia. In Washington that past was often on display. He was a frightfully hard-nosed interrogator at Senate hearings, and he took great pride in his mastery of detail. He had spent the entire summer reading Bork's articles and speeches and, by season's end, knew their tone and content better than anyone else in the Senate. Although his skilled staff helped out, he sought little guidance from academics. He had a nearly hubristic sense of his own constitutional learning.

That Thursday afternoon Specter began a line of questioning that would continue the next day and culminate in an extraordinary Saturday session. His exchanges with Bork were exhilarating in their scope and nuance. He pressed Bork on free speech, equal protection, and original intent. It was his questioning, more than anyone else's, that lent the hearings the feel of high-minded constitutional debate. Friday evening, when it was clear that Bork's testimony could not be finished that day, Biden decided there would have to be a Saturday session. He went around asking senators how much time, if any, they wanted the next day. Heflin said he needed about five more minutes, Kennedy wanted another ten. Specter wanted an hour and a half. When Thurmond heard that, he went up to Specter and said, "Arlen, what's this I hear about your wanting an hour and a half?"

Specter said, "I'm glad you're raising that because I'm not sure an hour and a half is enough."

Thurmond grumbled, "Okay, okay, take your hour and a half." And Specter was right. Toward the end of his questioning he was forced to hurry. It was clear he could have used at least the same amount of time again.

Specter's exchanges with Bork focused first on the question of the Constitution as a living and growing charter. Specter was intrigued by the fact that Bork had stated in an opinion that executive power was supposed to evolve under the Constitution. He quoted Bork as saying that the Constitution "was to allow room for the evolution of the powers of various offices and branches, that the Constitution's specification of those powers was made somewhat vague. The framers contemplated organic development, not a structure made rigid at the outset by rapid judicial definition of the entire subject as if from a blueprint."

Specter also referred to a recent libel decision of Bork's in which he had said that freedom of the press had to be understood expansively because the framers could not have envisioned the kind of harassment through libel trials characteristic of the late twentieth century. In that case, then Judge Antonin Scalia, who was also on the panel, dissented, saying Bork had abandoned the intent of the framers.

What Specter wanted to know was this: If executive power could undergo organic development, if press freedom had to be interpreted for the modern era, why not the rest of the Bill of Rights? Why not liberty? Why couldn't liberty be an organic concept? Why should judges interpret liberally when faced with the vague concept of press freedom but be held back when confronted with the equally vague concept of liberty?

There was the nub of the constitutional dispute over Robert Bork. He favored a strong executive branch, something clearly opposed by the framers. He championed an expansive view of freedom of the press, also unknown to the founders. If he was willing to see evolution in those areas, why couldn't "liberty" grow and evolve through judicial interpretation as well? If left to expand only through the workings of the majority, as Bork would have liked, those most in need of increased liberty would never get it.

Specter's question on evolving liberty was partly a reference to the volatile issue of constitutional privacy. Bork objected to the

Court's privacy decisions on contraception and abortion because the Court had never defined privacy sufficiently.

The Court's contention that government may not interfere in certain "private" decisions was a product of the 1960s but had its origins in a few isolated early cases. In 1923 it struck down an anti-German Nebraska law forbidding the teaching of foreign languages in elementary schools. The Court said that an individual's right "to acquire useful knowledge, to marry, establish a home and bring up children, to worship God according to the dictates of his own conscience and generally to enjoy these privileges long recognized at common law is essential to the orderly pursuit of happiness by free men."

In 1925 the Court reiterated its message. The Ku Klux Klan exercised enormous influence over the Oregon legislature for two years in that period and successfully lobbied to outlaw all private education in the state, as part of its anti-Catholic bias. The Court struck that down on similar grounds, speaking of parents' right to "direct the upbringing and education of children under their control."

For liberal scholars, the fact that one law was anti-German and the other anti-Catholic demonstrated the need for judicial intervention in such matters. Give the majority the exclusive right to define liberty and minorities suffer.

In 1942 the Court again acted in what was later seen as an antecedent to the privacy doctrine. It struck down an Oklahoma statute requiring that certain repeat criminals but not others be sterilized, holding that it violated the Equal Protection Clause. While such a distinction might have been allowed for lesser penalties, Justice Douglas wrote for a unanimous Court that it could not here. "We are dealing with legislation which involves one of the basic civil rights of man. Marriage and procreation are fundamental to the very existence and survival of the race," he said.

The notion that privacy rights fall within the evolution of liberty was well expressed by Justice John Marshall Harlan in 1961. The occasion was the Court decision not to rule on the Connecticut anticontraceptive law (it did so four years later in *Griswold*), and Harlan, one of the nation's most respected conservative justices, wrote: "This 'liberty' is not a series of isolated points pricked out in terms of the taking of property; the freedom of speech, press and religion; the right to keep and bear arms; the freedom from unreasonable searches and seizures; and so on. It is a rational continuum which, broadly speaking, includes a freedom from all substantial arbitrary impositions and purposeless restraints, . . . and which also recognizes . . . that certain interests require particularly careful scrutiny of the state needs asserted to justify their infringement."

In 1965 the Court struck down the Connecticut law banning the use of contraceptives by married couples. In that decision it first put forth the privacy doctrine over the angry dissent of justices who believed it was a license for the Court to roam at large in the constitutional field. Justice Douglas said privacy was implied by several amendments. Two years later, in striking down a law banning interracial marriage, the Court said that marriage was "one of the basic civil rights of man, fundamental to our very existence and survival."

Privacy, later extended to encompass single people's and minors' rights to purchase contraceptives, was best summed up in 1972 by Justice William Brennan: "If the right of privacy means anything, it is the right of the individual, married or single, to be free from unwarranted governmental intrusion into matters so fundamentally affecting a person as the decision whether to bear or beget a child." The next year the Court decided that privacy "is broad enough to encompass a woman's decision whether or not to terminate her pregnancy."

One of the rationales offered for the privacy right was the Constitution's Ninth Amendment, which states: "The enumeration in the Constitution, of certain rights, shall not be construed to deny or disparage others retained by the people." It was Justice Arthur Goldberg, in his concurrence in the *Griswold* case, who looked to the Ninth Amendment, thereby rescuing it from near obscurity in Supreme Court jurisprudence.

He wrote: "The fact that no particular provision of the Constitution explicitly forbids the State from disrupting the traditional relation of the family—a relation as old and as fundamental as our entire civilization—surely does not show that the Government was meant to have the power to do so. Rather, as the Ninth Amendment expressly recognizes, there are fundamental personal rights such as this one, which are protected from abridgment by the Government though not specifically mentioned in the Constitution."

Even conservative Justice Rehnquist, one of two dissenters to the 1973 *Roe* v. *Wade* abortion decision, which was based on an extension of the privacy doctrine, acknowledged in his dissent that the "liberty" protected by the Fourteenth Amendment "embraces more than the rights found in the Bill of Rights."

Most agree that the Ninth Amendment was put into the Constitution to make clear there were unenumerated rights retained by the people. But using the amendment to define those rights made lawyers and judges nervous because there were no guidelines. Only Justice Goldberg based a decision on it, and that was in concurrence. Other Court mentions of the amendment have been as supportive evidence for other arguments.

Bork had dismissed the amendment on several occasions. He compared it, in effect, with both a water blot and an inkblot on the document of the Constitution. His argument was that if you had no idea how to use it or what it meant, it was no different from a smudge.

For Bork, liberty was a finite commodity, not something that could expand in a cost-free manner. When you used the Fourteenth Amendment to increase the liberty of an individual, you took it away from the group. In other words, if the community was offended by pornography, it could exercise its liberty and ban it. But if the individual was granted the liberty to read pornography or to display it in his shop, then the community's liberty to determine the kind of environment in which it lived was reduced. It was pure arithmetic.

The misty-eyed liberal notion of progress based on the courts' expanding individual liberty was a myth, and a destructive one at that. All that expansion in the name of individuals was sapping the community of its liberty to govern itself as it chose. Bork had no problem stopping the majority where the Constitution specifically instructed. But otherwise it was an illegitimate exercise of judicial power. It was for those reasons that he objected to the privacy doctrine.

Bork had earlier told Biden that in privacy cases where the result was appealing to nearly everyone—a father's right to see his children, a grandmother's right to live with her grandchildren—he would certainly, as a judge, "do my utmost to see if there is a legitimate constitutional ground to uphold that freedom."

But Biden had been quick and clever in response: "I do not doubt that you would attempt to do that. What I doubt is, based on your writings and your cases, whether or not your philosophy of the law and the integrity with which you apply it—and I mean that sincerely—would allow you."

To Specter's question of why liberty was not organic, Bork said there had to be a proper anchor in the Constitution to a right, a guide to how something might evolve. Liberty, he said, was too elastic and vague for judges to apply their views to its evolution. He reminded Specter that there had been a time when judges used the word *liberty* to strike down minimum wage laws and laws regulating the hours of bakers.

Specter said that while of course, the Court could make mistakes, there were well-established expansions of liberty within the American tradition—he cited the privacy cases—and so the evolution was not contourless. Specter referred to decisions which evoked "the conscience of our tradition" and "fundamental considerations of fairness." What bothered him was that Bork seemed selective in choosing which principles could grow and evolve and which were bound by original intent. It appeared as if Bork's selection were based on *his* prejudices.

This was a profound critique of Bork, one made six weeks earlier by New York University Law Professor Ronald Dworkin in an influential article in the *New York Review of Books*. Dworkin said his problem with Bork was not that his judicial philosophy was conservative but that Bork seemed really to have no judicial philosophy at all. Bork, he charged, allowed for broad interpretation of some things but insisted on narrow original intent in other things. The selection was nothing but a thinly veiled New Right political agenda.

Dworkin wrote: "Unless he can produce some genuine argument for his curtailed view of original intention, beyond the fact that it produces decisions he and his supporters approve, his constitutional philosophy is empty: not just impoverished and unattractive, but no philosophy at all."

It was a harsh attack by a man many on the right considered extreme in his own views. Dworkin had nearly the opposite view of judging from Bork. He favored the judiciary's expanding rights for individuals and minorities based on universal moral precepts, precisely the kind of approach for which Bork had reserved his greatest contempt. Dworkin had been a colleague of Bork's at Yale, and their relations had always been cool.

Nonetheless, Dworkin made a powerful point. He took as an example of seeming inconsistency Bork's support for the landmark 1954 school desegregation case, *Brown* v. *Board of Education*. This was one of the most nettlesome cases for proponents of original intent because the decision was based on the Equal Protection

Clause of the Fourteenth Amendment. Nearly all evidence showed that those who had written and passed that amendment in the late 1860s had no intention of integrating the nation's schools, let alone other public places. Even the Senate gallery was racially segregated at the time.

Bork said the framers had thought it possible for racially separate facilities to be equal. We knew with hindsight that they were mistaken—as they were about women's inferiority—and so we were obliged to take the principle they wanted to enshrine and protect it without repeating their error. In other words, to reach "equal," we had to drop "separate." The principle of the amendment, Bork said, was that government may not discriminate on grounds of race.

Dworkin objected. Why not discern a more general principle—that government ought not to discriminate against any minority when the discrimination reflects prejudice? The Equal Protection Clause, after all, did not mention race. Dworkin said that if that were the principle, contemporary judges should protect the rights of homosexuals. Bork had ridiculed constitutional protection for homosexuals as law by judicial fiat and illegitimate since the framers had no such intention.

But, Dworkin said, we knew the framers were mistaken about homosexuals—superstitions regarding them had been exposed and discredited—just as they were about racial segregation and the "natural" role of women. Why not enforce their principle of equality with contemporary wisdom as in those other cases? In other words, said Dworkin, appealing to the framers' intention meant nothing until we decided which level of generality to apply.

Bork had argued that judges must choose "no level of generality higher than that which interpretation of the words, structure, and history of the Constitution fairly supports." Fair enough. But, Dworkin complained, Bork had never really proved that his own interpretation met that test any better than others.

Others attacked Bork's originalism by contending that the framers themselves were not adherents of original intent. If they had wanted future generations to follow original intent, wouldn't they have provided records of their deliberations at the Constitutional Convention? Yet they kept the proceedings secret at the time. It took nearly fifty years for Madison to publish notes reflecting a minuscule portion of debate in the convention itself and none of the talk in the taverns and smoke-filled rooms. Scholars estimate that

Madison was able to take down no more than 7 percent of what was said. Without knowing the words of the Founding Fathers, it was difficult to apply their intent. Moreover, Madison and Hamilton, two key framers, fell into vehement argument within a few years after ratification over the Constitution's allocation of powers in domestic and foreign affairs. If they did not agree, how could we?

Without knowing precise mind-sets, one then must return to the notion of core values and principles. And once again, one faced the difficulty of choosing among competing values enshrined in the Constitution.

At the Saturday session of the hearings Specter carried this line of questioning a step farther. He quoted Bork as having said on three occasions that judicial review—the role of courts as interpreters of the Constitution and laws—was illegitimate if the framers' intent could not be discerned. Specter asked Bork what would happen if a judge came to a point where he was quite certain that determining original intent was impossible. Would it follow that there would be no judicial review in the country?

Bork: "I think you would require a consensus of the people that they wanted judges to rule, even though the judges had no law."

Specter: "There is pretty much that consensus by the tradition of our Court, isn't there?"

Bork: "I do not think so, Senator. I think the American people want judges to interpret the law and not to make it. . . ."

Specter: "Well, I agree with you about that. But the interpretation of the law does not depend upon an understanding of original intent."

Specter reiterated his point that it was entirely unclear whether the original intent of the framers could ever really be known. But there were values rooted in the people and tradition and two hundred years of judging. From those one could continue to apply the Constitution.

Bork replied that he never claimed one could know with great specificity the intent of the framers, but one could take the principle they were seeking to protect and build on that. Judges had to read the many writings and discussions of the era to get a sense of what the framers of a law had intended. That provided a firm starting point. He said he had never advocated "a mechanical way to approach the problem."

Specter was perplexed. "Judge Bork," he said, "as you define it, it does not seem to me that original intent provides any more specificity than the . . . definition of 'rooted in the tradition and history of our society.' "

The framers, Specter went on, could not have known about electronic listening devices, and Bork agreed that judges had to extend search and seizure rights to cover those. But the framers equally could not have known about contraceptive devices. Why, Specter wanted to know, was the doctrine of original intent sacrosanct regarding the specificity of privacy, but not so for other areas?

The room was silent, all listening intently to the intellectual bout. Bork acknowledged for the first time all week that his opponents had a point. "Well, Senator, you are making a very powerful argument from a very strong tradition. I hope, I think what I am saying also comes from a very strong tradition in our constitutional law. . . ."

It seemed Bork was making a genuine concession. But he was not. Ray Randolph, his friend and counselor, had said to him that it might be a good idea to stroke Specter a bit by telling him he was making a powerful argument. Bork agreed and did so.

It did have an effect, however. Specter continued to question Bork for another hour, raising doubts about Bork's opposition to the privatization of morality and egalitarianism. Bork consistently maintained that those views had nothing to do with his job as a judge. Specter accepted that and, in summing up, said: "The hearings present a real opportunity for the senators to tell you what is on their minds, and to tell you what is on the minds of our constituents. . . . And when you talk, as you did, about a powerful argument from a strong tradition, perhaps that will have some influence as you consider some of the doctrines, as you apply them in the future—on the Supreme Court, if confirmed; and on the District of Columbia Court, if you are not confirmed."

Specter told Bork that he had not made up his mind yet on the confirmation, that he was still concerned about Bork's shifts in position. But he said later that he left the hearings that fifth day leaning firmly toward voting for confirmation.

Bolton felt encouraged. He had a sense that Specter had laid the groundwork for voting in Bork's favor by saying, in effect: "I've raised my objections. I've done what I could."

Before the end of that Saturday session Alan Simpson, Republican of Wyoming, would make one final effort for the judge. Throughout the five days, and thirty hours of testimony, Simpson used his rangeland humor and irreverence to attack Bork's enemies and support his candidacy.

Simpson, fifty-six, of Cody, Wyoming, had been named deputy majority leader in 1984 after only one term in the Senate, reflecting his status as perhaps the most popular member of the Senate on either side of the aisle. With Bob Dole running for president in 1988, Simpson was a natural to take over as Republican leader had Dole succeeded.

Simpson was an appealing man of uncommon charm and wit. He was one of the very few legislators who wrote all their own speeches. But he was also exceptionally tough. Six feet seven inches tall, stooped and balding, he seemed to stare over his half-frame glasses like a vulture and survey the Senate floor for prey, according to one reporter. Simpson once compared passing a difficult bill with "giving dry birth to a porcupine."

Simpson liked nothing better than to condemn the peculiar pre-occupations of Washington as out of step with the rest of the country. He mocked the idea that Americans cared about Bork's role in Watergate's Saturday Night Massacre. Simpson said the event was so long ago that no one paid it any mind except the capital's inbred political junkies.

"Fourteen years," he began. "This is a curious place. If you go out in the land and say, 'What were you doing on the night of the Saturday Night Massacre?' a guy will say, 'What are you talking about?' But in this town when you say, 'What were you doing on the night of the Saturday Night Massacre?' they say, 'I was just finishing shaving. I was going out to dinner. I will never forget it my whole life. I went limp. My wife and I talked and huddled together and had a drink and just shuddered in shock.' "

On the third day of hearings Simpson dropped another line that caused the entire room to dissolve in laughter. A Washington weekly called *City Paper* had obtained a list of videocassettes that Bork's family had rented from a store in the preceding two years. The article, called "Bork's Tapes," was satirical. Bork seemed to have a weakness for Cary Grant. But it was a frightening invasion of Bork's privacy, and the fact that privacy was a club with which Bork was being bludgeoned only enraged Simpson further.

He said, "You talk about the right to privacy. Well, I do not know how many in this room would like to have them go and check through Erol's or Freddy's Video and find out what they are check-

ing out down there; when you go to get the tape, and you tell them
you got one on bird-watching, and it is about a red-headed, double-
breasted mattress-thrasher."

Simpson, who relished displaying stylistic independence, spent a
major portion of his question time making small speeches complaining about what had been done to Bork. On that last day he recited
the familiar poem by Rudyard Kipling "If":

> If you can keep your head when all about you
>   are losing theirs and blaming it on you,
> If you can trust yourself when all men doubt you,
>   But yet make allowance for their doubting too;
> If you can wait and not be tired by waiting,
>   Or being lied about, don't deal in lies,
>   Or being hated, don't give way to hating,
>   And yet don't look too good, nor talk too wise. . . .

He recited more lines, weaving a small spell in the room. Then
Simpson built to a rhetorical climax. He said to Bork, "And I have
one final question. Why do you want to be an associate justice of the
United States Supreme Court?"

No softer ball could have been imagined, no greater opportunity
for Bork, finally, to talk about protecting rights and doing justice for
America. The man condemned as a heartless, intellectual gamesman
could tell his countrymen what really mattered. Any listener would
have been forgiven for assuming it was prearranged.

Yet the response showed otherwise:

> Senator, I guess the answer to that is that I have spent my life in
> intellectual pursuits in the law and since I have been a judge, I
> particularly like the courtroom. I liked the courtroom as an
> advocate and I like the courtroom as a judge and I enjoy the
> give and take and the intellectual effort involved.
>
> It is just a life—and that is, of course, the court that has the
> most interesting cases and issues, and I think it would be an
> intellectual feast just to be there and to read the briefs and
> discuss things with counsel and discuss things with my col-
> leagues. That is the first answer.
>
> The second answer is, I would like to leave a reputation as a
> judge who understood constitutional governance and contrib-

uted his bit to maintaining it in the ways I have described before this committee. Our constitutional structure is the most important thing this nation has and I would like to help maintain it and to be remembered for that.

Bork's "intellectual feast" line would live in infamy. Even he, months later, would agree that he might have found a more felicitous phrase. Bork himself seemed to be confirming what people had been told to fear about him: The bearded egghead from Yale just wanted to play with ideas. He didn't understand that beyond those elegant intellectual constructs, the lives of real people hung in the balance.

That was the rap against Bork, finally, and five days of testimony had done little to dispel it. Of course, if Bork's nomination had not been at the center of an extraordinary conflict of national visions, the comment would have stirred little interest. It was hardly a shocking sentiment for a constitutional lawyer. The love of intellectual challenge is common to all fine jurists. Lewis Powell, whom Bork had been nominated to replace, made much the same point when asked upon retirement what he would most miss at the Court: "First, working on opinions. I found the writing of opinions to be intellectually challenging and stimulating, at times quite exciting. . . ."

No one accused Powell of being unfeeling.

But against the background of his harsh conservatism and the portrait painted of him by his opponents, that answer made Bork look like Dr. Strangelove.

CHAPTER

13

Determined to Be Heard

The lead witness for the hearings' second week sat in his impeccable three-piece suit, a gold chain and a Phi Beta Kappa key spanning his ample midsection. At the age of sixty-seven, he was in the fullest sense a senior member of the American establishment. He was on a first-name basis with many of his interlocuters on the Senate Judiciary Committee. He served on the board of directors of nine of the nation's largest corporations. He earned nearly a million dollars a year as a Washington lawyer. He was a Republican.

And he was black.

William T. Coleman, Jr., was used to being among the first. He was the third black accepted on the *Harvard Law Review*, the first to serve as a clerk to a Supreme Court justice, and the first to reach the top of the corporate legal establishment. He was the second black to serve on a president's cabinet, having been transportation secretary under President Ford.

Bork's backers had once held high hopes of persuading Coleman to support the nominee. Coleman had known Bork well over the years. Both had frequently argued before the Supreme Court, and they had served together in the Ford administration. Coleman had also served on the American Bar Association committee that in 1981 rated Bork "exceptionally well qualified" for appointment to the federal bench. On the ABA committee he had headed the investigation of Bork's background.

Coleman's son, William, was in the Detroit office of the prestigious Philadelphia firm of Pepper Hamilton and Scheetz, of which he was a partner. He had studied under Bork at Yale. The younger Coleman, a known admirer of his former professor, was approached by Bork's friends to testify.

Bork's opponents also yearned for the Coleman nod. When Lloyd Cutler's piece defending Bork appeared on the *New York Times* op-ed page in mid-July, the anti-Bork coalition was shaken. In search of a man of equal stature, they approached Coleman, who demurred, saying he would remain neutral. His son followed suit.

Coleman was chairman of the board of directors of the NAACP Legal Defense and Educational Fund, a group that was fighting Bork vigorously. Eric Schnapper and Elaine Jones, the organization lawyers who worked full time on Bork, made sure that Coleman saw relevant material on the nomination. They never actually lobbied Coleman; dignified and strongheaded, Coleman was not a man one lobbied in a traditional sense. But they did what they could. So did others, including Zoe Baird, a former junior associate of Coleman's and the wife of Paul Gewirtz, the liberal Yale law professor advising Senator Simon.

Coleman kept his own counsel. While he hoped Bork would lose, he expected, as did most observers, that the nomination would gain confirmation. And as a frequent practitioner before the high court he feared antagonizing a future justice. So in the beginning he chose neutrality.

Two things happened. First, his conviction grew that anyone who had fought for legal equality for blacks—and who, like himself, had benefited from it—had to be offended by the positions Bork had taken in his life. After all, Coleman had not *floated* to the top of the heap in his hometown of Philadelphia. He had scraped. This was a man who remembered that "When I was in high school and I went out for the swimming team, they abolished the team rather than let me swim." Legal and social tides had tugged against black equality. A form of equality had been won nonetheless—without Bork's help.

Secondly, as the hearings approached, a Bork rejection seemed likelier. Enough prestigious lawyers had announced opposition to Bork that it had become legitimate for a member of the Washington establishment. On Wednesday, September 9, Coleman flew out to the Los Angeles headquarters of his law firm, O'Melveny and Myers. He wanted to probe the views of the senior partners regarding a possible announcement by him against Bork. They accepted the move.

Coleman called Elaine Jones and said he would oppose Bork publicly. She and the entire anti-Bork coalition were elated. The hearings were to start in less than a week, and there was much to do. Coleman invited Gewirtz down from New Haven, set him up in an office next to his own, and together—aided by Jones and Schnapper—they developed Coleman's opposition. Coleman made his helpers work exhaustive hours and constantly rewrite what had been done. He wanted his position to be airtight.

Coleman made his first move in an op-ed piece for the *Times*. It appeared two months after the Cutler article and so had lost the immediacy of a reply. But it was published on the day the Bork hearings opened and had a different, perhaps more potent effect.

In his article Coleman said there was an enormous difference between being qualified for a lower court and being qualified for the Supreme Court.

"A lower court judge is legally obligated to carry out Supreme Court precedents with which he or she disagrees. It was not unreasonable to assume that Robert Bork understood that obligation—and, in any event, there was the High Court to review him," Coleman wrote.

He added that Bork's pattern of opposition to important Court rulings was unmistakable.

"When it has counted, Robert Bork has often stood against the aspirations of blacks to achieve their constitutional rights and to remove the vestiges of racial discrimination," he wrote. "And as women and others move ahead to seek their equal share of the American Dream, there is the great risk that the pattern will repeat itself."

Six days after the op-ed piece had appeared, Coleman succeeded Bork in the witness chair. He recited an Aramaic phrase from the Book of Daniel meaning "Thou art weighed in the balances, and art found wanting," to explain to the Judiciary Committee why he could not stay out of the battle: "I have tried very hard to avoid this controversy. The Supreme Court has played such an important role in ending so many of the horribly racially discriminatory practices that existed when I first came to the bar. As one who has benefitted so greatly from this country's difficult but steady march towards a free, fair and open society, the handwriting on the wall—'mene mene tekel upharsin'—would condemn my failure to testify against Judge Bork."

Coleman made clear that he came to the hearing as a supporter of the president. He said he shared the president's goals of increased defense and decreased government spending. "But I find myself in disagreement with the president in indicating that the present Supreme Court is not functioning the way it ought to function, and somehow you have to put people on the Court which [*sic*], at least by their public statements, have said they would turn the thing back."

Coleman's testimony was unusually powerful. Not only was he a prominent black Republican, but he was also a gifted student of the Constitution. He had prepared for his testimony with the same energy and drive as he put into preparing for an oral argument before the high court. He had cases at his fingertips and ready reply to the objections of Republican senators.

On the Equal Protection Clause, Coleman assailed Bork's notion that, on issues beyond race, protection should be left to the legislative process. "I just ask you gentlemen sitting there and I ask the rest of the Senate and I ask the rest of the people in this room: Do you think that when there is a state statute which says that an illegitimate child cannot recover for the death of his or her mother, but a legitimate child can, that that illegitimate child can muster sufficient legislative force in the legislature that he or she could get that statute changed?"

Coleman then spoke of a 1948 ruling, *Shelley* v. *Kraemer*, which held that racially restrictive covenants on property—deeds that specified the buyer not resell the property to a nonwhite—were unconstitutional. Bork had criticized that decision, saying that the covenants were private, not state, action and so not covered by the Constitution.

Coleman said that restrictive covenants affected real people in real ways, and there was every reason to fight them on constitutional grounds. He told of a black judge from Philadelphia named Raymond Pace Alexander who wanted to buy a house covered by a restrictive covenant. So he purchased it through a third party, or straw. But Alexander wanted to see his property. And, Coleman recounted, barely controlling his rage, Alexander, a graduate of the University of Pennsylvania and Harvard Law School, whose wife held a doctorate, had to dress up as a house painter to get into his own house. The *Shelley* decision rendered such ignominy a horror story that would not be repeated.

Coleman was strongest in his exchanges with Bork's best-informed defender, Senator Hatch. Hatch always kept close at hand a list of cases Bork had signed on to as solicitor general or had ruled on as a judge in which the rights of women or blacks were upheld. Coleman called the list irrelevant since no one was accusing Bork of being a bigot or incapable of understanding the language of congressional statutes. The issue was Bork's reading of the Constitution's broad phrases. As he put it in his written testimony, "If it were claimed that Judge Bork's constitutional views derived from some animus towards minorities or women, the filing of briefs in statutory civil rights cases might be of some relevance. The objection set forth in this testimony, however, turns on the substantive injustices that Judge Bork's views of the Constitution would permit, so any claim of malice on his part is not reached."

Coleman corrected Hatch's version of events.

COLEMAN: [Bork] has not been exposed to the great cases as a judge. As a scholar, he has reached out, and he discussed them, and in the whole line of liberty cases, privacy cases, his discussions are completely contrary to what the Court said. . . .

HATCH: I might just give you a couple of significant civil rights issues that he voted on. The voting rights case in Sumter County, South Carolina; the equal pay for women case in Matthew v. Palmer; the Title VII cases that he decided. Those are all great cases.

COLEMAN: Now wait a minute. Look, to the two litigants every case is a great case.

HATCH: Well—

COLEMAN: But wait.

HATCH: Anybody looking at a great case—

COLEMAN: Each one of those cases—

SENATOR KENNEDY: Can he answer the question, Mr. Chairman? I am trying to follow the dialogue, and I would like to make sure that he is able to answer the question without interruption.

COLEMAN: Each one of those cases dealt with the interpretation of a statute. That great voting case that you described on television, I went back and I looked at it. All that case was, that you passed a statute saying that certain states, if you are going to make a change in your voting law, you have to get preclearance from the Attorney General's office. The state did not get preclearance. It tried to review that on the court of appeals, and Judge Bork wrote an opinion. I read the statute and that is all right. Now the other case you cited—and this one really surprised me at about one o'clock in the morning last night—and that is the Runyon case which is the, you know, the civil rights case.

HATCH: Versus McCrary which he argued as solicitor general.

COLEMAN: He did not argue, sir. With all due respect to you, when I pulled that book down, the oral argument, he did not make the oral argument. That was a case decided after Jones v. Mayer, and by that time you did not have to be much of a lawyer to say that I can go in and convince a court that the Act of 1866 applied.

HATCH: I agree with that, too . . . but it was his brief filed in that case, making that point that was argued by another attorney under his direction as solicitor general.

COLEMAN: No, no. The point was, the government did not argue the case. The government, along with about ten other amicuses, filed a brief.

HATCH: Okay. I understand he did not personally argue the case. . . . All right. You led the investigation resulting in then Mr. Bork receiving the highest rating of the American Bar Association back in 1981. There was not a single dissenting vote. All or most of the materials upon which you based your opinion, and your current opinion of Judge Bork, all of those materials were public then.

COLEMAN: That is not so, sir.

HATCH: Well—

COLEMAN: That is not so.

HATCH: Okay. Go ahead.

COLEMAN: Well, the fact is that since he has been on the bench in 1982, he has made a lot of speeches, and I have a footnote where you can see all the speeches—

HATCH: All right. That is fair. . . . Most of his writings that he has been criticized for occurred before that particular investigation back in 1981.

COLEMAN: With all due respect, sir, that is not true.

HATCH: Well, there have been some since, there is no question. Most of them, most of the ones—

COLEMAN: If you are examining a witness and you say most happened before such and such a date, and thirty percent of them happened after that date, I do not expect the witness to say yes.

    HATCH: Fine. . . .

And so it went. After Hatch, other Republican senators tried to rattle Coleman and with equally little success. The fact that they kept probing Coleman worked to the advantage of Bork's opponents. Coleman was superbly prepared, growing more convinced and convincing with each question. And because he stayed so long in the witness chair, the pro-Bork witnesses planned for the early afternoon were kept waiting, pushing their testimony beyond the deadline of some news organizations.

After Coleman came two other prominent blacks to testify against Bork. While Coleman's testimony was more legally sophisticated, theirs was emotionally stirring. Barbara Jordan, former Texas congresswoman and now professor of government at the University of Texas, and Andrew Young, mayor of Atlanta, spoke of their personal debt and that of all black Americans to the Supreme Court during the 1950s and 1960s. The two of them captivated the hearing room with the dignity and passion of their convictions.

Jordan, who gave up her career in the House and the promise of national leadership because of severe health problems, testified from her wheelchair. With her renowned oratorical flourish, she told the senators she opposed Bork not out of knee-jerk loyalty to civil rights groups but as a result of "living fifty-one years as a black American born in the South and determined to be heard by the majority community. . . . When you experience the frustrations of being in a minority position and watching the foreclosure of your last appeal and then suddenly you are rescued by the Supreme Court of the United States, Mr. Chairman, that is tantamount to being born again."

Jordan said she owed much to the Court's legislative reapportionment decisions of the mid-1960s, the so-called one person, one vote rulings. In her first two attempts at winning a seat in the Texas House of Representatives she failed because the Texas legislature was malapportioned. The Supreme Court forced reapportionment, and in 1966 Jordan ran again. She won.

Jordan quoted Bork's comment on the reapportionment decision: "I do not think there is a constitutional basis for it."

Then she said: "My word. 'I do not think there is a constitutional basis for it.' Maybe not, gentlemen. Maybe there is no theoretical basis for one-person one-vote. But I will tell you this much. There is a common sense, natural, rational basis for all votes counting equally." She added that if Bork's view of constitutional law had held sway, "I would right now be running my eleventh unsuccessful race for the Texas House of Representatives."

When Senator Kennedy asked Jordan how young Americans would react to Bork's confirmation, she replied: "I am talking to these young people you are talking about. I am talking to them, and they are meeting in their clubs, their sororities, their various organizations, and they are not having little cocktail parties. They are having letter-writing campaigns to their members of the United States Senate. And what are they writing about? They are writing about the nomination of Robert Bork. They sense there is something different about this nomination, and do not want to risk a diminution of the kind of life they have enjoyed so long and so well with the Supreme Court as guardian."

Andrew Young told the panel that for blacks, "the Supreme Court has never been just about issues and cases. It really could never be an intellectual feast. It is about people. It is about Rosa Parks wanting, as a seamstress, to sit down in the bus and not have to stand up when a white man comes on. It is about Charlayne Hunter and Hamilton Holmes wanting to go to school in the University of Georgia."

Young, whose city symbolized racial cooperation in the New South, said the Court's place in black hearts was summed up by its desegregation of the buses in Montgomery, Alabama:

> [W]hen it looked as though the Montgomery Improvement Association was going to have to close down its doors, when it looked like 381 days of nonviolent preaching and teaching would be a failure—on that very day Martin Luther King was about to announce that he would have to give in to this injunction—the word came down from the Supreme Court that buses in Montgomery, Alabama had been desegregated. And one good sister in the church just jumped up and shouted, "Great God almighty done spoke from Washington." . . . We

see the Supreme Court as the final protector and guarantor of those rights. And with a Supreme Court that is intellectualizing about those rights, or a Supreme Court that does not understand the passion and anguish of people whose rights are being denied is a Supreme Court which really does not live up to what I think the American dream is all about.

Neither Jordan nor Young challenged Bork's reading of the law. They opposed Bork because, as they saw it, his approach to the Constitution would not help blacks in their political battles. As Young stated, "We do not see this as a legal struggle. We see it as an intensely personal struggle, a struggle for survival and for continued coexistence and the right to keep on as we are going."

The fact that the lead witnesses in the battle against Bork were blacks, two of them from the South, was no accident. The original plan was for the opening group to include Bill Clinton, governor of Arkansas, as a white representative of the New South. Young, liberal, and dynamic, Clinton would have sent the message that a new generation had risen, that the clock could not be turned back. But because Bork's testimony took far longer than originally expected, Clinton ran into scheduling problems for a long-planned trip abroad and by the day of expected testimony had left the country.

Few political struggles in recent American history testified to black American power as persuasively as the Bork confirmation fight. The *Christian Science Monitor* had said of the 1930 defeat of Judge John Parker that it was "the first national demonstration of the Negro's power since Reconstruction days." Black opposition to Bork, without which he would surely have been confirmed, was a far more profound and detailed demonstration of that political might. In state after state in the South, blacks gathered their forces and sent a harsh message to their elected representatives: A vote for Bork means losing our support.

This was especially effective with four freshman Democrats elected the previous November. Several of them recalled a series of conversations in the Senate Dining Room held the week before the Bork hearings, just after Labor Day.

Presiding over the sessions was J. Bennett Johnston, Democrat of

Louisiana. Johnston, a three-term conservative, had well-known ambitions to gain the post of Senate majority leader and often served as guide and protector to his newer colleagues. He chaired the powerful Energy and Natural Resources Committee and the Appropriations Subcommittee on Energy and Water Development.

A product of the harsh political brawls of northern Louisiana, Johnston was under intense pressure on the Bork fight. The prolife lobby was pounding him, but so were organizations of blacks, women, and labor on the other side—and to greater effect. Late in September Johnston reached a decision to oppose Bork. At one point he turned to the young blacks in his office and, in an uncharacteristic but telling use of black slang, said, "We're gonna go with the brothers on this one."

Johnston had not yet reached that stage in early September, but he was heading firmly in that direction. At one late-night session around the table he listened to Richard Shelby of Alabama, one of the freshmen. Shelby was remarking how surprised he was that, with the hearings only a week away, President Reagan had not called any of the southern Democrats to ask for their vote. At town meetings in his state no overwhelming support for the northern judge had emerged.

Johnston turned to Shelby and said, "Shelby, you're not going to vote for Bork. You know why? Because you're not going to turn your back on ninety-one percent of the black voters in Alabama who got you here." Then Johnston pointed at others at the table and said, "I know how you're going to vote, and you, and you, and you."

Sitting there were, among others, John Breaux of Louisiana, Wyche Fowler, Jr., of Georgia, and Bob Graham of Florida. David Pryor of Arkansas, who was not a freshman, also was there. Breaux and Fowler had been elected with a minority white vote and more than 90 percent of the black vote. Graham had won 52 percent of the white vote and 86 percent of the black vote.

All voted against Bork.

All of the men at the table were Democrats, but few were traditional liberals. Breaux supported aid to the Nicaraguan contras and the MX missile. Conservatives rated him highly. But he fully understood the politics of this battle. As he put it a week before announcing his vote, "Those who helped us get elected—the black voters, the working people—are united in their opposition to Bork, and don't think for a moment that we are going to ignore that." He added that groups opposing Bork seemed more dedicated to Bork's defeat than his supporters were to his victory. "If you vote against Bork, those in favor of him will be mad at you for a week. But if you vote for him, those who don't like him will be mad at you for the rest of their lives."

Richard Shelby had come to the Senate from the House, where he had voted against extending the Voting Rights Act and against creating the Martin Luther King, Jr., holiday. Blacks and liberals helped him squeak by his opponent, freshman Senator Jeremiah Denton, only because they viewed Denton as the greater evil. Denton, among the Senate's staunchest Reagan backers, had spent much of his time promoting teenage chastity and exhibiting a stark looseness of words. During a hearing on spousal rape, for example, Denton proclaimed: "Damn it, when you get married, you kind of expect you're going to get a little sex." By contrast, Shelby had supported the Equal Rights Amendment while in the state legislature.

When Bork was nominated, Shelby expressed little doubt he would vote for confirmation. The day the nomination was announced, Dan Casey of the American Conservative Union, one of Bork's most avid champions, was in Shelby's office. He was lobbying the senator against the Civil Rights Restoration Act pending in Congress. As Casey remembered it, he said to Shelby, "Senator, I can't let this opportunity pass. The president has just nominated Judge Bork. What do you think?"

Shelby responded that unless there was a skeleton in Bork's closet, he would vote for him. He said that he really respected Bork for firing Archibald Cox during the Watergate episode. "Sometimes you've got to be tough and do things like that," Shelby said. Casey remembered Shelby's adding that if Ted Kennedy opposed the nomination, "a lot of us southern Democrats will have to be in bed with Bork."

But by September Shelby had understood things differently. Those late-evening chats with Johnston and the other southerners helped him gain a fuller perspective. Johnston, a shrewd conservative, told his colleagues that they owed the president nothing on this vote, that the politics were firmly on the other side.

Reagan had campaigned the previous year against those sitting around Johnston partly on the issue of judicial nominations. Speaking, for example, in Columbus, Georgia, in October 1986, Reagan

praised Senator Mack Mattingly, the Georgia Republican, as someone who "can make all the difference" on judicial appointments.
"Without him and the Republican majority in the Senate, we'll find
liberals like Joe Biden and a certain fellow from Massachusetts deciding who our judges are." Mattingly lost in an upset to Wyche
Fowler, who deflected attacks on his liberalism by invoking his
South Georgia roots through anecdotes and charm.

Earlier that month Reagan told a rally for Representative James
T. Broyhill of North Carolina that the proliferation of drugs in
America was due to "liberal judges who are unwilling to get tough
with the criminal elements in this society. We don't need a bunch of
sociology majors on the bench. What we need are strong judges
who will aggressively use their authority to protect our families,
communities and our way of life. . . . Since coming to Washington,
we've been putting just such people on the bench."

Broyhill, who failed to ignite the passions of the conservative
wing of his party at home, lost to Terry Sanford, a liberal former
governor and president of Duke University.

Liberal lobbyists were able to use those Reagan speeches as evidence that whatever politicization of the judiciary the Bork battle
represented was in response to the president. And while this was
partly true, Reagan's efforts on the issue in 1986 had been only half-
hearted and too late to make a difference. It was Dan Casey who had
argued for Reagan's using the judiciary as a campaign theme in the
off-term Senate races. Casey, who had been at the Republican National Committee at the time, urged a poll upon his party to test for
political sentiments regarding liberal and conservative judges. The
poll revealed that when the questions were properly designed,
nearly half the country preferred conservative to liberal judges with
only a quarter favoring liberal judges. Casey sent a note to Pat Bu-
chanan, White House communications director at the time: The
president should act on the poll's results. "They finally got the president cranked up on the judges issue," Casey recalled. "But it was too
little and too late."

Johnston's notion that the politics of the nomination went against
confirmation was vitally reinforced a couple of days after his late-
night session with freshmen colleagues. California Democrat Alan
Cranston, the majority whip, brought pollster and Biden adviser

Patrick Caddell to talk to Johnston about some very reassuring findings. The data were from the Marttila and Kiley poll done for the liberal anti-Bork coalition a few weeks earlier. When Caddell saw the results, he exploded with enthusiasm. He understood instantly that Bork could be stopped and that the data held good news for a Democrat such as Joe Biden in 1988.

"When I saw the data, I said, 'We're going to beat the shit out of this guy,'" Caddell remembered. "To see the reaction of white southerners afraid to go back on civil rights was overwhelming. I am a white southerner and I felt this stuff, but I had never seen it so dramatically demonstrated."

Caddell had his assistant, Michael Donilon—younger brother of Tom Donilon, Biden's campaign adviser—write up their conclusions from the poll. In a memo dated September 9 Donilon wrote that the conventional wisdom regarding white southern support for Bork was "just plain wrong." He said the incorrect assumption was based on three misconceptions: firstly, that Bork already enjoyed great support in the South; secondly, that white southerners had dramatically different views regarding the Supreme Court from the rest of the country; and thirdly, that as southern whites learned more about Bork, they would become more supportive of his nomination. On the last point, Donilon wrote: "In fact, the potential for the development of intense opposition to Bork is perhaps greater in the South than in any other region.

"The reason for this is three-fold: Bork poses the risk of reopening race-relation battles which have been fought and put to rest; Bork flouts the southern tradition of populism; and . . . Bork poses a challenge to a very strong pro-privacy sentiment among southern voters."

The conclusions were based on regional and racial comparisons of the Marttila and Kiley polling data. With very little variation, white southerners reflected the views of the nation as a whole regarding the Court, race relations, and privacy. The poll found that Reagan's popularity among white southerners had not been translated into support for Bork.

The data were striking. Of white southerners polled, 62 percent said they were less inclined to support Bork upon hearing that "he has strongly criticized most of the landmark decisions protecting civil rights and individual liberties." Moreover, 68 percent of white southerners said they were less inclined to support Bork upon hearing that the NAACP opposed him. The same percentage was also less inclined to support him because Bork opposed "a decision striking down a poll tax requirement for voting." Bork's 1963 opposition to the public accommodations law pushed to 77 the percentage of southern whites less inclined to support him. The numbers were similar when constitutional privacy and pro-big business questions were asked.

Donilon's summary also referred to a Scripps-Howard poll in early September showing white southerners about evenly divided on the nomination. As Donilon put it, "In sum, there is no groundswell of support for Bork in the South. Southern senators are not faced with a heated clamor for Bork in their home states. In fact, quite the opposite is true."

While overstated—the polling questions presented Bork in the least flattering light—the Caddell-Donilon message was powerful and welcome: Southern Democrats risked little in opposing Bork.

Cranston played a key but little publicized role from the beginning of the Bork battle, meeting frequently with liberal groups and encouraging senators against confirmation. He remembered how impressed Johnston was with the data. Caddell said Johnston was stunned. Cranston and Caddell made sure every southern Democrat received a copy of the poll and analysis.

"The polling data freed up people politically," Mike Donilon said. "It gave them evidence that the issue was not nearly as settled as conventional wisdom would have them believe. It said: 'Your constituencies are not screaming for this guy. You can take a look at him.'"

William Schneider, a political analyst at the American Enterprise Institute in Washington, had described the Bork nomination as trouble for southern Democrats a month earlier in the *Los Angeles Times*. He said that a vote for Bork would, of course, alienate the senator's black constituents. But blacks, after all, had nowhere else to turn in the South. They were not going to switch to the Republicans. On the other hand, black alienation could mobilize an angry black electorate. And that, in turn, Schneider said, could mobilize an angry white electorate.

"Confronted by militant and embittered black voters, whites would leave the Democratic Party in droves, just as they did in the 1960s . . ." Schneider wrote. "[T]he biracial basis of Southern Democratic politics would vanish. The South would end up with exactly what it doesn't need—a black party and a white party. . . . It is a law of politics that when the race issue heats up, Democrats lose. And Southern Democrats, elected by an extremely delicate biracial coalition, are likely to go first."

Bork's opponents had so successfully framed the issue, had so effectively "turned back the clock" for the debate that the natural wellspring of Bork support—white southerners—was dry. Southerners perceived the nomination as racially divisive and so a threat to their peace and prosperity. No matter what racial resentment many southern whites still harbored, they recoiled at the prospect of reviving the period of intense racial tension.

Tom Griscom, White House communications director during the Bork battle, explained why the opposition was so effective in the South, lamenting: "They resurrected the sixties because they knew our people would react back. That's where we got into trouble. There are so many people from the part of the country I'm from— the South—who don't like being tagged racists. We've worn that tag for too long as far as I'm concerned. We don't want to reopen those wounds. We don't want to live that again. We've passed that. Please don't make us go through it again. The sensitivity is more among whites in the South than anywhere else."

Griscom's view was amply demonstrated by the case of Lloyd Bentsen, a conservative Texas Democrat. Bentsen was known in the Senate as a smooth and hugely successful businessman whose views and votes were right of center. But Bentsen indicated early to anti-Bork lobbyists that if what they told him about Bork's attitude to key civil rights cases was correct, he could not support the nomination. Several lobbyists recalled telling Bentsen in a meeting early in September about Bork's criticism of a decision banning poll taxes. Bentsen had opposed poll taxes thirty years earlier as a young congressman and found it inconceivable that Bork could still defend their constitutionality. When they walked out of the meeting, the lobbyists were buoyed. They were convinced they had Bentsen's vote and probably that of many of his southern colleagues. Throughout September Bentsen dropped generous hints at Democratic events that Bork was a goner. Without yet officially announcing his vote, he told the *New York Times:* "My deep concern is that you could turn back the clock on civil rights. We've already fought those fights, and we're happy with the outcome." Despite many political differences, Bentsen was chosen ten months later by Democratic presidential nominee Michael Dukakis to be his running mate. His votes on Bork and civil rights issues were seen by many unhappy liberals as a saving grace.

As Mike Donilon had pointed out in his memo, the fear of racial tension was compounded by issues of populism and privacy. Southern whites' lack of enthusiasm for Bork as an individual was partly cultural. He was a bearded northern intellectual rumored at first to be Jewish and later an agnostic or atheist. No one was sure which of the three was correct—or worst—but as John Breaux, Democrat of Louisiana, put it, "This was not Jerry Falwell, after all."

By the time of the hearings many southern Democrats understood they would vote against Bork. A couple had actually made that clear earlier in the summer, either privately to Biden and Kennedy or publicly in coded fashion. Both Georgia's Wyche Fowler and North Carolina's Terry Sanford gave speeches in early August urging the Senate to take up with great care its advice and consent duty in the nomination. This was an early signal to anyone listening that they were likely to vote against.

Most of their colleagues, however, waited. One never knew if an extraordinary event might change the picture. Such an event soon grew unlikely. As Shelby analyzed it, by the beginning of the hearings, "Things were set in concrete politically."

Louisiana's Bennett Johnston reluctantly took the lead among southern Democrats because the senator widely expected to play that role, Howell Heflin of Alabama, held back. Heflin was the only Democrat on the Judiciary Committee from the Deep South; Robert Byrd was a West Virginian and also spent almost no time at the hearings because of his majority leader duties. Moreover, Heflin was a former chief justice of the Alabama Supreme Court. At first it was assumed that Heflin would run interference for his southern colleagues, offering them guidance on the nomination. Instead, he remained noncommittal and strangely aloof from the process, revealing his vote only after Johnston and several others had announced their opposition.

Slow-walking and slow-talking, Heflin was a huge mass of a man. He was feared by committee staffers because of his habit of stealing their sandwiches and doughnuts during late sessions. Six feet four inches tall, 275 pounds, Heflin had the homespun style and accent of a backroads country lawyer and the deliberateness of the judge he once was. Although in the Senate since 1978, Heflin continued to prefer the title Judge. On the basis of his court background, he was immediately made chairman of the Ethics Committee, becoming the first freshman senator since 1910 to head a committee in his first year.

His mix of country drawl and judiciousness reminded many of the late Sam Ervin, the North Carolinian who chaired the Senate's investigation into the Watergate scandal. In fact, Heflin was nearly given the chairmanship of the special Iran-contra committee in 1987, but that post went instead to Daniel Inouye of Hawaii. Heflin did serve on the committee but with little distinction. He was considered a plodding disappointment by many who had high expectations. His most famous utterance from those proceedings was in offhandedly accusing Fawn Hall, Oliver North's secretary, of smuggling documents from the White House by hiding them in her brassiere.

Heflin had a checkered background and a complex reaction to it. His father had been a traveling preacher, and his uncle, "Cotton Tom" Heflin, a U.S. senator from 1920 to 1931, earned a reputation as perhaps the most racist and anti-Catholic member of the nation's upper house. Many who knew Heflin, a staunch civil rights advocate, believed one of his goals was to make up for some of his uncle's misdeeds.

Heflin, sixty-six, served in the Marines during the Second World War and was wounded and decorated for bravery. He attended the University of Alabama law school and set up practice as a trial lawyer, quickly gaining a reputation as one of the craftiest in the state. Stories of his courtroom technique abounded. In one case, he laid his bulky frame across counsel's table to demonstrate the problems of an alleged assault. In another, he spread talcum on the courtroom floor as he made a point about footprints.

On the Judiciary Committee Heflin stayed crafty, never letting on his thinking about difficult confirmation battles. He voted with the Reagan administration on Rehnquist, Meese, and Manion. But in the case of a judge from his own state, Jefferson Sessions III, Heflin withstood strong political winds from home and voted no. There had been questions about Sessions's qualifications and sensitivity toward blacks, and Heflin cast the deciding vote against him. Some Alabama papers labeled Heflin a traitor.

At the Bork hearings Heflin tended to emphasize what he considered Bork's unusual background—the fact that Bork had begun life on the left and moved to the right—as well as reports of the nominee's agnosticism and questions about his beard ("Well, now there are those, and this is not my idea, that say, well, you can look at his attire and the way he wears his hair as some indication. I don't agree with that. I have got several members in my staff that have beards and everything else. Would you like to give us an explanation relative to the beard?"). It was not that Heflin avoided substance entirely, but he discussed more personal issues than the other members of the panel did.

In his opening statement, for instance, Heflin did something inexcusable. He raised the question of Bork's religion, claiming he was doing so merely to make the point that such rumors had no place in the august confirmation hearings. By pointing to the issue, he focused national attention on it. He said:

> There are those who charge that Judge Bork is an agnostic or a non-believer. These critics contend that such beliefs will affect the opinions of the courts and hence, our churches, our synagogues and, ultimately, our lives. While voicing concern about the propriety of a religious test, some critics contend, nevertheless, that this is a legitimate area of inquiry. For in determining the fitness of a nominee, they argue, one must look to the total man—his reasoning process and the reaches of his values and views.
>
> However, let me remind my colleagues that Clause Three of Article Six of the Constitution of the United States clearly provides that "no religious test shall be required as a qualification to any office or public trust under the United States." This clause, as well as the spirit of the freedom of religion clause in the First Amendment, should be observed in pursuing any inquiry, whether it be legitimate or not, as to one's personal religious feelings.

But after voting against Bork and hearing of the nominee's decision to stay in for a full Senate vote, Heflin returned shamelessly to the agnosticism theme. In a taped statement distributed by his office to Alabama radio stations, Heflin piled falsehood upon innuendo, accusing Bork of suffering from a martyr complex.

"This martyr approach," Heflin said, "is further evidence of his extremism. I was troubled by Judge Bork's extremism and admission that he'd been a socialist, a libertarian, that he'd nearly become a Communist and actually recruited people to attend Communist party meetings and had a strange life-style. I was further disturbed by his refusal to discuss his belief in God or the lack thereof. All of this as well as other reasons gave me doubts on risking him to a lifetime position on the United States Supreme Court."

Heflin's apparent aim, like that of some fellow southerners, was to base opposition on grounds acceptable to conservative voters. His no vote was enough of a payback to blacks and liberals. They demanded nothing further and would forgive him for hinging it on Bork's "strange life-style," a smear that could hardly have been farther from the truth.

Heflin provided Senator John Warner, Republican of Virginia, with some ammunition in choosing to vote against Bork. Warner was lobbied with extraordinary vigor by black groups, but his opposition infuriated his state's conservative Republicans. In voting no, he was able to quote on the Senate floor and to constituents Heflin's words that Bork had a "fondness" for the "strange."

A few other southerners chose equally inappropriate reasons. Tennessee's Jim Sasser wrote to a voter that he opposed Bork because he was not a southerner and the high court's "regional balance" would have been jeopardized. He also said that "scientifically conducted polls" showed that Bork was unpopular.

Shelby of Alabama offered few substantive points when he announced his opposition after the hearings. Instead of taking a stand on a controversial issue, Shelby chose to base his rejection of Bork on the very existence of a controversy. He made a veiled reference to civil rights, saying society would be rent in two: "As a senator from a Southern state, I am well aware of the adverse effects of division and polarization. The seams of our society could be torn apart. If the mere nomination has caused division, the appointment can only multiply the effects. We, as a country, cannot afford such disruption."

Shelby said later that he was deeply impressed by lobbying from conservative businesswomen who told him that Bork threatened two decades of progress for women. Asked if he thought that was a fair assessment, Shelby replied, "I don't know. That was the perception. . . . I was listening to the people. I think that's what you're supposed to do."

The Bork hearings lasted twelve days. Three former attorneys general testified on behalf of the nominee, as did former Chief Justice Warren Burger. Former President Jimmy Carter sent a letter against Bork aimed at blunting the impact of pro-Bork testimony by his own attorney general, Griffin Bell. Prominent and distinguished academics offered views in support and opposition. Pillars of the bar spoke both in Bork's favor and against.

Laurence Tribe testified for three hours, longer than any other witness. He contended that no justice in the nation's history had questioned the existence of unenumerated rights. With typical flair, Tribe made one of the hearings' most dramatic statements:

> Indeed, not one of the 105 past and present justices of the Supreme Court has ever taken a view at odds with this basic axiom of our Constitution. If he is confirmed as the 106th justice, Judge Bork would be the first to read liberty as though it were exhausted by the rights the majority expressly conceded individuals in the Bill of Rights. He would be the first to reject an evolving concept of liberty and to replace it with a fixed set of liberties protected at best from an evolving set of threats. It seems to me that in an age of biomedical and technological revolution, that frozen concept of liberty is dangerous."

Tribe also argued that Bork's preference for a reasonableness test over intermediate scrutiny in gender discrimination was "a request for a blank check" and "subjectivity run rampant." He said: "Women and other vulnerable groups are asked to gamble. Not to gamble on whether Judge Bork is a sexist; I do not believe for a minute that he is. But to gamble on his personal notion of what is reasonable according to his sense of community standards."

In addressing Bork's claim the previous week that a constitutional right to abortion might be found in a way hitherto unknown, Tribe said: "I do not think that constitutional law is a game of hide and seek. The idea that there might be a right hiding there from Judge Bork to be discovered in the next decade I think is not very plausible."

Alan Simpson, Wyoming Republican, accused Tribe of being a politician hiding behind the title of Professor. He said Tribe had volunteered to work for Ted Kennedy's presidential campaign, adding: "Now, everybody has the right to identify with a political party and a political person. But I think we have to be aware of your strong political leanings and of the fact that the title 'professor' does not just allow you to sit outside of the mainstream of politics."

Tribe took umbrage, replying: "[T]he fact that I have political views—which I surely do and which I am not ashamed of—does not have a lot to do with what I have testified here, or anything to do with why I am testifying here."

Simpson: "Well, I know you believe that, but I have a little problem with believing it."

Simpson had a point. Tribe *did* believe what he said, but his political affiliations, like his view of the Constitution, grew out of his convictions and vision for America. His was a liberal world view; when the Constitution's conflicting traditions and origins made the framers' intent hard to discern, Tribe usually opted for a more liberal interpretation. Just as Bork's partisan politics were not coincidentally conservative Republican, so Tribe's politics were liberal Democratic. Throughout the Bork battle participants saw with great clarity the link between politics and constitutional interpretation of their opponents, rarely of themselves.

But Tribe was also partly correct. He had not publicly opposed Sandra Day O'Connor or Antonin Scalia or the elevation of William Rehnquist to be chief justice. They all were Republicans and conservatives. Tribe believed that Bork needed to be opposed both because of the precarious balance on the Court and because Bork had specifically and consistently championed what Tribe considered a cramped interpretation of individual liberty under the Constitution. Tribe was saying: This one nomination is imbued with profound importance. I am not here as a Democrat. I am here as one who cherishes Court-protected personal and civil rights.

The Bork hearings were a watershed for Tribe. They greatly increased his national fame—and notoriety—outside legal circles. His profile appeared in numerous national publications. And the hearings made him a target of the right as never before. A few weeks after the Senate had rejected Bork, Harvard officials found the remains of a wiretap on Tribe's office telephone. Tribe's secretaries had reported strange noises on the line. No culprit was ever found, nor was it clear if Tribe's conversations had been monitored. But he couldn't help wondering if there was a link to the Bork hearings.

After Bork's defeat the right constantly referred to a Tribe judicial nomination as the one event for which they would, without hesitation, go to war. This was not only because Tribe was a feared liberal advocate but because he had taken such a public role in stopping Bork. During the summer of 1988, when it looked as if George Bush would lose to Democratic nominee Michael Dukakis, the issue of Tribe's nomination was widely discussed. Tribe was close to many in the Dukakis camp, especially campaign manager Susan Estrich, his Harvard Law colleague. He braced himself for nomination, either to the post of solicitor general or directly to the Court itself. Bush's victory eliminated any chance of Tribe's playing an official national role over the coming four years. But at forty-seven, Tribe recognized that his moment could still come.

Among those who testified after Tribe was Harvard colleague Richard Stewart, who argued that Bork's five years on the circuit court showed a judge of uncommon ability and fairness. He accused Bork's opponents of "highly selected culling, unrepresentative sample of cases, and an outright distortion or highly misleading account of those cases when they are discussed in the reports." Stewart stated that Bork clearly examined the arguments on all sides and often went "out of his way to state the position of the person against whom he rules in stronger terms than the advocate presented itself."

Carla Hills, secretary of housing and urban development under President Ford and later trade representative for President Bush, took issue with the notion that Bork's view of the Constitution would harm women's interests. She said that most gains for women had come from legislatures and that a strict parity of treatment for women and men ultimately harmed women more than it helped them.

Senator Kennedy introduced into the record letters from thirty-two law school deans and seventy-one professors of constitutional law who opposed Bork's confirmation. The letters had been drafted by William Taylor, the civil rights lawyer who played a key role in behind-the-scenes opposition to Bork. After urging by Melanne Verveer, of People for the American Way, and Kennedy, Taylor agreed to take on the thankless task of writing the letters and then rounding up professors who would sign them. The text read, in part:

> Judge Bork is a highly skilled lawyer. He has also been a colleague in the teaching of law where his skills and experience are widely respected. We have decided to oppose his nomination because of a substantive concern that we believe to be so important as to override matters of credentials or personal considerations. . . . If Judge Bork were to be confirmed, his vote could prove detrimental in turning the clock back to an era where constitutional rights and liberties and the role of the judiciary in protecting them were viewed in a much more restrictive way."

Michael McConnell, a young constitutional specialist at the University of Chicago, was on a pro-Bork panel at the witness table when Kennedy read the letters into the record. McConnell asked to respond and stated:

> I would like to acknowledge that this nomination is certainly controversial among law professors. I am not at all surprised that they were able to come up with 100 some odd law professors to sign a letter of that sort. What I think is even more remarkable, however, given the very politicized nature of my profession, is how many moderate, liberal and even very liberal law professors whom I know who have declined to sign letters of that sort who are not appearing in opposition not because they agree with Judge Bork—because they disagree with Judge Bork on many things—but because these charges that some people with the politicized portion of the legal community are making are so extreme, so outlandish and so obviously partisan and political.

A week later the opposition came up with an even more impressive assault by Bork's academic colleagues. Biden presented a list of 1,925 law professors—some 40 percent of all full-time law faculty—who signed a letter against Bork. They represented faculty members at 90 percent of the American Bar Association-accredited law schools, 153 out of 172. As a means of comparison, Biden pointed out that only 300 law professors signed letters opposing the nomination of G. Harrold Carswell, Nixon's failed appointee.

And so back and forth went the testimony. The projected witness list seemed to stretch on endlessly; the hearings looked likely to last more than three weeks.

Among the expected witnesses were scores of liberal activists who had put everything aside for three months in order to stop Bork. The hearings were to provide them an important public forum. The National Organization for Women, the Leadership Conference on Civil Rights, the National Association for the Advancement of Colored People all hoped to testify. They had done so at previous hearings, such as Rehnquist's and they felt it was their due as well as their duty. It provided proof to members around the country of the status and seriousness of their groups. And testimony helped fund raising.

During the first week of witness testimony, negotiations began within the coalition and with Hill staffers on who would testify. Biden and Kennedy feared that such testimony would do more harm than good, allowing their Republican colleagues to make an issue out of the groups themselves and their anti-Bork campaign. Biden could just imagine Alan Simpson going after those witnesses, picking apart their advertisements, probing them on unpopular positions their groups had taken, asking embarrassing questions on finance and structure and partisanship. In view of how angry the Republicans were, this would not be a pleasant event.

Some liberal activists, such as Kate Michelman of the National Abortion Rights Action League and Morton Halperin of the American Civil Liberties Union, felt the same way. A highly controversial movement developed first to limit any liberal group testimony and then to eliminate it entirely. Kennedy told a meeting of group representatives in Cranston's office toward the end of the second week that he hoped the hearings would end promptly so he could get to work on undecided senators. People were no longer paying attention to the Caucus Room. And things were going so well. Why threaten victory?

Stormy meetings among group representatives ensued. They met daily anyway, usually at the offices of the ACLU right around the corner from the Senate. As the hearings progressed, the subject turned away from Bork and toward themselves and the advisability of testifying.

Ralph Nader and NOW's Molly Yard were adamant. They had worked hard, and they deserved a chance to testify. Ultimately they were voted down; no one would testify. It was the most difficult coalition decision of the entire battle, the only one that left scars. But the decision manifested a political maturity and realism of the majority of those fighting Bork. They had come to understand that allowing themselves to become the focus of attention did their causes more harm than good under some circumstances.

As the groups ultimately understood, once Bork's own testimony was over, the case had been nearly decided. Those leaning against confirmation had little reason to change their minds. And if they had any doubts, they were buoyed by opinion polls taken right after Bork's five days on the witness stand. All polls were decisively against confirmation. A CBS News-*New York Times* poll showed 26 percent opposed to Bork and 16 percent in favor. An NBC News/ *Wall Street Journal* poll showed 42 percent opposed and 34 percent in favor of confirmation. The seven days of testimony by more than a hundred witnesses, as distinguished and thoughtful as many were, had marginal impact on the outcome.

There were, nevertheless, some extraordinary moments at the hearings. One was provided by former Chief Justice Burger. His handsome, chiseled midwestern features and shock of smooth white hair had always made Burger look like a television producer's hackneyed version of a chief justice of the United States. A Nixon appointee, Burger had stepped down from the Court in 1986 to take charge of the national celebration of the Constitution's bicentennial. It was his commission that had considered printing the Constitution on breakfast cereal boxes so as to bring the charter into the homes of ordinary citizens. If any man in America should have been an expert on the Constitution, this was the one.

Biden neatly summed up the controversy over Bork by reading to Burger part of his own opinion in the 1980 case of *Richmond Newspapers Inc.* v. *Virginia.* The decision reinforced open access to the courts for press and public. It relied heavily on the notion that there were unenumerated rights in the Constitution as expressed in the Ninth Amendment, which states, "The enumeration in the Constitution, of certain rights, shall not be construed to deny or disparage others retained by the people."

In the part of the opinion read by Biden, Burger had stated:

The State argues that the Constitution nowhere spells out a guarantee for the right of the public to attend trials and that, accordingly, no such right is protected. But arguments such as the State makes have not precluded recognition of important rights not enumerated. . . . For example, the rights of association and the right of privacy, as well as the right of travel, appear nowhere in the Constitution or Bill of Rights; yet these important, unenumerated and unarticulated rights have nonetheless been found to share constitutional protection with explicit guarantees.

Biden asked Burger if he would elaborate, since the statement seemed directly to contradict Bork's view with regard to unenumerated rights and the Ninth Amendment, which the nominee had compared with an inkblot.

Burger said good-naturedly that he had not come to the hearings "to give a lecture on constitutional law," adding: "I see no problem about that statement and I would be astonished if Judge Bork would not subscribe to it."

Biden, as surprised as most people in the room—there was a low murmur among the reporters—but seeking to appear deferential, asked the man who had been at the top of the nation's third branch of government for nearly two decades: "Does the Ninth Amendment mean anything?"

Burger manifestly couldn't remember what the Ninth Amendment was. (Lyle Denniston of the *Baltimore Sun*, who had covered the high court for nearly thirty years, muttered half aloud from the press section, "It's the one between the Eighth and the Tenth, Mr. Chief Justice.") Burger pulled out his copy of the Constitution, saying that Justice Hugo Black had never tried to remember exactly the words to any amendment, and he considered that the wisest course. While fumbling for the right place in the document, Burger said that "of course, it is one of the very, very important . . ." but did not finish his sentence. Instead, he launched into an anecdote about the word *persons* which he said was probably the amendment's key word. (It does not appear in the amendment.) He told a story about an opinion by former Chief Justice John Marshall saying that slaves could not be considered freight because they were persons. He then said: "It is hard to say which amendment is more important than any other amendment but, surely, this matter of 'persons' becomes terribly important."

Biden, out of respect for the nation's highest judicial office and the dignity of a man astonishingly out of his depth, backed off. With impressive self-restraint, the chairman concluded by saying: "I appreciate that answer. My time is up. I, even much more than you, Your Honor, have to look at this to make sure I have got the amendments right. And let me just read it into the record." He then read aloud the Ninth Amendment.

Biden's performance was remarkable not only as a combination of thoughtful questioning and self-restraint. The senator's political ambitions were crashing down around him. Two hours after questioning Burger, Biden killed a long-held dream by officially withdrawing from the presidential race.

Biden's troubles, which had begun with the Neil Kinnock speech, had expanded during the week of Bork's testimony amid charges that he had plagiarized from a law review article while a law student at Syracuse University. On the second day of Bork's testimony Biden got word of the law school issue. His campaign sent top New York lawyers to the university to seek and sort through the records. The next day Biden held a press conference saying he would stay in the race.

In fact, *plagiarism* was a harsh term for what young Biden had done. He had engaged in sloppy, perhaps deceptive footnoting in a legal writing course. He was given an F in the course and instructed to take it again, whereupon he received a B and his record was cleared.

At the weekend it seemed as if the issue had been put behind him. Biden was getting high marks for the hearings, and Bork looked to be going down. News organizations were turning their attention away from the law school issue and to the question of which competing campaign had the bad taste and ruthlessness to distribute the tapes of the Kinnock and Biden speeches on the eve of the Bork hearings. Biden's campaign staff asked him if they could plan a couple of trips to Iowa and New Hampshire, sites of the first primary contests.

"We figured if another shoe doesn't drop, we're fine," recalled one campaign staffer. "On Sunday Howard Fineman of *Newsweek* called to say his magazine was running a story that would appear the next day about a tape of Biden in New Hampshire. The other shoe had dropped."

On the videotape a fatigued and exasperated Biden was seen taking a question from a man identified only as Frank, who asked him where he went to law school and where he placed in his class. Biden replied: "I think I probably have a much higher IQ than you do, I suspect. I went to law school on a full academic scholarship, the only one in my, in my class to have a full academic scholarship. In the first year in the law, I decided I didn't want to be in law school and ended up in the bottom two-thirds of my class and then decided I wanted to stay, went back to law school and, in fact, ended up in the top half of my class.

"I won the international moot court competition. I was the outstanding student in the political science department at the end of my year. I graduated with three degrees from undergraduate school and one hundred sixty-five credits—only needed one hundred twenty-three credits. And I would be delighted to sit down and compare my IQ to yours if you'd like, Frank."

Biden did have a full scholarship to law school, and he and a partner had won an international moot court competition in Canada. But most of the rest was exaggeration or invention. He finished seventy-sixth out of a class of eighty-five in law school. He was graduated from the University of Delaware with a single degree, after majoring in history and political science. He had not been selected as the outstanding student in political science, although a professor had nominated him for that honor.

Other reports began to question claims he had made in his political career. Most of them were trivial, but Biden's presidential bid was unraveling. Campaign staffers remembered the Monday afternoon after the *Newsweek* story appeared as the fateful one. Biden was in the anteroom just outside the hearings. He was trying simultaneously to negotiate the witness list with Strom Thurmond, place a phone call to a former law school professor, and answer campaign staff about setting up an appearance that evening in New Hampshire.

"It had become untenable," one aide remembered. "The poor guy was stretched to the limit. When I advised Joe to discontinue his campaign, that was the example I gave."

That advice came the next day, as aides Tom Donilon, Larry Rasky, and Mark Gitenstein joined Biden on the train back to his home in Wilmington. The three of them went to a restaurant while Biden ate dinner with his family and discussed his possible withdrawal. Later they came to the house. Conspicuously absent from the meeting was Patrick Caddell, pollster and campaign adviser to Biden. He was the only member of the inner circle who wanted Biden to stay in the race. Blame the media, he suggested. He kept calling from a Washington pay phone and demanding to talk to Biden. At one point he screamed at Rasky: "You people have formed a vigilante group to get my candidate out of the race."

Against the pleadings of his family Biden reluctantly agreed to withdraw. He announced the decision at a press conference at midday on September 23. "Although it's awfully clear to me what choice I have to make . . . I do it with incredible reluctance, and it makes me angry," Biden said. "I'm angry with myself for having been put in the position—putting myself in the position—of having to make this choice. . . . I made some mistakes. But now the exaggerated shadow of those mistakes has begun to obscure the essence of my candidacy and the essence of Joe Biden."

Biden walked out of the press conference and returned immediately to the Caucus Room to begin questioning witness Lloyd Cutler. All of Biden's colleagues on both sides of the committee offered support. Staffers who had never felt warm toward the chairman found a new esteem for him. He had acted with grace and courage under pressure. His chairmanship of the hearings even seemed to take on a new and welcome crispness.

One former staffer felt the Bork hearings were therapeutic for the senator. They provided an outlet, forcing his mind off his sinking and often chaotic presidential campaign, concentrating it on a contest of national and constitutional import. Biden permitted himself the belief that he had acted nobly, putting aside personal ambition for a higher cause.

Within three months Biden had suffered two life-threatening aneurysms in the arteries of his brain.

Just before the first of three operations, which lasted nine hours, his doctors told him that the chances of brain damage or death were far from negligible. He called in his family members one by one. To his sons, who now faced the possibility of losing a second parent, he "told them what phenomenal promise they had and why I thought whether or not I lived, they would be great men. I guaranteed them that every single solitary time they had a problem, every time they had a tough decision to make, I'd be standing right there with them.... That was the thing that made me think I'd make it—I just didn't think it was going to happen to them twice in their life."

He missed seven months of work. His doctors told him that if he had stayed in the presidential race, he would have been under such strain that when the aneurysms hit, he would very likely have died.

Biden looked back philosophically on his extraordinary couple of years. He said he deserved to be forced out of presidential politics in 1987 since he acted foolishly, and he deserved to beat Bork since he acted wisely. His encounter with death was an exercise in self-awareness. It brought him greater serenity. But it did little to slake his political thirst. "I'm confident that I'm more qualified to run for president than before."

Biden's political and medical troubles also brought him closer to a career-long nemesis, Ted Kennedy. The man who had often ignored Biden's instructions on the Judiciary Committee, whose shadow covered him for fifteen years, became suddenly like a brother.

"Something changed once I was under attack," Biden mused. "Teddy has a strong streak of loyalty. He yielded more to my setting the agenda than before.... When you are down, when you are in jeopardy, he not only helps you, but he jumps in on all fours." Kennedy sought out doctors for Biden; he sent gifts to his family; he visited and called him in the hospital. And for seven months, while Biden was recuperating, Kennedy took over responsibilities on the Judiciary Committee, doing exactly what Biden's staff asked of him, making no effort to impose his own agenda. A bemused Biden claimed that had he been well and in the committee chair, Kennedy would have fought him every step of the way.

CHAPTER

14

"... How Many Are My Foes!"

Bork had finished his five days of testimony feeling fine. Specter seemed friendlier after their detailed Saturday exchange. Byrd, whose leadership duties kept him away from the hearings, had nonetheless posed for a photograph with the judge. Bork felt he had loosened up as the week went on and had displayed judiciousness and knowledge. He and those around him were persuaded that Kennedy, Biden, and Metzenbaum had made fools of themselves.

Of course, it had been an exhausting week. The day after he finished, Bork and his wife drove to Middleburg, Virginia, for three days of rest at the farmhouse of a friend. There Bork plunged into detective novels, staying away from television and newspapers.

Mary Ellen Bork, fervently dedicated to her husband, did not display the same equanimity. She could not close her eyes entirely to accounts of the hearings or of the confirmation battle waged in the media. She turned on the television occasionally. But most of the hearings and coverage seemed to be dedicated to Bork's opponents. What she saw incensed her. She urged Bork to watch the hearings and call the Justice Department lawyers with advice on correcting some of the slander. Bork would have none of it. He said he had done what he could do. Finally, disgusted with the proceedings, she gave up watching. But she developed a fierce sense of foreboding.

The Borks returned to Washington late Tuesday, September 23, to find a new atmosphere. Earlier the confirmation had been seen as a difficult struggle. Now it was portrayed, even by many supporters, as a losing battle. White House aides were quoted in the press as saying that Bork and the Judiciary Committee had been like two trains passing in the night, that Bork's testimony had been a disappointment.

John Bolton's mother-in-law died on the twenty-third. He left the hearings to go to his wife, and as he drove through Washington, he was beginning to feel defeat. Combined with his family tragedy, a grim, sinking sensation struck him.

Fueling the gloom were public opinion polls released that week showing a sharp movement against Bork. Before his testimony the polls had shown an even split on confirmation. Now, after his appearance before the committee, they showed marked opposition with margins of eight to ten points against confirmation.

During this period Bork went to his D.C. Circuit Court chambers daily, trying to work on opinions. But his time was increasingly taken up by long talks with friends and supporters about his chances for confirmation. He wrote a long, detailed letter to the committee restating some of his views he felt were misrepresented. He talked to columnist George Will and counsel Ray Randolph, and of course, he talked to his family.

Nearly everyone said the same thing: We're getting killed in the heartland through a massive effort by our opponents and no viable response from the White House. An urgent campaign is needed.

Mary Ellen Bork felt this keenly. She kept receiving letters from a nun she knew in Minnesota asking for Bork's position on the death penalty. Mrs. Bork realized that there were no simple pamphlets setting forth Bork's views of the Constitution, nothing that could be sent to people such as her Minnesota friend. And she herself was too busy to write back. Yet the nun kept writing, expressing rebuke in her letters that she had not yet received a reply. She became a symbol to Mary Ellen, who talked to her husband about it. The more she thought about that nun's letters, the more incensed she got.

"Something just suddenly happened to us," Mrs. Bork recalled. "We realized that only one side of the story was getting out there in the press. There was no response from the White House."

She urged Bork to do something about it. He agreed. On Friday Bork called Brad Reynolds. As Reynolds told it to a colleague later, Bork "hit the panic button." Bork also called Will Ball in the White House and asked for a meeting with Howard Baker for the next day.

Baker had just left for Tennessee and could not come back in time. Tom Griscom, the communications director and a close Baker ally, agreed to run the meeting.

The Borks arrived at the White House that Saturday, September 26, with a list of demands. They wanted a speech by the president on Monday evening, a stream of phone calls by the president and Baker to undecided senators, and some high-profile fund raising. At the meeting were Ball, Reynolds, Korologos, Culvahouse, and Griscom.

Griscom said, "Judge, I'll talk to Senator Baker [the chief of staff went by his title of Senator]. I'll tell you right now there is nothing wrong with the idea of a presidential speech. But we've got to look at the best time to do the speech, not only in terms of the nomination but also in terms of the president. I understand why you want it Monday. But things just don't turn that fast around here."

Mary Ellen Bork complained about what she saw as biased news accounts of the hearings and Bork's record. She couldn't understand why the White House was not responding.

Bork said it was time to go on a media counterattack, possibly doing a television commercial as a reply to the Gregory Peck one. The judge had heard that Charlton Heston had expressed interest in helping. Money had to be raised for the entire effort.

Griscom replied that the White House could not be involved in raising money in that fashion. He reminded Bork about the Iran-contra scandal and allegations that administration officials had raised money for the contras despite the congressional prohibition on such activity. The White House could not open itself to such accusations again. That was why We the People, a private pro-Bork group, had been formed in California.

But, Bork protested, the group had failed to raise any money or to set up an organization. "The president chose me," he said. "I'm *his* nominee. I don't see why he can't get more involved."

"Yes," Griscom replied. "He did choose you and was proud to have done so. The president has done a lot for you. But not all the responsibility falls on his shoulders. And we need to look at the impact of what he does and how he does it."

Korologos passed Griscom a note. He understood Reagan was in the White House. Perhaps the president could pop in and boost Bork's spirits.

Griscom decided against that. He feared the press would get word of it and the story would get out that the president had to cheer up Bork.

Recalling the meeting later, Griscom said his job was to protect the president of the United States, to look out for his interests. "I did that to the best of my abilities. We got into this thing of whether the president should speak now or later. I wanted to make sure the speech would make a difference. If not, it trivializes his word. What troubled me most when I arrived here in early 1987 was that people had the idea 'We'll just wheel out the president whenever necessary.' But if nobody is carrying the message on the outside, it gets diluted, and it doesn't have the same impact."

Culvahouse was deeply disappointed by the meeting. He had begun to worry that the White House was not doing the job for Bork. He told Bolton and Eastland at Justice that Griscom seemed no more committed to the nomination than before, that he had apparently seen the meeting as simply an opportunity for Bork to let off steam. Kenneth Duberstein, Baker's deputy, didn't even bother to show up at the meeting, Culvahouse complained. The men at Justice were surprised by Culvahouse's candor with them. He was a Baker loyalist. But he had become an admirer of Bork's.

The Borks were no less disenchanted. They also left the meeting dismayed. Bork told a few people that perhaps he had better begin to think about making other plans. While he and his wife were angered by Griscom's coolness, they could not reproach the aide for dissembling. The man had been honest: The president's interests were larger and more important than those of this nomination. It was precisely what Bolton and Judge James Buckley had warned Bork about the afternoon of the nomination.

The next day Bolton, Eastland, Reynolds, and Mike Carvin gathered in Reynolds's office to talk about the situation. The idea was to come up with some kind of plan. But frustrations were so high that nothing was accomplished. Although it was Sunday, and they all had better things to do, they spent two hours attacking the White House staff for lack of guts.

The third and final week of the hearings began, but few paid attention. No members of the public lined up outside the Russell Building. Seats in the Caucus Room remained unoccupied. Television news devoted almost no time to the proceedings, and newspaper stories on them were buried. Biden sought to move things along so that he and other Democrats could devote their time to persuading their colleagues to vote against confirmation. The hearings ended on Wednesday with a vote planned for the following week.

Bolton was calling Republicans all over the country, trying to see if anything could be done. He felt as if he were shoving ice off the deck of the *Titanic*. John Tuck, assistant to Howard Baker, wrote Bork a memo detailing all the work that the chief of staff had done for the nomination. Hearing that, Bork's son Bob wrote a note to himself: "The apologies begin."

On the last day of the hearings Arlen Specter called Bork for a face-to-face meeting. They had already spoken privately for more than three hours over the months. Specter questioned Bork for an hour that day. Later in the evening Specter met with Lloyd Cutler. The Pennsylvania Republican had made up his mind. He called Howard Baker and told him he had decided to vote against confirmation. It was devastating news. Specter's decision would provide cover to a whole range of unsure senators on both sides of the aisle. He was, after all, a Republican and the committee member who had distinguished himself as the most serious, the most high-minded constitutional student.

Baker asked if it would help for Specter to talk to the president. "I don't think there is any need, Howard," Specter replied.

The next day, just before noon on October 1, Specter called Bork to tell him of his decision.

"I'm disappointed to know that," Bork said. "I thought I addressed your concerns."

"You did address my concerns, but you didn't resolve the doubts that I had," Specter replied. He then went to the Senate floor to announce his vote.

The committee did not vote officially until the following week. But by the end of that day, Thursday, October 1, few doubted that Bork would be defeated. Specter's announcement was compounded by statements from southern Democrats David Pryor of Arkansas, Terry Sanford of North Carolina, and Bennett Johnston of Louisiana. All were against. Moreover, the *Atlanta Journal/Constitution* published a Roper poll showing strong opposition to Bork in the South.

At the Justice Department Bolton went to Meese's office and said what he had intimated on several occasions in the past: It was time to find another nominee. For the first time Meese did not disagree. Later in the day a meeting was held in Bob Dole's office. In attendance were Baker, Ball, Korologos, Bolton, and the committee Republicans—except Specter, who was asked not to come. Baker recommended taking the fight to the Senate floor unless there was massive Republican defection. The committee's conservatives—Charles Grassley, Orrin Hatch, and Gordon Humphrey—attacked Baker, saying he had mishandled the nomination from the beginning. Baker slumped in his chair. Dole did not come to his aid.

The next day nine more Democrats, including Lloyd Bentsen, announced their intention to oppose Bork. Brad Reynolds agreed with others in the department that the nomination was dead. A quiet search for a replacement should begin.

On Friday, four days before the vote, President Reagan invited Dennis DeConcini to the White House. DeConcini went with his committee aide, Ed Baxter. Reagan read them a list of prominent people supporting Bork.

"This is really important to me," Reagan told DeConcini. "It is my job to appoint justices, and this man is truly qualified. Politics shouldn't come into it."

"Politics *has* come into it—on both sides," DeConcini answered. The meeting lasted fifteen minutes.

On Monday there were more announcements. The *New York Times*, in an editorial that surprised no one, advised the Senate to turn Bork down. The *Washington Post*, which had harshly condemned the Bork opposition, accusing it of "intellectual vulgarity and personal savagery," also came out against Bork. It was an unusual editorial, half assailing Bork's critics and half assailing Bork.

The *Post* said that when Bork was nominated, it had fully expected to endorse him. It said he had suffered a "lynching" by special-interest groups. (It printed, on the same day, an op-ed piece by Bob Bork, Jr., bitterly complaining about the "evil caricature" of his father.) But in the end, the editorial said, what mattered most was Bork's written record and, especially, his five days of testimony. What was it that had changed the paper's initial strong feelings?

The impression, never disturbed throughout the hearing and never refuted by the nominee no matter how many questions just begged for such refutation, that he did not change in the one respect that matters most: Judge Bork has retained from his academic days an almost frightening detachment from, not to say indifference toward, the real-world consequences of his views; he plays with ideas, seeks tidiness, and in the process does not seem to care who is crushed. What people like ourselves needed when confronted with this impression was modest, but critical. . . . [I]t was a simple assurance that, in addition to the forensic brilliance, the personal integrity and the care for the law, Robert Bork's moral sensibility could be engaged with the questions on which he had pronounced so forcefully, that in these great cases that were to have so profound and intimate an effect on people's lives, he had a feeling for justice, not just for the law. They are not always the same.

The *Post*, which went on to say that the Constitution's genius lay partly in its elasticity, added of the nominee: "He does not read the Constitution generously."

The editorial pleased neither side in the fight, and in any case it came out too late to make any difference. The nomination was already sunk. The anti-Bork coalition, which had felt mistreated by the *Post*, accused the paper of jumping on the bandwagon when it no longer mattered. To Bork's supporters, the *Post* seemed to be siding, predictably, with liberals, taking the cowardly way out.

George Will, a *Post* columnist, lashed out at the editorial three days later on its op-ed page, saying the paper "should blush about its role in reducing liberalism to the politics of flaunted feelings."

On October 6 the Judiciary Committee held its vote. Hours before, the beleaguered Bork team held a meeting in Howard Baker's office. Griscom had an idea: The opposition had painted Bork in such harsh colors, wildly claiming he wanted to sterilize people and then, just to be sure, post policemen in their bedrooms, that perhaps an entirely new approach was needed. Humanize Bork; soften his image through a folksy television interview. He suggested the Borks grant an interview to Barbara Walters. Mary Ellen Bork would be able to say loving things about Bork that he himself could not. Barbara Walters was keenly interested.

Bork thought about it but rejected it on the advice of many around him. They said it was beneath his dignity. He did not want to campaign for the Court by showing he was a lovable guy.

By the time of the vote only Heflin's decision was still publicly unknown, although the Alabaman had told Biden the evening before of his plans to oppose. Biden called Howard Baker and told him there would be a clear vote against Bork and offered him the opportunity to withdraw the nomination. Baker refused.

Reagan then called Heflin, who declined to say how he would vote. Heflin joined the Judiciary Committee in recommending to the Senate by a vote of 9–5 that it turn down the Bork nomination. His words summed up what many felt:

> I am in a state of quandary as to whether this nominee would be a conservative justice who would safeguard the living Constitution and prevent judicial activism or whether, on the other hand, he would be an extremist who would use his position on the Court to advance a far-right, radical judicial agenda. The question is difficult. Frankly, I am not sure that I have the answer. I am reminded of an old saying, "When in doubt, don't." I see a great deal of wisdom to this warning. A lifetime position on the Supreme Court is too important to risk to a person who has continued to exhibit—and may still possess—a proclivity for extremism in spite of confirmation protestations.

Every morning for some time reporters and television crews had gathered on the Borks' lawn. Mrs. Bork felt their presence dramatically illustrated the psalms that she recited daily: "O Lord, how many are my foes! Many are rising against me." And: "O men, how long shall my honor suffer shame? How long will you love vain words, and seek after lies?" Prayer, she wrote later, helped her to "remain firm and patient and to rise above conflicting emotions. With all the turmoil and stress of those days I still experienced a peace and inner freedom that came from trying to *do* the truth. Jesus' promise, 'The truth will make you free,' has new meaning for me."

Supporters around the country were praying with her. The telephone at home rarely stopped ringing with the words of supporters. One anonymous woman left a message on the Bork answering machine suggesting the family read Psalm 35, which begins: "Strive, O Lord, with those who strive against me, Fight against those who fight me, Grasp shield and buckler and rise up to help me."

Some prayer groups held twenty-four-hour vigils during Bork's testimony. Others sent telegrams and letters to the Bork home. The family stored hundreds of them in large expanding envelopes. They came from all over. From Watchung, New Jersey: "I am deeply saddened by this shameful display of deceit and dishonesty by those selected to represent me in my government." From Bronxville, New York: "I don't remember having ever been as grateful for the existence of a single person as I am for your life, your thoughts and ways of reasoning and your actions." From Owensboro, Kentucky: "I think you need to know that the grassroots people of America are with you, and desire very much to see you appointed. . . . Praise the Lord, most people are no longer swayed by the media hype."

With Bork's withdrawal seen as imminent, television employees on motorcycles tailed him everywhere lest their networks miss the moment. Bork himself assumed he would withdraw.

He had told as much to his friend Leonard Garment, a prominent Washington lawyer, the evening after the committee vote. Garment had tried to push Bork into staying the course, but Bork hadn't the stomach for it.

Garment had known Bork for years. He and his wife, Suzanne, were great fans of the judge. It was Garment who first recommended Bork to the Nixon administration in 1970, on the advice of Alexander Bickel. The two men also played in a monthly poker game with Chief Justice Rehnquist, Justice Scalia, Walter Berns of the American Enterprise Institute, and, occasionally, Education Secretary William Bennett. It was a game of long standing. When Justice Potter Stewart was still alive, he, too, would occasionally play. Someone would send out to the deli for sandwiches, there was plenty of beer, and for a couple of hours the men would shed their titles and robes and just gossip. With all those judges and justices there you couldn't talk about cases or real work. Everyone was scrupulous about that. So they chatted about everything else. And Bork, while a pretty appalling poker player—he actually had a crib sheet to remind him that a full house beat a straight, which beat three of a kind, and so on—was always delightful.

Over the summer, as Bork's nomination ran into trouble, Garment had been busy helping former National Security Adviser Robert C. McFarlane through the Iran-contra labyrinth. Now, with the committee vote over, he decided he had to act.

He went to see Bork at home, bringing with him his son, Paul, twenty-seven, a clarinetist. Glum and exhausted, the Bork family was sitting around the living room, discussing the big question: Should they ask President Reagan to withdraw Bork's name? The air was funereal.

Bork looked like someone who wanted to go to sleep and not wake up for about four days. He had gained weight and was smoking more than ever. Before the nomination he had nearly quit cigarettes; he had taken up tennis again, getting back into shape. At his first White House meeting after the nomination was announced, he was still chewing Nicorettes. But the pressure got to him.

Early that evening Bork had fallen asleep in his study, unusual for him. The truth was, he hadn't wanted Garment to come over because it was late and he was washed out. But Garment had pushed, saying his son was in from out of town, admired Bork, and wanted to meet him. With the Garments settled in, Bork poured himself another martini. Garment had a couple of vodkas and felt energized. He and his son stayed for two and a half hours.

Bork was inclined to withdraw his name, and his family was feeling the same way. But Garment urged him, harangued him really, to stay in. Principles were at stake; pulling out would only legitimize the distortions and allow the lying rascals off the hook. Posterity deserved an honest record. As the vodka took hold, Garment grew grandiose, punching the air with his cigarette. He predicted that some moderate Democratic senator like Sam Nunn of Georgia or Daniel Patrick Moynihan of New York would grasp the significance of what was happening and deliver a historic and eloquent defense of Bork.

The Bork family said little. Mrs. Bork's demure nature offered a contrast with her husband's rumpled presence. She sat very still and listened. The children were restless.

Finally, Bork looked so wretched that even Garment took the hint and rose to leave. Bork thanked him. He would think about what Garment had said. Over the next couple of days Garment had trouble reaching Bork although he sent him little notes suggesting things to say about why he was going to stay in. Garment kept his fingers crossed.

The day after the Garment visit, Bork canceled a courtesy call with John Heinz of Pennsylvania, seeing it as no longer necessary. He drove with his wife and two sons to the Justice Department to tell Meese and Reynolds of his plan.

He found a receptive audience. Reynolds, who had lost his own acrimonious confirmation battle in the Senate Judiciary Committee two years earlier, told Bork he saw no reason to go through more humiliation and agony. Meese agreed. While the three of them spoke in Meese's office, Bork's family sat in the anteroom. Bob, Jr., remembered another time he had been in that room—fourteen years earlier as his father was sworn in as solicitor general. The contrast of that memory with the day's mission only added to his pain.

The family left the Justice Department and rode the few blocks to Bork's chambers at the D.C. Circuit Court. Mary Ellen, Bob, and Charlie ate lunch while Bork made some phone calls, including one to Alan Simpson, who had left a message. The previous day Bork and Mary Ellen had met with a score of conservative Republican senators on Capitol Hill. Their message to him: Take the confirmation to the full Senate; force the southern Democrats to go on record so we can use this against them in the 1988 elections; those who oppose you will pay politically. Gordon Humphrey of New Hampshire had said the same thing to Bob, Jr., on the phone. Only Simpson objected to that reasoning, saying that Bork should do what was best for himself and his family, and that probably meant withdrawing. Jake Garn, conservative Utah Republican, glared at Simpson. "If I'd known you were going to say that, I wouldn't have invited you," he said.

Bork appreciated Simpson's concerns. Dialing his number, he wondered what the Wyoming legislator wanted. But Simpson was not there, and Bork left a message.

At lunch, meanwhile, Bob, Charlie, and Mary Ellen began to discover that each secretly wished Bork would stay in for a full Senate vote. None harbored illusions about winning—fifty-three senators were already declared opposed—but they felt an honest record needed to be left.

They went into his office and told him of their conversation. Charlie argued that to withdraw would be to lend credence to the outrageous charges made against him. Bob urged his father to think back to the Watergate crisis, when he had had the courage to fire Archibald Cox and hold the Justice Department together. The easy move, politically and personally, would have been to step down like his two superiors, Elliot Richardson and William Ruckelshaus. All would have praised him. But the department would have fallen apart and the nation plunged into even greater chaos. He did what had to be done then. He should do the same now.

Bork was moved. As chance would have it, Senator Simpson called back right then. Bork said to him that he had been thinking it over, and at the urging of his family, he had changed his mind and would prefer to stay in for a full Senate vote. Simpson was pleased. The reason he was calling was that he, too, had reconsidered his view and believed Bork should stay in. Simpson promised that he and his Republican colleagues would offer history an honest picture of the maligned judge and of his small-minded and politically vicious opponents.

Bork called Meese to tell him that he wanted to take his nomination to the full Senate. "You're talking to a guy who is changing his mind every three and a half minutes," Bork averred. But he said he had talked to Simpson, who had agreed. And his family was in a fighting mood. Bork reiterated that he deserved a speech from the president. "The senators will rescue my character," Bork said Simpson had promised.

To his watching family, Bork seemed to have a new depth to his voice, a new energy, a new sense of mission. A calm settled over all of them as they set about helping him draft his statement. This was a situation in which the Borks felt at home—fighting against the odds, bucking prevailing wisdom. "We're going to lose, but they can't beat us" is how Bob, Jr., remembers feeling.

That night Ray Randolph and his wife, Eileen O'Connor, went to the Borks, where Randolph worked with Bork on his statement. At first the atmosphere was jovial, almost slaphappy. Later the three of them sat and talked and drank like battle-weary comrades. The evening was bathed in a surreal, almost religious peace. For unspoken reasons, it seemed that Claire Bork was present.

Friday, October 9, Bork and his family, steeled for their encounter, went to the White House to tell the president and the nation that he would not withdraw his name. The president was having lunch with his old friend Charles Wick, director of the United States Information Agency. The Borks, accompanied by Randolph, waited in the Map Room, so named because Franklin Roosevelt had kept his maps there during World War II. Meese arrived, and Bork showed him his statement. Bob, Jr., watched the attorney general intently as he read. What was going on in his mind? Meese exhibited no emotion. He was not eager for Bork to stay in, but he sympathized and was willing to help. He pronounced the speech "perfect." Vice President Bush arrived, read it, and said encouraging words. The Borks could not tell if they were sincere. Bush made small talk about mutual friends on the street where the Borks lived.

In the early 1970s Bush had lived next door to the house Bork bought in 1981. Randolph made small talk about the room's antiques. Bob noted that the couch on which he was sitting was rock hard.

An hour later Baker's assistant, John Tuck, announced that the president had finished his lunch. He would see first the attorney general and vice president and then the Bork family. While Meese and Bush met with Reagan, Bork and his eldest son discussed the possibility that Reagan would not allow the nominee to stay in. In their hour of need they trusted no one.

"When you get in there, they may gang up on you and try to bully you into withdrawing," Bob warned. Bork told his son that if Reagan forbade him from reading his prepared statement in the press room, he would go outside and recite it for the press there.

Five minutes later the group—except for Randolph, who chose to wait downstairs—was escorted up the elevator to the president's private living room, a lavish and beautiful chamber. As angry as the family had been at Reagan's ineffective efforts on Bork's behalf, they were smitten by his charm and easygoing manner. As they prepared to have their photograph taken with the president, Reagan told an old story about the actor Fredric March's having his picture taken. It seems that March always chose to stand on the right flank of any newspaper photo because his name would then appear first in the caption. It was nothing, and a story Reagan had doubtless told hundreds of times. But it came out with a freshness and spontaneity that made the Borks warm to him instantly. Reagan admired political conviction. He was consoling and told the family he supported Bork's decision to stay in and would issue a statement to that effect.

There were forty-five minutes before the announcement, and the family waited in Howard Baker's office. Bork paced furiously. Bob had never seen him so intense or anxious. Bork was not afraid. But he was consumed by his mission. Bob drank in the scene. Behind Baker was a computer screen with a minute-by-minute description of the whereabouts of the president and first lady. He also had a telephone linked to a briefcase. Inside was a scrambler for sensitive calls. The air was thick with history and anticipation.

Bob asked his father if he wanted the family to join him in the press room for the statement. It was a natural offer. The family had united behind him, had helped him understand the importance of staying in, had aided in drafting the statement, had accompanied him on the sensitive visits. No one needed to state it outright, but the unity was like the one they had felt when Claire Bork lay dying. Mary Ellen Bork, who had not shared in that trauma, was fully part of this one. It was serving as a rite of passage, drawing her in more tightly to the family web.

But Bork said, "No, I'm not trying to elicit that kind of sympathy."

At 3:00 P.M. Bork surprised the nation by announcing his intention to stay in for a full Senate vote.

> He declared: The process of confirming justices for our nation's highest court has been transformed in a way that should not and indeed must not be permitted to occur again. Federal judges are not appointed to decide cases according to the latest opinion polls. . . . A crucial principle is at stake. That principle is the way in which we select the men and women who guard the liberties of all the American people. That should not be done through public campaigns of distortion. If I withdraw now, that campaign would be seen as a success, and it would be mounted against future nominees.

From Baker's office Bob watched on television with tears in his eyes. He had never felt prouder of his father.

Garment watched from his office; delighted by Bork's speech, he set to work. He went on ABC's "Nightline" with Ted Koppel; he persuaded half a dozen lawyers to write defenses of Bork. And he told anyone who would listen that this was a moment to stand tall for what mattered. If they stuck together, this nomination—and the dignity of the judicial selection process—might be saved.

Some ordinary citizens felt equally moved. Another batch of letters and telegrams arrived at the Bork home and office, some quoting Scripture, some just praising the judge's bravery. "You dear courageous man! Judge Bork, how my heart breaks for you and how I admire you," wrote a woman from Cincinnati. "Your words today that you will not give up as nominee to the Supreme Court brought tears to my eyes. I said a prayer for you just then, asking God to be with you. I do not think I have ever witnessed such a stirring and fervent turn of events these past two months than I have with the issue of your nomination."

Vice President George Bush sent a handwritten note: "Dear Bob, Before I leave for Texas tomorrow, I wanted to send along this personal note. There was something very special about that little get together with your family the other day (Map Room). As one who has caught his share of arrows in public life, I could only think about your kids and family love. Seeing them and Mary Ellen steadfast in their support for you really got to me. Good luck. I'm very proud of you. George."

At the Justice Department there was little such sentiment. Reynolds, Carvin, Eastland, and Bolton had been discussing new nominees when Meese called them from the White House to say that Bork was staying in. They were shocked and, to be truthful, annoyed. No one wanted to push Bork, but he was, after all, defeated. They were afraid that his move would complicate, even jeopardize, their plans to get another strong conservative on the bench.

That night there was a meeting at the White House to set up a last-ditch strategy, but it was clear that nobody felt this battle could be won. Korologos said the aim would be to get forty-five votes for Bork. They agreed to a presidential speech the following week. It was delivered in the middle of the afternoon five days later, and as Griscom had predicted, the three major networks refused to carry it. They said it was politics, not policy. Only Cable News Network presented the full speech live.

As an apt symbol of the fate of the nomination, the evening of Bork's announcement ABC News named as its Person of the Week Ralph Neas of the Leadership Conference on Civil Rights, the man who had led the campaign to stop confirmation.

The men at Justice understood their duty and agreed to look as if they were fighting for Bork. On Sunday Bolton and Reynolds went to the White House for another Bork meeting. It was Gay Pride Day, and Bolton was unable to park near the White House. He had to walk through a throng of gay and lesbian activists who were shouting anti-Bork and anti-Reagan slogans such as "Reagan, Bork No Way! Sexist, Racist, Anti-Gay!"

This was just the sort of display that would have discredited the anti-Bork forces in the minds of most Americans, Bolton thought wearily. "Where were these people two months ago when we needed them?"

The Bork meeting was uneventful. The demonstration was still going on as Bolton and Reynolds left the White House together.

Bolton was virtually unknown to the public, but Reynolds had received press exposure over the years as an advocate for an agenda these demonstrators detested. Suddenly Bolton worried that with Reynolds at his side, he was walking into the jaws of hell. "What if some of these people recognize you?" he asked.

"No problem," Reynolds answered. "I'll just hold your hand."

The full Senate debate occurred after some delay—it began on October 21—and lasted just under three days. It was testy and predictable. But there were moments of eloquence.

Biden defended the work of the committee, stating that the nominee had been given every opportunity to make his case and that every courtesy had been extended to Bork and his supporters. He said the hearings took place at a historically high-minded level with witnesses who were uniformly intelligent and learned.

Biden spoke of the stark constitutional choice the Bork nomination represented: whether individuals, imbued with fundamental rights, cede some of those rights to government or whether individuals have rights only because government grants them. He argued for the former and said Bork was an advocate of the latter. He acknowledged that it was an old debate, as old as the Republic, and that both sides deserved respect.

"Judge Bork seems, sadly, to see a fatal vagueness in the protection of individual rights, and an expansive field for temporary majorities to wreak their will upon the minority and upon individuals," he said.

Biden pointed to what he regarded as a fundamental contradiction in Bork's testimony: Bork claimed that the only legitimate jurisprudence was one of original intent, saying dozens of cases were wrongly decided. But he assured the committee those same decisions represented settled law. How could Bork remain true to his own judicial principles and accept such decisions as precedents upon which to build?

Hatch answered Biden, accusing Bork's opponents of waging an extraordinarily nasty campaign. Armed with blowups of the anti-Bork ads and large, dramatic charts, Hatch pointed to what he said were scores of inaccuracies.

Hatch said Biden's formulation of the debate was wrong. Everyone agreed, he said, with the Declaration of Independence that "all men are created equal, that they are endowed by their Creator with certain unalienable Rights. . . ." That part was easy. The question, the Utah senator pointed out, was how to *identify* those natural rights. Should that awesome responsibility be left in the hands of unelected judges? No, said Hatch. "Because rights belong to the people, Judge Bork would let the people identify and define them. This process occurs either by constitutional amendment or by statute."

For Hatch, as for Bork, the "people" meant the majority. But to liberals, the very point of rights was to protect minorities. For that reason, judges, steeped in law and history and insulated from majority political pressures, were the appropriate identifiers of rights.

When Kennedy stood up to speak, Bob, Jr., and Mary Ellen Bork got up from the visitors' gallery to leave. Journalists noted it and reported it as proof of the family's special contempt for the senator from Massachusetts. Actually the Borks had been looking for a convenient moment to eat and had no interest in hearing Kennedy. But when their move was misinterpreted, they were not sorry.

Few outsiders were paying attention to this debate. It was seen by most as *pro forma.* But behind the scenes a fired-up Leonard Garment was busy. He was allowed to work in Vice President George Bush's Capitol office. On the evening of the second day he brought with him some hastily written analyses of Bork's judicial opinions, prepared at his request by a group of top lawyers. Piled up on a dolly he had brought from his law firm, they were the opening intellectual salvo in his pro-Bork offensive.

In between phone calls, Garment hopped out to the Senate waiting room or the press gallery to find out how the floor exchanges were progressing. The debate had been lackluster, and Garment hoped to keep it in motion till after the weekend so the senators would have a chance to read his reports—and possibly change their minds. He knew his mission seemed sisyphean, that Bork's fate was probably sealed. But it was worth trying. He figured if he could get a couple of senators to say they had jumped too quickly to a conclusion against Bork, he could get something going.

Having returned from a quick trip to the gallery, Garment suddenly found himself being pushed out of Bush's office. The Capitol police told him that since the vice president's office staff had left, they had to lock the doors. Garment couldn't believe it. Where was he supposed to work? Was that maybe the point? He banished the paranoia from his brain and proceeded. He wheeled his reports out of the Bush office, feeling more like a Brooklyn pretzel vendor than a top Washington attorney, to a table in the ornate waiting room, where he set up camp. He was reminded of his days trying cases in New York City courtrooms where there wasn't enough space for lawyers, who sometimes set up shop in a phone booth.

This was not the first setback Garment had suffered in his efforts for Bork. He was, for starters, *persona non grata* with the press. After working news reporters so hard, badgering them at their computer terminals while they were on deadline, he had been officially barred from the Senate press gallery. For another, he had hoped for a spot on David Brinkley's Sunday morning program ten days earlier, but fellow Washington attorney Lloyd Cutler was chosen instead. By then Cutler had decided that enough was enough, and contrary to Garment's last-minute pleas, he acknowledged on television that Bork seemed beaten.

Garment wanted to fight on. He genuinely believed that if the record were set straight, a few senators might change their minds.

At age sixty-three, Garment epitomized the Washington establishment. He was one of the anointed, a man who took special pleasure in lamenting the sorry state of the local power culture and enjoyed every minute of it.

Garment had come to Washington in 1969 to join the Nixon administration, having worked as Nixon's law partner in New York. In the Nixon White House, however, Garment was a bit of an oddball. A onetime Democrat who had voted for John F. Kennedy, he had also played jazz clarinet with Woody Herman years before. Many of Nixon's handlers mistrusted him. Now he was a registered independent and a political conservative.

In other circumstances Garment might have felt silly, stuck alone in the Senate waiting room with a dollyload of material no one seemed interested in reading. He'd have seen the absurdity of standing there, disheveled, on his quixotic mission. But tonight Len Garment was a man obsessed. He had convinced himself that if the senators would just read the truth about Bork, this thing wouldn't look so grim. And its being Thursday night, they could examine the material over the weekend and get some momentum going for the following week.

Now he was stuck in the Senate waiting room. Not only was he on the rhetorical defensive, but he was alone. The doors around him were locked. The normally bustling waiting room, with its ornately patterned tile floor and chandeliers and portraits of Calhoun and Webster, was empty. Garment paced the room. Out came Randall Rader, Judiciary Committee aide to Senator Orrin Hatch. Just the man Garment wanted to see. But Rader's news was unhappy.

A decision had been made: The vote on Bork would take place the next day. There would be no weekend for the senators to read Garment's material. There would be no changes of votes, no momentum.

Garment blew up.

"Who the hell do you think you are?" he demanded.

"It wasn't my decision," Rader replied, backing off. He said the majority leader, Robert Byrd, was sending signals that if there wasn't a vote on Friday, he would delay the thing indefinitely, making it very hard for the administration to get another name in after this one was defeated. This was not entirely true, although Simpson had told Bork the same thing on the phone earlier in the day to get him to agree to wrap it up. Bork had consented, saying he wanted only to set the record straight about himself. He had no intention of tying up the Senate forever and jeopardizing the Court, which had opened its term two weeks earlier with only eight of the nine justices on the bench.

"The whole family has decided. And everyone here agrees there is no point in dragging this out any further," Rader told Garment.

"Everyone doesn't agree, goddammit," Garment shot back.

Garment scribbled a note to Minority Leader Dole and asked a messenger to bring it to him on the floor. If anyone could stop this debate from ending, it was Dole, a professional hardball legislator. The problem was that Dole, a moderate Republican who hoped to beat Bush for their party's presidential nomination, had been tepid on Bork from the beginning. Earlier, when opposition to Bork around the country became heated, Dole told an aide: "I've been talking to the folks on the floor, particularly southern Democrats. They see a no vote as a no-lose proposition. They can please blacks, women, liberals. And in the end they figure the administration will get another conservative on the Court."

Dole was also concerned about the civil rights objections to Bork. All that constitutional theorizing was not his game. It made him uneasy, and he was a tad suspicious about Bork's motives. Moreover, there was no personal chemistry between Bork and Dole. They were vastly different people. Dole, a pragmatist of the first order, had never considered himself an intellectual. He was a how-ya-doin' kind of guy, a deal maker, a man of action. Bork, with his professorial manner, seemed unable to relax with Dole. He acted aloof. It rankled Dole, who felt the judge was putting him down.

Garment's note to the minority leader was short and simple: "Give me just 20 seconds of your time."

Standing outside the door to the Senate chamber, Garment watched Dole read it and, without so much as turn toward him, head out of the Senate in the other direction.

Simpson appeared. He saw no point in carrying on. There wasn't a glimmer in any senator's eye suggesting the possibility of a shift, as he put it later.

Garment began pleading for time. This thing could be won. All this work had been done. Just a few more days.

"There's no point, Len," Simpson said, and, pointing to the Senate floor, added: "That room is filled with a bunch of goddamned cowards. They don't have the guts to stand up to the pressure. No one's budging. It's over."

Garment began to make his case one more time.

Simpson interrupted. He had a gentle, homespun manner when he wanted it, and this was the moment. He started to tell Garment that he had once been a practicing lawyer himself, and he, too, had had cases where he had wanted to fight on even when the client hadn't. In this case, he said, the client had thrown in the towel. It was time for the lawyer to get the message.

And with that it clicked. The runaway train that Leonard Garment had become in the previous two weeks was finally derailed. The information seeped in. But he had no energy left for rage. Instead, out came tears. There, just off the floor of the United States Senate, Leonard Garment, counsel to the rich and powerful, began to weep. And Alan Simpson, Senate minority whip, cowboy lawyer with the rapier wit from Cody, Wyoming, a hardy soldier in the nation's most vicious of political wars, put his arm around him and said everything was going to be all right.

The debate dragged on. Bob Packwood, Republican of Oregon, spoke at great length about liberty and privacy, beginning with the Magna Carta. John Danforth, Republican of Missouri and a former

Bork student, said, "The man has been trashed in our house. Some of us helped generate the trashing. Others of us yielded to it."

Newspapers obligingly ran stories on the proceedings, but they were short and inside the paper. But toward the middle of the third day, as the historic moment approached, the visitor and press galleries grew packed. The often rarefied atmosphere of the Senate was crackling. Lobbyists had their reaction statements ready for the press.

Strom Thurmond, as mindful as anyone in the chamber of the inevitable result and of the prevailing sentiment, had the debate's final word: "Mr. President, I would like for the presiding officer to admonish the audience in the galleries there will be no outburst when the outcome is announced."

At 2:00 P.M. on Friday, October 23, the Senate defeated the Bork nomination by a vote of 58–42. Having spent the morning at home, Bork and his wife felt an urgent need to get out of the house as the hour of the vote approached. So while the yeas and noes were being solemnly registered and counted, a resigned Robert Bork sat with Mary Ellen Bork and friend Walter Berns sipping a martini in the lavish dining room of the Madison Hotel and contemplating his future.

CHAPTER

15

Endgame

For weeks the administration had been looking for a new nominee in a defiant mood. A few days after Bork announced his intention to stay in, Reagan told a cheering crowd in New Jersey that he would send up another name that the senators will "object to just as much as the last one."

The charged political atmosphere of the Bork battle exaggerated the shortcomings of many of the possible nominees. One was not sufficiently antiunion, another soft on abortion, still another too much of a lightning rod for liberals. One by one, the possibilities fell away until the only ones left standing were Anthony Kennedy from the Ninth Circuit Court of Appeals in California and Douglas Ginsburg, a young judge on the District of Columbia Circuit Court of Appeals, the same court as Bork. Both men were interviewed by administration officials. Kennedy was urged on Reagan by Baker and his aides; he was a solid conservative with many years' experience and no known enemies. Moderates spoke approvingly of the choice. He would win speedy confirmation.

But Ginsburg was the pick of Meese and Reynolds at Justice. They assured the others that Ginsburg, who had worked in the administration for three years before being named to the bench, was "one of us."

Anthony Kennedy was what Justice Department conservatives called an eighty percenter, meaning it was thought he could be counted on in 80 percent of the cases, but not more. He had handed down a ruling in the sensitive privacy area that made New Right advocates nervous. It was in a case similar to one Bork had ruled on, regarding the right of a branch of the military to bar homosexual activity. Both judges came to the same conclusion: that the military had such a right. But Bork went out of his way to say that homosexual activity enjoyed no protection under the Constitution, contrary to what many liberals advocated. He said further that the privacy doctrine itself was fundamentally flawed. Kennedy took a different approach. In a footnote he pointed out that there was an ongoing academic debate on whether the privacy doctrine protected homosexual acts. He did not take a stand on the debate but by recognizing its existence seemed to lend it legitimacy.

While that soothed many on the left, it incensed a number on the right, in particular Senators Humphrey, Grassley, and Jesse Helms, the North Carolina Republican, who threatened a boycott if Kennedy were chosen.

Grassley, a strapping, avuncular politician who liked to refer to himself as "a dirt farmer from northeast Iowa," had defended Bork with dedication on the committee. Backed by his Judiciary aide, Sam Gerdano, Grassley waxed indignant on what he saw as the unfair treatment of Bork. After the committee vote he favored taking the issue to the full Senate.

Following Bork's defeat, Grassley continued to feel deeply involved in the process and called the White House to lobby against Kennedy and for Ginsburg. Speaking of it later, he said he had done so on the advice of the Justice Department, advice he quickly came to regret.

"I wasn't as fully informed about Ginsburg to justify being that involved, and I should have stayed out till the nomination was made," Grassley lamented. "I wanted to support Justice over the White House. It was a decision made in haste. I wanted a justice who would overturn *Roe* v. *Wade*. . . . I felt we had to cut these people [at the White House] off at the pass."

The pressure from Justice and conservative senators persuaded Reagan to name Ginsburg. Bork himself had also recommended him highly. The president was particularly pleased about Ginsburg's age, forty-one. He would be on the bench a very long time.

White House aides felt outmaneuvered by Meese. As one put it, "The guys at Justice sandbagged us. They blindsided us. [Former

Attorney General] William French Smith had talked up Ginsburg to the president just before Baker and Meese went in to discuss their choices."

Another White House aide said, "The fallout was so heavy from Bork that people were screaming for cover. They just let Justice have the run of the field and push Ginsburg through. Baker was so stung on Bork he was unable to act."

Reagan nominated Ginsburg on October 29 at a carefully planned press conference populated by dozens of administration officials to applaud as the nominee entered. The judge's physician wife and young daughter were also present at the announcement. This act of the nomination process was well staged, but the play's conclusion was unexpected. Following the Bork tragedy would be the Ginsburg farce.

Doug Ginsburg had been on the District of Columbia Circuit Court of Appeals for less than a year. A graduate of Cornell and the University of Chicago Law School, he had been a clerk to Justice Thurgood Marshall and a professor at Harvard Law School for eight years before joining the Justice Department in the antitrust division in 1983. After a period at the Office of Management and Budget, he returned to the antitrust division before being named to the bench. His brief experience in the practice of law brought him the lowest ABA rating of "qualified" when he was made a judge.

Ginsburg was a University of Chicago market-oriented conservative who believed regulatory questions should be decided by strict comparisons of social costs and benefits. That meant he opposed much government role in achieving social equality. But his political and judicial views on a wide range of issues, including civil rights, privacy, equal protection, and free speech, were unknown. He had never written or spoken publicly on those questions. Even the man who described himself as Ginsburg's best friend, Professor Hal Scott of Harvard Law School, said he had no idea what Ginsburg thought about the issues. Advocacy groups and Hill staff combed the literature and queried former students and colleagues for some hint of where the nominee stood on divisive and sensitive constitutional questions. A few described him as a libertarian who believed the government should stay off the backs of people in all areas, including speech, bedroom privacy, and press.

As soon as the nomination was announced, Gordon Humphrey declared: "Conservatives are delighted the president is hanging tough." Hatch called Ginsburg "truly exemplary" and said that "intellectually, he's in the big leagues."

Liberals were suspicious. What did Meese and Hatch know that even Ginsburg's friends claimed not to know? Some expressed fears of Ginsburg being a Bork without the paper trail. There was a strong sentiment that this was a nomination of spite.

Ted Kennedy pledged to do all he could to block Ginsburg's confirmation if his judicial philosophy "is as extreme as Judge Bork's." But Kennedy faced the same potential embarrassment over Ginsburg that Biden had suffered over having once said he would support Bork. When Ginsburg was named to the D.C. Circuit, Kennedy, the senator from the nominee's state, had said, "He has an insightful mind to deal with complex and involved fact situations . . . with clarity and with a sense of compassion."

Kennedy never had to face the issue. Ginsburg's nomination lasted just nine days. During that period reporters uncovered several potentially damaging facts about his background. One was a possible conflict of interest over nearly $140,000 of investments he owned in a cable television company when, as a Justice Department official, he handled matters involving the cable industry. He had supervised an antitrust investigation of the cable industry and handled a brief in a Supreme Court case, arguing that the First Amendment protected cable operators against certain types of regulation.

Another problem involved irregularities at a computerized dating business Ginsburg had helped set up as a young man in Cambridge, Massachusetts, in the mid-1960s. The business was investigated by the Better Business Bureau after dozens of clients had complained they got nothing for their money. The company, called Operation Match, moved suddenly to New York and then disappeared. Ginsburg also received notably lackluster student evaluations during most of his eight years of teaching at Harvard. For a couple of years Ginsburg's evaluations were among the bottom few of more than 150 courses offered.

Still a fourth concern was that he had vastly overstated his trial experience on the Judiciary Committee questionnaire when he was named to the court of appeals. In answering the question "How many cases have you tried to verdict or judgment?," he had replied: "thirty-four." It turned out that his answer included all the cases he supervised as head of the antitrust division at Justice, a very different matter.

332]   BATTLE FOR JUSTICE

One liberal committee aide said that investigating Ginsburg's background reminded him of the opening credits to the old television show "The Beverly Hillbillies." Like Jed Clampett, reporters kept striking oil wherever they pointed their shotguns.

But in a twist that prompted enormous debate, it was Ginsburg's expected supporters—those on the right—who forced him to withdraw his name. The man touted by Meese loyalists as "one of us" turned out not to be, at least not in the vitally symbolic way the administration had imagined. That the problem would center largely on generational issues from the sixties—women's liberation, abortion, the use of soft drugs—made the Ginsburg affair a peculiar postscript to Bork, who had set out to undo much of the "damage" from sixties activism.

Unease about Ginsburg had surfaced among many conservatives for the same reason it had among liberals: He had no record on social issues. As the right-wing weekly *Human Events* put it in an article entitled "Ginsburg a Mystery to Conservatives," the nominee "may embrace, full-blown, the controversial 'right to privacy' doctrine, and thus refuse to vote to uphold curbs on homosexual conduct, pornography and abortion."

Social conservatives were also distressed to learn that Ginsburg's second wife, Dr. Hallee Morgan, had performed abortions as part of her medical training at Boston's Beth Israel Hospital. Orrin Hatch, ever the administration loyalist, quickly released a statement saying he had talked with Morgan, who had informed him that "As a result of that experience, she resolved not to perform any more abortions."

Both of Ginsburg's wives had kept their own family names and had passed on those names to their daughters. This also troubled movement conservatives, who felt the bearded Jewish Ginsburg resembled, in attitude and life-style, liberals and intellectuals, the very groups they were fighting against.

The sixties label was definitively pinned on Ginsburg when it emerged that he had smoked marijuana during the late 1970s while a professor at Harvard. It was first discovered by Nina Totenberg, the legal affairs reporter for National Public Radio. Totenberg suspected right away that Ginsburg would pose problems for the administration, and she dug vigorously into his background. She pursued his marijuana use as part of a larger profile. She planned to make the point prominent in her story but not to lead with it.

Al Kamen of the *Washington Post* also heard of the marijuana issue, and after confirming it, both he and Totenberg called the

Justice Department for comment to include in their stories. Those calls were made on Tuesday and Wednesday, November 3 and 4. By Wednesday morning a few other reporters had picked up similar rumors and were checking them. It was not difficult to confirm; Ginsburg had been relatively careless in his marijuana use and not especially popular on the faculty. Former colleagues were willing to talk.

When the press queries arrived, the Justice Department was plunged into panic. Officials immediately called Ginsburg, who said at first that he may have used the drug once or twice in the early 1970s, but that was it. Slowly he changed the story, acknowledging that he had done so in the presence of other Harvard law professors later in the 1970s. As Totenberg's reporting showed, Ginsburg's use went well beyond that. She had half a dozen sources for the story. Some said Ginsburg had smoked with students. While such activity was relatively common a decade or so earlier, it sounded alarmingly illicit in the Reagan era. In addition, it was felt that a man aspiring to the Supreme Court ought to have an unassailable respect for the rule of law.

Several Justice Department officials argued for Ginsburg's immediate withdrawal. They were already hearing disturbing noises about the nomination from the conservative groups that would have to be mobilized in support. Law enforcement leaders had felt betrayed by Bock's refusal to announce clearly a law-and-order position. The marijuana revelation would drive them away entirely from Ginsburg, who was being advertised as tough on crime.

In addition, Ginsburg's early courtesy calls on senators were not going well. He was ill prepared to talk about substantive constitutional law. Howard Baker went along for several of the visits in an effort to quash the perception that he had opposed the nomination. But it was not enough. There was a growing feeling that Ginsburg would be defeated just as Bork had been.

Wednesday afternoon John Bolton called Brad Reynolds from his car telephone to suggest that Ginsburg withdraw. The nominee should say he did not want to put his family through the strain of a confirmation proceeding. In Bolton's opinion, if Ginsburg stayed in, he would be forever known as the marijuana judge, tied ineluctably to the illegal substance. Others in the department agreed with him. They glumly envisioned the gags the following weekend on "Saturday Night Live" about the "high" court.

Ginsburg refused to pull out.

White House aides had originally asked the judge the "skeleton" questions they asked of all potential nominees, including: "What is there in your background that you don't want a U.S. senator to ask you about?" Ginsburg had referred only to circumstances around the divorce from his first wife but had made no mention of marijuana.

When the reporters' queries reached the administration, the White House aides held a second such session with Ginsburg. He owned up to some early marijuana use. He said he had not originally mentioned it because it seemed so insignificant. The aides went through all the other possible problems with Ginsburg that day, including his investments. They agreed to let him try to stick it out on the condition that he and the Justice Department release a statement saying he had used marijuana as a young man. That way it would come from them, not from the triumphant liberal press. It would be portrayed as youthful indiscretion from an earlier era and fully deserving of forgiveness.

Terry Eastland, the Justice Department spokesman, called the major media with the statement. He reached National Public Radio one minute before Totenberg had planned to go on the air with the story.

The statement from Ginsburg acknowledged that he had used marijuana on "a few" occasions in the 1970s and called it "a mistake."

Liberals, giddy over the irony of it all, quickly expressed indulgence. Conservatives were mortified. The administration had tried to build a reputation on law and order and a return to traditional morality. Meese and Reagan had risen to prominence in California by fighting pot-smoking Berkeley radicals in the late 1960s. Nancy Reagan had launched an antidrug campaign for youths with the slogan "Just say no." It was all just a little too delicious for the snickerers on the left—and a little too embarrassing for the stalwarts on the right. The edifice began to crumble.

The evening of the revelation Ginsburg called a top White House aide at home. The call came at nearly 11:00 P.M. Ginsburg sounded desperate. He said he and his wife had gone over everything that could possibly cause further problems, and he wanted to go through the list with the aide. He started recounting odd details from his life, including the fact that his wife had once taken second prize in a beauty contest. There might be photographs of the event somewhere. Would that pose a problem?

The aide felt acutely uncomfortable. "Look, Doug, none of that matters at all," he said. "Only things that would have a direct bearing on confirmation would worry us." The aide then asked to speak to Ginsburg's wife and told her the same thing. After hanging up, he felt like someone forced to watch an unnatural act. "I wanted to take a shower when it was over," he recalled.

By the next day a number of key conservative senators were jumping ship. Education Secretary William Bennett, a conservative spokesman, decided someone had to tell Ginsburg to get out. He asked the president for permission to call the judge. Reagan told him to do what he thought was right but publicly defended Ginsburg, saying: "He was not an addict . . . nothing of that kind. . . . Judge Ginsburg erred in his youth. He has acknowledged it. He has expressed his regrets."

Patience toward youthful indiscretion only went so far, Bennett thought. It was time to cut bait. He called Ginsburg on Friday and announced the call to the press. Ginsburg was noncommittal, but the next day he called the president at his Camp David retreat and informed him of his decision to withdraw.

Kenneth Duberstein, the deputy chief of staff at the White House, was at a McDonald's with his children near his Virginia home when his portable telephone rang. He was told that Ginsburg had asked to come to the White House that afternoon to announce his withdrawal. There was concern among the senior staff that Ginsburg would either say something inappropriate or do what Bork had done: make a surprise statement about his intention to stay in. Duberstein was asked to get to the White House immediately to vet Ginsburg's statement.

Duberstein's wife came to pick up the children, and he drove to the White House in jeans and a sweat shirt. Ginsburg's statement was unremarkable. He said his withdrawal was necessary because "all of the attention has been focused on our personal lives and much of that on events of many years ago. My views on the law and on what kind of Supreme Court Justice I would make have been drowned out in the clamor."

While enjoying the embarrassment for the administration, liberals were nonetheless troubled by what happened. If previous marijuana smoking disqualified people from the top ranks of public service, many of their number were in trouble. Moreover, they believed that Ginsburg could have been defeated on substantive grounds. With some luck, it would have taken longer, perhaps even months. In that case Reagan might have been deprived of a third try at filling Powell's seat, just as twenty years earlier, President Johnson could not get Abe Fortas confirmed so late in his administration. Now there was no question that Reagan would get that opportunity. And given the battle fatigue in the Senate and the unpleasantness involved in fighting another nomination, the next one was a certain bet for confirmation.

Twenty-four hours later Anthony Kennedy flew again to Washington from his home in Sacramento. This time the questioning of the potential nominee was thorough and meticulous: drugs; extramarital sex; family trouble. But if there was a judge in America with a more clean-cut past, he would have been hard to find.

"Fellas," the lanky, clean-shaven Kennedy told Culvahouse and Duberstein, "you're in for a very boring afternoon." It was music to their ears.

Tony Kennedy, fifty-one, had been a judge on the Ninth Circuit Court of Appeals in California for twelve years. He had three grown children and had been married to Mary Davis Kennedy, a schoolteacher, for twenty-four years. He was still living in the stucco and frame house in which he had been raised, playing golf with the doctors and lawyers with whom he had once been a Cub Scout. A devout Catholic, he went to nine-thirty mass every Sunday.

A stalwart of the Sacramento community, Kennedy exhibited a manner that harkened back to the way fathers were portrayed on television during the Eisenhower era. Although a graduate of Stanford University and Harvard Law School, he was no Ivy League intellectual nor an especially original thinker. He was bright, thoughtful, and politically astute. He seemed to be a man with no enemies.

Like Bork, Kennedy had been a lonely conservative on a liberal bench before Reagan began to appoint judges. But unlike the failed nominee, Kennedy had developed a consensus-building style to opinion writing by concentrating on narrow points of law. Kennedy was a conservative but not in the banner-carrying style. He seemed likely to be to the right of Lewis Powell, but perhaps more moderate than Scalia and Rehnquist.

In criminal law he had shown concern for helping law enforcement agents and preventing the accused from escaping justice through what he saw as legal trickery. In a number of civil rights cases he had drawn the anger of liberal advocacy groups. But his rulings were varied enough, his speeches were bland enough, his manner silken enough that as soon as he was named by Reagan later that week, there was universal accord that he would be confirmed. None of the groups that had opposed Bork took a stand on Kennedy, except the National Organization for Women, which opposed him. Larry Tribe made a point of praising the nomination, not only to blunt attacks on his role in the Bork battle but also because he found Kennedy both moderate and intelligent.

Kennedy understood immediately that to win confirmation, he had to emphasize his differences with Bork. He did so artfully. In the committee questionnaire he was asked what qualities a judge should have. He answered: "Compassion, warmth, sensitivity, and an unyielding insistence on justice are the attributes of every good judge. It must be remembered, however, that judges can and should follow those aspirations within the context of settled legal principles, lest either their motives or the authority of their decrees be drawn in question."

His hearings, which began a month later and lasted two and a half days, showed Kennedy to be either a markedly more moderate student of the Constitution than Bork or a master of soothing rhetoric. When asked, for example, why he had remained a member of clubs that excluded women and minorities, he said, "Over the years, I have tried to become more sensitive to the existence of subtle barriers to the advancement of women, and of minorities, in society. And this was an issue on which I was continuing to educate myself."

Bork's shadow hung over the proceedings. While, in theory, the aim of the Kennedy hearings was to examine the new nominee, the unstated goal was to shape the legacy of the Bork battle, to lay out why the previous nominee had lost. If, as Bork opponents claimed, Bork had been rejected because of his adherence to a radical judicial philosophy, then Kennedy's testimony would have to contrast sharply with Bork's. It would be a vindication for the Senate's aggressive examination of Bork's views.

Kennedy's testimony did so beyond the Democrats' fondest hopes. The nominee distanced himself quite specifically from Bork's views on key areas.

Asked about First Amendment protection, he said it applies not only to the news media but to "dance, art, music, and all the ways we express ourselves as people."

Asked about privacy, he said the Constitution's references to "liberty" included "protection of a value we call privacy." He made clear that there were unenumerated rights in the national charter, disavowing the approach of original intent. He spoke of a Constitution with a capacity for growth and of framers who had "made a covenant with the future," of contemporary interpreters bolstered by experience and better able to understand the Constitution than the men who had written it.

On using the Fourteenth Amendment to outlaw school segregation, Kennedy said, "The whole lesson of our constitutional experience has been that a people can rise above its own injustice; that a people can rise above the inequities that prevail at a particular time. The framers of the Constitution originally, in 1789, knew that they did not live in a constitutionally perfect society, but they promulgated the Constitution anyway. They were willing to be bound by its consequences. And in my view the Fourteenth Amendment was intended to eliminate discrimination in public facilities on the day that it was passed."

For many who had fought the Bork nomination, there seemed no more fitting conclusion to their efforts. Few liberals believed that Kennedy's voting record on the high court would please them. He was clearly conservative. But his expansive reading of rights and equality made Bork's opponents feel their fight had been worthwhile. As the *New York Times* stated after Kennedy's testimony: "[T]he Constitution lives. . . . [H]e looks like a justice all Americans, whatever their politics, can respect."

Robert Bork knew he would lose when he stayed in for a full floor fight in the Senate. He knew it, yet somehow he hoped his courage would help turn things around. The finality of the defeat that late October afternoon hit him with tremendous force. November and December proved to be a difficult time. More than anything else, he and his wife needed to rest, to rebuild their spirits. They went for five days to their neighbors' Virginia farmhouse, where they read and walked and talked. Five days were not enough. Back in Washington, all activities, even joyous ones, were chores. They moved like robots through Thanksgiving and Christmas.

"It is like being hit by a truck," Mrs. Bork recalled. "It just takes time to recover."

Bork followed the developments around Judges Ginsburg and Kennedy. He had supported Ginsburg avidly and recommended him to the administration. He did not know Kennedy and was troubled by some of his testimony. But Bork had it on good authority that Kennedy was a reliable conservative.

The question for Bork was what to do next. He yearned to write again, to speak, to enter the arena of ideas in the kind of free-wheeling way he had so enjoyed while a professor. He had given many speeches as a judge but sidestepped direct commentary on many of the nation's most sensitive questions. Bork cared about issues outside the law; he was, for example, deeply anti-Communist and favored a hard line with the Soviets.

One thing became clear: The judge would leave the bench. He had thought about stepping down even before his ill-fated nomination to the Supreme Court. He had vague plans to write a book about what was wrong with liberalism and American legal culture. Now he would move ahead with those plans. He harbored no desire to return to the administrative law load of the D.C. Circuit.

Bork finished up his court duties, sitting for another session and writing a few last opinions. He stepped down officially on February 5, 1988. Three days later he held a press conference at the conservative American Enterprise Institute, where he would be based as a resident scholar. His position was funded by the John M. Olin Foundation, which financed Allan Bloom's institute at the University of Chicago and many other conservative institutions and causes. Bork also contracted to write his book attacking what he regarded as the liberal stranglehold on the academy and courts. While long in the planning, now it would be leavened and informed by bitter personal experience.

Bork received somewhere in the low six figures for the book. For the high-minded reflections of a former appeals court judge—no matter how eloquent—that was an enormous sum of money. But it was a harbinger of a profound change in Bork's life: The man was now a star. Having spent five days on television and having his face on the cover of every major American publication had given him just the right mixture of notoriety and fame. In an unexpected way Robert Bork, the *enfant terrible* of law and politics, had arrived. And it was as if he had been reborn.

He signed with the Washington Speakers Bureau, which immediately received dozens of requests for his speeches. The former nominee charged between $12,500 and $15,000. He paid off his long-standing debts. He took on a few legal consulting jobs at a steep hourly wage. He began to think about buying an estate in Virginia with pool and tennis court.

Bork became a cult figure for the right. His provocative and well-expressed thoughts were demanded on television and in the press. He appeared on "Good Morning America" and "Nightwatch," explaining why *Roe* v. *Wade* was unconstitutional and why the executive branch needed more power. People stopped him at airports and on the street, asking for his autograph. Sometimes they had no idea who he was or confused him with C. Everett Koop, the nation's bearded surgeon general. No matter. Bork was a man one saw on television; for that he was the object of a new esteem.

Bork also paid back those who had worked for his confirmation. He spoke at fund raisers for Senators Orrin Hatch of Utah and John Danforth of Missouri. He spoke free of charge to the Federalist Society, the group of conservative young lawyers who so strongly supported his nomination.

While Bork recovered, his son, Bob, Jr., continued to take the defeat quite hard for some time. In recent years, he had filled his apartment with photographs and drawings of his father. There was Bork with Reagan at the White House, Bork in New Haven, Bork in England. Bob paid hundreds of dollars each for original caricatures of his father that had appeared in publications such as *The Nation* and the *New York Review of Books*.

He left his job at the newsmagazine, got a small fellowship at the Heritage Foundation, and began work on a book that would vindicate his father. But after Bork himself announced book plans, the publisher interested in Bob's book pulled out, and he could not find another taker. Publishers kept telling him he was "too close" to the subject. They probably did not realize how true that was. Several people who cared for Bob silently breathed a sigh of relief when the project was abandoned. They feared that for him to relive the process all over again would only tear him apart. After months of living on adrenaline, Bob suddenly felt helpless and angry. His book contract gone, his father defeated, he floundered. Slowly he looked around for employment in the conservative movement, as either a writer or an editor. Ultimately he was hired as a speech writer by Senator Gordon Humphrey, New Hampshire Republican, one of Bork's most avid defenders.

Bob Bork, Jr., continued to use his father's defeat as a touchstone for his political world view. He judged public figures first and foremost by what stand they had taken on the controversy. And like a number of those hurt by the defeat, he changed his standards for political debate. He had been scandalized by the oversimplification of his father's record. But when the same was done later to Democratic politicians, he shrugged it off, saying he had become battlehardened. He could no longer muster moral indignation, only a fighting spirit for the causes and candidates in whom he had a stake.

The newly liberated Judge Bork offered essentially the same speech everywhere. He told his audience—mostly business and conservative groups—that his had been "the first all-out political campaign with respect to a judicial nominee in the country's history." He said the campaign, which "reached record lows for mendacity, brutality and intellectual vulgarity," had a small virtue: It brought out of the closet something the country ought to know. "And that is that a war is going on, a war to control the legal culture."

Bork argued that those who opposed him had done so because their radical ideas stood outside the American mainstream. He referred to efforts to establish rights to cocaine use and prostitution as typical of his adversaries' program. Those people sought to control the law schools and future judges being trained there. That way they could get their agenda in place without having to go through the proper legislative channels. His opponents were not liberals, but nihilists, he warned; they had no interest in policy, only in power: "I sometimes think that the issues raised in these kinds of contests are not about ideas at all but simply about power, that the people I'm talking about do not seek power to implement their ideas but hold the ideas as weapons in the fight for power."

The struggle, Bork said, as he had in the past, was between "the knowledge class"—liberals in "the idea business"—and the rest of society. He insisted that liberals cared about judges more than the rest of society because "that class would prefer to be governed by members of the knowledge class who are not disciplined by elections, that is, judges, rather than by legislators."

Bork also signed advertisements warning against trusting Soviet leader Mikhail Gorbachev and his programs of *perestroika* and *glasnost*. He urged support for the Nicaraguan contras and for greater American military strength. He constantly found himself wearing a tuxedo at long-winded dinners in his honor in the nation's far-flung corners. And while the travel wore him down physically, it rebuilt him spiritually. His friends said that while Bork had been seared by his rejection, he seemed increasingly relaxed and buoyed by continued interest in him and his views. If Bork had lost his only really important professional battle, he was at least turning defeat into a lucrative and interesting new life. As he enjoyed telling audiences, "I can offer you a unique perspective. Who wouldn't like George Armstrong Custer's version of events at the Little Bighorn?"

Bork's harsh conservatism served as a vindication for liberals, evidence that here was no moderate. If any distortion or exaggeration had occurred during the confirmation battle, his opponents said, it had come from the White House trying to sell this man as a centrist. Just listen to those speeches! Of course, Bork had never claimed to be anything but a political conservative. He maintained simply that he could separate his politics from his judging. But as he crisscrossed the country, thundering against contemporary liberalism, as his familiar face and voice appeared on television screens, seeking to inspire a new generation in law and politics, his adversaries breathed a sigh of relief. Ralph Neas of the Leadership Conference on Civil Rights summed up the feeling: "I'd far prefer to hear his opinions on the lecture circuit than read them on the Supreme Court."

Conclusion

To appreciate the passion that fueled the anti-Bork movement, John Hope Franklin must be heard. A victim of luckless timing, he found that his words at the confirmation hearings went largely unreported. The day Franklin testified, former Chief Justice Warren Burger spoke and Joe Biden withdrew from the presidential race.

A soft-spoken seventy-two-year-old academic, Franklin did not compare constitutional theories; he did not contrast original intent with a living evolving charter. He talked about himself. The black historian and author had no interest in discussing Bork's nomination from the perspective of a scholar. The work of the postwar Court had been for Franklin no intellectual feast. It had been a lifeline.

Franklin's long, productive life had suffered more barriers than most Americans would care to dwell on. An early memory involved a train trip he, his sister, and their mother tried to take in Oklahoma in 1922. His mother refused to move to the "Negro coach," half of which was for baggage. The conductor stopped the train and threw the family off into the woods. They returned home on foot.

In 1945, after attending a college commencement, Franklin was returning by train to his home in Durham, North Carolina. Blacks were uncomfortably crowded into the half baggage car while five white men had the entire next coach to themselves. The five were German prisoners of war, who, Franklin recalled, "seemed to relish our discomfort. They laughed at us all the way to Durham. They could have wondered what we had been fighting for."

As a graduate student Franklin was forbidden from using the North Carolina state archives; no one dared force upon the white employees the indignity of serving a black man. As a professor at Howard University in Washington he couldn't get a cup of coffee at local restaurants while doing research at the Library of Congress.

Time and again the Supreme Court came to his aid. As he put it, "If we did not derive much benefit from fighting the Nazis and the Japanese as far as equal rights and transportation at home were concerned, we fought and won that battle in the courts. The Supreme Court decreed that people such as my mother and her family, and those blacks traveling to Greensboro from Durham, would never again be subjected to degradation and humiliation while traveling in the land of their birth to which they had given so much."

It was the Supreme Court that made it possible for blacks to attend public universities. The Supreme Court opened the restaurants of Washington, D.C., to blacks.

Franklin said he opposed Bork because:

There is no indication in his writings, his teachings or his rulings that this nominee has any deeply held commitment to the eradication of the problem of race or even of its mitigation. One searches his record in vain to find a civil rights advance that he supported from its inception. The landmark cases I cited earlier have done much to make this a tolerable, tolerant land in which persons of African descent can live. I shudder to think how Judge Bork would have ruled in any of them had he served on the Court at the time that they were decided.

Bork would hardly have been the first justice lacking passion for the plight of black Americans. But the harsh nature of his writings, the well-established aims of his sponsors, and the political circumstances of the moment conspired to elevate his nomination into a Rorschach test of American values. His rejection, inspired by the personal pleas of men like John Hope Franklin, served as a kind of constitutional amendment on the questions of civil and personal rights. Like the Lincoln-Douglas debates of a century before, the Bork debates forced the nation to stare into its soul.

Not everyone saw the same thing, of course. Mike Carvin of the Justice Department said afterward: "I'm not sure I can live in a country that would reject Bob Bork as a Supreme Court justice."

But the majority felt differently. It spoke, and did so with conviction.

The fight over Bork cannot be understood outside the context of Reaganism. The Reagan years marked a radical turn away from traditional approaches to civil rights. All administrations since Lyndon Johnson's believed, with varying degrees, that the power of government had to be harnessed to provide special help to black America because of a legacy of slavery and discrimination.

Reagan, Meese, and Reynolds believed otherwise. They contended that the playing field had been leveled. They sought to redefine discrimination. It was no longer a multitiered set of indignities, both blatant and subtle, suffered by political and social minority groups. It no longer required constant and active government and court vigilance. Discrimination existed solely at the level of the individual, in other words, when a specific illegal act had occurred. Blacks, Hispanics, women, the handicapped did not, as groups, require or deserve government help any more than did white men. The administration rejected the notion, expressed by the Supreme Court as early as 1938, that the courts owe special protection to "discrete and insular minorities" because they have less access to the political process than the majority. Reagan and his aides saw such help as a new form of discrimination as reprehensible as the original kind.

Wittingly or not, the administration denied minorities the ineffable: a sense that government cared.

Under Reagan, the administration petitioned the Supreme Court to change its approach to discrimination. It attempted to authorize the granting of tax exemptions to private schools that bar nonwhites. It attacked some voluntary plans to end segregation in schools and others aimed at overcoming the effects of employment discrimination. It urged federal courts to interpret the Voting Rights Act narrowly. It sought to persuade local governments and major corporations to abandon the use of goals and timetables in affirmative action. And with the end of its term near, it pulled a trump card: It nominated Robert Bork to the Supreme Court. Bork had built a reputation by attacking Court expansions in civil and personal rights over the preceding thirty years. He was the intellectual side of Reaganism, the administration's final attempt at a lasting legal legacy.

For men like John Hope Franklin, the Court had been a barricade against Reaganism. It had held the line on regression. With the Bork nomination, black Americans suddenly felt vulnerable again. They felt their barricade being dismantled. The one government branch that had looked out for them would be vitally altered. Battle was joined.

The fact is that Reagan's efforts on race over the years had been a surprising failure. They had been rebuffed not only by the courts but by Congress, business leaders, and the public at large.

Perhaps the most telling of those failures—until the Bork defeat—occurred in the summer of 1985, when the White House staff drafted an executive order to change requirements that federal contractors set numerical goals to remedy possible job discrimination. The document was aimed at reversing an existing executive order, signed in 1968, that required thousands of government contractors to hire and promote blacks, women, and Hispanics in rough proportion to the number of qualified candidates in a given labor market.

The proposed change met with a storm of resistance. Scores of congressmen and advocacy groups, even Labor Secretary William Brock opposed the move. When the National Association of Manufacturers, the epitome of the American industrial establishment, objected to abolishing the executive order and came out unanimously in favor of goals and timetables, the plan was abandoned.

"A lot of longtime NAM watchers couldn't believe it in their wildest dreams," said William S. McEwan, chairman of the NAM equal opportunity subcommittee. "Many of our members were brought into affirmative action kicking and screaming. But there has been a change in this country."

Like the Senate's rejection of Brad Reynolds's promotion within the Justice Department, the failure of the executive order was a stark demonstration of the nation's rejection of Reagan's agenda on civil rights. Even those who fought for the program acknowledged defeat. Gary L. McDowell, a chief speechwriter for Meese, said in 1988 after leaving the administration: "Domestically, Ronald Reagan did far less than he had hoped, he did far less than he had promised, less than people wanted—and a hell of a lot more than people thought he would." McDowell spoke of "an enormous gulf between rhetoric and reality."

Terry Eastland, who served as Justice Department spokesman, wrote afterward that "it may be too late to stem the tide of racial preference that has been engulfing the nation during the past decade."

The Bork defeat must be understood within this context. The same forces that had fought other Reagan efforts in civil rights mobilized against his confirmation. Bork's attacks on a few cherished civil rights decisions, his oft-repeated contention that numerous high court rulings had to be overturned, and his belief that egalitarian trends were dangerous rendered him a threat to future, and perhaps some existing, civil rights advances. No one can predict with precision how a future justice will rule, but Bork's record offered a reasonably precise foretaste.

Bork, one of the most eloquent and courageous advocates of the right, had provided a legal framework for Reaganism. His unrelenting efforts to uproot a liberal, rights-based understanding of the national charter were keenly, perhaps uniquely admired by conservatives because he challenged liberals on turf they had claimed as their own for so long—constitutional law. The Senate's refusal to seat Bork on the highest court signaled a counterattack. It manifested a new assertiveness on judicial matters in the Democratic-controlled legislature, one likely to play a bigger role as the Court grows more conservative. It pointed to a broad acceptance of individual and civil rights in constitutional law.

Distortions of Bork's record, the dehumanization to which he was subjected, and the shameless fears raised about him as a godless technocrat complicate analysis of his defeat. But a pattern emerges. Had Reagan succeeded in gaining wide acceptance for his agenda on civil and individual rights, then a Bork defeat might have been written off as a frightening example of image manipulation. But his rejection fitted a pattern so closely that one is compelled to place it in that context.

The fact that Bork's defeat hinged partly on the masterly use of media manipulation and message framing raises troubling questions about the tight braiding of style and substance in public debate. But it hardly diminishes the impact of his defeat, certainly no more so than Reagan's scripted mastery of television diminished his administration's stature or accomplishments. In fact, because Bork's nomination ran aground on shoals that had been well charted over the previous seven years—civil and individual rights—its significance was enhanced.

When Howard Baker and his aides felt the need to soft-pedal

Bork's harsh criticisms, that was a sure sign that much of what had been handed down by the Warren and Burger courts had come to be seen as inescapably mainstream. Had there been a ground swell of support for a pronounced shift in the nation's rights agenda, there would have been no need to downplay Bork's statements or his fervent right-wing support. As Baker said later, "I can't think of a single vote Bork would have gotten if we had had a mobilization of conservative rhetoric on those issues." That may be a self-serving assessment, yet it seems right. President Bush, who owed his victory to Reagan's popularity, quietly abandoned Reagan's civil rights approach, further evidence that it had failed to gain a proper foothold among the electorate.

A poll conducted at the end of the Bork debate showed significant results: Americans would be inclined by overwhelming margins to disapprove of a prospective Supreme Court candidate who had criticized recent civil rights gains or revealed a reluctance to acknowledge a constitutional right to privacy.

Bork argued that the constitutional changes of the past generation had been wrought by a cabal of law professors and judges acting as social engineers. They had stretched the national charter beyond its capacities, stitching together new rights with random bits of constitutional cloth. Their work was an exercise in the usurpation of power away from the people. Yet the results of his nomination indicated that most Americans disagreed.

The changes that so offended Bork resulted from a push toward pluralism. Women, racial minorities, the poor, those born out of wedlock, aliens, and the politically unorthodox were recognized as members of groups whose "rights" had been abridged in the past. Precisely because the new rights were enjoyed by members of political minorities, the rights had come principally from the nonmajoritarian branch of government—the courts. Had the legislatures been left to offer those rights, some might not have come at all.

Since those changes were driven by the courts—although in cases such as women's rights pushed along equally by other societal forces—contemporary political dialogue has become increasingly delineated by legal, especially constitutional, issues. It was no surprise that the questions that animated the 1988 presidential election were constitutional ones: treatment of criminal defendants; the death penalty; the program of the American Civil Liberties Union. Issues that were once restricted to law school discourse have in recent years come to define the contours of national political debate. Law has evolved in the public's mind from a technical specialty, such as engineering or medicine, to a terrain for the struggle over public policy. Delicate social issues had been taken up increasingly by the Supreme Court in the 1960s and early 1970s. Reflecting larger trends, the Court was informed by liberal views on those issues. To Bork's chagrin, the law became an exciting area for social reformers, a field to push the boundaries of pluralism and tolerance, to expand the newfound rights for minorities.

For conservatives such as Bork, the pluralism had come at the expense of traditional values. Reagan and Meese, who had built political careers upon opposition to 1960s Berkeley radicals, advocated a return to a pre-sixties sensibility. But to do so would have meant to dilute the political gains of minorities. This was no mere philosophical debate; it was a power struggle.

The fight over Reaganism, like the fight over Bork's confirmation, was part of a cultural war between those buoyed and inspired by the 1960s and those for whom it represented moral and social derailment. On one side were those who believed in continuing human progress through the development of self-expression; on the other were those who saw humans less as flowers to be nurtured than as beasts to be tamed.

Many who organized against Bork had come of age politically during the student movement. Their work against his confirmation was an updated version of that activism. When the nomination was defeated, they were exhilarated. It brought back to many the power that the huge protest demonstrations against the Vietnam War had mobilized. As Eric Schnapper, of the NAACP Legal Defense and Educational Fund, put it, Bork was the first battle since the Vietnam War in which he saw his cause expressed in graffiti on urban walls. More than a year after the defeat anti-Bork activists still proudly displayed "Block Bork" buttons and banners on their walls and doors; Bork supporters displayed their slogans. To both sides these were medals of war in the battle for justice.

Some of the tactics used against Bork resembled those used against Democratic presidential candidate Michael Dukakis a year later. Just as the American Cyanamid case was used to raise fears about Bork, so the case of Willie Horton—a Massachusetts murderer who raped while on a prison furlough—was used to raise fears that, under Dukakis, Americans would be unsafe in their own homes. Both cases tapped into deep-seated psychosexual fear in a dishonest fashion.

Both Bork and Dukakis were accused of being "outside the mainstream" and generally portrayed as too process-oriented to care about average Americans and the impacts of policy decisions on "real people."

Dukakis, like Bork, responded to the charges ineptly, dismissing them as absurd or offering legalistic explanations that missed the mark of popular fears and concerns.

Both the fight against Bork and the campaign against Dukakis point up troublesome trends in public debate. When a half-truth is repeated enough, it often gains acceptance. Most people assume that telling accusations would not be raised if untrue, so unless the charges are promptly and effectively countered, they tend to stick. Since outright lies, when denied, work against the accuser, slander by half-truth and innuendo—which is hard to counter effectively—is far more potent.

There is another, equally disturbing trend that emerges: In order to "frame the debate," in the now oft-repeated phrasing of public relations practitioners, it helps to go on the attack. By placing your opponents on the defensive, you oblige them to answer charges and to engage in debate on your terms.

A comparison of the campaign against Bork and against Dukakis shows that both efforts caused the public to fear the nominees. Yet, in fairness, the Bork charges and actuality were closer to each other than was true for Dukakis. Bork answered questions for thirty hours over five days. Inside the hearing room there was posturing, but there was also real intellectual give-and-take. Bork had the opportunity to lay out his constitutional vision. The dispute over Bork can be summed up as a substantive debate with some slander. The Bush campaign against Dukakis had the inverse balance.

This key difference became evident in polls after both events. Many voters told exit pollsters they had voted for Bush because they feared that Dukakis was soft on crime and would let murderers out on furloughs—claims of the Bush campaign. In the Senate debate on Bork, on the other hand, no senator mentioned the American Cyanamid case in announcing opposition to Bork. Public opinion polls showed that concern over Bork centered almost entirely on civil and personal rights. Asked to name their concerns about Bork, some Americans said he was "insensitive to minorities" and had the "wrong temperament," but they did not name his supposed penchant for sterilization. Polls also showed that few Americans recall seeing any advertising at all against Bork, that 17 percent saw newspaper ads and 24 percent television ads, a tiny percentage when compared with those who saw the Bush advertisements. At the same time, 60 percent of those surveyed claimed to have watched portions of the actual hearings.

If there was a tragic aspect to Bork's defeat, it lay in his failure to articulate appealingly a concern shared by many: Americans have grown accustomed to letting judges and bureaucrats make difficult social policy choices for them. They seem resigned to allowing courts and government agencies take responsibility on issues that a self-governing people ought to work out in greater detail through the democratic process.

Participation at the polls has gone down steadily since World War II even as barriers to voting have been removed. The percentage of voters who went to the polls reached an all-time low of 50 percent in the 1988 presidential election. Voting in local elections is well below that in many cities. Party loyalty has been eroded. The most popular candidates for office have often been those who portray themselves as common-man outsiders to the system. Individualism and individual rights have come so to dominate political discourse that Americans feel increasingly alienated from the "We" in "We the people." As Americans have been freed to choose their life-styles, they have felt less attached to their roles as members of a self-governing society. That role has come to be perceived as a burden, something else we are free under our system to shed. Such is the underbelly of liberalism.

This concerns rightists like Bork, who are bothered both by the fact of increased judicial activity and by its results. But left-leaning and centrist thinkers have also, in the past decade, raised the question of whether tolerance and moral neutrality are enough of a value system to serve as the glue of American society. Have the American people given up something vital by failing to promote positive values from the courts and the federal government? If communities are forbidden to regulate pornography or racist speech, do citizens feel further alienated from control over their own lives? Must the free speech slope be that slippery?

There is an irony to the fact that fewer and fewer Americans participate in the political process, yet they turned out in massive numbers to play a role in the Bork controversy. Since the work of the Supreme Court has come to provide so much of the framework for social policy issues, democracy—in which citizens make choices through public debate, local referenda, and elected representatives—was replaced with a substitute form: debate over a nominee to the Supreme Court. Average citizens with little role in public affairs were ignited by the Bork dispute and hoped to have an impact on the nation's philosophical direction. They watched hours of hearings, wrote letters, made phone calls, and attended meetings. But it was democracy by proxy.

Bork never stated this in an appealing way, but his point is that Americans have relinquished the power of self-definition to the courts. It is an important message even if overstated and by the wrong messenger. Bork had spent most of his life as a hell raiser, as a gadfly of the intellectual and judicial communities. He entered debate with jutted chin. After he lost his Supreme Court nomination he left the bench and took to the lecture circuit to exhort the right to wrest control of the nation's legal culture from power-hungry liberals. His was not a manner that inspired communal cooperation. Although he claimed to be interested more in process than in results, many found this hard to believe him. His behavior after leaving the judiciary only added to that incredulity.

It is likely to be a long time before a New Right legal agenda will be openly supported by a Republican or Democratic presidential candidate or a Supreme Court nominee. The scope of individual and civil rights will continue to be vigorously debated. But the Bork defeat showed that most Americans, in and out of power, think the politically weak and the ideologically extreme have special "rights." They believe, further, that it is the role of the Supreme Court to guarantee those rights and thereby to promote equality. Rejecting Bork required defiance of one of the century's most popular presidents, a man grown used to setting the terms of national debate. His inability to frame this momentous debate and its coincidence with the Constitution's two hundredth anniversary lent the Bork defeat a monumental quality, one which will resonate through the nation and its institutions for decades to come.

Notes

Chapter 1: The Most Powerful Man in America

15 "Toni, this is Lewis Powell" . . . House's recollection of events that day were offered in interview, June 8, 1988.

16 "It was odd" . . . Interview with Richard Carelli, August 3, 1988.

18 "Only the chief knows" . . . Interviews with Justice Lewis Powell, September 12, 1988, and Toni House.

18 "When Powell said" . . . The hardcover edition of this book tells a different story. It says that when Rehnquist finished his conversation with Powell, he called Baker and told him the news. Baker then told the president. That account was based on a tape-recorded interview with Baker on June 21, 1988, in which he repeatedly said he had gotten word of the Powell retirement twenty-four hours in advance in a telephone conversation with Rehnquist. The chief justice had turned down my written interview request. When the book appeared, Rehnquist complained publicly that the story was incorrect. He said that his secretary had called the previous day but he had not spoken with Baker. Asked to back up his story, Baker said that he had misspoken based on faulty memory. After discussions with Rehnquist, Baker, and Baker aides John Tuck, Thomas Griscom, and A. B. Culvahouse, I have concluded that Baker did, in fact, get it wrong.

18 [S]olicited a solemn promise . . . Interview with Powell.

19 Chief Justice Warren Burger had paid the White House . . . Interview with White House Counsel Arthur B. Culvahouse, April 27, 1988.

19 "I did not want it to have any implication" . . . Interview with Powell.

20 "Everyone realized immediately" . . . Interview with Ralph Neas, April 22, 1988.

20 "Our worst fears" . . . Interview with Kate Michelman, May 17, 1988.

20 "There was this explosion" . . . Interview with Paul Gewirtz, May 31, 1988.

20 "[T]he President may slip" . . . Alexis de Tocqueville, *Democracy in America* (Garden City, N.Y.: Anchor Books, Doubleday, 1969), p. 151.

21 During the Constitution's 150th . . . See Michael Kammen, *A Machine That Would Go of Itself* (New York: Vintage Books, 1987), especially pp. 282–312.

21 government ought to remove itself as much as possible . . . I thank Michael Sandel, associate professor of government at Harvard University for introducing this notion to me and discussing it with me in several conversations. It is an idea developed at length by Sandel in a forthcoming book.

21 "For the past fifteen years" . . . Statement issued by Senator Edward Kennedy's office, June 26, 1987.

22 "justice for women" . . . *Hearings Before the Senate Judiciary Committee on the Nominations of William Rehnquist and Lewis Powell* 92d Congress, November 3, 4, 8, 9, 10, 1971, p. 424.

22 "The views expressed by both men" . . . Ibid., p. 456.

22 "The outcry against wiretapping" . . . First published in the *Richmond Times-Dispatch* on August 1, 1971. Reprinted in *U.S. News & World Report* (November 8, 1971), p. 41.

23 "History abundantly documents" . . . *United States* v. *United States District Court,* 407 U.S. 297 (1972). Discussed and quoted by Anthony Lewis in the *New York Times,* June 30, 1987, p. 31. The opinion was 8–0. Rehnquist did not take part, and two justices filed concurring opinions.

23 "It is different when you" . . . Interview with Powell.

24 "Coming from the South" . . . Ibid.

24 *Allan Bakke* case . . . *Regents of University of California* v. *Bakke,* 438 U.S. 265 (1978). The *Batson* case . . . *Batson* v. *Kentucky,* 476 U.S. 79 (1986). "I was glad" . . . Interview with Powell.

24 "I have seen so many changes" . . . Interview with Powell.

25 "I am authorized by the President" . . . Ibid., and Bob Woodward and Scott Armstrong, *The Brethren* (New York: Simon and Schuster, 1979), pp. 160–61.

26 "Dad, it's a whole lot better" . . . Press conference of Justice Lewis F. Powell, Jr., following announcement of his retirement, June 26, 1987. Interview with Powell and interview with Lewis Powell III, July 20, 1988.

26 "We have researched his background" . . . Interview with Michelman.

26 "Oh, my God. That's Bork" . . . Interviews with Althea Simmons, June 16 and June 20, 1988.

26 But Bork himself was skeptical . . . Interview with Robert Bork, Jr., June 23, 1988, based on his interviews with his father.

27 "If Sir Thomas had had" . . . From Robert H. Bork, "Law, Morality, and Thomas More," delivered to Thomas More Society on June 26, 1985, p. 1.

27 A friend remembered Bork . . . Confidential interview.

27 In fact, friends recalled . . . Among them was Harry Wellington of Yale Law School. Interview with Wellington, May 31, 1988.

28 "The administration has a well-entrenched tradition" . . . Interview with Robert Bork, Jr.

28 "I immediately called John Richardson" . . . Interview with Patrick McGuigan, July 11, 1988, and recounted in Patrick B. McGuigan and Dawn M. Weyrich, *The Ninth Justice* (forthcoming from the Free Congress Foundation).

28 Bork's admirers in the Justice Department . . . Background interviews with Justice Department officials.

30 "If you can't get Bob Bork" . . . Interview with Justice Department official.

Chapter 2: High Stakes

31 Culvahouse might have pressed . . . Interview with Arthur B. Culvahouse, April 27, 1988.

32 The choice of Scalia . . . Interviews with William Bradford Reynolds, June

15 and June 23, 1988; Edwin Meese, September 16, 1988; and other Justice Department officials.

32 Many conservatives had a unique . . . See, for example, Suzanne Garment, "The War Against Robert Bork," *Commentary* (January 1988), p. 18.

32 "There was a feeling that Bob" . . . Background interview with senior Justice Department official.

32 "Sometimes you have to" . . . Ibid.

33 "They were anything from highway patrol" . . . Interview with J. Anthony Kline, July 1987. See *Boston Globe,* July 28, 1987, p. 53.

33 His aging mother . . . See Kate Coleman "The Roots of Ed Meese", *Los Angeles Times Magazine,* May 4, 1986.

34 "He tends to surround" . . . *Boston Globe,* July 28, 1987.

34 After he left office . . . see *New York Times,* September 13, 1988, p. A23.

34 A subsequent report . . . *Washington Post,* January 17, 1989, p. 1.

35 "You don't have many suspects" . . . *U.S. News & World Report* interview, October 10, 1985. "people go to soup kitchens" . . . Said in Washington on December 10, 1983. "criminals' lobby" . . . Said before the California Peace Officers Association, Sacramento, California, on May 14, 1981.

35 He preached a return . . . See, for example, address by Edwin Meese before the American Bar Association, July 9, 1985, pp. 14–15.

35 "I kept track of" . . . Interview with Edwin Meese, September 14, 1988.

35 Baker and Culvahouse realized . . . Interviews with Howard Baker, June 21, 1988, and Culvahouse.

36 Ralph Neas called the White House . . . Interviews with Thomas Griscom, April 15, 1988; Howard Baker; and Ralph G. Neas, May 8, 1988.

36 When Reynolds and Meese heard . . . Interviews with Reynolds and Meese.

37 "It appears he would not allow" . . . Quoted in *Washington Times,* June 29, 1987, p. A8.

37 From the first . . . Interviews with Laurence H. Tribe, March 22 and July 6, 1988.

38 would not "compel children" . . . Quoted in *New York Times,* November 20, 1981, p. 14.

39 "liberal criminal lobby" . . . See, for example, address by William Bradford Reynolds to the Joseph Story Society, March 1988.

39 "a minority of one" . . . Address by William Bradford Reynolds in Amherst, Massachusetts, April 1983. Quoted in *Hearings on Confirmation of William Bradford Reynolds to Be Associate Attorney General of the United States,* Senate Judiciary Committee No. J-99-29, June 4, 5, and 18, 1985, pp. 184–85.

39 "In order to get beyond racism" . . . *Regents of University of California* v. *Bakke,* 438 U.S. 265 (1978) at 91, Justice Blackmun concurring.

40 "shadow solicitor" . . . See Lincoln Caplan, *The Tenth Justice* (New York: Alfred A. Knopf, 1987), pp. 81–114.

40 "we've just won the White House" . . . Interview with Patrick McGuigan, July 11, 1988.

41 "far too many of the Court's opinions" . . . Meese address to the ABA, July 9, 1985, pp. 14–15, 10.

41 "This doctrine of Mr. Lincoln" . . . *The Annals of America,* Vol. 9, 1858–1865,

"The Crisis of the Union," *Encyclopaedia Britannica*, 1968, pp. 8–9.

41 "Now I believe if we could" . . . Ibid., pp. 13, 15.

43 For the first time in fifty years . . . Discussed in Caplan, op. cit., pp. 121–24.

43 "feigns self-effacing deference" . . . William J. Brennan, Jr., "The Constitution of the United States: Contemporary Ratification" Georgetown University, Washington, D.C., October 12, 1985, p. 4.

43 "subsequent developments in the law" . . . Address of Justice John Paul Stevens to the Federal Bar Association, October 23, 1985, p. 9. "simplistic" . . . quoted in Caplan, op. cit., p. 122.

43 "the least dangerous" . . . Alexander Hamilton, "The Federalist No. 78," in Michael Kammen, ed., *The Origins of the American Constitution* (New York: Viking Penguin, 1986), p. 228.

44 Originally, Supreme Court justices . . . For history and explanation of the Court for the general reader, see Archibald Cox, *The Court and the Constitution* (Boston: Houghton Mifflin, 1987); William H. Rehnquist, *The Supreme Court: How It Was, How it is* (New York: William Morrow and Co., 1987; David M. O'Brien, *Storm Center: The Supreme Court in American Politics* (New York: W. W. Norton and Co., 1986).

45 "there is no liberty" . . . Hamilton in Kammen, op. cit., p. 230.

45 "It is emphatically the province" . . . *Marbury* v. *Madison*, 5 U.S. 137 (1803).

46 a follower of Jehovah's Witnesses . . . *West Virginia State Board of Education* v. *Barnette*, 319 U.S. 624 (1943).

46 "We are a Christian people" . . . *United States* v. *Macintosh*, 283 U.S. 605 (1931). Not until 1947 . . . *Everson* v. *Board of Education*, 330 U.S. 1 (1947). Court outlawed prayer in school . . . *Engel* v. *Vitale*, 370 U.S. 421 (1962).

47 to place the right people on the federal bench . . . For further discussion, see Herman Schwartz, *Packing the Courts: The Conservative Campaign to Rewrite the Constitution* (New York: Charles Scribner's Sons, 1988) and Caplan, op. cit.

47 Bork, in a 1987 speech . . . Robert H. Bork, "The Crisis in Constitutional Theory: Back to the Future," address to the Philadelphia Society, April 3, 1987, p. 3.

47 the ratio was reversed . . . Schwartz, op. cit., p. 58.

48 "Mr. Reynolds and the Department of Justice" . . . *Reynolds Hearings*, op. cit., pp. 178–79.

49 Their message was that . . . Ibid., pp. 312–44.

49 Reynolds's earlier shading of the truth . . . Ibid., pp. 888–89.

50 "Because of their extremism" . . . Interview with Ralph Neas, May 8, 1988.

52 It was also surprising that Neas . . . The following profile is based partly on interviews with Neas, April 21, May 8, June 11, and December 13, 1988, numerous less formal encounters with him, and his writings and speeches.

55 "everyone agrees" . . . Interview with Neas.

Chapter 3: Levity and Ferocity

56 "Wreak yourself upon the world" . . . *Washington Post*, July 26, 1987, p. 1. Bork said in an interview with the author on January 13, 1989, that he got the

expression from Alexander Bickel of Yale and that he used it jokingly. Bickel got it from Justice Frankfurter, and it is a variation of a statement by Justice Oliver Wendell Holmes in 1886 that a man "may live greatly" in the law. "There, as well as elsewhere he may wreak himself upon life . . ." he said.

56 What Bork had written of antitrust law . . . The title of his 1978 book is *The Antitrust Paradox: A Policy at War with Itself.*

56 "He was always competitive and aggressive" . . . Interview with Robert Bork, Jr., June 20, 1988.

57 Bork began verbal jousting . . . Interviews with Robert Bork, Jr.; William Karn (childhood neighbor of Bork's), August 18, 1988; Robert Espy, (faculty adviser to Bork's student newspaper), August 19, 1988; profiles in *Washington Post,* July 26, 1987; *Time* (September 21, 1987), *Newsweek* (September 14, 1987), *Philadelphia Inquirer,* July 26, 1987. "reading books and arguing with people" . . . *Washington Post,* July 2, 1987, p. 1.

57 "She tricked me" . . . *Philadelphia Inquirer,* July 26, 1987.

57 Snakes as pets . . . Photo of Bork with snakes appears in both *Washington Post* and *Time* profiles.

57 "The Russian army" . . . Interview with Karn.

58 "It hit me like a ton" . . . *Philadelphia Inquirer,* July 26, 1987.

58 Bork wanted to join the Marines . . . Interview with Robert Bork, Jr.

59 Bork remembered . . . Ibid.

59 "Chicago was the kind of place" . . . Interview with Karl Weintraub, August 12, 1988.

59 "It seems that there was" . . . Interview with Wayne Booth, August 11, 1988.

59 the dissolution of the West . . . Richard M. Weaver, *Ideas Have Consequences* (Chicago: Phoenix Books, 1948).

60 "[c]hange and reform" . . . Russell Kirk, *The Conservative Mind* (Chicago: Henry Regnery Co., 1953), p. 8.

60 "Strauss opened up" . . . Interview with Ralph Lerner, August 12, 1988.

61 New Deal type of socialism . . . Interview with Bork, January 13, 1989.

61 "take philosophy into the marketplace" . . . Cited by Bork in "We Suddenly Feel That Law Is Vulnerable," *Fortune* (December 1971), p. 115.

61 "I won't keep you long today" . . . Robert Bork, "A Whig View of the Republic," address to University of Chicago Alumni Association, Washington, D.C., May 7, 1976, p. 3.

62 "the logic of" . . . *Los Angeles Times,* September 13, 1987.

62 "I learned some basic" . . . *Philadelphia Inquirer,* July 26, 1987.

63 Director did not remember . . . Interview with Aaron Director, August 18, 1988.

63 A Bork law school classmate . . . Confidential interview.

63 "the most savagely honest" . . . *Los Angeles Times,* September 13, 1987.

63 "Recognition of the need for principle" . . . Robert Bork, "Neutral Principles and Some First Amendment Problems," *Indiana Law Journal,* vol. 47, no. 1 (Fall 1971), p. 6.

64 "a new way of looking at the world" . . . Cited in *Washington Post,* July 26, 1987, p. A8.

64　Howard Krane came to the firm . . . Interviews with Howard Krane, August 10, 1988; with Bork, January 13, 1989; and *Hearings Before the Committee on the Judiciary United States Senate on the Nomination of Robert H. Bork to Be Associate Justice of the Supreme Court of the United States,* Part 3, pp. 1500–28 (hereafter cited as *Bork Hearings*).

65　He remembered that Bork was shaken . . . *Washington Post,* July 26, 1987, p. A8.

65　"He told me he didn't want to spend his life" . . . *Time* (September 21, 1987), p. 16.

66　He recommended Bork for the position . . . Interview with Ward Bowman, August 19, 1988.

66　Yale had built a reputation . . . See Laura Kalman, *Legal Realism at Yale 1927–1960* (Chapel Hill: University of North Carolina Press, 1986).

66　One could count on a rousing debate . . . Interview with Harry Wellington, May 31, 1988.

67　between the time he walked out of his house . . . *Bork Hearings,* Part 1, p. 290.

67　Bork wrote an article . . . Recounted by Bork in a speech to the New England Legal Foundation, Boston, Massachusetts, June 2, 1988.

67　Bork wrote a fateful article . . . "Civil Rights—A Challenge," *New Republic* (August 31, 1963), p. 21.

67　"I agree that the attack" . . . *Philadelphia Inquirer,* July 26, 1987.

67　"The discussion we ought to hear" . . . Bork, "Civil Rights—A Challenge," loc. cit., p. 22.

68　"Government without principle" . . . *New Republic* (August 31, 1963), p. 24.

69　A decade later . . . *Hearings on the Nomination of Robert H. Bork to be Solicitor General Before Senate Judiciary Committee,* January 17, 1973, p. 14.

69　He provided Goldwater . . . Reported in *Chicago Tribune* at the time and cited in *Washington Post,* July 26, 1987, p. A8, and July 27, 1987, p. A8.

69　the man he really wanted . . . Confidential interview. Judge Bork, in an interview, said he remembers being impressed by Reagan when Reagan was a Chubb Fellow at Yale in the late 1960s and might well have made that remark.

69　"[A]s audiences lose confidence" . . . Robert Bork, "Why I Am for Nixon," *New Republic* (June 1, 1968), p. 19.

69　"Laws that raise" . . . Ibid., p. 22.

70　"The text of the Constitution" . . . Robert Bork, "The Supreme Court Needs a New Philosophy," *Fortune* (December 1968), p. 141. "my freedom to swing my fist" . . . p. 177.

71　"Mr. Bickel's legal philosophy" . . . Cited by Bork in his eulogy of Bickel, reprinted in *The Alternative: An American Spectator* (April 1975), p. 28.

72　During one long student strike . . . Interview with Robert Bork, Jr., October 13, 1988.

72　"One precipitating factor" . . . Robert Bork, "A Remembrance of Alex Bickel," *New Republic* (October 18, 1975), p. 22.

73　Bork's wave theory of law reform . . . Discussed in Robert Bork, "The Crisis in Constitutional Theory: Back to the Future," address to the Philadelphia Society, April 3, 1987, pp. 6 and 10–13.

74 This thinking Bork laid out . . . "Neutral Principles and Some First Amendment Problems," loc. cit.

75 One old acquaintance recalled . . . Confidential interview.

Chapter 4: Public Figure

77 Had it not been for his wife Claire . . . *Washington Post,* July 27, 1987, p. A8.

77 One day Bork showed up . . . Interview with Charles Bork, October 26, 1988.

78 "But the thing that Claire was" . . . Eulogy for Claire Bork by Barbara Black, Dwight Memorial Chapel, Yale University, New Haven, Connecticut, December 12, 1980.

78 Black was like a mother to Ellen . . . Interviews with Robert Bork, Jr., and Harry Wellington.

79 Bork almost forsook his tradition . . . and . . . One close friend of Bork's said . . . Confidential interview.

79 advising Nixon on legislation . . . Interview with Robert Bork, January 13, 1989. See Robert Bork, "Constitutionality of the President's Busing Proposals," American Enterprise Institute for Public Policy Research, no. 24, May 1972.

80 they ought to involve a smart Republican . . . Interview with Leonard Garment, April 29, 1988.

80 "Only you can save us" . . . *Washington Post,* July 27, 1987, p. A8.

81 "you would have had massive resignations" . . . *Senate Judiciary Committee Hearings on the Confirmation of Robert Bork to the Circuit Court of Appeals of the District of Columbia,* January 27, 1982, p. 10.

82 Some of those serving him . . . See the testimony of Henry Ruth and George Frampton at *Bork Hearings,* Part 3, pp. 1712–37.

82 Bork's three-and-a-half-year tenure . . . Interviews with Andrew Frey, September 15, 1988, and Justice Powell, July 12, 1988; and *Philadelphia Inquirer,* July 26, 1987.

82 A secretary told La Fontant one day . . . Jewel LaFontant testimony in *Bork Hearings,* Part 3, pp. 1444–49.

83 Chief Justice Warren Burger . . . Reported originally in *Los Angeles Times,* November 1974, and cited in *Washington Post,* July 27, 1987, p. A8.

83 At Christmas 1974 . . . Confidential interview.

83 "I had worked hard" . . . Interview with Harry Wellington, May 31, 1988.

84 "Alex Bickel's gifts" . . . Reprinted in *The Alternative: An American Spectator* (April 1975), pp. 28–29.

86 "There is no prospect" . . . Robert H. Bork, *The Antitrust Paradox* (New York: Basic Books, 1978), p. 423.

86 "The trend now" . . . "Morality and Authority," Robert Bork address to Carleton College, 1977–78, pp. 2 and 4.

87 "Contrary to the assertions made" . . . Memorandum from Robert Bork to the faculty of Yale Law School, April 27, 1978.

87 "It's tough enough" . . . *Washington Post,* July 28, 1987, p. A8.

88 "You remember those last" . . . Quoted in *Los Angeles Times,* September 13, 1987.

88 "It was a real shock" . . . *Philadelphia Inquirer,* September 26, 1987.

89 "He really cared about" . . . Confidential interview.

89 "We would find it impossible" . . . *Dronenburg* v. *Zech,* 741 F.2d at 1388, 1396–97 (D.C. Circuit, 1984).

89 "Look, Bob" . . . Interview with Abner Mikva, May 17, 1988. "extravagant exegesis" . . . *rehearing en banc denied,* 746 F. 2d 1579,80.

90 In a 1987 case . . . *United States* v. *Meyer,* No. 85-6169, Slip op. at 2 (D.C. Circuit, July 31, 1987).

90 "Nobody knows exactly what effect Claire's death" . . . Confidential interview.

91 As a young woman . . . Interview with Mary Ellen Bork, October 27, 1988. "It came as a great shock" . . . Quoted in V. V. Harrison, *Changing Habits* (New York: Doubleday, 1988), pp. 220–21.

92 "love at first listen" . . . The quip was by Eileen O'Connor, wife of Raymond Randolph, Bork's counsel during the hearings: interview with Randolph.

92 "I am convinced" . . . Testimony of Robert Bork, *Hearings on a Bill to Provide That Human Life Shall Be Deemed to Exist from Conception,* April 23, 24, May 20, 21, 1981, Serial No. J-97-16, p. 310.

92 friends from the mid-1970s . . . Confidential interviews. Judge Bork confirmed in an interview that his views had evolved.

93 Senator Bob Packwood . . . Senate debate on confirmation of Robert Bork to Supreme Court, Thursday, October 22, 1988, *Congressional Record,* vol. 133, no. 166, p. S14808.

93 "A relaxation of current rigidly" . . . Untitled address by Robert Bork to the Brookings Institution, September 12, 1985, pp. 10–12. Judge Bork confirmed in an interview that his attitude toward religion had changed over the years.

93 "[M]atters such as abortion" . . . Robert Bork, "Federalism and Gentrification," address to the Federalist Society, Yale University, April 24, 1982, p. 7.

93 "When the Constitution" . . . Robert Bork, "Federalism," address to the Attorney General's Conference, Williamsburg, Virginia, January 24–26, 1986, p. 7.

94 Asked to name the book . . . Interview with Raymond Randolph.

94 opposed by the majority of Americans . . . Robert Bork, "Tradition and Morality in Constitutional Law," the Francis Boyer Lecture to the American Enterprise Institute, December 6, 1984, p. 9.

95 "It is questionable whether" . . . Interview with Judge Richard Posner, August 11, 1988.

95 At 6:30 A.M. on Wednesday . . . This account is based on interviews Robert Bork, Jr., conducted with his father and passed on to the author.

97 "Judge Bork, widely regarded" . . . President Reagan's press conference, July 1, 1987.

Chapter 5: Advice and Dissent

98 Ball flicked on the television . . . Interview with William Ball, May 5, 1988.

99 "Now we better win" . . . Interview with Jeffrey Blattner, April 5, 1988.

100 "I wanted to make clear" . . . Interview with Edward Kennedy, October 9, 1987; see *Boston Globe,* October 11, 1987, p. 1.

100 "Four presidential elections hence" . . . *New York Times,* November 6, 1987.

101 "Running for president" . . . Interview with Edward Kennedy, September 16, 1988.

102 "They were both my best friends" . . . Ibid.

102 one wit proposed . . . Told in Peter Collier and David Horowitz, *The Kennedys: An American Drama* (New York: Summit Books, 1984), p. 326.

102 On that grim California day . . . Ibid., p. 364.

103 the black readers . . . *Ebony* (April 1988), p. 42.

103 Once, toward the end of a long day . . . Interviews with Mary Ellen Bork, October 27, 1988, and Kennedy, April 13, 1988.

104 When the Bork nomination . . . Told by Phil Gramm at a gathering of Bork supporters after the nomination was defeated and repeated to the author by two of those present, especially Robert Bork, Jr.

104 "He's absolutely professional" . . . Interview with Kennedy in *Rolling Stone* (November 5, 1987).

104 "Look, the masses" . . . Confidential interview.

105 Kennedy called Ernest Morial . . . Interview with Anthony Podesta, Carolyn Osolinik, and Jeffrey Blattner, October 9, 1987.

106 Stopping in at Marshall's island retreat . . . Interview with Burke Marshall, June 1, 1988.

106 "I thought for a moment" . . . Interview with Jeffrey Blattner.

106 "The question was how to convince" . . . Interview with Anthony Podesta, May 16, 1988.

106 The letter Kennedy sent . . . Interview with Michael Frazier, June 14, 1988.

107 Ed, we don't call often . . . Confidential interview.

107 "Our opponents complained" . . . Interview with Podesta.

108 Kennedy's speech . . . Interview with Kennedy, October 9, 1987.

108 Freund hadn't talked with Kennedy . . . Interview with Paul Freund, March 15, 1988.

109 "this was a swing seat" . . . Interview with Jeffrey Blattner, April 5, 1988.

109 "When the people elect" . . . Interview with Sheldon Goldman, September 7, 1988.

109 The traditional concept of judging . . . I thank Burt Neuborne of New York University School of Law for lending me his course materials on these issues and discussing them with me. He calls the first model the syllogism machine and provided me with the short-order cook analogy of the second model of judging.

110 judges "must fill in gaps" . . . Paul Simon, "Judging Judges: The Senate's Role in Judicial Appointments," address to the National Press Club, March 10, 1986.

111 "Each of us" . . . William Rehnquist, "Judicial Selection for Constitutional Courts," address to the Bicentennial Australian Legal Convention, August 29, 1988, p. 12.

112 From the beginning . . . See, among others, Henry J. Abraham, *Justices and Presidents* (New York: Oxford University Press, 1974) and Laurence Tribe, *God Save This Honorable Court* (New York: Random House, 1985).

113 Brandeis "not a fit person" . . . *New York Times,* March 15, 1916, p. 7.

114 "The significance is not that" . . . *Subcommittee Hearings of the Judiciary Committee, U.S. Senate, on the Confirmation of Judge John J. Parker,* 71st Congress, 2d Session, 1930, p. 27. Cited in Olive Taylor, *Two Hundred Years, an Issue: Ideology in the Nomination and Confirmation Process of Justices to the Supreme Court of the United States* (Washington, D.C.: NAACP, 1987), p. 49.

114 "participation of the Negro in politics" . . . Abraham, op. cit., p. 43.

114 "In Judge Parker's case" . . . *New York Times,* April 27, 1930, III, p. 1.

115 "the first national demonstration" . . . Cited in Taylor, op. cit., p. 55.

115 Justice Hugo Black once commented . . . Black made the comment to Paul Freund, who recounted it to the author in an interview.

115 Senator Strom Thurmond . . . *New York Times,* July 30, 1967, Section IV, p. 10.

115 Johnson nominated Fortas . . . For a detailed and fascinating account, see Bruce Allen Murphy, *Fortas: The Rise and Ruin of a Supreme Court Justice* (New York: William Morrow and Co., 1988).

117 "I yield to no man" . . . Abraham, op. cit., p. 16.

117 Carswell "was not qualified" . . . Cited in Taylor op. cit., p. 77. Carswell "was not qualified to carry" . . . Abraham, op. cit., p. 17. Senator Roman Hruska . . . Ibid.

117 The Senate, following a concerted effort . . . See Richard Harris, *Decision* (New York: E. P. Dutton, 1970).

117 "When all the hypocrisy" . . . Televised address by Richard Nixon to the nation, April 9, 1970, text in *New York Times,* April 10, 1970, p. 1.

118 "Rather (and to my surprise), all the relevant" . . . Henry Paul Monaghan, "The Confirmation Process: Law or Politics?," *Harvard Law Review,* vol. 101, no. 6 (April 1988), p. 1204.

118 "Any inclination by anybody" . . . Interview with Eric Schnapper, June 1, 1988.

119 nominees were being vetoed by the right wing . . . See Herman Schwartz, *Packing the Courts* (New York: Scribner's, 1988), pp. 77–89.

120 "It became evident" . . . "Judging the Judges," *Newsweek* (October 14, 1985), p. 73.

120 During Reagan's first term . . . Schwartz, op. cit., pp. 59–60.

120 potential nominees were asked about . . . Ibid., pp. 60–61.

121 A comparison of the ratings . . . Sheldon Goldman, "Reagan's Second Term Judicial Appointments: The Battle at Midway," *Judicature* (April–May 1987), and interview with Sheldon Goldman, September 7, 1988.

121 Ratings of some of these nominees were very low . . . See Peter J. Ferrara "Qualifications and Confirmation of Reagan's Judges," *The Judges War,* ed. Patrick B. McGuigan and Jeffrey P. O'Connell (Washington: Free Congress Foundation, 1987), pp. 160–61.

121 "[I]n recent years" . . . Michal Freedman, "Assembly-Line Approval: A Common Cause Study of Senate Confirmation of Federal Judges," January 1986, p. 1.

122 "What are the nominee's views" . . . Paul Simon, "Judging Judges: The Senate's Role in Judicial Appointments," address to National Press Club, March 10, 1986.

122 justices' votes are not traded . . . David P. Bryden, "How to Select a Supreme Court Justice," *American Scholar* (Spring 1988), pp. 204–05.

123 "The Senate had not been paying" . . . Interview with Patrick Leahy, September 16, 1988.

123 Asked his view . . . Interviews with Edwin Meese, September 16, 1988, and Edward M. Kennedy, September 16, 1988.

123 Gewirtz had been informally debating . . . Interview with Paul Gewirtz, May 31, 1988.

124 "People need to understand" . . . Tribe, *op. cit.,* p. ix.

125 "[I]f the appointment" . . . Ibid., p. 129.

Chapter 6: Self-Made Men

128 if he could have rewritten the Constitution . . . See Laurence H. Tribe, "On Reading the Constitution," Tanner Lectures on Human Values delivered at the University of Utah, November 17 and 18, 1986 (forthcoming), p. 14, and interview with Tribe, July 6, 1988.

128 the Supreme Court case he lost . . . *Bowers* v. *Hardwick,* 106 2841 (1986).

129 one of the nation's most widely used treatises . . . Laurence H. Tribe, *American Constitutional Law,* ed. (Mineola, N.Y. Foundation Press, 1988).

129 "probably the most creative" . . . Interview with Henry Paul Monaghan, September 19, 1988.

129 "more decency than dogmatism" . . . Cited in *New York Times,* November 14, 1987, Section 1, p. 8.

130 "Larry's a complicated person" . . . Cited in *Wall Street Journal,* December 18, 1987, p. 25.

130 he entertained a roomful of guests . . . Interview with Polia Tribe, September 13, 1988.

131 "I was a really driven kid" . . . Interview with Tribe, July 6, 1988.

132 "It may well be" . . . Cited in *Wall Street Journal,* December 18, 1987, p. 25.

133 the Senate was obliged . . . Letter to the Senate Judiciary Committee from Kurland and Tribe, June 1, 1986.

136 "We're as different" . . . Interview with Joseph Biden, December 7, 1988.

137 "What's going to happen" . . . Confidential interview.

138 Aides gently warned him . . . Ibid.

139 "[T]he new Justice" . . . *Philadelphia Inquirer,* November 14, 1986, p. A13.

139 Biden was so touched . . . Confidential interview.

139 Biden acknowledged . . . Interview with Biden.

141 When Biden had spoken . . . Ibid.

141 Gitenstein, aware of the *Inquirer* gaffe . . . Interview with Mark Gitenstein, April 11, 1988.

141 Biden told White House Chief . . . Interview with Biden

141 As Stuart E. Eizenstat . . . cited in *Washington Times,* July 6, 1987.

141 When he emerged from his meeting . . . *Washington Post,* July 1, 1987, p. A8.

141 Biden pointed to the meeting . . . Interviews with Biden, Meese, and Baker.

142 "It was no accident" . . . Interview with Thomas Donilon, June 14, 1988.

143 "I learned a lot" . . . Interview with Gitenstein.

144 "We will fight it" . . . *USA Today,* July 6, 1987.

Chapter 7: Raw Meat

146 "Actualities are free" . . . Interview with Henry Griggs, July 14, 1988.

147 Prior's products . . . Interview with James Prior, July 14, 1988.

147 The organization spent . . . Interview with Melanne Verveer, April 26, 1988.

147 "The idea was to frame" . . . Interview with Phil Sparks, July 15, 1988.

148 If you could have a headline . . . Interview with Emily Tynes, June 23, 1988.

148 Over the course of the summer . . . See Anthony Lewis, *New York Times*, August 27, September 3, 6, 10, 13, and 24, 1987; Ronald Dworkin, "The Bork Nomination," *New York Review of Books* (August 13, 1987), p. 3; *New Yorker* (August 3, 1987), p. 17; Renata Adler, "Coup at the Court," *New Republic* (September 14 and 21, 1987); Philip Kurland, "Bork: The Transformation of a Conservative Constitutionalist," *Chicago Tribune*, August 18, 1987. See *Wall Street Journal* editorials on July 2, 8, 30, September 15, 28, October 5 and 20, 1987.

149 Paid advertising amounted to . . . This is based on a pooling of figures offered by the major organizations involved. People for the American Way, the biggest spender, said it spent $650,000, Planned Parenthood spent $150,000, the National Abortion Rights Action League $200,000. There was more advertising at the local level but not much.

149 "Never before had I felt" . . . Interview with Linda Greenhouse, July 25, 1988.

149 "It's different from all those" . . . Interview of David Kusnet by members of the Advocacy Institute and provided to the author.

150 This was also true . . . "The Judicial Record of Judge Robert H. Bork," Public Citizen Litigation Group, Washington, D.C., August 1987.

151 "the topics covered most often" . . . *Media Monitor*, Center for Media and Public Affairs, Washington, D.C., October 1987.

152 Louis Harris and Associates . . . National telephone poll October 2–7, 1987, by Louis Harris and Associates.

153 "In the past decade" Interview with Phil Sparks, July 15, 1988. "A shot in the arm" . . . Interview with Emily Tynes, June 23, 1988.

153 "When Powell resigned" . . . Interview with Jackie Blumenthal, June 20, 1988.

154 a budget of more than ten million . . . Interview with Melanne Verveer.

155 it was aired only eighty-five times . . . Interview with Jackie Blumenthal; Few Americans saw it . . . Marttila and Kiley poll, October 1987, showed that 24 percent of those polled said they saw anti-Bork television ads.

156 "What the camera always focuses" . . . Arthur Kropp, address to the Stanford Business School, April 27, 1988.

157 "We could have all the substance" . . . Interview with Ricki Seidman, May 4, 1988.

159 "Then we had the idea" . . . Interview with Nikki Heidepriem, June 13, 1988.

160 "From day one" . . . Interview with Ricki Seidman, May 4, 1988.

160 It involved a unanimous 1984 decision . . . *Oil, Chemical and Atomic Workers International Union* v. *American Cyanamid Company*, 741 F. 2d 444 (D.C. Circuit 1984).

177 "I have seen nothing in the law" . . . Words of the administrative law judge at a prehearing conference. The judge ultimately dismissed the claim. His

statement was cited by Robert Bork in an October 5, 1987, letter to Senator Biden

178 "To treat the choice" . . . Interview with Laurence Tribe, March 22, 1988.

179 "They made Bob look" . . . Confidential interview.

179 "Simply stated" . . . *Bork Blocker,* September 1987, Charleston, West Virginia, the West Virginia Network for Peace, Freedom and Justice, p. 1.

180 This referred to Bork's ruling . . . *Vinson* v. *Taylor,* 753 F. 2d 141 (D.C. Circuit 1985).

181 For a campaign that would normally . . . Interview with Mimi Mager, May 17, 1988.

181 "People were lining up to volunteer" . . . Interview with Michael Mac-Dougall, August 18, 1988.

182 An example of the latter . . . Reported in *Richmond News Leader,* September 8, 1987, p. 15.

183 At the annual meeting . . . *Washington Post,* July 7, 1987, p. 1. "I have the votes in New York" . . . *Washington Post,* July 8, 1987.

184 Something similar happened . . . Interviews with Frank Jackalone, June 17, 1988; Carlton Moore, September 20, 1988; and Lawton Chiles, July 13, 1988.

184 He contacted Bill Gunter . . . Interview with Frank Jackalone.

184 In Pennsylvania . . . Interview with Arlen Specter, June 22, 1988.

184 In Washington State . . . Interview with Michael MacDougall.

185 "It is always in the back" . . . Interview with Dennis DeConcini, May 10, 1988.

185 "The ease with which" . . . George Will, "The Scale and Intensity of the Anti-Bork Campaign," *Washington Post,* October 1, 1987, p. A21.

186 "Here were all the issues" . . . Interview with Monica McFadden, September 6, 1988.

186 "I thought I was throwing" . . . Interview with Patrick Caddell, October 25, 1988.

Chapter 8: Let's Not Ballyhoo It

189 "Look, Bob" . . . This account is based on several confidential interviews.

190 "Conservatives have waited" . . . Quoted in "Liberal Groups Jump into Fight," *Fort Worth Star-Telegram,* July 2, 1987, p. 24.

191 "the president could advance" . . . *Human Events* (July 11, 1987), p. 1.

191 "The idea was to" . . . Interview with William Ball, May 5, 1988.

192 "Judge Bork is recognized" . . . Quoted in "Reagan Wants Confirmation of Bork to Be Apolitical," *Washington Post,* July 5, 1987.

192 "There was a determined effort" . . . Interview with Authur B. Culvahouse, April 27, 1988.

192 "Our strategy was" . . . Interview with Howard Baker, June 21, 1988.

193 "It's basically a coaching operation" . . . This discussion and later account of visit to Bork based on interviews with Thomas Korologos, April 7, 14, and 27 and May 2, 1988.

193 "How much do you charge" . . . George Will, "Bork Up Against a Stall Defense," *Washington Post,* August 2, 1987, p. C7.

194 They said they would not . . . Interview with Al Kamen, April 8, 1988.

195 "He thinks *he's* under pressure?" . . . Confidential interview.

195 "His centrism was woefully" . . . Interview with William Bradford Reynolds, June 15, 1988.

196 "It's hard for a fair-minded" . . . "Reagan, Opening Bork Fight, Calls Judge a Moderate," *New York Times,* July 30, 1987.

197 he wrote at least three . . . Interviews with Terry Eastland, March 4, 1988, and Michael Carvin, April 13 and 25 and May 6 and 17, 1988.

197 "If we're going" . . . Carvin *ibid.*

197 "In my view" . . . Interview with Eastland.

198 "Judge Bork's appointment" . . . "The White House Report" reprinted in *Cardozo Law Review,* vol. 9, no. 1 (October 1987), p. 214.

198 "I nixed that" . . . Interview with Thomas Griscom, April 15, 1988.

199 "The sky was clear" . . . Interview with Raymond Randolph, April 14, 1988.

199 "If the Democrats beat up" . . . "Polarized Senate Prepares for September Hearings on Bork," *Congressional Quarterly* (July 11, 1987), p. 1499.

199 "I personally regard him" . . . *New York Times,* August 1, 1987, p. 1.

199 "I don't think in more" . . . *San Diego Union,* August 12, 1987, p. 1

199 a poll commissioned . . . "Half of Judges Polled Back Bork Confirmation," *Washington Post,* August 2, 1987.

199 "To me, Reagan was like" . . . Interview with Terry Eastland.

200 "No way. I'm not" . . . Interview with Patrick McGuigan, July 11, 1988.

201 "My wife Pamela" . . . McGuigan and Weyrich, op. cit.

201 "prayerfully consider writing" . . . Quoted ibid.

201 "Robert Bork does not" . . . quoted in *New York Times,* September 9, 1987.

202 The name suggested . . . Interview with Steven Baer, June 13, 1988.

202 McGuigan called one of his friends . . . Told in McGuigan and Weyrich, op. cit.

203 Another serious setback . . . Interview with Dan Casey, director of the American Conservative Union, June 15, 1988.

204 "It was inconceivable" . . . Ibid.

204 "I really think" . . . *Legal Times,* (July 20, 1987).

205 It was the first time . . . Interview with Irene Emsellem, staff liaison for the ABA Standing Committee on Federal Judiciary, December 13, 1988.

205 "his compassion, open-mindedness" . . . Report on Robert Bork of ABA Standing Committee on Federal Judiciary to Senator Biden. Reprinted in *Bork Hearings,* September 1987, p. 959.

206 "Politics has never come up" . . . Quoted in *New York Times,* September 11, 1987.

206 The weekend before the ABA . . . Interviews with several Justice Department and other administration officials, including Brad Reynolds, John Bolton, Mike Carvin, Peter Keisler.

207 The previous Tuesday . . . Interview with Terry Eastland.

207 After the meeting broke up . . . Confidential interview.

Chapter 9: The Main Event

208 Illinois Senator Paul Simon . . . Interview with Paul Simon, June 24, 1988. The telephones of Senator Leahy . . . Interview with Patrick Leahy, September 16, 1988.

208 "Wherever you go" . . . *Bork Hearings,* Part 1, p. 6.

208 Senator Arlen Specter . . . Interview with Arlen Specter, June 22, 1988. See also Dale Rusakoff, "Toned-Down Nominee has Conciliatory Manner but Strong Words," *Washington Post,* September 16, 1987.

209 Senator Kennedy and his staff . . . Interviews with Jeffrey Blattner, April 18 and 25 and May 15, 1988.

210 When Larry Tribe playacted . . . Interview with Joseph Biden, December 7, 1988.

211 During Iran-contra . . . Interview with Thomas Donilon, June 14, 1988.

211 "Calling it an opportunity" . . . Interview with Biden.

212 a front-page story reporting . . . *New York Times,* September 12, 1987, p. 1.

214 the longest delay . . . *Bork Hearings,* Part 1, p. 19.

215 The National Abortion Rights Action League . . . Interview with Kate Michelman, May 17, 1988.

215 "Biden did everything but" . . . Tom Shales, *Washington Post,* September 16, 1987, p. D1.

215 No one within earshot . . . Interview with senior Justice Department official.

216 "Mr. President" . . . *Bork Hearings,* Part 1, pp. 4–5.

217 "Ford had requested" . . . Interview with Dennis DeConcini, May 10, 1988.

217 "And so let us make" . . . *Bork Hearings,* Part 1, pp. 65–69.

219 "As late as 1961" . . . William J. Brennan, Jr., "The Constitution of the United States: Contemporary Ratification," address at Georgetown University, Washington, D.C., October 12, 1985, p. 12.

220 Not until 1925 . . . Abraham, op. cit., pp. 193–94.

220 "I should think it improper" . . . Quoted by Paul Freund in *Harvard Law Review* (April 1988), p. 1159.

220 there had been some debate . . . Interviews with Justice Department officials and with Peter Keisler, December 26, 1988.

222 "The truth is that the court" . . . Bork, "Neutral Principles and Some First Amendment Problems," loc. cit., p. 9; *Griswold* v. *State of Connecticut,* 381 U.S. 479 (1965).

222 "You have been a professor now" . . . *Bork Hearings,* Part 1, p. 88.

222 "I have never found it" . . . Ibid., p. 125.

223 Kennedy's aide . . . Interview with Jeffrey Blattner.

224 Kennedy had expected it . . . Ibid.

224 "The point that I would make" . . . *Bork Hearings,* Part 1, pp. 127–28.

224 In the 1966 case . . . *Harper* v. *Virginia State Board of Elections,* 383 U.S. 663 (1966). See Bork's discussion of this in his introduction to Gary L. McDowell, *The Constitution and Contemporary Constitutional Theory* (Center for Judicial Studies, 1985), pp. v–xi.

225 "I think the people of this country" . . . *Bork Hearings,* Part 1, p. 132

226 "He looked, and talked" . . . *Washington Post,* October 9, 1987, p. B1.

Chapter 10: Missed Opportunities

227 "He's good on substance" . . . Interview with John Bolton.

228 Thurmond was not enthusiastic . . . Confidential interviews.

228 In the old days . . . Cited in Alan Ehrenhalt, ed. *Politics in America: The 100th*

Congress (Washington D.C.: Congressional Quarterly Press, 1987), p. 1366.

228 "I might say" . . . *Bork Hearings,* Part 3, p. 1617.

228 "I'm not a racist" . . . Cited in Ehrenbalt, op. cit., p. 1367.

229 When Biden decided in July . . . Confidential interviews.

229 "It appears to me" . . . *Bork Hearings,* Part 1, p. 122.

230 "You know how much water" . . . Confidential interviews.

230 "I subscribe to what" . . . Interview with Orrin Hatch, April 12, 1988.

230 He later said . . . Ibid.

230 "I think what you have" . . . *Bork Hearings,* Part 1, p. 153.

232 "It was very frustrating" . . . Interview with Hatch.

232 "You accept in *Bolling v. Sharpe*" . . . *Bork Hearings,* Part 1, pp. 262–63.

233 Bork's advisers . . . Confidential interviews.

233 Bolton and Korologos decided to ignore . . . Interviews with Bolton and Korologos.

234 ". . . no view of literacy tests" . . . *Bork Hearings,* Part 1, p. 324.

234 "What responsibility" . . . *Bork Hearings,* Part 1, pp. 441–444.

235 Afterward he expressed anger . . . Interview with Gordon Humphrey, April 27, 1988.

235 "In the U.S. Senate" . . . *Wall Street Journal,* June 29, 1988, p. 1.

236 "Some of them, I guess" . . . *Bork Hearings,* Part 1, pp. 448–50.

236 Eric Schnapper and Elaine Jones . . . Interview with Eric Schnapper, December 14, 1988.

236 "I had surgery because" . . . *Bork Hearings,* Part 1, p. 654.

237 DeConcini and his wife . . . Interview with committee aide.

238 "Judge, goddamn, surely" . . . Interview with William Ball.

238 "You're doing a wonderful job" . . . Interview with Randall Rader.

239 "I think you did really well" . . . Interview with Robert Bork, Jr.

Chapter 11: Confirmation Conversion

242 "He can't in forty-eight hours" . . . *Washington Times,* September 18, 1988, p. A11.

242 "Constitutional protection" . . . Bork, "Neutral Principles and Some First Amendment Problems," loc. cit., p. 20.

242 "The notion that all valuable" . . . Ibid., p. 28.

243 In 1911, for example . . . *United States* v. *Press Publishing Co.,* 219 U.S. 1 (1911) and *Gompers* v. *Bucks Stove and Range Co.,* 221 U.S. 418 (1911); both are cited in Tribe, *Constitutional Choices* loc. cit., p. 190.

244 In the infamous . . . *Abrams* v. *United States,* 250 U.S. 616 (1919); see Richard Polenberg, *Fighting Faiths: The Abrams Case, the Supreme Court and Free Speech* (New York: Viking Press, 1987).

244 In 1925 the Supreme Court . . . *Gitlow* v. *People of State of New York,* 268 U.S. U.S. 652 (1925), and *Whitney* v. *People of State of California,* 274 U.S. 357 (1927).

244 "the constitutional guarantees" . . . *Brandenburg* v. *Ohio,* 395 U.S. 444, 447 (1969).

245 "If our president" . . . Ibid., at 446.

245 "long since concluded" . . . 70 ABA Journal 132 (February 1984).

245 Moreover, two years before . . . *Judiciary Committee Hearings for Confirmation of Robert Bork to the Circuit Court of Appeals,* January 27, 1982, p. 4.

245 "I have expanded" . . . *Bork Hearings,* Part 1, p. 245.

246 "The Supreme Court has come" . . . Ibid., p. 247.

246 "I think these confirmation hearings" . . . Ibid., p. 252.

246 In the anti-Bork war room . . . Interviews with William Taylor, December 14, 1988, and Eric Schnapper, December 14, 1988.

247 "Judge Bork does not believe" . . . *A Response to the Critics of Judge Robert H. Bork* (Washington, D.C.: Department of Justice, September 12, 1987), pp. 57, 60.

247 "I have not changed my mind" . . . *Bork Hearings,* Part 1, p. 311.

248 "Senator, we are talking about" . . . Interview with Raymond Randolph.

248 "These include the lewd" . . . *Chaplinsky* v. *New Hampshire,* 315 U.S. 568, 572 (1942).

249 In 1969 . . . *Stanley* v. *Georgia,* 394 U.S. 557 (1969).

249 In a 1973 Indiana case . . . *Hess* v. *Indiana,* 414 U.S. 105 (1973).

249 "One man's vulgarity" . . . *Cohen* v. *California,* 403 U.S. 15, 24 (1971).

250 The federal appellate court . . . *Collin* v. *Smith,* 447 F. Supp. 676 (N.D. Ill.), aff'd 578 F. 2d 1197 (7th Circuit), *cert. denied,* 439 U.S. 916 (1978).

250 "The fundamental issue raised" . . . Robert Bork, "The Individual, the State and the First Amendment," address at the University of Michigan, 1978, p. 24.

250 some political and legal theorists to the left . . . See Michael Sandel, "Democrats and Community," *New Republic* (February 22, 1988), pp. 20–23.

250 he was thinking of pre-Nazi Germany . . . *Bork Hearings,* Part 1, p. 249.

251 This sort of waffling . . . Both the Fein and Viguerie quotes are from *Boston Globe,* September 20, 1987, p. 1.

251 And Pat Robertson . . . *Washington Times,* September 29, 1987, p. A10.

252 "The natural and proper timidity" . . . *Bradwell* v. *Illinois,* 83 U.S. 130, 141 (1872).

252 "That woman's physical structure" . . . *Muller* v. *Oregon,* 208 U.S. 412, 421–22 (1908).

252 In 1948 . . . *Goesaert* v. *Cleary,* 335 U.S. 464–46 (1948).

252 And as late as 1961 . . . *Hoyt* v. *Florida,* 368 U.S. 57 (1961), at 61–62. The defendant, a woman who had murdered her husband with a baseball bat, was eager for women on her jury.

252 invalidated an Idaho statute . . . *Reed* v. *Reed,* 404 U.S. 71 (1971).

253 "a child, male or female" . . . *Stanton* v. *Stanton,* 421 U.S. 7, 14–15 (1975).

253 In 1976 the Court . . . See *Craig* v. *Boren* 429 U.S. 190 (1976)

254 The only thing . . . Bork, "Neutral Principles and Some First Amendment Problems," loc. cit., p. 11, 17.

254 "I think the Equal Protection Clause" . . . Interview of Robert Bork on World Net, May, 1987, p. 12.

254 Bork's new position . . . Confidential interviews.

255 The book stated . . . "A Response to the Critics," loc. cit., pp. 139–40.

255 "I do not think" . . . *Bork Hearings,* Part 1, p. 267.

256 During hearings . . . *Hearings on a Bill to Provide That Human Life Shall Be Deemed to Exist from Conception,* J-97-16, April, May, June 1981, p. 310.

256 As Laurence Tribe . . . *Bork Hearings,* Part 2, p. 26.

256 why should courts . . . Address by Robert Bork at Catholic University, 1982, p. 19.

256 "The desire for judicial" . . . Speech reproduced in *Bork Hearings,* Part 1, p. 147.

257 "You know, democracy" . . . *Bork Hearings,* Part 1, p. 619.

258 "It may take ten years" . . . Robert Bork, "The Crisis in Constitutional Theory: Back to the Future," address to the Philadelphia Society, April 3, 1987, pp. 14–15.

258 "An originalist judge" . . . Quoted in *Bork Hearings,* Part 1, p. 523.

259 "Yes I can" . . . "A Talk with Judge Robert H. Bork," *District Lawyer,* vol. 9, no. 5 (May–June 1985) p. 32.

260 "I don't think" . . . *Bork Hearings,* Part 1, pp. 523–24.

Chapter 12: Intellectual Feast

261 On the third day . . . *Bork Hearings,* Part 1, pp. 398–99.

262 "I think we ought to" . . . Interview with Gordon Humphrey, April 27, 1988.

262 Humphrey had to apologize . . . "Humphrey: Motherhood Remarks 'Just Plain Stupid,' " *Boston Globe,* September 9, 1988, p. 21.

263 "Were those years" . . . *Bork Hearings,* Part 1, p. 408.

264 "I'm sure Judge Bork" . . . Interview with Arlen Specter, June 22, 1988.

265 "He was going to win it" . . . Quoted by Rich Scheinin in "Arlen Specter Always Told People He'd Be a Senator—Now That He Is One, He Has Changed," *Philadelphia Inquirer Magazine,* April 15, 1984, p. 22.

265 "Arlen, what's this I hear" . . . Interview with Specter.

266 He quoted Bork as saying . . . *Bork Hearings,* Part 1, p. 575.

266 something clearly opposed . . . See, in particular, Leonard W. Levy, *Original Intent and the Framers' Constitution* (New York: Macmillan, 1988).

267 In 1923 . . . *Meyer* v. *State of Nebraska,* 262 U.S. at 399 (1923).

267 In 1925 . . . *Pierce* v. *Society of the Sisters of the Holy Names of Jesus and Mary,* 268 U.S. at 534–35 (1925).

267 For liberal scholars . . . See, for example, Tribe, *American Constitutional Law,* loc. cit., p. 1320.

267 Justice Douglas wrote . . . *Skinner* v. *Oklahoma,* 316 U.S. at 535 and 541 (1942).

267 "This 'liberty' is not a series" . . . *Poe* v. *Ullman,* 367 U.S. 497, 543 (1961).

268 Two years later . . . *Loving* v. *Virginia,* 388 U.S. 1, 12 (1967).

268 "If the right of privacy" . . . *Eisenstadt* v. *Baird,* 405 U.S. at 453 (1972).

268 privacy "is broad enough" . . . *Roe* v. *Wade,* 410 U.S. 113, 153 (1973).

268 "The fact that no particular" . . . *Griswold* v. *State of Connecticut,* 381 U.S. at 495–96 (1965), Goldberg concurring.

268 Even conservative Justice Rehnquist . . . *Roe* v. *Wade,* 410 U.S. 113 at 172–73 (1973).

269 Bork had dismissed the amendment . . . See, for example, Bork's testimony, *Bork Hearings,* Part 1, p. 224, and his speech on October 25, 1984, to the

University of Southern California, p. 12: "When the meaning of a provision, or the extension of provision beyond its known meaning, is unknown, the judge has in effect nothing more than a waterblot on the document before him." See also the exchanges on the issue between Laurence Tribe and the editors of the *Wall Street Journal*, October 5 and October 7, 1987.

269 Bork had earlier told Biden . . . *Bork Hearings,* Part 1, p. 299.

270 This was a profound critique . . . See Ronald Dworkin, "The Bork Nomination," *New York Review of Books,* vol. XXXIV, no. 13 (August 13, 1987).

271 Bork had argued . . . He did this in a speech to the University of San Diego School of Law on November 18, 1985, reprinted in *San Diego Law Review,* vol. 23, no. 4 (1986), p. 823. Bork had made the identical point in his October 25, 1984, lecture at the University of Southern California.

272 choosing among competing values . . . It is said that the great logician Kurt Godel refused for a long time to become an American citizen because it meant pledging allegiance to the Constitution, whose principles, to his eye, were internally inconsistent.

272 At the Saturday session . . . *Bork Hearings,* Part 1, p. 682.

273 it might be a good idea to stroke Specter . . . Interview with Raymond Randolph.

273 But he said later . . . Interview with Specter.

273 Bolton felt encouraged . . . Interview with Bolton.

274 he seemed to stare . . . Steven Komarow, "Wyoming's Simpson Not Promoting Himself as Running Mate for Bush," Associated Press, June 23, 1988.

274 "Fourteen years" . . . *Bork Hearings,* Part 1, p. 212.

274 "You talk about the right to privacy" . . . Ibid., p. 361.

275 "Senator, I guess the answer" . . . Ibid., p. 720.

276 Even he, months later . . . See accounts of Bork's first news conference upon leaving the bench, February 8, 1988.

276 "First, working on opinions" . . . The interview was conducted by the Supreme Court's quarterly public relations magazine, *Docket Sheet,* vol. 24, no. 2 (Fall 1987), p. 14.

Chapter 13: Determined to Be Heard

278 Coleman's son, William . . . Interview with Raymond Randolph.

278 Coleman kept his counsel . . . Based on several confidential interviews.

278 "When I was in high school" . . . Quoted by Stuart Taylor, Jr., *The New York Times,* April 20, 1982, p. D21.

279 Coleman invited Gewirtz . . . Based on several confidential interviews.

279 "A lower court judge" . . . William T. Coleman, Jr. "Why Judge Bork Is Unacceptable," *New York Times,* September 15, 1987, op-ed page.

279 "I have tried very hard" . . . *Bork Hearings,* p. 734.

281 "If it were claimed" . . . Ibid., p. 782.

281 "[Bork] has not been exposed" . . . Ibid., pp. 744–746.

283 "living fifty one years" . . . Ibid., p. 785.

284 "I am talking to these" . . . Ibid., p. 788.

284 "[W]hen it looked as though" . . . Ibid., p. 803.

285 "We do not see this" ... Ibid., p. 809.

286 "We're gonna go with the brothers" ... Confidential interviews.

286 Johnston turned to Shelby ... Interview with Richard Shelby, May 11, 1988; see also Dale Rusakoff, "How the South Was Swayed," *Washington Post*, October 8, 1987, p. 1.

286 "Those who helped us" ... Quoted by Nathaniel C. Nash, "Bork Is Losing Southern Democrats While Picking Up G.O.P. Moderates," *New York Times*, September 27, 1987.

287 "Damn it" ... Cited in Ehrenhalt, op. cit., p. 11.

287 As Casey remembered it ... Interview with Dan Casey, June 15, 1988.

288 "Without him and the Republican majority" ... This and following Reagan quotes were cited by Lou Cannon, *Washington Post*, October 8, 1987, p. A18.

288 Johnston's notion ... Interviews with Alan Cranston, April 21, 1988, and with Patrick Caddell.

290 "The polling data freed" ... Interview with Michael Donilon, June 17, 1988.

290 "Confronted by militant" ... *Los Angeles Times*, August 23, 1987, p. V-1.

291 "They resurrected" ... Interview with Thomas Griscom.

291 "My deep concern" ... Nash, op. cit.

292 "This was not Jerry Falwell" ... Rusakoff, op. cit.

292 "Things were set in concrete" ... Interview with Richard Shelby.

293 Many who knew Heflin ... This point is made fully by Terence Moran, "Heflin and the Bork Question," *Legal Times*, vol. X, no. 11 (August 10, 1987), pp. 1, 12, 13.

293 Stories of his courtroom technique ... Ibid., p. 13.

293 Some Alabama papers ... Patrick Leahy tells the following story: When Heflin voted against Bork—maintaining the suspense until the moment before he actually cast his vote—he was attacked at home as Bennett Johnston's "lap dog" for following the Louisiana senator's lead. Shortly after that accusation was leveled, Heflin walked into the Senate's private dining room and spotted Johnston at a table. The Alabama senator proclaimed, "Here I am, your lap dog," and dropped himself into Johnston's lap. Johnston groaned, "I'll never get out of this chair again." (Patrick Leahy "Judgment Days," *Washingtonian* [April 1988], p. 97.)

294 "Well, now there are those" ... *Bork Hearings*, Part 1, p. 270.

294 "There are those who charge" ... Ibid., p. 58.

295 Tennessee's Jim Sasser ... Cited by George Will, "What They're Saying Now About Judge Bork," *Washington Post*, January 21, 1988, p. A23.

295 "As a senator from a Southern state" ... Statement issued by Richard Shelby, October 7, 1987.

295 "I don't know" ... Interview with Shelby.

296 Laurence Tribe testified ... *Bork Hearings*, Part 2, p. 7.

297 Harvard officials found ... See *Boston Globe*, November 7, 1987, p. 1.

298 "highly selected culling" ... *Bork Hearings*, Part 2, p. 179.

298 Carla Hills ... Ibid., Part 2, p. 99.

299 "Judge Bork is a highly skilled ... Ibid., p. 206.

299 "I would like to acknowledge" ... Ibid., p. 207.

299 Biden presented a list ... Ibid., Part 3, p. 1899.

302 In the part of the opinion . . . *Bork Hearings*, Part 1, pp. 698–99. For one liberal scholar watching, there was a neat symmetry to the moment. Burger's opinion had been taken largely from the brief of the lawyer in the case—Larry Tribe.

303 "We figured if another" . . . confidential interview.

305 "Although it's awfully clear" . . . Stephen Kurkjian, "Biden Quits His Quest for the Presidency," *Boston Globe*, September 24, 1987, p.1.

305 Just before the first of three operations . . . *Washington Post*, January 12, 1989, p. C14.

306 Biden looked back philosophically . . . Interview with Joseph Biden.

Chapter 14: ". . . How Many Are My Foes!"

307 Bork and his wife drove . . . Interview with Mary Ellen Bork.

308 "Something just suddenly" . . . Ibid.

309 "Judge, I'll talk to" . . . Interview with Thomas Griscom.

310 Culvahouse was deeply disappointed . . . Confidential interviews.

311 Bork's son Bob . . . Interview with Robert Bork, Jr.

311 Specter called Bork . . . Interview with Arlen Specter.

312 a meeting was held . . . Confidential interviews.

312 President Reagan invited . . . Interview with Ed Baxter, April 15, 1988.

312 It was an unusual editorial . . . *Washington Post*, October 5, 1987.

313 Griscom had an idea . . . Interview with Griscom.

314 Mrs. Bork felt . . . See Mary Ellen Bork, "My Ordeal," *Crisis*, vol. 6, no. 5 (May 1988), p. 8.

315 He went to see Bork at home . . . Interview with Leonard Garment, April 29 and July 25, 1988. The scene was also described by Robert Bork, Jr., and Ray Randolph, who had heard of it from Bork.

317 Bob, Jr., remembered . . . Interview with Robert Bork, Jr.

318 Simpson was pleased . . . Interview with Alan Simpson.

318 That night . . . Interview with Ray Randolph.

321 At the Justice Department . . . Interviews with top Justice officials.

322 "No problem" . . . Ibid.

322 Biden spoke of . . . *Congressional Record*, October 21, 1987, p. S14659.

323 "Because rights belong to the people" . . . *Congressional Record*, October 21, 1987, p. S14684

323 Actually the Borks had been . . . Interview with Robert Bork, Jr.

324 barred from the Senate press gallery . . . Interview with Garment and with Senate Press Gallery coordinator, October 22, 1988.

324 Cutler was chosen instead . . . "This Week with David Brinkley," October 11, 1987.

325 Garment blew up . . . Scene described by Garment and by Randall Rader, May 5, 1988.

325 Bork had consented . . . Interview with Alan Simpson, May 12, 1988.

325 "I've been talking to the folks" . . . Confidential interview.

326 There wasn't a glimmer . . . Interview with Simpson.

327 Strom Thurmond . . . *Congressional Record*, October 23, 1987, p. S15011.

327 Bork and his wife felt . . . interview with Mary Ellen Bork.

Chapter 15: Endgame

328 Reagan told a cheering crowd . . . *New York Times,* October 14, 1987, p. 1.

329 Both judges came to the same conclusion . . . The Kennedy case was *Beller* v. *Middendorf,* 632 F. 2d 788 (9th Cir. 1980); the Bork case was *Dronenburg* v. *Zech,* loc. cit.

329 "I wasn't as fully informed" . . . Interview with Charles Grassley, June 10, 1988.

329 "The guys at Justice" . . . Confidential interview.

330 "Conservatives are delighted" . . . Quoted in *Congressional Quarterly,* October 31, 1987, p. 2670.

331 a possible conflict of interest . . . See the *New York Times,* November 4, 1987, p. D30.

331 irregularities at a computerized dating business . . . See the *Boston Herald,* November 7, 1987, p. 1.

331 lackluster student evaluations . . . See the *Boston Globe,* November 4, 1987, p. 1.

331 overstated his trial experience . . . See the *New York Times,* November 8, 1987, p. A36.

332 As the right-wing weekly . . . See *Human Events* (November 14, 1987), p. 3.

332 It was first discovered . . . Interview with Nina Totenberg, November 1, 1988.

333 Ginsburg's early courtesy calls . . . Confidential interviews with Justice Department officials.

333 Others in the department . . . Ibid.

334 The evening of the revelation . . . Confidential interview with White House aide.

335 Kenneth Duberstein . . . Interview with Duberstein.

338 "[T]he Constitution lives" . . . *New York Times,* December 20, 1987, p. 18.

Kennedy's voting pattern in his first term and a half on the bench gave rise to early commentary that liberals who defeated Bork had won the battle but lost the war because Kennedy was proving to be even more conservative than Bork.

While Kennedy proved especially disappointing for liberals in a string of employment discrimination cases, he has in fact shown himself to be markedly more moderate than Bork. In the 1989 *Croson* case regarding a minority set-aside program, Bork would surely have joined Justice Scalia in saying there was no place in the Constitution for any such reverse discrimination. In his concurrence, Kennedy said one could not ignore more than a decade of rulings allowing for some affirmative action and that the Court traditionally took a "case-by-case approach." Regarding the abortion case, *Webster* v. *Reproductive Health Services,* Bork has publicly stated that he would have voted to overturn *Roe* v. *Wade,* whereas Kennedy joined the plurality which narrowed its scope. In *Texas* v. *Johnson,* the 1989 decision declaring the burning of the American flag to be a protected form of political speech, Kennedy was in the majority. Bork was a leader in the movement for a constitutional amendment to overturn that ruling. And in the 1990 case of *U.S.* v. *Verdugo-Urquidez,* which said the Fourth Amendment's stricture against unreasonable search and seizure did not apply to foreigners abroad, Kennedy wrote separately to make clear he did not agree with Rehnquist's sweeping originalist analysis. Bork would surely have agreed with Rehnquist. Bork's 1989 book *The Tempting of America* calls the Rehnquist Court too liberal and lays out a belief in strict constitutional originalism that Kennedy does not seem, so far, to share.

339 "It is like being hit" . . . Interview with Mary Ellen Bork.

339 Bork received . . . Interview with Robert Bork, Jr.

340 Bob paid hundreds of dollars . . . Ibid.

341 "the first all-out" . . . This and the following excerpts are taken from speeches at Grove City College in Pennsylvania, February 8, 1988; the Federalist Society in Charlottesville, Virginia, March 5, 1988; the Worcester Economics Club, Worcester, Massachusetts, March 22, 1988; the New England Legal Foundation, Boston, June 2, 1988.

342 "I'd far prefer" . . . Interview with Ralph Neas, February 8, 1988; see *Boston Globe,* February 9, 1988, p. 10.

Conclusion

343 An early memory . . . *Bork Hearings,* Part 2, pp. 717–20.

344 a kind of constitutional amendment . . . Edward J. Bloustein made this point in "Did the 'Bork Case' Change the Meaning of Our Constitution?," *Judicature,* vol. 72, no. 3 (October–November 1988), p. 145.

344 "I'm not sure I can live" . . . Interview with Michael Carvin.

346 "A lot of longtime NAM watchers" . . . Interview with William S. McEwan, March 1987; see *Boston Globe,* March 29, 1987, p. 1.

346 "Domestically, Ronald Reagan" . . . *Baltimore Sun,* January 8, 1989.

346 "it may be too late" . . . Terry Eastland, "Racial Preference in Court (Again)," *Commentary* (January 1989), p. 32.

348 "I can't think of a single" . . . Interview with Howard Baker.

348 A poll conducted . . . Confidential Marttila and Kiley poll conducted October 1987 for the anti-Bork coalition. On civil rights, 50 percent to 7 percent said they would disapprove of a nominee who had criticized many of the civil rights advances of the past thirty years, and 40 percent said they needed more information. On privacy, the percentages were 48 percent disapproving to 8 approving of a Court nominee if he does not believe the Constitution recognizes a general right of privacy, with 40 percent saying they wanted more information.

349 Bork was the first battle . . . Interview with Eric Schnapper.

350 Many voters told exit pollsters . . . See Thomas B. Edsall, "Poll Shows GOP Attacks Worked Against Dukakis," *Washington Post,* November 16, 1988 p. A12

351 Asked to name their concerns . . . Marttila and Kiley poll, November 1987; ABC News/*Washington Post* poll, October 13–14, 1987.

351 Polls also showed . . . The numbers are from Marttila and Kiley, October 1987. The ABC News/*Washington Post* poll of October 13–14, 1987, shows that 28 percent said they saw or heard or read some anti-Bork advertising while 71 percent saw none.

351 That role has come . . . I thank Michael Sandel of the Harvard Government Department for his helpful discussions with me on this issue.

Bibliography

Abraham, Henry J. *Justices and Presidents, a Political History of Appointments to the Supreme Court.* New York: Oxford University Press, 1974.

Adler, Renata. "Coup at the Court." *New Republic* (September 14 and 21, 1987).

Beckwith, David. "A Long and Winding Odyssey." *Time* (September 21, 1987), pp. 16–21.

Berger, Raoul. *Government by Judiciary: The Transformation of the Fourteenth Amendment.* Cambridge, Mass.: Harvard University Press, 1977.

Bickel, Alexander M. *The Supreme Court and the Idea of Progress.* New York: Harper and Row, 1970.

Blasi, Vincent. *The Burger Years: The Counter-Revolution That Wasn't.* New Haven: Yale University Press, 1983.

Bloom, Allan. *The Closing of the American Mind.* New York: Simon and Schuster, 1987.

Blumenthal, Sidney. *The Rise of the Counter-Establishment: From Conservative Ideology to Political Power.* New York: Harper and Row, 1986.

Blumenthal, Sidney, and Thomas Byrne Edsall, eds. *The Reagan Legacy.* New York: Pantheon, 1988.

Bork, Mary Ellen. "My Ordeal." *Crisis,* vol. 6, no. 5 (May 1988).

Bork, Robert H. "Civil Rights—A Challenge." *New Republic* (August 31, 1963), p. 21.

———. "The Supreme Court Needs a New Philosophy." *Fortune* 138 (December 1968).

———. "Why I Am for Nixon." *New Republic* (June 1, 1968), p. 19.

———. "We Suddenly Feel That Law Is Vulnerable." *Fortune* (December 1971), p. 115.

———. "Neutral Principles and Some First Amendment Problems." *Indiana Law Journal,* vol. 47, No. 1 (Fall 1971).

————. "Alexander M. Bickel 1924–1974." *The Alternative: An American Spectator* (April 1975), p. 28.

————. "A Remembrance of Alex Bickel." *New Republic* (October 18, 1975), p. 22.

————. *The Antitrust Paradox: A Policy at War with Itself.* New York: Basic Books, 1978.

————. "Tradition and Morality in Constitutional Law." The Francis Boyer Lecture, the American Enterprise Institute, December 6, 1984.

————. "The Crisis in Constitutional Theory: Back to the Future." Address to the Philadelphia Society, April 3, 1987.

Brennan, Jr., William J. "The Constitution of the United States: Contemporary Ratification." Georgetown University, Washington, D.C. October 12, 1985.

Bryden, David P. "How to Select a Supreme Court Justice." *American Scholar* (Spring 1988).

Caplan, Lincoln. *The Tenth Justice.* New York: Alfred A. Knopf, 1987.

Cardozo Law Review. The Bork Nomination: Essays and Reports, vol. 9, no. 1 (October 1987).

Chambers, Whittaker. *Witness.* Washington, D.C.: Regnery Gateway, reissued 1980 (originally 1952).

Coleman, Kate. "The Roots of Ed Meese." *Los Angeles Times Magazine,* May 4, 1986.

Collier, Peter, and David Horowitz. *The Kennedys: An American Drama.* New York: Summit Books, 1984.

Cox, Archibald. *The Court and the Constitution.* Boston: Houghton Mifflin, 1987.

Curtis, Michael Kent. "Individual Rights and Original Intent." Washington, D.C.: People for the American Way, 1987.

Dennis, Frank L. *The Lincoln-Douglas Debates.* New York: Mason and Lipscomb, 1974.

Dworkin, Ronald. "The Bork Nomination." *New York Review of Books* (August 13, 1987), p. 3.

————. "From Bork to Kennedy." *New York Review of Books* (December 17, 1987).

Eastland, Terry. "Racial Preference in Court (Again)." *Commentary* (January 1989).

Ehrenhalt, Alan, ed. *Politics in America: The 100th Congress.* Washington, D.C.: Congressional Quarterly Press, 1987.

Ely, John Hart. *Democracy and Distrust: A Theory of Judicial Review.* Cambridge, Mass.: Harvard University Press, 1980.

Encyclopaedia Britannica. *The Annals of America.* vol. 9, 1858–1865, "The Crisis of the Union," 1968.

Fish, Daniel. "Legal Phases of the Lincoln and Douglas Debates." Annual Address Before the State Bar Association of Minnesota, July 14, 1909.

Freedman, Michal. "Assembly-Line Approval: A Common Cause Study of Senate Confirmation of Federal Judges," January 1986.

Friedman, Lawrence M. *American Law.* New York: W. W. Norton, 1984.

Gans, Herbert J. *Middle American Individualism: The Future of Liberal Democracy.* New York: The Free Press, 1988.

Garment, Suzanne. "The War Against Robert Bork." *Commentary* (January 1988).

Gottfried, Paul, and Thomas Fleming. *The Conservative Movement.* Boston: Twayne Publishers, 1988.

Harvard Law Review, vol. 101, no. 6 (April 1988).

Harris, Richard. *Decision.* New York: E. P. Dutton, 1970.

Harrison, V. V. *Changing Habits.* New York: Doubleday, 1988.

Hearings on the Nomination of Clement F. Haynsworth, Jr., to Be an Associate Justice of the Supreme Court of the United States. Senate Judiciary Committee. 91st Congress., 1st session, September 16–19, 23–26, 1969.

Hearings on the Nomination of G. Harrold Carswell to Be an Associate Justice of the Supreme Court of the United States. 91st Congress, 2d session, January 27–29 and February 2–3, 1970.

Hearings on the Nominations of William Rehnquist and Lewis Powell to Be Associate Justices of the Supreme Court of the United States. 92nd Congress, 1st session, November 3, 4, 8, 9, 10, 1971.

Hearings on Confirmation of William Bradford Reynolds to Be Associate Attorney General of the United States. Senate Judiciary Committee No. J-99-29. June 4, 5, and 18, 1985.

Hearings on the Nomination of William H. Rehnquist to Be Chief Justice of the Supreme Court of the United States. 99th Congress, 2d session, July 29–31 and August 1, 1986.

Hearings on the Nomination of Robert H. Bork to Be Associate Justice of the Supreme Court of the United States. United States Senate, 100th Congress, 1st session, September 15–19, 21–23, 25, 28–30, 1987.

Hearings on the Nomination of Anthony M. Kennedy to Be an Associate Justice of the Supreme Court of the United States. 100th Congress, 2d session, December 14–16, 1987.

Judicial Roulette: Report of the Twentieth Century Fund Task Force on Judicial Selection. New York: Priority Press, 1988.

Kalman, Laura, *Legal Realism at Yale 1927–1960.* Chapel Hill, N.C.: University of North Carolina Press, 1986.

Kammen, Michael. *A Machine That Would Go of Itself,* New York: Vintage Books, 1987.

———, ed. *The Origins of the American Constitution.* New York: Viking Penguin, 1986.

Kirk, Russell. *The Conservative Mind.* Chicago: Henry Regnery Co., 1953.

Kramer, Michael. "The Brief on Judge Bork." *U.S. News & World Report* (September 14, 1987).

Kurland, Philip. "Bork: The Transformation of a Conservative Constitutionalist." *Chicago Tribune,* August 18, 1987.

Lasser, William. *The Limits of Judicial Power: The Supreme Court in American Politics.* Chapel Hill, N.C.: University of North Carolina Press, 1988.

Levy, Leonard W. *Original Intent and the Framers' Constitution.* New York: Macmillan, 1988.

Macedo, Stephen. *The New Right v. the Constitution.* Washington, D.C.: Cato Institute, 1987.

Magill, Frank L., ed. *Great Events from History, American Series, 1831–1903.* New Jersey: Salem Press, 1975.

Markman, Stephen J., ed. *Original Meaning Jurisprudence: A Sourcebook.* U.S. Department of Justice, 1987.

Materials on the Senate Confirmation Proceedings of Judge Robert H. Bork. Washington, D.C.: Committee for a Fair Confirmation Process, 1987.

McDowell, Gary L. *The Constitution and Contemporary Constitutional Theory.* Center for Judicial Studies, 1985.

McGuigan, Patrick B. and Jefrey P. O'Connell, eds. *The Judges War,* Washington, D.C.: The Free Congress Foundation, 1987.

Meese, Edwin. Address before the American Bar Association, July 9, 1985.

Moran, Terence. "Heflin and the Bork Question" *Legal Times,* vol. X, no. 11 (August 10, 1987).

Murphy, Bruce Allen. *Fortas: The Rise and Ruin of a Supreme Court Justice.* New York: William Morrow and Co., 1988.

Oates, Steven B. *With Malice Toward None: The Life of Abraham Lincoln.* New York: Harper and Row, 1977.

O'Brien, David M. *Storm Center: The Supreme Court in American Politics.* New York: W. W. Norton, 1986.

Perry, Michael J. *The Constitution, the Courts, and Human Rights.* New Haven: Yale University Press, 1982.

Pertschuk, Michael. *Giant Killers.* New York: W. W. Norton, 1986.

Polenberg, Richard. *Fighting Faiths: The Abrams Case, the Supreme Court and Free Speech.* New York: Viking, 1987.

Press, Aric, and Ann McDaniel. "Where Bork Stands." *Newsweek* (September 14, 1987), pp. 24–34.

Public Citizen Litigation Group. "The Judicial Record of Judge Robert H. Bork," Washington D.C., August 1987.

Rehnquist, William H. *The Supreme Court: How It Was, How It Is.* New York: William Morrow and Co., 1987.

Report on the Civil Liberties Record of Judge Robert H. Bork. American Civil Liberties Union, 1987.

Report on the Nomination of Robert H. Bork to Be an Associate Justice of the Supreme Court of the United States. Senate Judiciary Committee, 100th Congress, 1st session, 1987.

Report on the Nomination of Anthony M. Kennedy to Be an Associate Justice of the Supreme Court of the United States. Senate Judiciary Committee, 100th Congress, 2d session, 1988.

Russakoff, Dale, and Al Kamen. "The Shaping of Robert H. Bork." *Washington Post,* July 26, 27, 28, 1987, p. 1.

Sandel, Michael. "Democrats and Community." *The New Republic* (February 22, 1988), pp. 20–23.

Scheinin, Rich. "Arlen Specter Always Told People He'd Be a Senator—Now That He Is One, He Has Changed." *Philadelphia Inquirer Magazine,* April 15, 1984.

Schwartz, Herman, ed. *The Burger Years: Rights and Wrongs in the Supreme Court 1969–1986.* New York: Viking, 1987.

———. *Packing the Courts: The Conservative Campaign to Rewrite the Constitution.* New York: Charles Scribner's Sons, 1988.

Simon, James F. *In His Own Image.* New York: David McKay Company, Inc., 1973.

Simon, Paul. "Judging Judges: The Senate's Role in Judicial Appointments." Address to the National Press Club, March 10, 1986.

Sowell, Thomas. *A Conflict of Visions.* New York: William Morrow & Co., 1987.

Taylor, Olive. *Two Hundred Years, an Issue: Ideology in the Nomination and Confirmation Process of Justices to the Supreme Court of the United States.* Washington, D.C.: NAACP, 1987.

Taylor, Stuart, Jr. "Who's Right About the Constitution: Meese v. Brennan." *New Republic* (January 6 and 13, 1986), pp. 17–21.

Tocqueville, Alexis de. *Democracy in America.* Garden City, N.Y.: Anchor Books, Doubleday, 1969.

Tribe, Laurence. *God Save This Honorable Court.* New York: Random House, 1985.

———. *Constitutional Choices.* Cambridge, Mass.: Harvard University Press, 1985.

———. *American Constitutional Law,* 2d ed. Mineola, N.Y.: The Foundation Press, 1988.

———. "On Reading the Constitution." The Tanner Lectures on Human Values delivered at the University of Utah, November 17 and 18, 1986.

Tushnet, Mark. *Red, White and Blue: A Critical Analysis of Constitutional Law.* Cambridge, Mass: Harvard University Press, 1988.

Weaver, Richard M. *Ideas Have Consequences,* Chicago: Phoenix Books, 1948.

White, John Kenneth. *The New Politics of Old Values.* Hanover, N.H.: University Press of New England, 1988.

Witt, Elder. *A Different Justice: Reagan and the Supreme Court.* Washington, D.C.: Congressional Quarterly, 1986.

Woodward, Bob, and Scott Armstrong. *The Brethren.* New York: Simon and Schuster, 1979.

Zubrensky, Michael Arthur. "Politics and the Supreme Court Confirmation Process in the Modern Era." Undergraduate honors thesis, Harvard College, March 1988.

Index

ABOUT THE AUTHOR

ETHAN BRONNER, a graduate of Wesleyan University and of the Columbia University School of Journalism, covers the Supreme Court and legal affairs for the *Boston Globe*. He lives with his wife Naomi and their two sons in the Washington, D.C., area. *Battle for Justice*, Mr. Bronner's first book, received *The Washingtonian* Book Award and was selected by the New York Public Library as one of the twenty-five outstanding books of 1989.